The Truth Will Out

The Truth Will Out

Unmasking the Real Shakespeare

Brenda James and
William D. Rubinstein

PEARSON
Longman

Harlow, England • London • New York • Boston • San Francisco • Toronto
Sydney • Tokyo • Singapore • Hong Kong • Seoul • Taipei • New Delhi
Cape Town • Madrid • Mexico City • Amsterdam • Munich • Paris • Milan

PEARSON EDUCATION LIMITED

Edinburgh Gate
Harlow CM20 2JE
United Kingdom
Tel: +44 (0)1279 623623
Fax: +44 (0)1279 431059
Website: www.pearsoned.co.uk

First edition published in Great Britain in 2005

ISBN-13: 978-1-4058-2437-8
ISBN-10: 1-4058-2437-9

British Library Cataloguing in Publication Data
A CIP catalogue record for this book can be obtained from the British Library

Library of Congress Cataloging in Publication Data
James, Brenda, 1944–
    The truth will out : unmasking the real Shakespeare / Brenda James and W.D. Rubinstein.
        p. cm.
    Includes bibliographical references and index.
    ISBN-13: 978-1-4058-2437-8
    ISBN-10: 1-4058-2437-9
    1. Shakespeare, William, 1564–1616 – Authorship. I. Rubinstein, W. D. II. Title. PR2937.J36 2005
822.3'3 – dc22   2005044979

10 9 8 7 6 5 4 3 2 1
10 09 08 07 06 05

Set by 3
Printed by Clays Ltd, Bungay

The Publisher's policy is to use paper manufactured from sustainable forests.

Contents

List of Plates

Note on Calendar Discrepancies and Dating

During the period covered in this book, the English year started on 25 March. This means that in citing some primary sources, we have occasionally given two years – 1600/01, for example.

The situation is further complicated by the fact that the then continental calendar was ten days ahead of our own. Neville and Winwood (being diplomats) would often specify which calendar they were using, but this information was not always available to researchers. So confusing was the situation that many letter-writers of the time simply omitted the actual year. Discrepancies in the dating of some events and letters cited in this book may therefore occur. (These problems are in addition to the general uncertainties regarding the dating of Shakespeare's plays.)

Foreword

Theatre artists hide themselves to reveal themselves. We use an indirect communication in order to be more direct. We speak or write through the mask of a character in an imagined situation. We, ourselves, appear to be at a remove, while actually sharing the most intimate secrets and fears and foolish behaviour imaginable. We pretend to be someone else in order to be ourselves. Other people don't feel the need to do this, they speak or write directly as themselves.

Whoever Shakespeare the writer actually was, he seems, from his plays, to have known very well the advantages and dangers of hiding oneself: Imogen, Rosalind, Celia, Julia, Portia, the Duke of Vienna in *Measure for Measure*, Henry V on the eve of the battle of Agincourt, Kent to protect his beloved Lear, Hamlet to protect himself and, of course, Viola. They all use disguise to protect themselves, discover, test, and prove truths about others, or just get closer to people without being discovered. Shakespeare is the master of hiding and revealing. He's obsessed with it as a theme and device and one of the great delights of his plays is the recurring experience of things not being as they seem. I include his obsession with punning on an apparent and resonant meaning out of one word. He loves to display the Achilles heel of our minds: that we are susceptible to and very often deceived by appearances. The mystery of his own apparently secretive life and identity might just be no more than an elaborate practical and philosophic joke!

In a very real sense, all the authorship candidates have been secretive about their identity for one reason or another. I include William Shakespeare of Stratford in this thought, as there must be a reason for the lack of any letters to or from him, the lack of any indication of books in his ownership, or access to the kind of book learning he clearly demonstrates in his work, not to mention the lack of any indication of his access to the kind of life experience which he clearly demonstrates in his work. All possible answers to these aspects of the little we know about him imply someone who was extremely private. But, how did such an unparalleled genius inspire others not to remark on him in his youth, as he moved among the learned courtiers he wrote about so searchingly, and even when he died? Indeed Ben Jonson's Dedication of the First Folio implores us to focus on the *wit* not the *picture* of the man. The other authorship candidates necessarily have a wish to be secretive, hidden behind the mask of Shake-speare. 'Why?', is the question most asked about them. 'How?', follows close behind.

Like famous victories in sport, or heroic self-sacrifice in battle, great works in the theatre are born of a great need and an equivalent, and therefore refining, obstacle to that need. Something forces the expression into the secret channels of theatrical characterization and imagined situation. Also, in any artist, there may be something given at birth, a genius in the unknown atom, be your science mystic or genetic, but the experience of life provides the matter, and the learning of the mind moulds the artist's ability to express their need.

As would be expected, the works of Shakespeare have a distinctive and recognizable character, and an apparent age and growth. They cannot be attributed to anyone. They have dates, not necessarily of birth, but first known performance, first mention, publication, registration; the implications of these dates are debated, but cannot be ignored. What is undeniable is a development in the writing style, particularly the verse.

There are patterns in the use of genre, histories, comedies, tragedies; also, in the depth and quality of the subject matter. As this book rightly points out, these developments should correspond with the author's life and learning, and we should weigh that correspondence when considering any authorship candidate. The Sonnets are clearly attributed to the author and must be owned, philosophically and personally by any candidate. Their images and date of publication must have had a cause. Their dedication to Southampton must be possible and likely. The reason and ability to conceal oneself as the author of these works must be tackled, not just during life but for hundreds of years after life as well. For those proposing that the author was not the actor, the connection to the actor Shakespeare, the Burbage brothers, and the workings of the professional theatres, must be possible. The incredible knowledge from books, from travel, in Italy particularly, via five or more languages, and of matters legal and courtly, all of this must be possible in a candidate.

As this book rightly suggests, if the plays had not been attributed to Shakespeare in 1623, he would be the last person you would imagine able to write such matter. It would be like searching for the author of John Steinbeck's *Grapes of Wrath* among the green light gazers of the East Coast of America, or the author of Charles Dickens' work walking on the lonely moors of Yorkshire. But, of course, they were attributed to William Shakespeare and so Ms James and Professor Rubinstein must establish the need for their candidate. This they do with some force, and some may feel at times perhaps unnecessary force, given the strength of their case, but this is to be expected in a book where they must open their biographical case, like lawyers in an academic courtroom, expectant of a vigorous defence.

This is a pioneering book. No one has considered this candidate before as the author of the works attributed to Shakespeare, so you will not be alone in having your image of the author shaken by these pages, as I have. If Brenda James has found the true author, and she certainly appears to have found a person who could have done it – his learning, his life experience and the dates of his life are as good as they could be; if Professor Rubinstein has been as careful as I imagine he has, given his extensive knowledge and experience of history and this controversial question; if the authors have not avoided any difficult aspects of his biography in relation to the plays, then this is an historic book. It must certainly be a major piece in the puzzle of the creation of the Shakespeare works and potentially a central piece which will unblock many other pieces. For those of us approaching this puzzle with an open mind it provides countless new paths of enquiry. I long to read more examples of this man's writing, his account of his meeting with the King of France, for example, but especially the notebook that Ms James has discovered. I long to study his tutor's commonplace of their travels in Europe. I can't imagine that any scholar or student, actor or enthusiast of Shakespeare will be able to ignore this book. I can't imagine they won't find the life of this man, the new document discovered, and the detailed links to the Shakespeare works a compelling window into the cause and possible authorship.

It was in the late eighties, while I was playing Hamlet and Romeo for the RSC in Stratford upon Avon, that I became sceptical that my hero, the actor known as William Shakespeare, could have written the plays and especially the poems, attributed to him. This was, at first, a big surprise to me. Then for a while I was on fire with all the implications of my new understanding, and amazed by the reaction of friends and strangers, who treated me like some sort of religious heretic! I was even named so in *The Times* newspaper, no less. Gradually I stepped back from any need to contradict other people's story. It's enough for me that my scepticism has lead me to a much wider awareness of the works of Shakespeare, a much deeper appreciation of their beauty, their wit, and their mystery than I possessed before. I have become aware of the context of their creation and not been limited by one theory of creation, so to speak.

Just lately I compare the biographical perspective to any number of perspectives via which we encounter the Shakespeare plays and poems: Historical, Linguistic, Political, etc. Within each perspective there are different interpretations. These perspectives and interpretations are only windows into something. They will each yield a view of the plays and poems. That is perhaps their real value. One of the windows will be more familiar than the others because it will be the closest to your imagination of the author, but each will only yield a view of the author's works. I prefer many windows into a house. This book opens up a new one but doesn't board up the others. They also have their light.

I will never regret the fact that I believed at one time that the Stratford actor wrote the plays. I know what it is to travel from a small town to the big city, pursuing a life in the theatre. I was inspired and encouraged by the story of William Shakespeare, when I arrived obscure and far from home in London.

If your language is English, the primary 'author' of how you express your life, how you question your actions, how you ask for what you want in speech and writing is arguably the man we know as William Shakespeare. Some would go further and say he is also a huge influence on how we live our lives. I believe he is the major influence on how I live mine.

Perhaps this is why the perfectly reasonable doubt about his identity – a doubt that flourishes within the university grounds of orthodox Shakespearean biography just as much as beyond where the name changes and is replaced by other names – perhaps this is why the topic of his persona, the topic of this book, seems to enflame so many intelligent people into quite uncharacteristic behaviour: repression of debate, denial of evidence, lack of objectivity, personal slander, wild conspiracy theory and paranoia, death threats, and threats of unemployment in academia, as one American professor was warned when he shared his scepticism about the authorship of the works attributed to Shakespeare.

I for one welcome and celebrate this book not only for its discoveries and clear style of expression, but for the wonderful partnership of a professional academic and an independent scholar which gave it birth. Surely, this is the way forward, and a momentous publication in the history of authorship studies. How many wild authorship discoveries outside accepted academia would have been helped to expression by a trained scholar like Professor Rubinstein? How many professors would have found their studies enriched by new evidence away from the petty repetitive squabbling over the agreed subject matter that seems sometimes to define the concept of a university? We must move away from the harmful idea that university-based knowledge is the only knowledge, and also accept that a university-trained mind is a marvellous instrument for gathering, weighing and communicating knowledge.

If I had never doubted the authorship, I would never have received this little Penguin book of Great Ideas, which lies in front of me next to my computer; sent to me by my sister, just the other day. Its cover provides a good quote on which to exit the page and make way for the lead players:

> *Read not to contradict and confute;*
> *nor to believe and take for granted;*
> *nor to find talk and discourse;*
> *but to weigh and consider.*

Mark Rylance
Actor
Artistic Director Shakespeare's Globe 1996–2005
and Chairman of the Shakespearean Authorship Trust

Preface

I came across the name of Sir Henry Neville while researching various issues relating to the background of Shakespeare's Sonnets. At that moment of discovery I had no idea who he was, and I felt compelled to investigate the shadowy figure of this virtually forgotten 16th-century aristocratic politician.

Readily available secondary historical sources concerning his personality and career were soon exhausted, though even these suggested that he was just the man to have written Shakespeare's works. (Sir Henry had been in the Earl of Essex's circle and was also a friend of the Earl of Southampton – Shakespeare's patron – as well as possessing the learning and 'inside knowledge' of Court and State affairs one would expect from the 'real Shakespeare'.)

Next, I travelled to record offices all over the country on a quest to search out any papers Sir Henry had left behind. One trail led to another until I had uncovered a web of connections and associations between Sir Henry Neville and the works attributed to William Shakespeare. Then the timeline also became clear – at every step, the chronology of the plays coincided with Sir Henry's life events. For instance, when 'Shakespeare' was completing *Henry V*, with many of its scenes set in France, and others written in perfect French, Neville was beginning his Ambassadorship in France; at the very moment 'Shakespeare' was writing *Hamlet* – the first of the dark tragedies – Neville experienced a reversal of fortune (following the Essex rebellion) which ended with his imprisonment in the Tower. And in this same manner, the list of coincidences continued relentlessly.

Sir Henry's personal and diplomatic letters were a delight to read, displaying the lively style and linguistic constructions reminiscent of

Shakespeare's language. The texts of, and knowledge encapsulated within, the plays and poems also overlapped with the knowledge and interests Sir Henry demonstrated in these letters. Even such *documentary* evidence as remained after four hundred years was also confirmatory of his secret authorship. The mysterious Tower Notebook contained references to the deposition of Richard II and notes towards directions for the coronation scene in *Henry VIII* – a play produced eleven years after the date of these preliminary notes. Then came the relatively well-known Northumberland Manuscript, with Neville's name at its head, Neville's family motto and poem beneath it, and Shakespeare's signature being practised at the foot of that document. One document owned and annotated by Sir Henry even hinted at a hitherto unexpected source for some of Shakespeare's history plays. Within that same document too, came hints that the character of Hamlet could well have been based on the personality and life experiences of Neville's admired nobleman, the Earl of Essex.

Eventually, I presented my case and first manuscript to Professor William D. Rubinstein, who had long studied and written about the Shakespeare Authorship Question. He procured a number of additional, specialist academic secondary sources on Sir Henry for me, and we were both further convinced that Sir Henry Neville was the author of the plays and poems which have for so many centuries been attributed to William Shakespeare. Professor Rubinstein also cleverly steered his way through my over-long manuscript, refocusing my work and cutting it down to size. The result of our subsequent collaboration on the text is now presented in this book.

In addition to Professor Rubinstein, whose unstinting support and assistance was so essential to the production of this book, I would like to thank a number of wonderful people whose aid also helped me on my way. During the first four years of my lonely quest, my task of researching the life of a man named in a masquerading code was necessarily a very secretive one. Having taken the difficult decision to leave my post-graduate studies and lecturing for a while, I was embarking on a trail of long-envisaged, very independent research. Only with my family could the matter be discussed, so my first thanks go to my dear husband, children and son-in-law. They all took much time and trouble to involve themselves in my work and its progress. To Christina Wipf-Perry and Benjamin Roberts – my editors at Longman – go thanks for their patient attention to detail, and to Elie Ball and the other staff at Longman I send my gratitude for all their hard work in promoting the further progress of the book.

It is also a pleasure to thank Gareth Hughes of English Heritage for his assistance in guiding me through the house of Neville's descendants and the treasures of portraiture and books it contains. Dr Geoffrey Parnell, Keeper of Tower History at the Royal Armouries HM Tower of London, discussed with me the true background of the Tower of London prisoners and their situation, and was a great supporter of my efforts to ascertain the truth from primary sources.

The very first personal friend to whom I showed the first draft of my book was David Jenkins, M.Phil, alongside whom I had lectured in English and Civilisation for many years. His extensive knowledge of history and esoteric symbolism supplemented and surpassed my own, thus enabling us both to traverse in conversation a very entertaining pathway of the more hidden connections between the works of Shakespeare and Sir Henry Neville. I am indeed grateful for his steadfast belief in my work, and for his trustworthiness.

Among the many reference centres I have visited, I would like to point out the especial kindness I received years ago from the staff at Maidenhead library. Then come the curators at the Public Archives at Kew, who made copies of some key documents for me. Also the very helpful staff at Berkshire Record Office, and at the Lincolnshire Record Office too. The staff at Essex Record Office patiently searched for some difficult-to-locate documents, while I am also grateful for being able to search the archives of Chichester Record Office.

Last, but by no means least, come my warm thanks to Robin Wade and Broo Doherty, my Literary Agents, without whose friendship, constant support, sage advice and management this book would not have gained an audience.

Brenda James
West Sussex
August, 2005

Publisher's Acknowledgements

The publishers are grateful to the following for permission to reproduce copyright material:

Plate 1: The Bridgeman Art Library, London; Plate 2: Bodleian Library, University of Oxford; Plate 3 © English Heritage Photo Library; Plates 4 and 5: Berkshire Record Office; Plates 6 and 7: © English Heritage, National Monuments Record; Plate 8: John Bethell/The Bridgeman Art Library, London; Plates 9, 11 and 12: Lincolnshire Archives; Plate 15: The National Archives, Kew; Plate 16: © English Heritage NMR, The Private Collection of Lord Braybrooke, Audley End House, Essex.

In some instances we may have been unable to trace the owners of copyright material, and we would appreciate any information that would enable us to do so.

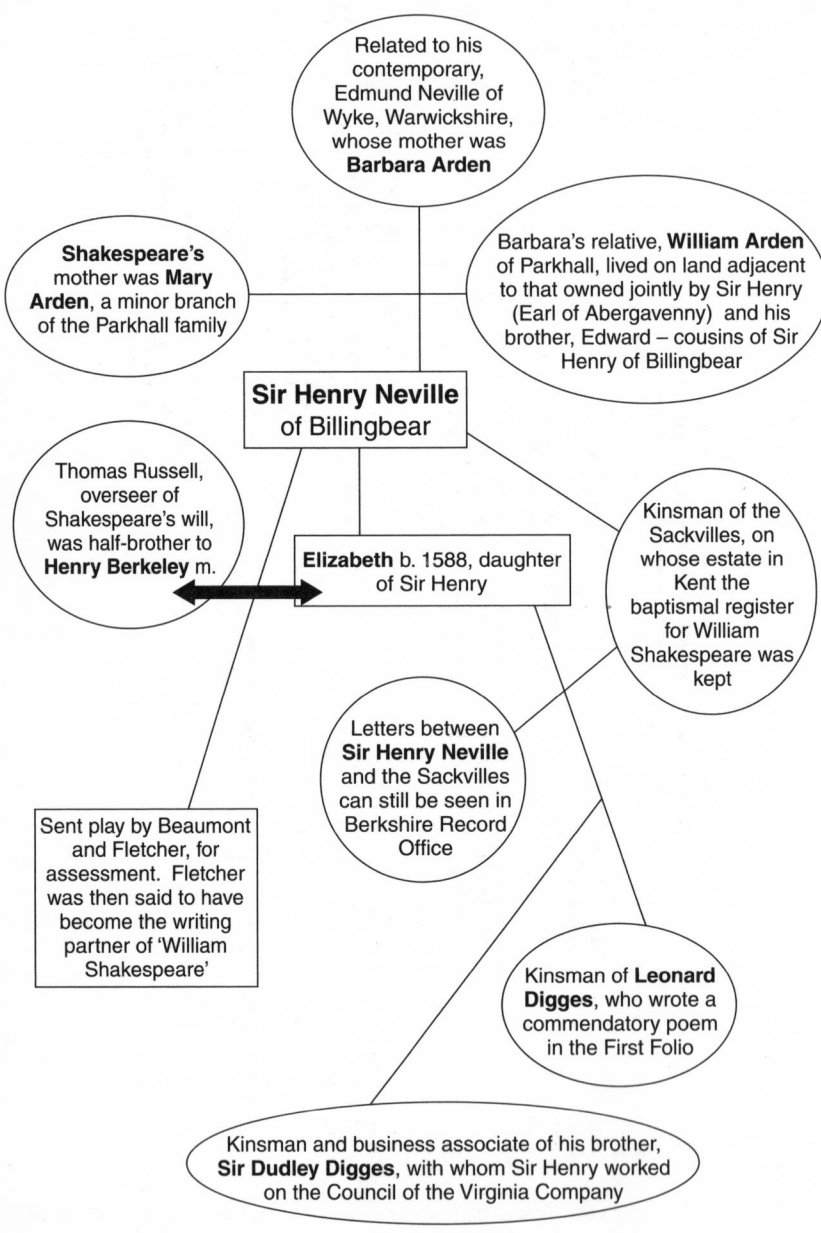

Related to his contemporary, Edmund Neville of Wyke, Warwickshire, whose mother was **Barbara Arden**

Shakespeare's mother was **Mary Arden**, a minor branch of the Parkhall family

Barbara's relative, **William Arden** of Parkhall, lived on land adjacent to that owned jointly by Sir Henry (Earl of Abergavenny) and his brother, Edward – cousins of Sir Henry of Billingbear

Sir Henry Neville
of Billingbear

Thomas Russell, overseer of Shakespeare's will, was half-brother to **Henry Berkeley** m.

Elizabeth b. 1588, daughter of Sir Henry

Kinsman of the Sackvilles, on whose estate in Kent the baptismal register for William Shakespeare was kept

Letters between **Sir Henry Neville** and the Sackvilles can still be seen in Berkshire Record Office

Sent play by Beaumont and Fletcher, for assessment. Fletcher was then said to have become the writing partner of 'William Shakespeare'

Kinsman of **Leonard Digges**, who wrote a commendatory poem in the First Folio

Kinsman and business associate of his brother, **Sir Dudley Digges**, with whom Sir Henry worked on the Council of the Virginia Company

Family tree 1   Henry Neville's links to William Shakespeare of Stratford

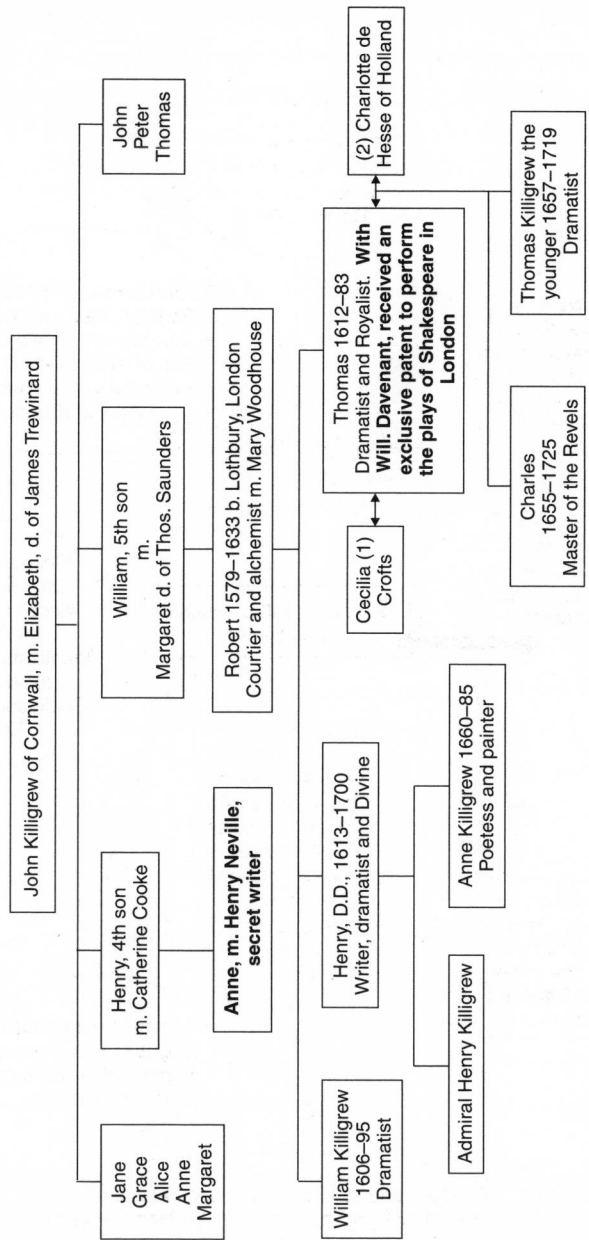

Family tree 2 The Killigrew connection. Henry Killigrew and his brothers produced a remarkable number of literary descendants, one of whom worked with Sir William Davenant, rumoured to be the illegitimate son of Shakespeare. Robert Killigrew, son of Henry's brother William, was an amateur alchemist involved with the Overbury murder. William Killigrew lived with his wife and children at Lothbury, along with Sir Henry Neville

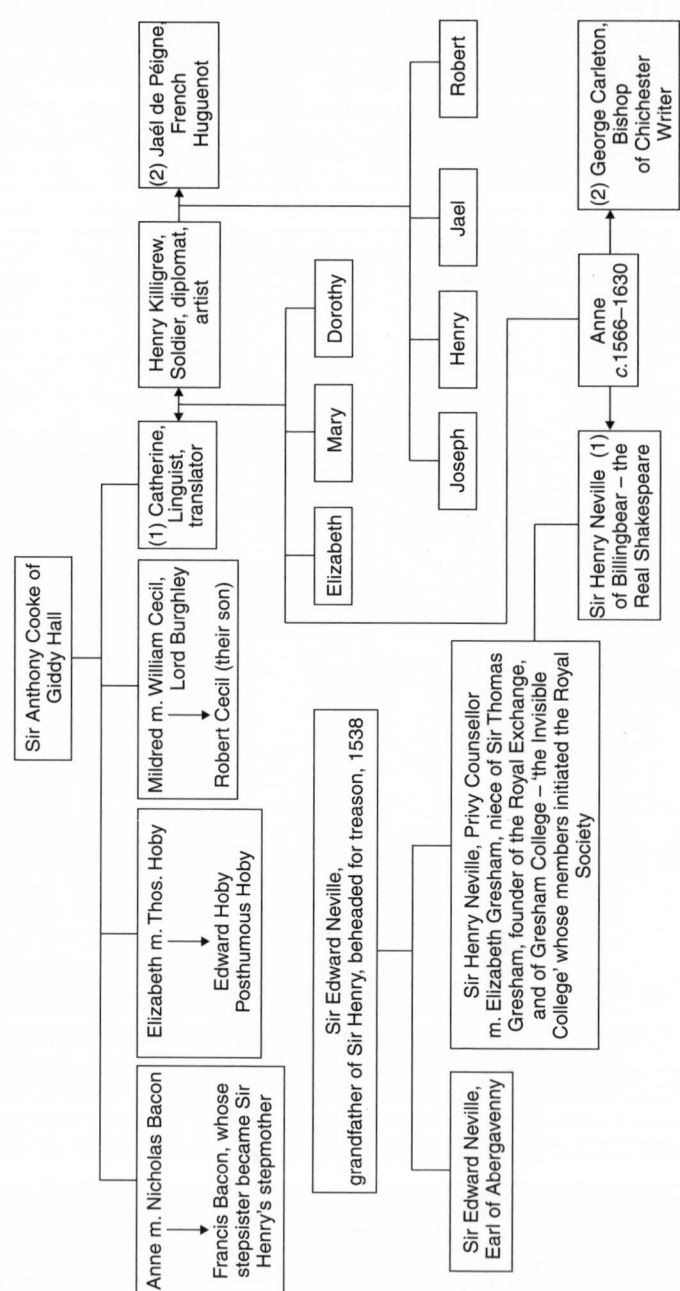

Family tree 3 Sir Henry Neville's political connections, reinforced through marriage to Anne Killigrew (this family tree also illustrates the interconnected nature of the Neville, Killigrew, Cecil and Bacon families)

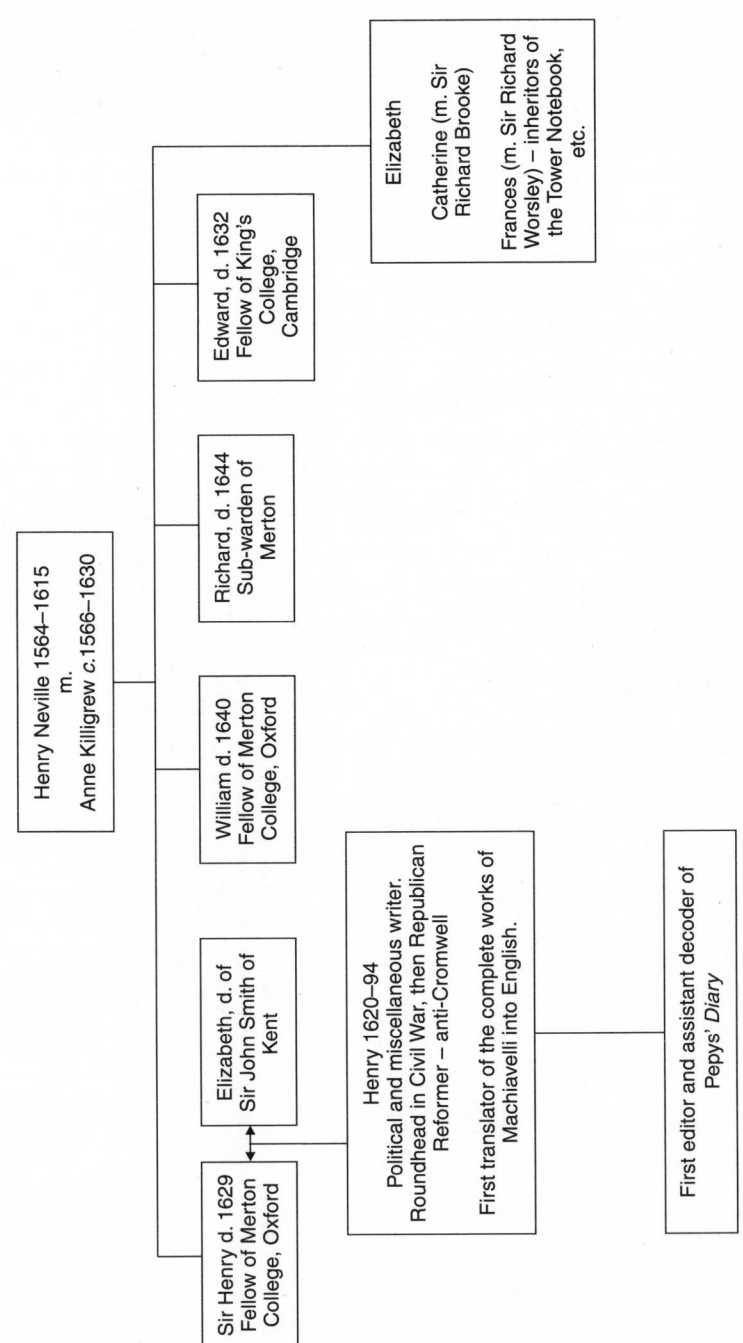

Henry Neville 1564–1615
m.
Anne Killigrew c.1566–1630

Sir Henry d. 1629
Fellow of Merton
College, Oxford

Elizabeth, d. of
Sir John Smith of
Kent

Henry 1620–94
Political and miscellaneous writer.
Roundhead in Civil War, then Republican
Reformer – anti-Cromwell

First translator of the complete works of
Machiavelli into English.

First editor and assistant decoder of
Pepys' *Diary*

William d. 1640
Fellow of Merton
College, Oxford

Richard, d. 1644
Sub-warden of
Merton

Edward, d. 1632
Fellow of King's
College,
Cambridge

Elizabeth

Catherine (m. Sir
Richard Brooke)

Frances (m. Sir Richard
Worsley) – inheritors of
the Tower Notebook,
etc.

Family tree 4   Literary, academic and political descendents of Anne and Henry Neville

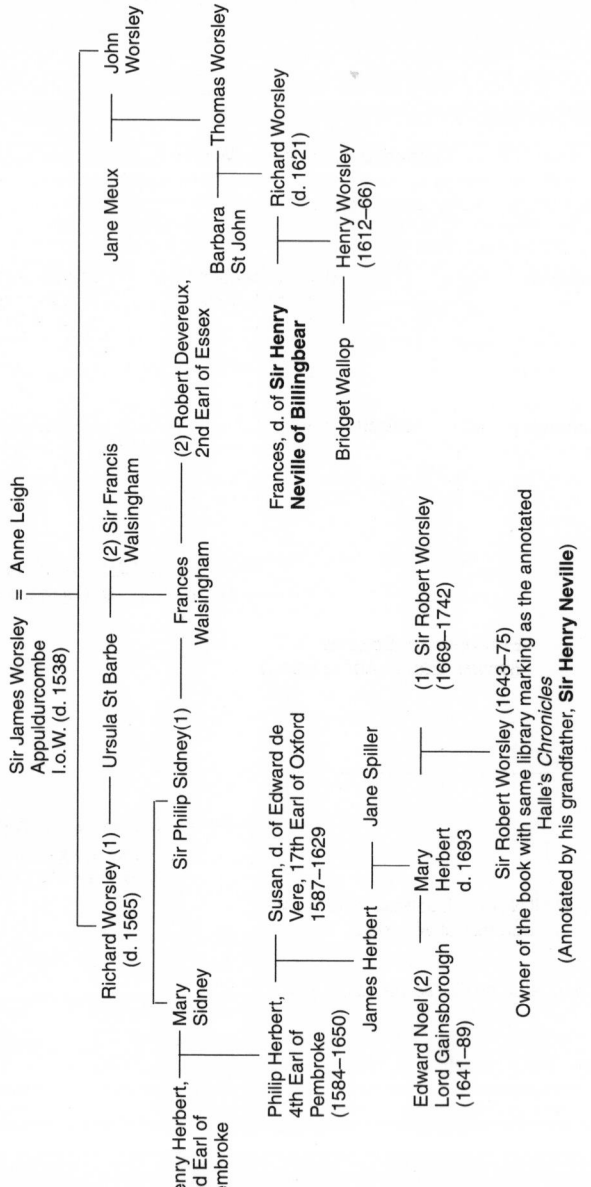

Family tree 5 The Isle of Wight Worsleys of Appuldurcombe House and their relationship with the Herberts, Nevilles and Sidneys. The Worsleys owned the library in which Sir Henry Neville's Tower Notebook and the annotated Halle's *Chronicles* were housed. Some of Sir Henry Neville's books were therefore inherited by his daughter, Frances, who married Richard Worsley (d. 1621)

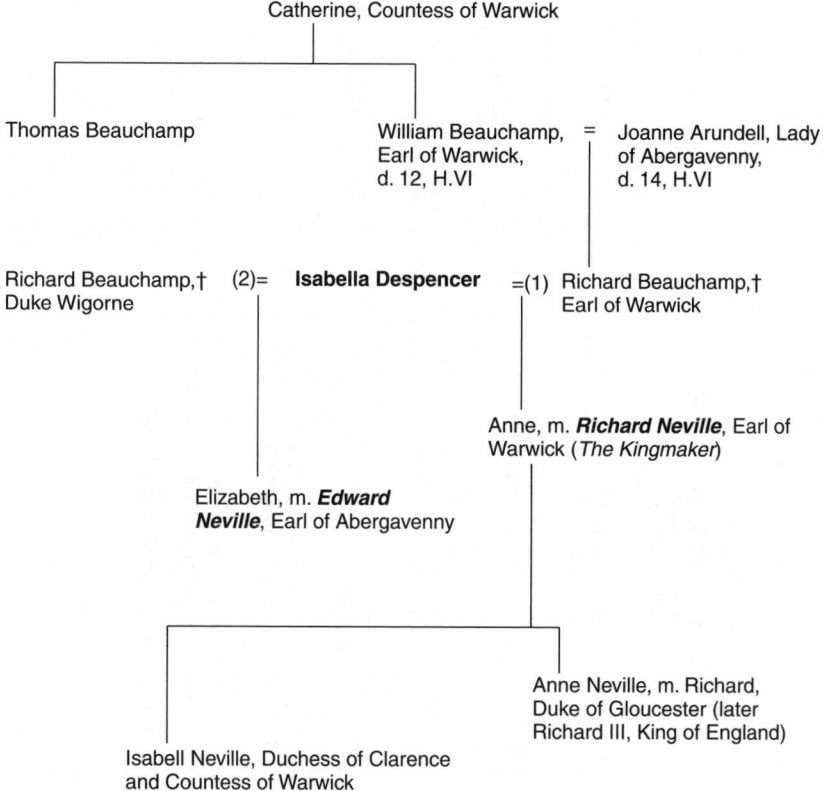

Catherine, Countess of Warwick

Thomas Beauchamp

William Beauchamp,
Earl of Warwick,
d. 12, H.VI

= Joanne Arundell, Lady
of Abergavenny,
d. 14, H.VI

Richard Beauchamp,† (2)= **Isabella Despencer** =(1) Richard Beauchamp,†
Duke Wigorne   Earl of Warwick

Anne, m. *Richard Neville*, Earl of
Warwick (*The Kingmaker*)

Elizabeth, m. *Edward
Neville*, Earl of Abergavenny

Anne Neville, m. Richard,
Duke of Gloucester (later
Richard III, King of England)

Isabell Neville, Duchess of Clarence
and Countess of Warwick

† *These two men, sharing the same name, were cousins*

Family tree 6   Some pedigrees illustrating the Nevilles' link with the Earls of Warwick and the Spencers (originally called Despencer or Despensator). Besides showing the link with the Spencers, this family tree also illustrates one reason why Sir Henry Neville would have been so interested in Warwickshire as a county from which his 'alter ego' might originate. One of his friends, the writer, Thomas Overbury, came from Gloucestershire and wrote a book about Warwickshire. There was also a marriage between a Spencer and a Neville during the eighteenth century

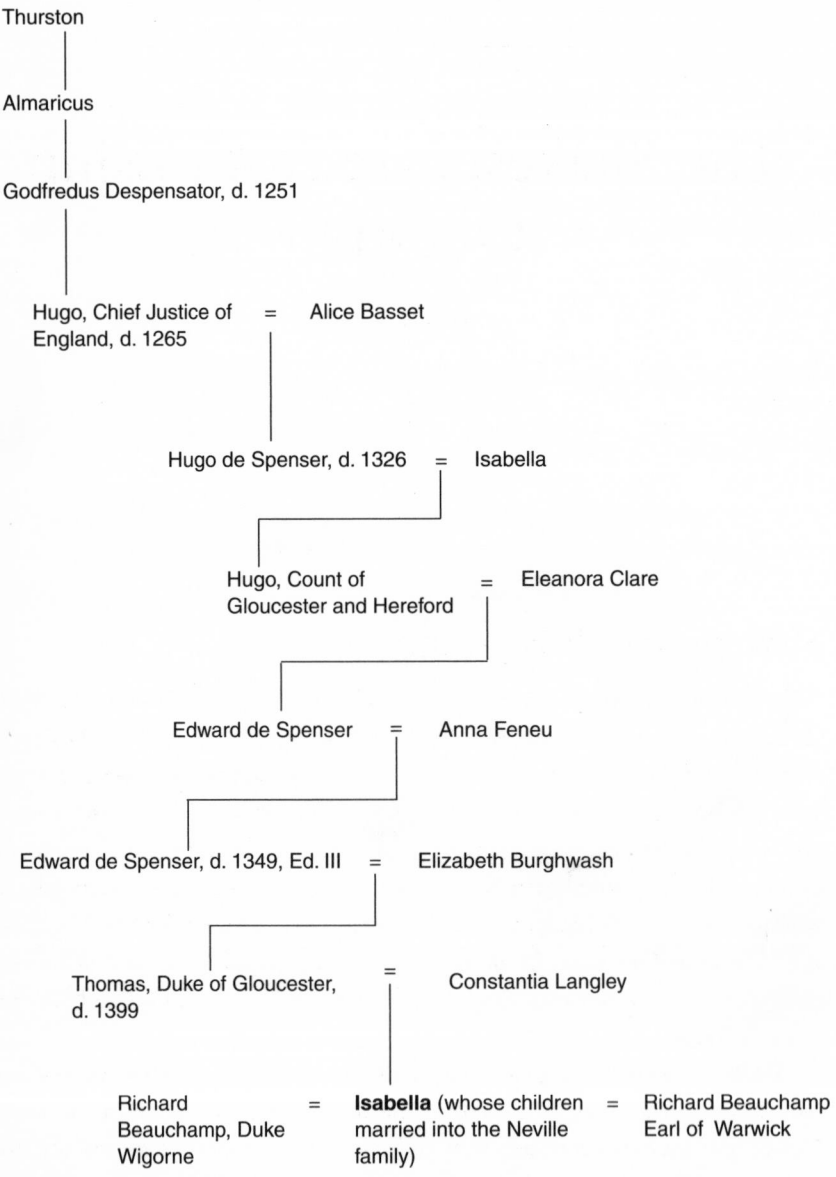

Thurston
|
Almaricus
|
Godfredus Despensator, d. 1251
|
Hugo, Chief Justice of   =   Alice Basset
England, d. 1265

Hugo de Spenser, d. 1326   =   Isabella

Hugo, Count of   =   Eleanora Clare
Gloucester and Hereford

Edward de Spenser   =   Anna Feneu

Edward de Spenser, d. 1349, Ed. III   =   Elizabeth Burghwash

Thomas, Duke of Gloucester,   =   Constantia Langley
d. 1399

Richard   =   **Isabella** (whose children   =   Richard Beauchamp
Beauchamp, Duke   married into the Neville   Earl of Warwick
Wigorne   family)

Family tree 7   An abbreviated Spencer pedigree showing the male dependency up to Isabella, the originator of the Spencer–Neville line

Chapter 1

The Shakespeare Authorship Question

Shakespeare's background

At the heart of our awareness of the writings of William Shakespeare there is a great mystery, which is often known as the Shakespeare Authorship Question. For over 150 years this question – whether the actor who was born in Stratford-upon-Avon in 1564 and died there in 1616 actually wrote the plays – has continued to perplex well-educated and intelligent people. Although often dismissed by orthodox Stratfordian scholars (those who believe that Shakespeare of Stratford wrote the works attributed to him), it shows no signs of disappearing and, indeed, in recent years has returned with a vengeance as a subject of intense debate, especially in the United States.

While William Shakespeare may well have been the greatest author the world has ever known, as a man his life has proved to be one of the most elusive and mysterious of any human being of his achievement and stature in history. Virtually everything known of the facts of his life seem to belie the transcendent genius of his plays and poems. His parents were illiterate; he grew up in a small provincial town in which lived no more than a handful of educated men; his schooling ended at around 12; there is no evidence that he ever owned a book. No manuscript definitely known to have been written by him survives, nor do any letters, memoranda or notes he wrote on any subject, let alone literary documents. Shakespeare's only writings which survive, in fact, consist of just six signatures scrawled on legal documents, three of which are on his will. While Shakespeare is named in 75 known contemporary documents, not a single one concerns his career as an author. Most are legal and financial documents which depict him as a rather cold, rapacious and successful local landowner, grain merchant and moneylender.

Shakespeare's life between his marriage in 1582 to Anne Hathaway and his emergence as an actor and presumed author nearly ten years later is a blank, a mystery period known as 'the lost years' in which biographers, lacking any hard evidence for their views or any way to explain Shakespeare's apparent wide erudition, have credited him with being – amongst other things – a law clerk, schoolmaster, traveller on the continent and soldier. At the age of about 47, after a quarter-century allegedly at the centre of one of the world's greatest cultural renaissances in London, the nation's capital, suddenly and for no obvious reason Shakespeare retired to his home town of Stratford, living there quietly until his death about five years later. No one, it seems, marked his passing at the age of 52 in any way, let alone by the publication of memorial verses or funereal tributes.

In 1623, seven years after Shakespeare's death, an enormous memorial volume containing nearly all of his plays, including many published in full for the first time, was edited and produced by a number of his former theatrical associates. The First Folio, as this volume is known, does not mention or acknowledge his family in Stratford, although it seems surprising that they did not retain some manuscripts or effects left by him which would have been useful to the Folio's compilers. There is no evidence that any member of his family – or anyone else in Stratford-upon-Avon – owned a copy of the First Folio; its literary glories would in any case have been lost on Shakespeare's two surviving daughters, who were illiterate.

Since Shakespeare's recognition in the late eighteenth century as England's preeminent national writer, hundreds of historians, researchers and archivists have pored over thousands of Elizabethan and Jacobean documents to discover anything there is to find about Shakespeare the man, and, in particular, Shakespeare the writer. Despite all their efforts, they have found little on the former and nothing on the latter.

There is thus a Shakespeare Authorship Question which has continued to perplex thousands of admirers of Shakespeare's works over the past two centuries: or rather, there are two separate but interconnected authorship questions which, for innumerable readers of Shakespeare's works and others, constitute one of history's most abiding and intriguing mysteries. The first of the two Shakespeare authorship questions is how satisfactorily to explain the seemingly unbridgeable gap between the magnitude of his achievement and the meagreness of his apparent background, while the second is why so little has been discovered about his life as a man and, particularly, as a writer, regardless of how thoroughly we research. As a result, over the past century and a half, many intelligent and perceptive persons have come to doubt whether William Shakespeare of Stratford, the man who was born in Stratford-upon-Avon in 1564 and died there in 1616, and who was unquestionably an actor and theatre-owner in London as well as a businessman and landowner in Stratford, could conceivably have written the plays and poems attributed to him. Over time, a variety of other authorship candidates (as they are known) have been proposed, the best-known of whom are Sir Francis Bacon (1561–1626) and Edward De Vere, seventeenth Earl of Oxford (1550–1604).

To gain a clearer understanding of why so many people have questioned whether Shakespeare of Stratford wrote the plays and poems attributed to him, it may be useful to examine the reasons under three headings: the meagreness of his early life and background and the difficulty of explaining the complexity and erudition of Shakespeare's works in terms of what is known of his educational achievements; the inability of scholars and historians to discover any new evidence about Shakespeare's life, including his career as a writer; and the incongruities between what is known of Shakespeare's life and the evolution of his plays.

Lack of learning

Perhaps the most striking way to approach the sheer inadequacy of William Shakespeare as the author of the plays and poems which bear his name is to consider the following: if the First Folio and the other works attributed to him had been published anonymously and, like *The Letters of Junius*, their author remained genuinely unknown and a matter of continuing controversy and debate, no one anywhere would regard, or ever have regarded,

William Shakespeare of Stratford as their likely author. Virtually everyone (including assuredly most of today's experts who have no doubts that Shakespeare wrote the works attributed to him) would certainly believe that their author was an aristocrat or some other well-connected member of the Elizabethan upper classes, and debate would in all likelihood centre, and have centred for generations, on those figures like the Earl of Oxford and Sir Francis Bacon who have long been the leading alternative authorship candidates. Almost certainly Shakespeare of Stratford would never have been proposed as an authorship candidate; if someone today were somehow to propose the Stratford-born actor and theatre-owner as the likely author, he or she would be greeted with ridicule, with critics of the suggestion quickly pointing out the extent to which Shakespeare lacked the educational background or Court and political connections which the author of the plays must obviously have possessed. The meagreness of Shakespeare's background, and the lack of any documented fact in his life which might lead one to believe that he was a playwright or poet, would rule him out as an authorship candidate among the overwhelming majority of scholars and historians. It is, indeed, safe to say that no one would ever have proposed him as the author of the plays and poems at any time from their original publication to the present day.

The many people who have, for the past 150 or 200 years, doubted whether William Shakespeare of Stratford wrote the plays and poems which bear his name have focused on a number of striking inadequacies and inconsistencies in what we know about the life of the Stratford man, which seem to call into question whether he could have been the real author. Probably the most serious is the extraordinary inconsistency between the verbal facility of Shakespeare's work and the limited educational background of the man from Stratford. We have no certain knowledge of where Shakespeare went to school; the assumption is that he attended the local grammar school in Stratford (the King's New School on Church Street), since his father, John Shakespeare, was entitled, as a burgess of the town, to send his son to this school. (No sixteenth-century enrolment records survive for the school; apart from pure supposition, our only evidence that Shakespeare attended this school comes from the 1709 remark of Nicholas Rowe, Shakespeare's earliest biographer, that he was educated 'for some time at a Free School'.[1]) If Shakespeare did attend this school, he would only have done so between the ages of about 7 and 12. In 1576, when Shakespeare was 12, his father experienced financial difficulties and ceased serving on the Stratford council. Many historians believe that Shakespeare was withdrawn from school at this time; this was the belief of Nicholas Rowe. John Aubrey suggested that young Will often worked alongside his father as 'a butcher' during his teenage years.[2]

The education Shakespeare would have received at Stratford Grammar School, though wide-ranging in some respects, would be viewed with despair by modern educational theorists. It would have consisted of endless hours of repeating memorized Latin grammar and texts, in a classroom full of bored local boys of radically unequal ability from perhaps 6.00 a.m. until 5.30 p.m. (with breaks).[3] Recalcitrant scholars would have been beaten at the drop of a hat by the schoolmaster. Although – perhaps – young Shakespeare would eventually have read Latin classics by the likes of Cicero and Virgil, and the Bible, the experience was infinitely stultifying and narrowing, with no opportunities for individual expression or recognition of personal ability except at mastering Latin grammar. Nothing taught in the school touched in any way on any of the liberal arts or any of the remarkably wide range of subjects with which the author of Shakespeare's plays was evidently familiar, from the new sciences to the law. Perhaps the most crucial point is that all, or virtually all, the lessons the young Shakespeare would have experienced were in Latin and designed to ensure that students mastered Latin, at least after a fashion. It is unnecessary to point out that Shakespeare is not known for his ability in the Latin language, but for his mastery of English, a subject which was not taught at his school and was not used in lessons. How on earth could such a school conceivably have equipped Shakespeare to become the world's greatest writer? This is for Stratfordian biographers to explain: some speculate that one among the (rapid) turnover of schoolmasters at the school, recognizing the remarkable talent of his young charge, gave him special lessons. Thus, according to Park Honan, it was schoolmaster Thomas Jenkins, an Oxford graduate who worked in Stratford from 1575 to 1579, who 'apparently … introduced William to Ovid's *Metaphorphoses* and perhaps to Arthur Golding's famous [translation].'[4] There is no evidence for this piece of speculation.[5] As Stratford schoolmasters taught dozens of boys via rote-learning for eleven hours a day, six days a week; the likelihood that such a schoolmaster would have found the necessary time for private tutoring seems very remote.[6]

Nor is it very likely that Shakespeare had much educational encouragement from his family. Shakespeare's father was illiterate, indicating that it is unlikely that his childhood home contained a single book. Nor is there any clear evidence that Shakespeare's mother, Mary Arden, could write: on a land deed of 1579 which survives, she made her 'marke' by 'signing' the initials S.M. instead of M.S., next to the place where the scrivener had written her name. A 'small, neat, rather complex design', 'the "S"' Honan states, 'is exampled in the handwriting of literate persons; the "M" (if such was intended) lacks a final stroke or minim'.[7] Among all of Stratford's 1,300 or so inhabitants, it is likely that only the vicar and the schoolmaster could remotely be described as educated men, and almost certainly a majority of its adult inhabitants were illiterate. The town did not possess a library, bookshop or newspaper, nor even a school above the elementary level.

Most importantly of all, perhaps, the fundamental and guiding aim of Stratford's local elite in its educational policy was to instil and enforce conformity among its youth. The 90 years or so preceding Shakespeare's education had seen the overthrow of a dynasty and dynastic turmoil, the replacement of one national religion by another, economic crises, numerous foreign wars and treasonous threats, and a continuing sense of insecurity and potential danger to everyone in authority, especially to local officials of no national consequence. Its aim was to enforce intellectual, political and religious conformity in the local community by any means, in particular to avoid being noticed as a hotbed of nonconformist or seditious sentiment. In startling contrast, Shakespeare's works are driven by precisely the opposite animating force: the author's unprecedented ability to empathize with all his characters, among them foreigners, Catholics, Jews, Moors and women, and to bring them all to life. This belies rather than supports the black-and-white view of English society he would have received in his youthful lessons in Stratford. Some biographers have suggested that Shakespeare's Catholicism – he may well have been a Catholic, though this is far from certain – made him sensitive to the plight of social outsiders, but Shakespeare's plays, as most critics agree, were emphatically Protestant in orientation throughout his career, becoming even more markedly Protestant in his latter years.[8]

Perhaps, however, Shakespeare's verbal facility and wide knowledge were the product of some formal education he received after Stratford Grammar School? Unfortunately for this theory, there is no record that Shakespeare received any formal education past the age of about 12. Comprehensive admission records survive for England's two universities, Oxford and Cambridge, and for the Inns of Court, the lawyers' training institutions in London often regarded as a 'third university'. Shakespeare attended none of these. If he wrote the plays attributed to him, the educational sources of his incredible range of knowledge remain largely unknown.

This is the sum total of Shakespeare's known educational background, what was formally implanted into the supposed writer. The outcome – what Shakespeare actually produced – is so totally different as to be at the very heart of the Shakespeare authorship question. First of all, Shakespeare had the largest vocabulary of any writer who ever lived. His works employ nearly 18,000 different and separate words, about twice as many as Milton used (although Milton was one of the most accomplished graduates of his time at Cambridge University), and perhaps five times as many as the average educated person today. Shakespeare also coined more new words than any other writer in the history of the English language, about 1,500 in all, among them not merely archaisms but dozens of common words in everyday use today, such as 'addiction', 'assassination', 'birthplace', 'circum-stantial', 'cold-blooded', 'courtship', 'dawn', 'denote', 'dialogue', 'discontent', 'divest', 'downstairs' and 'dwindle', to cite only those words he coined which begin with the letters A to D, to say nothing of 'alligator', 'amazement' and 'bandit'. Further along the alphabet there is, if one prefers, 'embrace', 'employer', 'eventful', all the way down to 'well behaved', 'widen', 'worthless' and 'zany', while along the way there is everything from 'eyeball' to 'outbreak', 'hurry', 'luggage' and 'retirement'. It may well be that no educated English-speaking person goes more than (at most) a few hours without using one or more words coined by Shakespeare, almost certainly without knowing it. It is quite possible that no book, news-paper or magazine published in English in the past century or more fails to contain at least one word coined by Shakespeare, and probably a great many. Then there are the innumerable common phrases coined by Shakespeare, which most people would assume to be proverbial, but which first occurred in Shakespeare's works: 'into thin air', 'time-honoured', 'be-all and end-all', 'pith and marrow', 'seamy side', 'shooting star', 'the dogs of war' and literally dozens of others.

Even this, however, is only a small part of the story. Not only was Shakespeare unique in his coining of new words and phrases, he was profoundly learned in the Western world's scholarship and intellectual inheritance. He read ubiquitously and almost omnisciently in classical litera-ture and in the recent literature of many European languages. His works apparently cite or rephrase more than 200 classical and later writers, only a handful of whom (nearly all authors of Latin classics) could have been studied by him at Stratford Grammar School. The list of works apparently used by Shakespeare includes many books which had not been translated into English. For instance, *The Rape of Lucrece* is seemingly based on the untranslated *Fasti* of Ovid. Scholars have traced dozens of other untrans-lated Latin writers whose works were read and digested in the original. Although Shakespeare was famously credited by Ben Jonson with having 'small Latin and less Greek', the Bard was also familiar with many of the great writers of ancient Greece. Even orthodox Stratfordians admit that the author read relatively recent books in French, Italian and Spanish which had not been translated into English, among them Belleforest's *Histories Tragiques*, Ser Giovanni's *Il Percorone*, Jorge de Montemayor's *Diana* and Cinthio's *Epitia and Hecatommihi*.[9] Rather oddly, Schoenbaum – probably the leading scholar of Shakespeare's life and biography of the past gener-ation, an expert who was well known for instantly dismissing all unorthodox theories of the authorship of the plays – states that 'Shakespeare did not have access to translations' of these and other works, but offers no sugges-tions as to how, then, he might have read and absorbed them.

If Shakespeare had an excellent reading knowledge of Greek, French, Spanish and Italian, where did he, a young struggling itinerant actor, acquire this knowledge? Where did he read so many obscure books, given that no public libraries existed and we have no evidence that he ever owned a book? The evidence that Shakespeare read voraciously in foreign works is often startling, and difficult for orthodox biographers to explain. For instance – to cite but one example – Diana Price points out that where *Romeo and Juliet* deviates from Arthur Brooke's poem on which it is sup-posedly based, as it does in four important instances, it agrees with the original Italian version by Luigi da Porto of which no known English or even French translation existed.[10] Where did Shakespeare read or obtain da Porto's version, and why did he use it rather than Brooke's well-known English language 1562 *Tragicall Historye of Romeus and Juliet*? Anyone who has researched the sources of Shakespeare's works is aware that this problem is encountered literally dozens of times: the author of the plays was manifestly a deeply learned and well-educated linguist with immediate access to a very large library, with works in many languages, which he used extensively in writing a play or poem, and with abundant spare time to read and write. In addition, Shakespeare's library evidently contained works accumulated over a long period of time, with books published many decades earlier as well as the latest works from the presses of Europe.

Again, how did the Stratford man, an itinerant actor whose formal education probably ended at the age of 12 (and did not include instruction in modern languages), conceivably obtain, read or use the many, varied and expensive works, which he must have read and digested? This has never been explained by orthodox biographers, who, in the absence of much concrete evidence, resort to speculation. A favourite – the favourite – mooted likely source of Shakespeare's material is Richard Field, the son of a Stratford tanner who moved to London in 1579 and became a leading printer, registering Shakespeare's *Venus and Adonis* in 1593 and publishing his *Rape of Lucrece* in 1594 and *Phoenix and Turtle* in 1601. That Field was a successful printer in London who knew the Stratford man cannot be doubted. But biographers of Shakespeare often go far beyond this to credit Field with being the main source for Shakespeare's wide-ranging library. '[It] is . . . probable that he borrowed any books he needed from his publisher Field', R.C. Churchill has concluded, after examining the books which Field and his partner actually published.[11] 'My contention is that Shakespeare derived most of his information, accurate and otherwise, either from earlier plays on the same subject or from books and pamphlets borrowed from Field.'[12] Similarly, the usually hard-headed Katherine Duncan-Jones suggests that a 'possibility, or even likelihood, is that Shakespeare regularly used Field's printing house in Blackfriars, near Ludgate, as a working library, and even did his writing there. This gave him unlimited access to the historical sources he needed.'[13] Shakespeare may very well have used Field's printery to produce the poems on behalf of the real author, but it is difficult to believe that, as a busy actor, with only a limited primary education behind him, he would have had the time and comprehension to read the weighty tomes Field's business may have included.

The theory itself also contains a number of serious flaws. We do not know if Field's office contained all, or even most, of the obscure and arcane foreign language books used by Shakespeare; in all likelihood Field's office retained only works which he had printed, and did not function as a miscellaneous library with a wide range of books. Proponents of the theory have given us no idea how, or why, Field obtained the dozens of foreign books used by Shakespeare which his shop did not print. The pro-Baconian writer N.B. Cockburn lucidly summarized the difficulties in the Field theory:

> *Field's business was a rather small one, and most of the books he printed were for other publishers and so presumably would not have been on display in his own shop. Of the books he did publish himself, about one-third were theological works. One can say that he published very few books used by Shakespeare. (For a detailed account of Field's business, see A.E.M. Kirwood in* The Library, *4th series, xii (1931), pp.1–39).*[14]

There is, secondly, the continuing mystery of how Shakespeare read and absorbed books in foreign languages which there is no evidence he understood. Another unsubstantiated theory is that Shakespeare 'made use of some nobleman's library'.[15] (Ben Jonson was known to have used Sir Francis Bacon's library.)[16] The fact that there is no equivalent account of where Shakespeare read a much wider range of books is in itself interesting – but then, there is virtually no information of any kind on the details of his career. The only nobleman, or cultivated man of the upper classes previously associated in any way with Shakespeare in his lifetime was Lord Southampton, to whom Shakespeare's two poems *Venice and Adonis* and *The Rape of Lucrece* were dedicated in 1593–94. But it must be reiterated that there is no evidence that Southampton ever even set eyes upon the Stratford man, let alone gave him free access to his library. It seems even more improbable that Shakespeare, an unknown actor, could have gained access to, for instance, the large library certainly owned by Lord Burghley, who was, in effect, prime minister. There is certainly no evidence he did and the likelihood that this ever happened diminishes still further when it is appreciated that Shakespeare's plays after about 1595 were highly political works, pro-Essex, with *Richard II* famously being performed on the eve of the Essex rebellion.

There is also another logistical puzzle of how Shakespeare read the sources he must have used. Shakespeare was, presumably, travelling every few months between London, where he was employed in the theatre, and Stratford, where his family lived and where, increasingly, he invested for his retirement. Shakespeare may, perhaps, have had access to a large library in

London, but what books did he read as sources in Stratford? Stratfordians who still argue that he used the putative library of Richard Field or a nobleman in London never explain how he might have been allowed by their owners to transport books to his Midlands home. Perhaps Shakespeare did no writing in Stratford, but this is very difficult to equate with the fact that, from around 1604 if not earlier, he apparently spent most of his time at home, yet continued to write plays. The question of where and how Shakespeare of Stratford obtained – and retained – the hundreds of works, many in foreign languages, which the author certainly used in writing his plays has yet to be satisfactorily answered by Shakespeare's biographers.

Even more mysterious, perhaps, is explaining how Shakespeare came to have the detailed knowledge of Europe, especially France and Italy, which he did. His immensely detailed knowledge of Italy's famous cities and the roads between them has been repeatedly commented upon, with an impressive list of scholars expert on Italy regularly suggesting that Shakespeare must have visited the country. Strikingly, few of the scholars who are best known for advancing the view that the young Shakespeare visited Italy are anti-Stratfordians: most accept that the Stratford-born actor wrote the plays.[17] Dr Ernesto Grillo, an eminent Italian scholar of Shakespeare resident in Britain, stated that 'we are forced to conclude that Shakespeare must have visited Milan, Verona, Venice, Padua and Mantua'.[18] Fourteen of Shakespeare's plays are set in whole or in part in Italy, among them the majority of his comedies. Time and again Shakespeare's often minutely detailed descriptions of places in Italy appear, to experts, to have been startlingly accurate and perforce based on eye-witness experience. To take only one or two examples, Shakespeare's *Taming of the Shrew* (Act I, Sc. I, l. 42) states that someone is said to 'come ashore' at Padua. As Padua is an inland town, this reference seems curious. But Grillo discovered that in Shakespeare's time Lombardy was intersected by a network of rivers and canals which many travellers used in preference to the roads, which were roughly made and infested with bandits. Padua was also connected to the Adriatic by waterways.[19] In *The Merchant of Venice* (Act III, Sc. IV, ll. 53–4) Portia speaks of 'the traject . . . the common ferry / which trades to Venice'. This was the *traghetto* which took travellers from the mainland to the city. In both the Quarto and Folio editions of the play, the word is misprinted as 'tranect', the compositors apparently never having heard of it. Since Shakespeare explained that the 'traject' was a ferry, he must not have expected his English audiences to have heard of it; indeed, in the nineteenth century Karl Elze, a German Shakespearean scholar, claimed that Shakespeare could not have read of the *traghetto* in any book.[20]

Prior to about the Second World War, orthodox and eminent biographers of Shakespeare often concluded that, given apparently compelling evidence of this kind, the playwright must have visited Italy. Both Sir Sidney Lee, in the revised (1915) edition of his *Life of Shakespeare*, and even Sir E.K. Chambers, believed that it was possible that Shakespeare visited Italy around 1592–95, when four plays set in that country were apparently written.[21] Even in the sixteenth century, hundreds of Englishmen probably visited Italy every year, and there is no *a priori* reason why Shakespeare of Stratford should not also have done so, except that he almost certainly did not. Historians have searched the passport records which survive at the Public Record Office in London. These record, after a fashion, the names of Englishmen who went abroad, whose journeyings were followed with keen interest by the English government, anxious as always to learn of possible subversives and trouble-makers. They contain no record of Shakespeare travelling abroad; if they did, this would by now be common knowledge, endlessly advanced by orthodox historians as evidence that he wrote the plays. (Notably, one does not find this embarrassing lack of evidence of foreign travel discussed in any biography of Shakespeare.) It is possible that he might have journeyed abroad in the entourage of a wealthy or noble traveller, whose servants and retainers were sometimes not named, but there is no evidence that he did. Trips to Italy, a prototype of the Grand Tours so common in the eighteenth century and later, often lasted months, sometimes years, and it would certainly have taken several months at least to travel from England to the range of Italian cities which it appears that the author visited. When, then, did Shakespeare go? During the 'lost years' (*c.*1582–90), when he had a growing family to support, and was also allegedly – according to some – a schoolteacher, an apprentice lawyer, the proprietor of a horse-parking concern in London, and, certainly, an actor in a busy, itinerant theatre company? Or (as Chambers suggests) during the early 1590s? But the plague only closed London's theatres from February 1593 to June 1594, and Shakespeare is also believed to have spent this time writing *Venus and Adonis* (published April 1593), *The Rape of Lucrece* (published May 1594) and possibly several plays.

Faced with the obvious difficulties, both in the lack of evidence and in the absence of a plausible opportunity for Shakespeare to have visited Italy, nearly all recent biographers simply ignore the question, never examining how Shakespeare could have gained so much evidently direct knowledge of the minutiae of Italy's geography, so publicly paraded in his Italianate plays.[22]

Shakespeare of Stratford was an actor whose father was an illiterate butcher, glove-maker and wool merchant in a small provincial town; yet the author of the plays and poems was obviously familiar with Court life and Elizabethan high politics, and apparently addressed senior members of the aristocracy on intimate and equal terms. Virtually everyone who has questioned Shakespeare of Stratford's alleged authorship of his works has pointed to this glaring incongruity, and the implausibility of someone of Shakespeare's background writing in the terms he repeatedly did. No one from Shakespeare's background could possibly try to address powerful aristocrats in such terms: such effrontery would, sooner or later, meet with its obvious reward. Many, perhaps most, critics believe that the Sonnets are autobiographical and that many of the earlier ones in the sequence were addressed to Henry Wriothesley, third Earl of Southampton (1573–1624). Southampton was a senior and powerful member of the aristocracy and, in his youth, the ward of Lord Burghley, who as noted was, in effect, England's prime minister. Sonnet 10 implores the addressee, presumably Southampton, to marry and 'make thee another self for love of me'. It has often been pointed out that it is highly unlikely that, in Elizabethan England, the actor son of a small-town butcher would urge a powerful earl to marry and beget children 'for love of me'; and the tone of the Sonnet is markedly different from the abject flattery employed by Shakespeare in the outward dedication to Southampton in his two poems.

Similarly, Sonnet 125 begins 'Weren't aught to me I bore the canopy, / With my extern the outward honouring'. It seems clear that the 'canopy' was the canopy of state, borne by powerful courtiers at an important state ceremonial such as a coronation, and that the author is saying, in effect, that although he expected to bear the canopy but did not, this doesn't really matter to him.[23] Clearly, because of his relatively low social standing, Shakespeare of Stratford would not have been asked to 'bear the canopy' at a ceremonial occasion. However, orthodox Stratfordian historians are, so far, at a loss to explain what this phrase might mean.[24]

In the same vein, it is often believed that Polonius, the chief minister in Hamlet, was included as a depiction of Lord Burghley, England's Lord High Treasurer, who had died in 1598, four years before Hamlet was first performed.[25] After Burghley's death, his son Sir Robert Cecil had succeeded as Lord High Treasurer. It is again very unlikely that someone of Shakespeare's background would have engaged in a parody of English high politics, however heavily disguised. It would have been extremely difficult for someone outside the circle of governance to have gained the knowledge or possessed the confidence to touch on such a sensitive and potentially dangerous subject.

Yet another area where many have seen Shakespeare as having possessed an implausible degree of knowledge, given his background, is in the law. Numerous legal experts, including eminent judges and legal scholars, have claimed that Shakespeare's plays demonstrate extraordinary legal knowledge. Shakespeare's apparent expertise in the law has impressed many of his biographers from the time of Edward Malone[26] onward, leading many to believe that he was trained in the law at one of the Inns of Court. Edgar I. Fripp, a well-known Shakespearean historian of the early twentieth century, stated that

> Contemporary dramatists use legal terms, some frequently, but their employment is quite unlike Shakespeare's. It is intermittent, decorative, self-conscious; Shakespeare's is persistent and inherent and often involuntary. It is impossible, in fact, for Shakespeare to write anything of any length without betraying the attorney ... His law slips from him unawares.[27]

Fripp's view has been repeated frequently, and one popular view of Shakespeare's 'lost years' is that he was for a time clerk to an attorney.

The problem with this view is that no evidence exists to support it or explain how Shakespeare acquired the legal knowledge manifest in his writings. Comprehensive admissions books exist, which list all the entrants at the Inns of Court, the barristers' training schools in London, and Shakespeare's name does not appear among them. He might have served as a solicitor's clerk, but no records exist to indicate that he did. It has also been noted that had Shakespeare been a solicitor's clerk, he would presumably have witnessed and signed his share of legal documents; none has ever been seen. There is also the very pertinent question of why, if Shakespeare was training to become a solicitor, the archetypal middle-class profession and the gateway to assured prosperity, he abandoned this course to become an itinerant actor.

Although Shakespeare's knowledge of the law does seem substantial to many experts, it must be noted that many other legal authorities have doubted whether he was a qualified lawyer: the apparent majority view, it must be said, is that he was never formally trained as a lawyer. John Light, the Attorney-General of Connecticut, stated in 1914 that 'he never studied law as a science, but that he had a natural aptitude for it'.[28] 'The weight of opinion, among those who accept William Shakespeare of Stratford as the author of the works attributed to him, is that the internal evidence does not indicate that Shakespeare had legal training or experience' O. Hood Wilson has concluded.[29] Shakespeare did apparently have an excellent knowledge of the law of property, but his knowledge of the law, according to an early twentieth-century conveyancing barrister, 'was neither profound nor accurate'.[30] Shakespeare also apparently had a first-hand knowledge of the local administration of justice, especially the country magistrates or justices of the peace.[31]

There the matter stands. Whoever wrote Shakespeare's works must have had a good working knowledge of the law, particularly the law of property and the local administration of the legal system (as caricatured in Justice Shallow). He quite possibly had some legal training but might well not have been a lawyer. Shakespeare of Stratford might fit this description, since he was certainly engaged in buying and selling property, although on a comparatively small scale and chiefly after about 1597, when many of his plays (including *The Merchant of Venice*, with its celebrated courtroom scene) had been written. Shakespeare's father had been a local Justice of the Peace and bailiff (mayor) of Stratford, although his son, in contrast, held no legal or quasi-legal positions of any kind and was, notably, not asked to become a Justice of the Peace when he retired to Stratford, although he was by then a comparatively wealthy man (in Stratford terms) who had been awarded a coat-of-arms.[32] It might also be noted that none of Shakespeare's relatives ever became a lawyer. The likelihood thus seems strong that this is yet another glaring inconsistency between what we know of the life of the Stratford man and what we can infer about the author from the plays.

Apart from the law, Shakespeare's plays reveal a degree of expertise in a wide variety of other topics, ranging from falconry to gardening to heraldry, for which we simply cannot rationally account, given what we know of the life of the Stratford man. Most of these topics were strongly associated with the English upper classes and those of courtier rank, and certainly not with a lower-middle-class provincial actor. But possibly the most genuinely puzzling topic may be Shakespeare's knowledge of the sciences, especially astronomy. Shakespeare's plays, especially *Hamlet*, are full of what one professor of astronomy described as a knowledge of 'cutting-edge astronomy', such as the Copernican theory of the sun as centre of the solar system and even of the Red Spot on Jupiter, thought to be unobserved until 1664–65, but quite possibly seen much earlier through the telescopes of sixteenth-century astronomers.[33] It is also well known (and frequently noted) that at least nine plays by Shakespeare written prior to 1608 describe the circulation of the blood, a central fact of anatomy first formally announced by William Harvey in 1616, the year of Shakespeare's death.[34] Is it really likely that Shakespeare of Stratford, whose formal education ceased at around 12, and who was employed by a troupe of actors, would have known (or cared) about astronomy or anatomy? And had he cared, where could he have acquired the requisite knowledge?[35]

Many biographers of Shakespeare, faced with these obvious difficulties, have seen the 'lost years' as the period when Shakespeare travelled on the continent, learned the law, or practised as a country schoolmaster. 'Others have argued that Shakespeare spent those undocumented years as an acting apprentice, a soldier, a sailor, a medical student, a printer, a gardener, a bookworm, a spy or a secretary or tutor in a noble household. The Lost Years are not infinitely elastic', Diana Price has sagely observed, 'yet the various conjectural assignments, when laid end to end, stretch decades beyond the available seven years.'[36] As she also notes, the young Shakespeare could not have been all of these things (or any of them, for that matter), yet he must have garnered his genuinely extraordinary range of knowledge from somewhere. None of this tallies, even remotely, with what is known of Shakespeare of Stratford, a young man from a provincial town with a wife and three young children who was, presumably, occupied most days with memorizing parts from plays and then performing them on virtually a daily basis, sometimes travelling throughout the country; a man of scant means and limited time.

From all of this it is hard to see how Shakespeare of Stratford could have gained the experience, or learned enough in his preparatory years, to have written the plays and poems attributed to him. Time and again, in trying to account for the learning found in his work, biographers of Shakespeare have had to fall back upon guesswork and supposition rather than real evidence. This leads to the second very general point which makes it unlikely that Shakespeare was the author of the works attributed to him: the complete lack of evidence linking him directly to his supposed works.

The lack of evidence

William Shakespeare of Stratford probably ranks among the most intensively studied men in history. Over the centuries, literally hundreds of researchers, historians, archivists, writers and serious amateur investigators have attempted to add to the meagre stock of knowledge which exists about him.

Virtually everything firmly based in evidence about Shakespeare of Stratford – none of which links him unequivocally to the plays – had been discovered by the late eighteenth century and would probably have been known to his first full-scale biographer Edmund Malone (1741–1812). For instance, Shakespeare's will, with its celebrated legacy to Anne Hathaway of Shakespeare's 'second-best bed', first came to light in 1747 and was first published in 1763.[37] By the late or even the mid-nineteenth century it was fast becoming evident that, barring a genuine miracle such as the proverbial discovery of an old trunk in the basement of a country house with the man-uscripts of Shakespeare's plays, it was unlikely that anything of major importance would be discovered about the Bard of Avon. Researchers and historians had already investigated all plausible archives and repositories for any scrap of paper which existed about the man who was, by the mid-eigh-teenth century, Britain's national poet. Today, hardly six months pass without yet another new biography of him; no university in the English-speaking world (and few outside it) is without a chair or lectureship exclusively in Shakespearean studies; several dedicated, well-funded research institutes, such as the Folger Library in Washington, DC, exist in large part to conduct research on Shakespeare's life and times. Many of the researchers who devoted their lives to studying Shakespeare, such as Sir Edmund K. Chambers, were plainly men and women who were unarguably of the highest intellectual calibre. Even the most trivial bona-fide new discovery about Shakespeare's life, never mind one which provided some direct new piece of evidence about his role as the author of plays and poems, would make the reputation of its discoverer, bringing him or her renown and professional esteem. During the twentieth century, moreover, research into Shakespeare's life and times has become markedly easier than in the past. Most Elizabethan and Jacobean documents are now housed in public archives rather than in private collections; mobility, both internationally and within England, is much easier than in the past; there is a recognized, well-funded research infrastructure at the world's universities and research institutes; the last decade has seen the development of the internet and other computer-based aids to learning. Despite all this, however, nothing has been learned about Shakespeare's life in the past half-century or more which sheds any light on his alleged career as a writer. Indeed, probably 95 per cent or more of what is known to us today about all aspects of Shakespeare's life would have been equally well-known in the late Victorian period, for instance to Sir Sidney Lee, who wrote Shakespeare's biographical notice in the *Dictionary of National Biography* in the 1890s.

Throughout the entire twentieth century, in fact, it would seem that only three new discoveries of any significance have been made about the life of Shakespeare of Stratford: the Bellot–Mountjoy deposition of 1612, discovered in 1909; the possibility, first brought to light in the 1920s but not explored until the 1940s or later, that Shakespeare was the 'William Shakeshafte' mentioned in the 1581 will of Alexander Houghton of Lea, Lancashire, a Catholic landowner; and the 1596 document unearthed in 1931 by Dr Leslie Hotson, a writ for the arrest of Shakespeare and three others in Shoreditch. Each of these is important as much for what it fails to tell us about Shakespeare's career as for what it does.

The Bellot–Mountjoy deposition

In 1909 the indefatigable American husband-and-wife team of Charles William (1865–1932) and Hilda Wallace discovered the Bellot–Mountjoy lawsuit. Charles Wallace, born in Missouri while the Civil War was still raging and the state was only a generation removed from frontier settlement, held a doctorate from a German university and was a professor at the University of Nebraska.[38] On an extended research visit to London (lasting from 1907 to 1916), the Wallaces turned over 5 million documents at the Public Record Office, finding many things, previously unknown, of keen interest to Stratfordian scholars; above all, in 1909, they discovered the Bellot–Mountjoy lawsuit, which included as part of it the sixth known signature of William Shakespeare, and the last one to be discovered prior to the end of the twentieth century. This discovery made the Wallaces world famous and added an authentic item to the meagre stock of verifiable information we have about Shakespeare's life.

Nevertheless, the Bellot–Mountjoy lawsuit is extraordinarily mundane. Christopher Mountjoy was a Huguenot tire-maker (a manufacturer of women's wig-like headdresses) living in Cripplegate ward just north of the City (approximately where the Barbican project stands today). In 1604, apprentice Stephen Bellot married Mountjoy's daughter; in 1612 Bellot sued Mountjoy for failing to provide his daughter with a promised dowry. Shakespeare comes into this trivial domestic matter because he lodged with Mountjoy for about two years, approximately from 1602 until 1604. The Stratford man deposed that he had indeed known the parties concerned, had persuaded Bellot to marry, but could remember nothing about the terms of the dowry. This was the sum total of the Bellot–Mountjoy lawsuit; Shakespeare signed his deposition, exited the court, and left the stage, his role unrecalled for 300 years.

From this minor domestic dispute, in which Shakespeare's only part was to state that he had forgotten all about it, a mountain of far-fetched inference has been constructed by later historians eager to seize on an unquestionably true anecdote, however trivial, about Shakespeare's life. Since the Mountjoys were Huguenot refugees, many historians have, for instance, seen the two years Shakespeare spent with them as his opportunity to learn French. While this is at first glance understandable, a moment's consideration will show the implausibility of this inference. The fact that some of Shakespeare's plays were written *before* his residence with the Mountjoys – for instance, *Henry V*, which was certainly written in 1599 – shows that their author already knew French. Indeed, one striking conclusion which might be drawn from considering Shakespeare's plays assumed to have been written after 1602–04 is that France disappears as a setting for the later plays, as do things French.[39] Moreover, if Shakespeare the playwright profited in any way from his residency in a Huguenot household, it would surely have been through hearing horror stories of the appalling persecution of Huguenots in France, especially the massacre of St Bartholomew (23–24 August 1572), when thousands of French Protestants were slaughtered or fled abroad, among them the Mountjoys. Shakespeare's position would have closely paralleled that of an English author of the 1960s or

1970s who lived for two years with a household of German Jewish refugees in London. It is highly probable that this author would have heard innumerable harrowing accounts of Nazi persecution of the Jews, which would almost certainly have been used as a part of the fiction or drama he wrote. Given Shakespeare's universal empathy, and the evident popularity and 'political correctness' of a play which recounted the savage persecution of Protestants by foreign Catholics, it seems strange that no part of the tribulations of the Mountjoys and their co-religionists figured in any work by Shakespeare. Some historians have claimed that Shakespeare's experience as a kind of marriage broker for Stephen Bellot was used in *All's Well that Ends Well* and *Measure for Measure*, where, in Honan's words, 'reluctant bachelors need to be nudged into marriage'.[40] But, apart from the sheer banality of urging reluctant bachelors to marry as a dramatic device, Stephen Bellot's reluctance was based, it seems, on the meagreness of the dowry, not on any opposition to marriage per se, while Shakespeare stated on oath ten years later that he had trouble remembering very much about the incident.[41]

The main point, however, about the Bellot–Mountjoy depositions discovered by the Wallaces is that they cast no light on any literary role which Shakespeare allegedly had. Shakespeare is not described as a writer by any of the witnesses in this affair, even by those who had apparently known him well. Shakespeare was unquestionably an actor and theatre-owner in London, so his residency during 1602–04 in Cripplegate is not surprising, just as in 1612, when the lawsuit occurred, he is described in the deposition as resident in Stratford. The Bellot–Mountjoy lawsuit, in fact, sheds no light on Shakespeare's writing career, about which it is totally silent; historians who have inferred that it does have done so with no evidence, employing the circular reasoning that one is entitled to use the lawsuit as evidence about his writing career because he must have been a writer.

The Lancashire connection

The second new alleged biographical evidence about Shakespeare's life to emerge in the twentieth century concerns the possibility that he might well have spent two years as a tutor and 'player' in two Catholic gentry households in Lancashire.[42] Prior to the 1920s, when this possibility first emerged, no one had ever linked Shakespeare with Lancashire, and thus the 'Lancashire connection' came as a genuine novelty. In 1923 Oliver Baker, a well-regarded antiquarian who investigated Shakespeare's life, found an intriguing reference in the 1581 will of Alexander Houghton of Lea, Lancashire (originally published in 1860). Houghton, a Catholic squire, left his 'musical instruments and play clothes' to his brother or, if he were unwilling to 'keep and maintain players' to Sir Thomas Hesketh, another prominent Catholic landowner in Lancashire. Furthermore, he did 'most heartily require the said Sir Thomas to be friendly unto Foke Gyllome and William Shakeshafte now dwelling with me, and either to take them into his service or help them to some good master'.[43] This 'Shakeshafte' was also left £5. Baker asked whether 'Shakeshafte' was in fact William Shakespeare, 'Shakeshafte' being a name sometimes found in both Warwickshire and Lancashire. The suggestion was picked up – although not discussed at length – by the great E.K. Chambers, the doyen of twentieth-century Shakespeare scholars, and made familiar in a number of more recent works such as *The Annotator* (1954) by Alan Keen and Roger Lubbock and, in particular, by the highly respected and influential contemporary Shakespeare scholar, Professor E.A.J. Honigmann, whose *Shakespeare: The 'Lost Years'* (1985) popularised the thesis.[44]

On the face of it, there would appear to be nothing to link Shakespeare of Stratford with Lancashire, let alone with employment in two Catholic households, while, as Schoenbaum notes, Shakespeare was 17 at the time and 'would have had to be back in Stratford to woo, impregnate, and marry Anne Hathaway before his nineteenth birthday'.[45] Both Keen and Lubbock and Honigmann have, however, intriguingly identified apparent oral traditions that Shakespeare was indeed so employed. According to Honigmann, for instance, local historian Philip Ashcroft heard 'the oral tradition that Shakespeare had been employed [by Sir Thomas Hesketh] as a young man', and that this tradition could apparently be traced to the early–mid-nineteenth century at least, long before it was publicly voiced.[46] There are also a few other pieces of circumstantial evidence to support the Lancashire theory, for instance that one of those who assisted Shakespeare and four others to acquire a half-interest in the Globe Theatre in 1599, Thomas Savage, came from Rufford, the home village of Sir Thomas Hesketh.[47] This is, nevertheless, very thin and the acceptance of the Lancashire theory on this evidence alone obviously requires considerable credulity. Yet the 'Lancashire connection' has become a stock-in-trade of many recent biographies of Shakespeare. The theory most usually put forward is that Shakespeare, the son of a recusant Catholic father (there is some evidence for this) was directed to Lancashire by his Stratford school-masters, many of whom came from Lancashire, especially John Cotton of Tarnacre, schoolmaster in Stratford in 1579–81. After two years of service as a tutor and 'player' in gentry households, Shakespeare was set on the road to London by joining Lord Strange's Company. (Ferdinando, Lord Strange, later the Earl of Derby, was the patron of an actors' company that frequently toured in Lancashire.[48])

The 'Lancashire connection' theory may, of course, be true: there must be some explanation as to why the glovemaker's son from the Midlands came to London, while Shakespeare must have been doing something during the so-called 'lost years'. Yet the Lancashire theory seems to build an enormous superstructure on a virtually non-existent foundation. First of all, the supposition that 'William Shakeshafte' was the Stratford man could be seen as far-fetched: Alexander Houghton knew and liked young 'Shakeshafte' well enough to leave him a legacy and specifically commend him to another patron, yet could not correctly remember his name? No one would, in fact, accept this as evidence were another, similarly implausible supposition about names involved. If one were to find an Elizabethan will describing a legacy to a 'Ben Jackson' or a 'John Dunstan', and an author claimed that the testator really meant Ben Jonson or John Donne, he would be laughed at and, in the absence of a great deal of confirmatory evidence, his claims regarded as absurd. Yet, so great is the desire to learn something more about Shakespeare, that the implausible transformation of 'Shakeshafte' into Shakespeare has been widely accepted by excellent scholars, and, indeed, an important strand in recent Shakespearean biography built upon it.

Secondly, the Lancashire theory flies in the face of everything which has come down to us about how Shakespeare came from Stratford to London. Every account of Shakespeare's life from the earliest has him leaving Stratford for London soon after his marriage, possibly driven by fear of a prosecution for poaching launched (almost certainly mythically) by Sir Thomas Lucy; in London he allegedly held horses at the theatre door, building up a business as the equivalent of valet car-parking. Whatever one might think of the plausibility of these accounts, they have the merit of being the only part of Shakespeare's biography which was apparently vouched for by a member of Shakespeare's own family, albeit a very distant one 200 years later. In 1818 Richard Philips, writing in *The Monthly Magazine*, interviewed J.M. Smith, a descendant of Joan Hart, Shakespeare's sister:

> *Mr. J.M. Smith said he often heard his mother [née Hart] state that Shakespeare owed his rise in life, and his introduction to the theatre, to his accidentally holding the horse of a gentleman at the door of the theatre, on his first arriving in London. His appearance led to enquiry and subsequent patronage. . . .*[49]

All pre-1930 accounts of Shakespeare's arrival in London and introduction to the theatre are variations on this theme: the footloose youth, driven by necessity to London, and alone, whose introduction to theatre life was somehow connected with horses. Nothing in any account of Shakespeare's arrival in London mentioned Lancashire or Lord Strange's Company. Admittedly, John Aubrey's famous claim (made around 1681) that Shakespeare 'had been in his younger years a schoolmaster in the country' is – perhaps – not totally inconsistent with the Lancashire account, although there would seem to be a very great difference between being a 'player' and a tutor in a gentry household and a 'schoolmaster in the country', the latter a post normally reserved for university graduates.[50]

Finally, the Lancashire account depends crucially on Shakespeare having emerged from a recusant Catholic family: given the odium and oppression of Catholics in Elizabethan England, it seems difficult to believe either that Shakespeare would have been invited to stay in a Catholic household, or would have been allowed to go there by his family, unless he were a Catholic sympathizer. As is well known, around 1700 one Richard Davies, formerly chaplain at Corpus Christi College, Oxford, wrote, on no known authority, that Shakespeare 'died a papist'.[51] This may well be true, although Shakespeare's will and burial were straightforwardly Anglican. Nevertheless, everything the author of Shakespeare's plays wrote was emphatically and increasingly Protestant in its orientation, and – as will be shown in this work – 'Shakespeare' was indubitably a Protestant. He was unsympathetic to Catholicism, and felt deeply the persecution of Protestants in Catholic Europe.[52]

Owing to the lack of real evidence for the Lancashire theory, some of Shakespeare's recent biographers have kept it at arm's length, despite the light it purportedly throws on the 'lost years'. Schoenbaum discusses it in one page of his 612-page account of how we came to know what we do about Shakespeare, despite its claim to being the most important new fact learned about the man during the twentieth century; his conclusion is that it is 'not ... the most plausible of scenarios'.[53] Katherine Duncan-Jones's account of the life of 'ungentle Shakespeare', which refreshingly concentrates on the darker elements in what is genuinely known about his life, deliberately omits the entire theory. 'I have yet to be convinced that these documents have anything to tell us about Shakespeare ... and the possible means by which William Shakespeare of Stratford, aged seventeen, might have been recruited into the household of Alexander Houghton of Lancashire ... have never been explained to my satisfaction', she notes, with considerable honesty.[54] It is, however, easy to account for the popularity of the Lancashire theory when it is remembered that it not only seemingly provides information about the 'lost years', and about how Shakespeare might have got his start as an actor, but also how he might well have begun as a playwright, since among his duties in the Lancashire gentry household might well have been the writing of plays, there being little or nothing in the way of a published stock of plays to draw upon. Such a theory is obviously enticing; unfortunately there is no evidence for it at all.

Shakespeare's summons

The third of the important new discoveries made about William Shakespeare in the twentieth century is in some ways the most peculiar of all: that Shakespeare, so far from being the 'gentle Will' of his historical image, was associated with criminals and other unsavoury types in London. In 1931 Dr Leslie Hotson, an eminent American academic who, like the Wallaces, specialized in looking for (and often finding) new literary evidence, unearthed a remarkable document among the 'Controlment Rolls' at the Public Record Office which had somehow been missed by the Wallaces and everyone else. Written on 29 November 1596, it improbably consists of a writ of attachment (the equivalent of a summons) for Shakespeare's arrest (along with three others). 'Let it be known that William Wayte craves sureties of peace against William Shakespeare, Francis Langley, Dorothy Soer wife of John Soer, and Anne Lee, for fear of death.'[55] What lay behind this is unclear. Hotson argued that Shakespeare became involved in what, in effect, was a 'turf war' among London's criminal gangs, Wayte being a known criminal and henchman of

William Gardner, a corrupt magistrate of Surrey. It has also been speculated that the women were prostitutes and all were somehow involved in London's vice trade.[56] Others more charitably suggest that Wayte and Gardner were trying to enforce a theatre closure notice on Shakespeare and Langley (the builder and owner of the Swan Theatre in Southwark), and met determined resistance, although who the women might be is uncertain.[57] Duncan-Jones and others have also recently pointed out that one of Shakespeare's known associates at the time of the Bellot–Mountjoy affair was George Wilkins, who also gave evidence in the lawsuit. Wilkins, a minor writer who (according to some) might have collaborated with Shakespeare in writing *Pericles*, was a sadistic beater of women, allegedly a brothel-keeper, and possibly in touch with the London underworld.[58] 'Shakespeare is not to be blamed for the company he kept', Honan urges, although one might have assumed that, in common with every other adult, he would be.[59] Most biographers have done little with this new disturbing image of 'ungentle Shakespeare', although it is fairly consistent with what we know about his apparently unfeeling behaviour as a money-lender, grain merchant and property developer in Stratford.

Remarkably enough, this represents the sum total of everything of significance which has been learned about Shakespeare of Stratford since the late Victorian period. If other discoveries have been made about him, they are relatively petty findings about yet another common field enclosed in Warwickshire or the like. It will be seen, as well, that the Lancashire theory, the most important of these recent 'discoveries', is based on speculation so insubstantial that it would be dismissed as far-fetched if not preposterous if employed by a writer in the biography of anyone but Shakespeare. The totality of Shakespeare's written works in his handwriting remains as it was in 1910: six known signatures, all on legal documents.[60]

Much more importantly, what all of these discoveries have in common – as will be seen – is that they have nothing to do with Shakespeare's life as a playwright and poet, and cast no light on his career as an author. In fact, no document has been found in modern times (or earlier, for that matter) which sheds any light on Shakespeare's career as a writer. The handful of discoveries outlined here all date from the earlier part of the twentieth century, which was apparently the very last period when the existing records remained insufficiently examined to yield some genuine new information about Shakespeare of Stratford, however irrelevant to his supposed writing career. Strikingly, not a single important new fact about Shakespeare's life has been discovered since 1945, although the post-war years have seen a vast and unprecedented increase in the number of university-educated academics and researchers.

Certainly, occasional discoveries continue to be made around the peripheries of his life. Michael Wood's 2003 BBC television series *In Search of Shakespeare* mentioned one such typical discovery, that John Shakespeare, William's father, engaged in illegal wool trading in Stratford in 1569: he was a 'brogger', a freelance wool dealer working without the required licence. This came to light only in the 1990s, from documents discovered in the Public Record Office.[61] *In Search of Shakespeare* trumpeted the finding as one which 'may cause the experts to look again at other aspects of the Shakespeare "myth"'.[62] In reality, it is difficult to see how this discovery could be of importance as it casts no more light on William Shakespeare's career as a writer than the discovery of a parking ticket issued to the father of Lee Harvey Oswald in the 1930s sheds any light on whether Oswald assassinated President Kennedy alone or as part of a conspiracy. It is completely irrelevant to the alleged career of Shakespeare the writer; one might ask, instead, why all that assiduous searching ever produces is meaningless records of the business dealings of Shakespeare's father, rather than new evidence about the authorial career of the world's greatest writer.[63]

This situation, that nothing of importance has been discovered about Shakespeare's life in many decades, seems very difficult to mesh with the life of an author of his standing. During a career spanning 25 years, Shakespeare must have written to many people for different reasons, especially as he was likely to be migrating several times a year between the two homes he maintained in London and Stratford. Some of these documents would have survived, and the ever-widening network of research would have uncovered them by now. Similarly, Shakespeare's contemporaries must have written to each other, or set down direct accounts of his life as a writer, in works written during his lifetime as immediate contemporary evidence by those who knew him. Yet, despite the fact that Shakespeare's life has been researched arguably more minutely than that of any other human being, no such evidence of this kind – direct evidence of his career as a writer made by contemporaries during his lifetime – has ever been discovered. As Diana Price has observed, the 'paper trail' which exists in Shakespeare's case is uniquely meagre – in fact, non-existent – in a way which sets him apart from all his contemporaries among writers of note, even those who are hardly known except to specialist experts, about whose lives only a tiny fraction of the research aimed at Shakespeare down the ages has ever been conducted. And far from more research, by well-funded experts with access to new sources, discovering more contemporary evidence on Shakespeare's life, less new information has been found about his life in the past half-century than in the previous eras. Both before and during the twentieth century scholars have, increasingly intensively, researched the lives of all Shakespeare's literary contemporaries, often using previously unseen archival sources. Something to, from, or about Shakespeare should have turned up, yet absolutely nothing ever has. 'Scholars have retrieved literary fragments for those lesser contemporaries with far fewer man-hours and fewer research grants behind them. Still, in every case, the personal documents reveal writing as a vocation for the individuals in question. If we had the sort of evidence for [Shakespeare] that we have for his colleagues', Diana Price has noted, 'there would be no authorship debate.'[64] Surely one is forced to the obvious conclusion that there is nothing to discover. It is hard to imagine that any amount of further research on Shakespeare's life will uncover any new source about his life as a writer. If any important new information about Shakespeare of Stratford is ever found – which it may well be – it is most likely to relate in great part to the subject of this book and his relationship with the true author of Shakespeare's works.

The evolution of the Plays

The third very general point to be made against Shakespeare of Stratford as the author is the complete lack of any nexus between his life and the evolutionary development of the plays: the two appear to be so wholly unconnected that it is difficult to believe that they truly converge at any point. 'No biographer has successfully integrated the life of Shakspere with the works of Shakespeare', Diana Price has stated, adding that 'the synthesis of what we know about the writer is the antithesis of what we know about the man from Stratford.'[65] Shakespeare's plays exhibit an unusually clear evolutionary pattern, arguably as clear as in any other prolific writer of great stature. First and famously put forward by Edward Dowden, a professor at Trinity College, Dublin, in the 1870s, Shakespeare's writing career may plainly be seen as being divisible into four phases: the young playwright (*c*.1588–94) specializing in comedies and romances; the author of the triumphalist history plays (*c*.1595–1600); the great tragedian (*c*.1601–06); and the writer of the 'problem plays', emphasizing the necessity of forgiveness before reaching a final reconciliation, even a return to earlier forms, in *The Tempest* and *Henry VIII* (*c*.1606–13). While there are, of course, exceptions in the Shakespearean canon to this pattern, in general it seems as accurate a developmental matrix as may be inferred from the texts of any great author. It is absolutely clear that a central, seminal boundary line, a continental divide in his work, occurred in Shakespeare's career around 1601, presumably at or about the time of the Essex rebellion. Every biographer of Shakespeare is well aware of this dividing line, but no one can satisfactorily explain it. Indeed, some of the most influential twentieth-century scholars of Shakespeare's life, in particular C.J. Sisson and R.W. Chambers, have gone out of their way to emphasize that there was no linkage between the biographical facts of Shakespeare's life and the evolutionary pattern of his works.[66] Sisson's reputation is based in large part on his 1934 paper 'The Mythical Sorrows of Shakespeare', in which he denied any connection between Shakespeare's life and his works. Chambers endorsed this view (very much in keeping with the mood of the 'New Criticism' coming to the fore at the time), which insisted that only the text be studied and viewed the life of the author as irrelevant to the text.

Yet each and every biographer must grapple with this plain evolutionary pattern. Several possible linkages with the facts of Shakespeare's life have become very popular, and are certainly still encountered in recent biographies by authors who are otherwise at a loss to explain the change in Shakespeare's mental outlook. Probably the most popular explanation still offered is the death of Shakespeare's only son Hamnett, in August 1596. 'As befits a poet born, Shakespeare would grieve for his son throughout his remaining work', Anthony Holden has recently explained. 'The shade of young Hamnett would stalk his father's lines for many a play to come.'[67] Obviously the loss of his son must have been a terrible blow – although his two daughters survived him – but E.K. Chambers long ago pointed out the fallacy in this explanation: Hamnett Shakespeare died in 1596, but the next few years in Shakespeare's writing career were not marked by grief, but by what R.W. Chambers termed 'his most joyous work ... to this period belong Falstaff, Rosalind and Orlando, Beatrice and Benedick, and Sir Toby Belch'.[68] In particular, it seems impossible to believe that a writer deep in grief and depression would produce the slapstick buffoonery of Falstaff, one of Shakespeare's most famous and revered characters, yet all the plays in which Falstaff appears were written, it is generally believed, between about 1597 and 1599, that is immediately after the death of Shakespeare's son. Another theory sometimes offered to explain the great divide of 1601 is the passing of Shakespeare's father John, who died in September 1601, probably aged 70 or more. While John Shakespeare's death occurred at the right time chronologically to explain the change in Shakespeare's work, as an explanation it seems fairly implausible. There is no evidence that Shakespeare was close to his father: he did not follow his father's trade, and, as a youth, apparently lost no time in leaving his father's home. William Shakespeare erected no funereal memorials or tributes to his father, whose death, indeed, is only known to us because of a routine two-line entry in the parish register.

Other historians have attempted to account for the 1601 dividing line in more rational ways, with, for instance, Katherine Duncan-Jones ingeniously seeing the period of the early 1600s as a period when Shakespeare was between patrons, with Southampton, his first patron, imprisoned in the Tower for his part in the Essex rebellion, but before he had established a working relationship with William Herbert, third Earl of Pembroke, the eventual co-dedicatee of the First Folio; Sir George Carey, Patron of the Lord Chamberlain's Company, was old and ill. 'For Shakespeare, therefore,' Duncan-Jones argues, 'the two years from February 1601 until Elizabeth's death in March 1603 were ones in which aristocratic patronage was at an all-time low'.[69] As a result, Shakespeare no longer had to gratify aristocratic tastes, but was sufficiently well established to write whatever he wished, and thus produced the great tragedies such as Hamlet.

This is a clever and perceptive thesis which – if William Shakespeare wrote the plays – might well be correct. Nevertheless, even taken on its own terms, it has a number of dubious features. As has been noted repeatedly, there is no evidence that Southampton was Shakespeare's patron. There are no references to Shakespeare in any of Southampton's surviving papers, and the fact that Shakespeare dedicated nothing to his 'patron' after the two poems of 1593 and 1594 is, even for orthodox Stratfordian historians, evidence that no patronage relationship existed between the two men.[70]

There is even less evidence that Shakespeare had anything to do with the Earl of Pembroke in his lifetime; Pembroke clearly enters the Shakespeare saga only as the co-dedicatee of the First Folio seven years after the Bard's death. As for Sir George Carey's son Lord Hunsdon, apparently his only known comment on a Shakespeare play was 'his great Contentment' at seeing 'Sir John Old Castell [i.e. Falstaff]' acted by 'his Plaiers' in March 1600.[71] There is no evidence that he either approved or disapproved of *Hamlet*, which was first performed sometime before July 1602.

In fact, there appears to be no straightforward or rational way to link the evolution of Shakespeare's works with any event around 1601, although the change in his mood and outlook was so far-reaching that one must inevitably look for a wider or more compelling source. The most obvious major political event which occurred at this time was the Essex rebellion, involving a half-hearted but far-reaching attempt by much of the aristocracy, including Shakespeare's supposed patron Lord Southampton, to compel Queen Elizabeth to name a Protestant as her heir and successor; some of the conspirators wished to go further and place Robert Devereux, second Earl of Essex (1566–1601) and a distant relative of the Queen, on the throne. The 'rebellion' failed dismally, with Essex being executed in February 1601, and Southampton jailed for life and imprisoned in the Tower. (He was released when James I succeeded to the English throne in 1603.) The Essex rebellion was also aimed at curbing the great power of the Cecil family and its followers. As is well known – but still most remarkably – Shakespeare's works played a direct role in the rebellion, for on the day before the rising, the Chamberlain's Company was paid by the conspirators to perform *Richard II*, apparently with the idea that a play depicting the deposing of an English king would influence the people in London in favour of the rebellion. Rather incredibly, no action was taken against the actors nor – even more amazingly, if he was indeed the author of the play – against William Shakespeare, who was neither interviewed nor arrested.

To orthodox Stratfordians, the Essex rebellion may indeed have had a powerful influence on Shakespeare, since his supposed patron Southampton was tried and sentenced to death, with his sentence later being commuted to life imprisonment in the Tower. Yet it is extraordinarily difficult to see how the Essex rebellion could have had the profound and seminal influence required to produce the great divide in his works. William Shakespeare spent the next few years turning his growing prosperity into an enhanced and enviable position in Stratford, for instance buying 127 acres of land in Old Stratford from William and John Combe in May 1602 for £320, an enormous sum. Yet this is also the very period when Shakespeare was allegedly writing *Hamlet* (*c*.1602), *Troilus and Cressida* (*c*.1601–02), and *Othello* (*c*.1602–03). Based on this information, there is, apparently, no convincing way of linking the known facts of Shakespeare's life with the great divide in the writing career of the playwright.

Convincingly to explain and account for the great divide of 1601 in the career of the playwright, especially its linkages, if any, to the Essex rebellion, is arguably the central aspect of Shakespeare's life which any authorship theory of any kind must satisfactorily address. No authorship theory, whether it entails the candidacy of William Shakespeare or anyone else, can be truly persuasive unless it offers a cogent explanation of the 'continental divide' in Shakespeare's writing career. As we have seen, the known facts of Shakespeare's life fail to explain the great divide, to the extent that many recent historians have been forced to argue that there was no linkage between the author's life and the evolution of his plays. Explaining the 1601 divide is also a requirement for any other serious authorship candidate; how well the best-known alternative candidates meet this requirement will be considered below.

The great divide of 1601 is the only important aspect of the playwright's writing career which it would be useful to be able to link to the known facts of his life; plainly, one would want to mesh the life story of the author with the evolution of his works at every point. Since so little is really known of the biography of William Shakespeare, there is little which appears flatly to contradict the evolution of his works, while Shakespeare's career as an actor and theatre-sharer, roughly from the late 1580s to around 1613, three years before his death, has the very considerable merit of fitting the chronology of the plays as we understand it very well, certainly better than for popular alternative authorial candidates such as the Earl of Oxford (who died in 1604) or Sir Francis Bacon (who lived on until 1626, long after the last play was apparently written). This confluence of dates between the man William Shakespeare and the chronology of the plays is certainly among the most powerful arguments in favour of his claims to the authorship of the plays and poems, and it is probably fair to say that no alternative theory of the authorship can be convincing (and certainly not without a great deal of further evidence and explanation) in any case where the dates and chronology of the proposed author's life stray far from the accepted chronology of Shakespeare's plays.[72]

The evidence in favour of Shakespeare

Given the general implausibility of the case that Shakespeare of Stratford wrote the plays attributed to him, why would any rational person believe that he did? One might point to several reasons which are obviously crucial to understanding why the great majority of persons still unquestionably believe that Shakespeare wrote the plays: his name on the title page of the works attributed to him; during Shakespeare's lifetime few doubted that he wrote the plays and poems; there appeared to be contemporaries who said that he was the author; and finally, and most crucially, there is the First Folio, with its dedicatory material, famously inadequate Droeshout portrait of Shakespeare, and the poems and later remarks by Ben Jonson.

Anti-Stratfordian writers have long had answers, implausible or otherwise, to these obviously well-taken points. Since the discoveries revealed in this book provide evidence that Shakespeare did not write the plays, there must be answers to the questions raised by these points, many of which are examined in the subsequent pages. Briefly, 'William Shakespeare' (or 'Shake-spear') is a deliberate pseudonym used by the actual author, with Shakespeare the actor and theatre-owner functioning as the real author's 'front man' and agent in the theatre. The author's identity was a secret which few cared sufficiently about to penetrate; a few knowledgeable contemporaries hinted at the real identity of the author, especially John Davies of Hereford in 'to our English Terence, Mr. Will. Shake-speare'. Contrary to widespread belief, apart from Ben Jonson's there are no anecdotes about Shakespeare by those who actually knew him which unquestionably link the Stratford man to the authorship of the plays.[73] The best-known apparent contemporary reference to Shakespeare made in his lifetime is, of course, the celebrated reference by Robert Greene (1558–92) in *Greene's Groatsworth of Wit*, allegedly written on his deathbed, which condemns the 'upstart Crow ... with his Tygers hart wrapt in a Players hyde' who 'supposes he is as well able to bombast out a blanke verse as the best of you – and keep an absolute Iohannes fac Totem, is in his own conceit the only Shake-scene in a countrey'. But this passage (which may well have been written by Henry Chettle) asserts only that Shakespeare was an actor, not a playwright. In any case,

Chettle (*c*.1560–*c*.1607), a printer and dramatist, had to apologize for this attack after 'divers of worship' complained about it; it is far from clear that Shakespeare was intended at all in Chettle's apology.

Like much Elizabethan writing, the Greene/Chettle passages are highly ambiguous. But as apparently unambiguous as anything can be is the dedicatory material, portrait and poems in the First Folio, especially the material supplied by Ben Jonson (with the famous encomium to the 'Sweet Swan of Avon!') and his later (*c*.1630) remarks about Shakespeare's having 'never blotted out a line'. The First Folio and Jonson's remarks are obviously crucial to the orthodox case for Shakespeare's authorship. As will be demonstrated in this book, however, they are part of an elaborate hoax to conceal the actual identity of the author, to which Jonson was almost certainly a party. Historians are, rightly, very reluctant to accept conspiracy theories of this sort and would regard it as both ludicrous and, in its complexity, virtually impossible to carry out in practice without the truth eventually coming to light from the discovery of contemporary documentation. Yet, as difficult as it may be to credit, such a conspiracy must have occurred, crucially involving Ben Jonson.

There is, however, another crucial reason why Shakespeare of Stratford continues to be almost universally credited with writing the plays and poems: the lack of a genuinely credible alternative authorship candidate. It is now time to consider the best-known alternative Shakespeares.

The authorship candidates

During the nineteenth century, and possibly even earlier, doubts began to arise as to whether Shakespeare of Stratford was the author of the works ascribed to him. During the past two centuries innumerable works have appeared claiming that someone else was really Shakespeare; they continue to appear on a regular basis and, after something of a period of diminution, these theories seem to be more popular than ever.[74]

The first man to question, in a considered way, whether Shakespeare wrote the plays was apparently the Rev. James Wilmot (1726–1808), a Warwickshire clergyman who lived near Stratford. Wilmot's doubts were aroused by his inability to find a single book belonging to Shakespeare, despite searching in every old private library within a 50-mile radius of Stratford. Wilmot was also unable to locate any authentic anecdotes about Shakespeare from any source in or around Stratford. Wilmot's father, it should be noted, was also a Warwickshire clergyman who might conceivably have met persons who had met Shakespeare or his daughters, but he, too, had evidently heard nothing about him from any local source. From this and other evidence, Wilmot concluded that the real author of Shakespeare's plays was Sir Francis Bacon, whose activities, it seemed, would have provided much of the knowledge of Court life and politics found in the plays.

Wilmot allegedly burned all the notes he had made on his findings, but not before confiding them to one James Corton Cowell, who supposedly presented his findings at the unlikely venue of a meeting of the Ipswich Philosophical Society in 1805. Neither Cowell's 1805 paper nor the works of Wilmot came to public light until 1932, when a handwritten copy of the Ipswich paper was found in the extensive library of Sir Edward Durning Lawrence, a wealthy pro-Baconian solicitor who had died some years earlier, leaving his immense collection to London University. A summary of the Ipswich paper was published in the *Times Literary Supplement* in 1932, and immediately became famous in anti-Stratfordian circles. Considerable doubt has recently been cast on the entire story.[75]

If the Wilmot story is untrue, the earliest sceptics who doubted that Shakespeare wrote the plays appeared in the mid-nineteenth century, especially the American Delia Bacon (1812–59), who visited Carlyle, Emerson and other notables to advocate her theory that her apparently unrelated namesake Sir Francis Bacon wrote Shakespeare's works.[76] By the late nineteenth century the 'Baconian heresy', as it came to be known, achieved the status of a world-wide cult, and was taken quite seriously by an enormous range of intelligent and perceptive writers and intellectuals. In the earlier part of the twentieth century, Bacon, who had previously held the anti-Stratfordian stage to himself, was joined by other authorship candidates, most notably Edward De Vere, seventeenth Earl of Oxford (1550–1604), Christopher Marlowe (1564–93) and Francis Manners, sixth Earl of Rutland (1578–1632), among many others. In part because, around the time of the Second World War, university-based knowledge came to be considered the only authentic and legitimate knowledge, the previous well-established tradition of amateur autodidactical writers being almost entirely marginalized, and in part because of the implausibility of the views advanced by the anti-Stratfordians, especially the wilder Baconian theories, all anti-Stratfordian writings went into a long period of decline. Towards the end of the twentieth century, however, they returned with a vengeance, especially in the United States, where the case against Shakespeare of Stratford as the author is regularly debated in mainstream magazines and television programmes. It is fair to say that today many thousands of well-educated and well-read people have the gravest doubts that the Stratford man could possibly have written the works ascribed to him, for the reasons examined earlier in this section. Perhaps only the fact that no truly viable alternative authorial candidate, backed by clear-cut and original evidence, has hitherto appeared, has prevented a stampede away from belief and credence in the Stratford man as the author.

The case for Sir Francis Bacon

As noted, for many decades the leading anti-Stratfordian candidate was Sir Francis Bacon (1561–1626). Superficially, the case for Bacon is strong, and he obviously possessed all the intellectual and political qualifications which Shakespeare lacked. Educated at Cambridge, he was probably the foremost English thinker and philosopher of his time, a universal genius of Renaissance thought. Bacon was also one of the greatest lawyers of his generation, entering Parliament in 1584, and holding a wide variety of legal positions culminating in his appointment as Lord Chancellor (with the title of Lord Verulam and, later, Viscount St Albans) in 1617. In 1621, however, Bacon was charged by Parliament with bribery, confessed and was stripped of his offices, and eventually died in rather impoverished circumstances.

Proponents of Bacon as Shakespeare argue that the plays were written as a component of his project, the 'great insaturation', aimed at deliberately creating an all-embracing view of science and humanity. They argue that Bacon wrote on virtually every topic except psychology, and that Shakespeare's works comprise this portion of his overall enterprise, written under a pseudonym, as no courtier or Member of Parliament would write plays under his own name.[77]

As with so many other alternative Shakespeares, there are a few bits of very intriguing evidence in favour of Bacon's claims. In 1867 a paper cover, evidently used as a folder to hold literary works, was discovered in

Northumberland House, the Duke of Northumberland's London residence. Known as the Northumberland Manuscript, it contains innumerable examples of scribbled writings and words, including the names of Bacon and Shakespeare, and even a sequence stating 'By mr. ffrauncis Bacon/Essaies by the same author/William Shakespeare'.[78] The Northumberland Manuscript has never been satisfactorily explained, although it also contains other crucial names.

In 1985 a painting was discovered by workmen renovating some panelling in an old inn dated from Elizabethan times, the White Hart Hotel, near St Albans, Hertfordshire, where Bacon's country seat was situated. It apparently depicts the hunt scene from Shakespeare's *Venus and Adonis*, and contains a picture of a boar similar to the boar's head used by Bacon in his crest. Baconians were, naturally, gleeful, and it is certainly the case that had such a discovery been made in an old inn near Stratford-upon-Avon, it would immediately have been seized upon by orthodox Shakespeareans as proof positive that the Stratford man wrote the plays and poems, and would have been remarked upon in every subsequent Shakespeare biography. Once again, it is difficult to know what to make of the White Hart mural, which is certainly a point in favour of Bacon. Baconians have also made a lengthy list of literary and other references from the Elizabethan age, which they say hints at Bacon as the author.[79]

There is, however, also quite a bit which might be said against Bacon's candidacy. First and foremost, Bacon's turgid, elephantine philosophical style is very different from that of poetry and drama, let alone Shakespeare. Baconians point out that Bacon did write some poetry under his own name, but these works were few and far between.[80] There are other fairly crucial points which might also be made against Bacon. Rather surprisingly, he never visited Italy, even as a young man. Baconians suggest that he could have learned anything he wanted to know about Italy from his brother Anthony, who lived on the continent for 12 years, or from one of his many friends who toured Italy.[81] While Bacon must certainly have known Southampton (to whom Bacon wrote after his release from the Tower in 1603), they were not particularly close, and Southampton is hardly mentioned in the latest full-scale biography of Bacon, *Hostage to Fortune* (1998) by Lisa Jardine and Alan Stewart.[82] It is not obvious why Bacon would have dedicated two long, abjectly flattering poems to him (as Shakespeare did). While Bacon was initially a general supporter of Essex, he turned forcefully against him as a result of the 1601 rebellion and helped to prosecute him; it is difficult to see why this should have marked the climacteric that it did in his works, if Bacon was indeed Shakespeare. Bacon was, apparently, a homosexual who remained a lifelong bachelor until, at the age of 45, he married a 14-year-old heiress by whom he had no children. This might explain the apparently homoerotic components of the Sonnets, but not the 'dark lady' or the enthusiastic heterosexuality of most of Shakespeare's works. Shakespeare's last plays were probably written in 1612–14, which is quite consistent with the Stratford man as author, but inconsistent with the life of Bacon, who lived for another 12 years after 1614. Baconians argue that Bacon was enormously busy in his legal offices from about 1613 onwards, but he was also busy as Solicitor-General from 1607 to 1613, while the last plays were being written. In any case, since Shakespeare died in 1616, believers in Baconianism ought to be looking for a subsequent pseudonymous 'front man', but none seems to exist.

Finally, as with the other authorship candidates, there is simply no compelling evidence that Bacon wrote Shakespeare's works. After more than 150 years of Baconianism, if any existed it surely would have surfaced long ago. Instead, for decades the Baconians did everything possible to discredit their own cause by 'discovering' absurd and preposterous codes, anagrams and cyphers in Shakespeare's works which allegedly 'proved' that Bacon wrote his works. These cryptograms became a stock-in-trade of Baconianism from around 1880 until about 1925, especially in the works of Ignatius Donnelly (1831–1901), a well-known American radical politician who also wrote the first modern book on Atlantis, and Elizabeth Wells Gallup, another American, and nothing did more to discredit the entire anti-Stratfordian endeavour. It has taken many decades for the legitimate anti-Stratfordian cause to recover from the harm done to it by these excesses, as most of today's Baconians freely acknowledge. It has also taken a long time for any cryptographical work concerning Shakespeare to recover from some of these latter Baconians' attempts to prove that the whole body of the works is encrypted. This is a great pity, since *some* encryption might be legitimate.

The case for the Earl of Oxford

In the twentieth century, the most popular authorship candidate was Edward De Vere, seventeenth Earl of Oxford (1550–1604), who today has a widespread following around the world. Whenever the anti-Stratfordian position is contested in the United States, it is normally argued by Oxfordians, who are thus well-known to the informed public. At first glance, De Vere appears to be an ideal candidate, bearing in mind the crucial difficulty that he certainly died in 1604: a well-educated courtier and a poet and playwright under his own name. The case for Oxford was first made around 1918 by a Gateshead schoolmaster named J. Thomas Looney, who became widely known in 1920 with the publication of his *'Shakespeare' Identified*.[83] Looney was convinced that 'Shakespeare' was a pseudonym, but was unconvinced that Bacon was the real author. Instead, he made a list of 18 characteristics which in his view the real Shakespeare must have had. Some of these appear likely and useful ('of superior education – classical – the habitual associate of educated people'; 'an enthusiast for Italy' – although many would argue that he must have visited Italy), others are dubious ('of probable Catholic leanings but touched with scepticism'; 'apparently eccentric and mysterious') while still others appear contradic- tory ('a mature man of recognized genius' but also 'not adequately appreciated'). Searching through the ranks of Elizabethan poets and writers he came across De Vere's poem 'Women' (which begins 'If women could be fair and yet not fond'), traced all he could find on him, and decided that he was the man. He soon attracted a considerable following among anti-Stratfordians on both sides of the Atlantic, which has continued over the decades and has probably grown markedly in recent years. Sigmund Freud was an early and committed enthusiast.

There are a number of excellent points to be made in Oxford's favour. Oxford was educated at Cambridge and was a ward of Lord Burghley; Burghley had an enormous library, and Arthur Golding, the translator of Ovid, was Oxford's tutor. In 1574–76 he travelled widely in Europe, vis- iting many places in Italy. Besides being a poet and playwright, he was a patron of the theatre, with a theatre company, Oxford's Men, under his patronage. As a playwright, Francis Meres in 1598 said that he was 'the best for Comedy amongst us', although this can be taken either way, since Meres also praised 'Shakespeare' in the same passage of his work *Palladis Tamia: Wits Treasury*. (Evidently Meres believed that Oxford and Shakespeare were two different men.) Oxford was (under his own name) what might be described as a major-minor poet; some of his poems have become anthology pieces.

Up to a point, De Vere's biography also strengthens his case. If he was indeed Shakespeare, a number of passages in the Sonnets seem autobiographical, as does some part of *Hamlet*. Many believe that most of the Sonnets were written in the early 1590s, when De Vere was in his early forties, echoing Sonnet 2 ('when forty winters shall besiege thy brow . . .'). He was apparently lame, and was probably bisexual, being accused by a courtier in 1576 of being a 'buggerer of boys'. In 1590 he tried unsuccessfully to arrange a marriage between his daughter Elizabeth and Lord Southampton, which could have been the occasion for writing the Sonnets advising a young man to wed. Certainly the Earl of Oxford was more likely to address another earl in the manner of these Sonnets than was an actor from the provinces.

Oxfordians also maintain that Polonius in *Hamlet* is a caricature of Lord Burghley, Oxford's father-in-law, and that other aspects of the play seem to comprise an autobiography of De Vere. It has also been found that Oxford invested and lost £3,000 with a London merchant named Michael Lok (or Lock), possibly the prototype of Shylock, a name unknown in Jewish nomenclature. In *The Merchant of Venice*, Antonio posts bond for 3,000 ducats with Shylock, his security being 'a pound of flesh'.

Although the case for De Vere is thus genuinely intriguing, there is also much about it which is seemingly wrong. Most obviously, De Vere's dates are apparently all wrong: while Bacon is the man who died too late, De Vere is the man who was born and died too soon. When Shakespeare's first plays appeared around 1589–90, De Vere was already nearly 40. Oxfordians argue that the works he published under his own name represent his 'juvenalia', and (apparently forgetting *Titus Andronicus* and other works) that this explains the apparent maturity of Shakespeare's earliest plays. They also claim that many of the plays were written much earlier than is credited in the orthodox chronology. It is certainly true, for instance, that in 1589 Thomas Nashe referred to 'whole Hamlets, I should say handfulls of tropical speeches', indicating that an earlier version of *Hamlet* (known as the 'Ur-Hamlet', and thought by orthodox scholars to have been written by Thomas Kyd) certainly existed: Shakespeare's *Hamlet* was first registered in 1602.[84]

The greatest single stumbling block to accepting the Oxfordian case is plainly that he died in 1604, and around 11 of Shakespeare's plays appeared after that date. Oxfordians argue that they were written earlier and subsequently 'released'. They point out that the mysterious dedication of the

Sonnets, published in 1609, refers to 'our ever-living poet', a phrase used only about the dead, and that the strange preface to *Troilus and Cressida*, also published in 1609, refers (very ambiguously) to 'the grand possessors will', indicating that the play was in other hands. This preface is also headed 'A never writer, to an ever reader. Newes', which Oxfordians claim is a pun on Oxford's name De Vere.

Opponents of De Vere claim that the later plays contain references to events after Oxford died, especially to the Gunpowder Plot of 1605 in *King Lear* and *Macbeth*, and to William Strachey's 1610 account of a shipwreck in the Bermudas which, it seems, formed the basis of *The Tempest*. If these references are accurate, this of course automatically rules out De Vere as a possible author; that the apparent references are post-1604 is strenuously denied by Oxfordians.

As with Bacon, another major point against Oxford is the lack of any direct evidence that he wrote the plays: surely a clear-cut 'smoking gun' would have been found in the more than 80 years since De Vere was first proposed as a candidate, if it existed. Recently, something much like this has (according to Oxfordians) come to light, in Oxford's 1579 Bible, owned by the Folger Library in Washington DC. The book contains about 1,000 underlined or marked passages and 40 marginal notes, apparently in De Vere's handwriting. In 1992 a detailed examination of these annotations was made by Roger Stritmatter and Mark Anderson, two American Oxfordians, who found that more than a quarter of the marked passages were direct references to Shakespeare's plays, among them more than 100 not previously noted by Shakespearean scholars, but which may be the sources of Shakespeare's phraseology. (It must be noted, however, that the majority of the marked passages have not been linked with Shakespeare's works.) Some historians who have studied De Vere's life also believe that he was simply too violent, quarrelsome and moody to have written the plays (he was once wounded in a duel with the uncle of his mistress), and while his early verse shows talent, it lacks the complexity and intelligence we associate with Shakespeare. In 1601 Oxford served as a juror when Southampton was convicted of treason for his part in the Essex rebellion; there is no reason to suppose that 1601 marked any kind of a climacteric in the evolution of his later plays, which, in any case, must have been written earlier, given his death in 1604. On the other hand, Oxford's son-in-law was Philip Herbert, Earl of Montgomery, one of the dedicatees of the First

Folio, who may have had a role in its publication. (However, Philip did not marry De Vere's daughter until after the death of her father.) The evidence about De Vere is thus very confusing. It is easy to see why he has been the strongest authorial candidate in recent years, but also easy to see why he has not swept everything before him.

The other candidates

There are several other well-known candidates. Christopher Marlowe (1564–93) was the second greatest playwright of the Elizabethan age, and has often been proposed as a collaborator (in his lifetime) with Shakespeare.[85] In 1955 Calvin Hoffman, an American, suggested in his book *The Murder of the Man Who Was Shakespeare* that Marlowe survived the affray at Deptford, Kent, in which he was allegedly killed, moved to France or Italy, and continued to write Shakespeare's plays. Hoffman cited a 1910 study of the word-lengths in the works of Marlowe and Shakespeare to show that the two authors were virtually identical in this respect. Yet their world-views would appear to be utterly different, with Marlowe's two-dimensional ferocity completely unlike Shakespeare's universal empathy. Since Marlowe died in 1593 (as officially certified by a legal inquest), the theory that he wrote Shakespeare's works would appear to be *a priori* absurd, unless dramatic evidence to the contrary can be found.

Another authorial candidate sometimes proposed is Roger Manners, fifth Earl of Rutland (1576–1612), whose case is arguably a strong one as he visited Italy, served as temporary Ambassador to Denmark in 1603, and took part in the Essex rebellion, serving five months in the Tower. As Rutland was born in 1576, however, this means that he would have been as young as 13 when Shakespeare's first play appeared.

Yet another candidate earl was William Stanley, sixth Earl of Derby (1561–1642), whose initials are the same as Shakespeare's, toured Europe, and was the patron of a theatre company. His partisans believe that *Love's Labour's Lost*, set in Navarre, contains clear-cut references to Stanley's visit. As with Rutland, the case is at least arguable.[86]

Dozens of other possible candidates have also been proposed down the years. One of the most intriguing is Mary Sidney, Countess of Pembroke (*c.*1561–1621), sister of Sir Philip Sidney, and famous intellectual, writer and patron of literature in her own right.[87] What has been lacking in each of these cases is the concrete documentation to link the candidates to Shakespeare's writings. Without such evidence, it is not surprising that virtually every educated, reasonably well-born man and woman in Elizabethan England has been proposed as an authorship candidate at one time or another.[88]

Chapter 2

The Real Shakespeare

W e seem to have reached an impasse. The evidence suggests that William Shakespeare lacked the background and education necessary to have written the works attributed to him, but also that the cases which have been made on behalf of the other authorship 'candidates' are unconvincing and lacking in evidence. Is there a way forward? Is it possible that, for centuries, we have actually overlooked and ignored the real author of Shakespeare's works, despite the wide range of persons who have been suggested, over the past 200 years, as the 'real Shakespeare'? Remarkably, this appears to be the case.

Our contention is that Sir Henry Neville (*c.*1562–1615), a wealthy, well-educated landowner, Member of Parliament, and Ambassador to France in 1599–1601, wrote the works of William Shakespeare. Although the name and fairly important role of Sir Henry Neville in English politics in the early 1600s is known to specialist historians, it is safe to say that not one reader in a thousand has ever heard of him. He published no literary works under his own name and has never previously been suggested as the author of Shakespeare's works – although one well-known primary source bears evidence to his connection with the Authorship Question as his name is on top of the Northumberland Manuscript, the mysterious document which was discovered in 1867 and which has often been taken by Baconians in support of their case.

The rest of this book will be devoted to providing the evidence for our contention: first, an overview of some direct evidence from Elizabethan sources which supports our conclusions, and then a biography of Sir Henry Neville, showing how his life meshes literally at every point with the accepted chronology of Shakespeare's works. We will also offer our suggestions as to how and why the First Folio was compiled in 1623, wrongly attributing the works to the Stratford actor instead of to the rightful author.

Documentary evidence

We believe that a number of primary sources from the Elizabethan period exist which corroborate the great weight of other evidence that Sir Henry Neville wrote Shakespeare's works. Probably the most important is the Tower Notebook of 1602, which for the past 50 years has been held in the Lincolnshire Record Office. Formally titled 'Extracts Copyed and collected out of the Recordes in the Tower Ann: 1602', it was written towards the end of Sir Henry Neville's confinement in the Tower of London in 1601–03 for his part in the Essex rebellion. This handwritten 196-page notebook consists in large part of extracts copied from the historical sources held at the Tower of London concerning 'personal services' afforded to the kings of England down the ages. Some of these extracts, copied out in a Gothic-like hand, are concerned with the coronations of the English monarchs. In a separate hand, a writer – presumably but not certainly another man – has annotated these notes, adding further remarks. The last coronation to be commented upon by the annotator – and the only one about which he has written an entire page – is that of Anne Boleyn, consort of Henry VIII and mother of Queen Elizabeth I, the reigning monarch who would die in March 1603. It contains many parallels with the coronation scene in Shakespeare's play *Henry VIII*, although *Henry VIII* was not written or performed until 1613, more than ten years later.

The first section of the page in question describes a great feast, such as the Lord Mayor and Aldermen of London held following a coronation. The second section of the page seems to concern the identity of the almoner at the time of Henry VIII's coronation and mentions the family name of the almoner at Anne Boleyn's coronation. In the third section, the author discusses the role of the Cinque Port barons who 'cary the canapie' over royalty at a coronation. Transcribed in full the page reads:

London *maior of London to serve the k[ing] in p[er]son in the halle and*
his chamb[e]r with a cup gold, & that his fee to cary awaye
other ciitzens. serve that daye in the butlers office
w[i]th the chefe butler, aslike at table in the halle, as afor
dinner in the chamb[e]r.
they claym this the maior & ciitz[en]s. that the Ald[ermen] & citizns
have a place to sit at dynner at table on the right
syde of the halle, as the k[ing] sitts, at the up[er] part of
the foresayd table.
that to this service the maior & citizns have bin admit[te]d
& never gayn sayde.
The Lo[rd] Steward made repeat of this clayme to the k[ing]
& by his ma[jes]ti[e]s comm[and] it was ord[er]ed for that he soe
clayms. and the maiors de ciph[?] aureo [=cup gold] services, &
have the cipho[?]& that p[er]tayns to it as the k[ing's] guest
And the Alder[men] shall have ther place to syt at dyn[n]er
at the sayd right side table.

Eli[?]

Jon Lo[rd] Latimer for [?] & Tho Mowbray. for the
office of allmoiynerie to k[ing].
Jon & Tho Gray claymed it also: that the clothe under
the k[ng] p[?] from the chamber Royall to the pulpit
in Westm[in]st[e]r p[er]tayns to the almoi[ne]r. and that p[ar]t of
the clothe w[it]hin the church where the k is coron[ate]d ptayns
to that churche, and that part out of the churche[?]
the Alm[oine] to give the poore. Those of Westm[in]str
alayd[?] it came not to them, neither co[u]ld the [?]
thinge ag[a]inst this [?]
orderd that them of Westm[in]st[e]r churche, that have part of the
clothe, betwixt the gate & dore [?] & restore it to
the Alm[on]er. to satisfye [harrie]? for the clother in that
place. savinge all rights.

. . .

Wm. Vernon to make wafers [lysten?] [?]
Barons 5 ports claym to cary the canapie on 4

> *Lances gilt sylver. 4 men at a lance And so at*
> *the Q[ueen's] cro[w]ninge. to syt in the halle at dyn[n]er at*
> *the first table next the k[ing]. on the right hand & so at*
> *the Q[ueen's] crowninge. Abbott Westmst[minste]r clayms canapie and*
> *staves[or stars] but had it not.*

It appears that some of this material was used in some form in the opening of *Henry VIII*, and in its Act IV, Scene I:

> *Lord Mayor, Aldermen, Lords and Ladies in the Dumb Shows; Women*
> *attending upon the Queen; Scribes, Officers, Guards, and other*
> *Attendants; Spirits [citizens] –*
>
> ### The Prologue
>
>
>
> *I come no more to make you laugh; things now*
> *That bear a weighty and a serious brow,*
> *Sad, high, and working, full of state and woe,*
> *Such noble scenes as draw the eye to flow,*
> *We now present . . .*
>
>
>
> *A canopy borne by four of the CINQUE-PORTS; under it the QUEEN in*
> *her robe; in her hair richly adorned with pearl, crowned. On each side her,*
> *the BISHOPS OF LONDON and*
> *WINCHESTER . . .*
> *. . . FIRST GENTLEMAN. They that bear*
> *The cloth of honour over her are four barons*
> *Of the Cinque-ports.*
> *SECOND GENTLEMAN. Those men are happy; and so are all*
> *are near her. . . .*
> *. . . SECOND GENTLEMAN . . . These are stars indeed,*
> *And sometimes falling ones.*
> *FIRST GENTLEMAN. No more of that.*
> *Exit Procession, with a great flourish of trumpets*
>
>
>
> *Act IV, Sc. I*
>
>

In addition, Shakespeare's famous Sonnet 125, published in 1609, contains well-known lines about bearing the canopy:

Were't ought to me I bore the canopy,
With my extern the outward honouring,
Or laid great bases for eternity,
Which proves more short than waste or ruining?

These lines are normally taken to mean that the poet does not regret the fact that he did not in fact bear the canopy over some high dignitary. But is the writer really saying (in that Sonnet, published in 1609) 'As if I ever cared about such things, I bore the canopy', or is he saying, 'Would it have meant anything to me, even if I had have borne the canopy?'. Grammatical and semantic arguments can be made for both interpretations. It is logical to assume, in either case, that the writer had a special interest in this. There has so far been no other authorship candidate who was qualified to carry out this office and who, at the same time, left notes foregrounding that role.

It appears that Neville, who was a Knight of Sussex and a Baron of the Cinque Ports, was therefore entitled to bear the canopy over the King at his coronation, and could well have expected to have done so at the coronation ceremony of James I, held in 1604. (This Sonnet can thus probably be dated to about 1604–05.)

There are several important points about the extract from the Tower Notebook. First, its provenance is unquestionably from Sir Henry Neville: he was a prisoner in the Tower in 1601–03, when he was freed by James I. At Neville's death in 1615, the notebook was inherited by his favourite daughter and her husband Sir Richard Worsley, who were ancestors of the family which became Baron Yarborough in 1794 and Earl of Yarborough in 1837. This family owned land in the Isle of Wight and in Lincolnshire, and in about 1954 donated the Tower Notebook and other associated material to the Lincolnshire Record Office. There it has remained, unnoticed and apparently little read, until it was discovered in the course of researching this book.[1]

Secondly, while this extract is somewhat similar to the portions of the third volume of Holinshed's *Chronicles* which is normally cited by scholars as the main source for Shakespeare's *Henry VIII*, and also has some phrasing in common with portions of Halle's *Chronicles*, another important source for Shakespeare's history plays, it is certainly not identical, and arguably represents a new, unknown source for the coronation material in the play. It may be useful to compare the Tower Notebook extract, and the rest of the coronation scene in *Henry VIII*, Act IV, Sc. I, with the relevant extract from Halle's *Chronicles*:

> ... *Lady Anne, marquess of Pembroke, was received as queen of England by all the lords of England. And the mayor and aldermen, with all the guilds of the City of London, went to Greenwich in their barges ... And on Saturday, the last day of May, she rode from the Tower of London through the City with a goodly company of lords, knights and gentlemen, with all the peers of the realm, richly appareled ... She herself rode in a rich chariot covered with cloth of silver, and a rich canopy of cloth of silver borne over her head by the four Lords of the Ports, in gowns of scarlet, crimson velvet decorated with ermine, and a robe of purple velvet decorated with ermine over that, and a rich coronet with a cap of pearls and stones on her head; and the old duchess of Norfolk carrying her train in a robe of scarlet with a coronet of gold on her cap, and Lord Burgh, the queen's Chamberlain, supporting the train in the middle*
>
> ... *And when the mass was done they left, every man in his order, to Westminster Hall, she still going under the canopy, crowned, with two sceptres in her hands ... earl of Arundel butler ... Viscount Lisle panter, and Lord Grey almoner.*[2]

From this extract, it can therefore clearly be seen that the Tower Notebook (with its mention of Lord Grey as almoner) was referring to Anne Boleyn's coronation. (Lord Grey was certainly not considered for the role in James I's coronation, because that Lord was imprisoned at the time on suspicion of being involved in a conspiracy.)[3]

More basically, the fundamental question one might ask of this coronation extract is what it, and other material relating to coronations, is doing in a notebook compiled by Sir Henry Neville in the Tower of London? Neville expected to be pardoned and freed by James I as soon as he became king (as in fact he was, along with his fellow prisoner and participant in the Essex rebellion, the Earl of Southampton, Shakespeare's supposed patron and dedicatee), and expected to play a role in the coronation, as well as to be rewarded by James I with high office. However, at the time he held no obvious position that would have entitled him to play a role in organising the coronation, which, in any case, would have had to have been approved by the new king and his senior officials. The inference is that these extracts were copied out as background material for a pageant or play of some kind to celebrate the parents of Queen Elizabeth I – Henry VIII and Anne

Boleyn – and the birth of Elizabeth herself. Perhaps Neville was hoping that if he were ever to be revealed as the author of the plays attributed to Shakespeare, then Elizabeth might be more disposed to free him if he could present her with a play written to celebrate her dynasty. This supposition is strengthened by the fact that the notebook extract concerns the coronation of Anne Boleyn. However, so far as anyone knew or knows, Sir Henry Neville was not a playwright. Yet here he was, in 1602, writing sketches which found their way into a play, in a notebook which also proclaimed itself to be principally concerned with 'Pastime'. The frontispiece of the Tower Notebook declares:

> *Serieantiez*
> *of sundrie kindes*
>
> *Namely*
>
> *Personall Services appertaining to*
> *the thronne and kings of this*
> *Realme aswell in tymes of*
> *warre as of peace and*
> *pastime Especially*
> *at there*
>
> *Coronation*
>
> *Copied and collected out of the*
> *Recordes in the tower*
> *Anno 1602*

He wrote nothing under his own name and had no apparent interest or *locus standi* in any such pageant or play; moreover, he was a prisoner in the Tower of London. Yet here is direct evidence of his interest in just such a play or pageant – one which, 11 years later, was actually written or co-authored by William Shakespeare as his final work.

(Almost all authorities regard *Henry VIII* as having been co-authored with John Fletcher. In 1613 Fletcher – and his collaborator Francis Beaumont – were certainly close friends and political supporters of Sir Henry Neville. Beaumont and Fletcher's play *A King and No King* was dedicated to Neville, who apparently owned the manuscript copy of their play).[4]

The fact that the Tower Notebook does not appear to be in Neville's hand does not present a problem. The employment of scribes was entirely permissible for wealthy prisoners in the Tower, and Neville's long-time scribe, John Packer, was probably employed for this purpose. Packer was, in later years, known to be a friend of Sir Richard Worsley, Neville's son-in-law, who inherited the Notebook. The Tower Notebook, which remains to be analyzed in full, may well contain many other indications of its Shakespearean links. Indeed, within the pages of that Notebook, there is also mention of 'three-fours' and choirs 'trilling', which is also described in the stage directions to Anne Boleyn's coronation in Act IV, Sc. I of *Henry VIII:*

THE ORDER OF THE CORONATION.
1   *A lively flourish of trumpets.*
2   *Then, two JUDGES.*
3   *LORD CHANCELLOR, with the purse and mace before him.*
4   *CHORISTERS singing. Music.*

The second Elizabethan primary source which we believe may well come directly from Sir Henry Neville and clearly show his Shakespearean links is the copy of Halle's *Chronicles* described in a well-known work published in 1954 by Alan Keen and Roger Lubbock, *The Annotator: The Pursuit of an Elizabethan Reader of Halle's Chronicles, Involving Some Surmises About the Early Life of William Shakespeare.* Halle's *Chronicles* is a sixteenth-century work on English history which is universally regarded as one of the major sources for Shakespeare's history plays; it is regarded by some as more significant a source than the better-known *Chronicles* by Holinshed.[5] In 1940 Alan Keen, an antiquarian bookseller, purchased an uncatalogued copy of Halle which contained numerous handwritten marginal annotations that Keen and Lubbock later argued were in Shakespeare's handwriting and represented his own copy, used by the playwright in writing his history plays. Keen and Lubbock traced the provenance of the annotated copy to the Worsley family, without realizing the connections of this family with Sir Henry Neville, of whose secret career as 'William Shakespeare' they obviously had no inkling. Our contention is that the marginal annotations are by Neville. The book was casually bought by Keen, who found it at the bottom of an unmarked box of miscellaneous works at an auction in York (the nearest city to Lord Yarborough's

Brocklesby estate). A friend of Keen's possessed a similar book, which had identical library markings on it to Keen's.[6] Inside his friend's book was the signature of one 'Robert Worsley'. The library mark inside the book was 'App'. Sir Robert Worsley (1669–1742) was a descendant of Neville's daughter and son-in-law, Sir Richard Worsley of Appeldurcombe on the Isle of Wight. In addition to this, the Worsley family had married into the Herbert family earlier in the seventeenth century, and there is evidence that William Herbert, Earl of Pembroke, had himself been a friend of Sir Richard Worsley, Henry Neville's son-in-law, as well as a friend of Sir Henry Neville himself. (William and Philip Herbert were the patrons of the First Folio.)

Keen and Lubbock claimed that this copy of Halle came from another branch of the Worsley family resident in Lancashire, and was thus somehow connected with the young Shakespeare and his alleged stay for two years as a youth in Lancashire. There is no evidence for any of this, and the case that the Isle of Wight branch of the Worsley family is much more likely to have owned the book was convincingly made – again, while knowing nothing whatever of Sir Henry Neville – in a pro-Oxfordian source in 1993, the *Edward De Vere Newsletter*, No. 56, published in British Columbia, Canada, and available on-line.[7]

The third primary source is the so-called Northumberland Manuscript, which, as has been noted earlier, was discovered in 1867 in the London mansion of the Dukes of Northumberland. It contains a vast number of scribblings, among them the names of Bacon and Shakespeare, as well as a listing of some of Shakespeare's plays, a line from *The Rape of Lucrece*, and the word 'honorificabiletudine', an abbreviation of the mysterious long word found in *Love's Labour's Lost*. The significance of the Northumberland Manuscript for this discussion lies in the fact that it is headed with the word 'Nevill' written twice, his family motto *Ne vile velis* and a whole poem in Latin based on this penned below it. A number of commentators on the manuscript (for instance John Michell, in *Who Wrote Shakespeare?* (1996), p.131) have speculated that the 'Nevill' in question was Sir Henry, who – in their view – may have owned the document. The manuscript apparently dates from about 1598–99, several years after Neville and Bacon (his kinsman by marriage and of virtually the same age) almost certainly collaborated during the 'night of errors' at Gray's Inn. Neville might have used the manuscript as a wrapper for holding copies of Shakespeare's plays or other works. No one, however, has satisfactorily explained the manuscript, while its provenance remains a mystery. No Duke of Northumberland was related, by ancestry or marriage, to Sir Francis Bacon. On the other hand, the wife of Henry Percy, eighth Duke of Northumberland, was Katherine, daughter of John Nevill, Lord Latimer (or Latymer) (the very man mentioned in the 'coronation' extract from the Tower Notebook' on p.45), a distant relative of Sir Henry's; she died in 1585. It is thus possible that the manuscript came into the possession of her son, Henry, the ninth Duke (d. 1632), who in 1594 married the sister of the Earl of Essex, with whose circle Sir Henry Neville had many contacts and paid a severe penalty for supporting in 1601. That the manuscript somehow links Neville with Bacon (a kinsman by marriage) but also with Shakespeare, with whom Neville had no publicly known contact, has been ignored by commentators, who have passed over Neville's connection with it in a few brief words.

In considering these contemporary manuscript sources, it is also important to note that nothing equivalent exists for William Shakespeare or for the other authorship 'candidates'; that is, contemporary documents which directly imply that they were the authors of the works of 'Shakespeare'. If, for instance, the annotated copy of Halle's *Chronicles* can be shown beyond a reasonable doubt to have been owned by Neville's son-in-law, with the annotations emanating from Sir Henry Neville himself – as seems very likely – this would arguably provide more in the way of strong *prima facie* authorship evidence for Neville as the author than for anyone else, including Shakespeare of Stratford.

Sir Henry Neville's life

The remainder of this work is devoted to providing a full biography of Sir Henry Neville, linking his life at every point with the accepted chronology of Shakespeare's works. Nevertheless, it is worth summarizing some of the main points here, in order to see the strength of the case which exists for accepting Sir Henry Neville as the real author of the works of Shakespeare. All of these points will be discussed at greater length, with full references, in the biographical section of this book:

- Sir Henry Neville was descended from the brother of 'Warwick the Kingmaker' (and, more remotely, from John of Gaunt). His father's lineage was that of a wealthy landed aristocrat. In contrast, his mother was the niece and heiress of Sir Thomas Gresham, the great London merchant. Neville was educated at Merton College, Oxford, where he was a brilliant student. He knew many foreign languages and owned a large library. He was related by marriage to Lord Burghley, Sir Francis Bacon and many other well-known Elizabethan figures. Neville served as a Member of Parliament for almost all of his adult life, and in the 1600s became well known as one of the leaders of the so-called 'popular party' in Parliament. He served in a variety of local, quasi-judicial offices, such as Justice of the Peace. For much of his life he lived in a large mansion, Billingbear, about six miles from Windsor in Berkshire (where *The Merry Wives* is set), and owned a house in London.

- In 1577–81, while a student at Oxford, Neville travelled for four years throughout Europe as part of an academic visit, led by the great Oxford scholar Sir Henry Savile, whose aim was to procure books and manuscripts for Merton College's library. Neville toured throughout Italy and elsewhere, visiting many leading scholars and intellectuals. He also went to Scotland in the early 1580s, visiting many of the places in *Macbeth*.

- Neville married Anne Killigrew, daughter of one of the famous 'Cooke girls' of Gidea Hall, who were known as the most educated ladies in England. Henry and Anne Neville then had six daughters, of whom Henry was extremely fond. His own sisters were also strong, educated women (which all echoes the strong female roles in the works of Shakespeare.) Neither Shakespeare nor any other of the authorship 'candidates' to date has ever had such respect for women's intelligence as Neville. Other of the Cooke girls married Lord Burleigh, Sir Nicholas Bacon and Sir Thomas Hoby. The Hobys lived at Bisham in a palace which was once the home of Richard Neville, Earl of Warwick, while the Hoby household has often been thought of as providing a backdrop for *Twelfth Night*. Similarly, the Cooke household of Gidea Hall has been thought by scholars to find its echoes in *Much Ado About Nothing*.

- William Shakespeare was, apparently, distantly related to Neville through his mother Mary Arden, whose family claimed a relationship with the Barons Bergavenny (Neville's grandfather) with a similar coat of arms. Shakespeare may have been introduced to Neville through this family linkage.

- Neville was a lifelong friend and political ally of Lord Southampton, 'William Shakespeare's' patron. In 1601–03 Neville spent two years imprisoned in the Tower of London alongside Southampton for their roles in the Essex rebellion. They were fellow directors of the London Virginia Company and, by 1610, were so close that one observer referred to Neville as Southampton's 'dear Damon', a bosom friend like the classical Damon and Pythias.

- Neville was increasingly fat, and was apparently known as 'Falstaff' to his friends. 'Oldcastle', Falstaff's original name, is an obvious pun on Neville's name. Neville apparently looked on Falstaff as an alter ego, but then banished and killed him off in 1598–99 when he was appointed Ambassador to France, which he openly hinted at in the Epilogue of *2 Henry IV*:

Epilogue
...If you be not too much cloyed with fat meat, our humble author will con-tinue the story, with Sir John in it, and make you merry with fair Katharine of France; where, for anything I know, Falstaff shall die of a sweat, unless already a' be killed with your hard opinions; for Oldcastle died martyr, and this is not the man. My tongue is weary; when my legs are too, I will bid you good night.
Exit

In contrast, why Shakespeare of Stratford, if the author, should have killed off his most popular character, remains inexplicable, just as why Shakespeare would have set *The Merry Wives* in Windsor remains a mystery.

- While Ambassador to France, Neville wrote a number of plays, including *Henry V*. In mid-1600 he got word that he was to be per-mitted to return home, which he had been attempting to do for many months. Just as he arrived at Dover, four of Shakespeare's plays were 'staied' by the Chamberlain's Men, clearly in anticipation of discussing them with their real author, who had been absent from the country for two years.

- Neville ultimately became catastrophically involved with the Essex rebel-lion, to which Earl his eighteenth-century descendant wrote that he had an 'excessive attachment'.[8] The mysterious production of the arguably treasonable *Richard II* by the Chamberlain's Men, Shakespeare's company, took place several days after Neville had long conversations with the leaders of the rebellion, and was promised that he would be made Secretary of State if the rebellion succeeded. After both Essex and Southampton gave evidence against him, Neville was sentenced to life imprisonment in the Tower and a huge fine. In the Tower, Neville wrote *Hamlet* – which is 'about' the Essex rebellion, and also wrote many of his Sonnets, which are addressed to his fellow prisoner Southampton, whom he forgave for betraying him. In the Sonnets, Neville often addressed the 'disgrace' and 'stain' which had befallen him. His imprisonment marked a seminal break in his writing career, with the previous works by 'Shakespeare', the Italianate comedies and the history plays, being succeeded by the great tragedies and the so-called 'problem plays'. This break in Shakespeare's career has been noticed by many critics but remains inexplicable in terms of the known life of William Shakespeare.

- Freed in 1603 when James I came to the throne, Neville clearly refers to his experience in the first play he wrote after leaving the Tower, *Measure for Measure*. His plays in the 1600s can clearly be linked to the 'oppositionist' politics he increasingly pursued as it became clear that the new king would not reward Neville with office or money.

- Neville was also a director of the London Virginia Company, which he hoped would restore his much reduced fortune. *Shakes-peares Sonnets* was published in 1609 as a thank-offering to his great friend and fellow director Lord Southampton upon the launch of the second London Virginia Company in June 1609, a few days after *Shakes-peares Sonnets* was published. Neville himself wrote the celebrated Dedication to *Shakes-peares Sonnets*, not Thomas Thorpe. As a director, Neville had access to the Strachey Letter about the famous Bermuda shipwreck of 1609, which he used as one of the bases of *The Tempest* of 1611.

- Ill and disappointed at the end of his life, Neville increasingly collaborated with other playwrights such as John Fletcher. A play by Beaumont and Fletcher, *A King and No King*, was dedicated to Neville, whose political stance they admired; Neville owned the manuscript copy of the play. Neville's last play, *Henry VIII*, written in 1613, was based in part on material he had copied out while in the Tower in

1602, originally in the hope of writing a play or pageant for Queen Elizabeth.

- Seven or eight years after Neville died in 1615, Neville's family apparently employed Ben Jonson to coordinate the writing of the dedicatory material for the First Folio of Shakespeare's plays, which attributed the works to the obscure Stratford actor and theatre-owner rather than to their real author. They apparently procured for Jonson a prestigious teaching position at Gresham College, London – founded by Neville's great-uncle – where Jonson apparently wrote the dedicatory material in the First Folio, including the famous 'sweet swan of Avon' poem.

Why both Neville and his family wished to keep the real authorship a secret remains a mystery, although the highly and dangerously political nature of the plays might well be a factor, added to the problem that both his father and his cousin – the eventual Lord Bergavenny – shared his name. It would be completely understandable if Henry did not wish these – and possibly other – contemporary namesakes to take the 'blame' for any unpopular opinions expressed in the works. There is also the fact that Neville's major ambition in life was to gain high political office. Not only was he a politician from the early age of 22 onwards, but even before then, when he travelled Europe, he sought out the great political and social thinkers of the day. These great men, who included the Hungarian humanist, André Dudith, were highly impressed with the then teenager's intellect and kept up a correspondence with him – in Latin. There can be little doubt, therefore, that he saw himself as a social and political thinker from his youth and planned accordingly. His social concerns were always linked with the expansion of wealth through international trade, so that he was able to become involved with the founding of Virginia and mapping trade routes to Russia and the Baltic on the macro level, at the same time as raising funds for the founding of free grammar schools in Yorkshire and being the major shareholder in the New River Company (which was a scheme to bring a water supply to North London) on a more local level. Great wealth was needed for his great schemes, and most Elizabethans were beginning to see that wealth was created through trade. With position and money behind him, Neville obviously planned to put new social policies into place, should he ever be placed in a position of power that would enable him to do so, but the process of obtaining that position of power might well be prejudiced if he was perceived by any monarch as the writer of the plays in which – for the first time – the aristocracy and other powerful persons revealed their very thought processes through the Shakespearean soliloquies they declaimed on the public stage. In fact, if anything at all in those plays were to be taken amiss, then Sir Henry's chances of obtaining the high office he sought would probably instantly have been dashed.

Several contemporary writers, such as John Davies of Hereford, did hint at the actual author at the time. John Donne and Inigo Jones spoke alongside Neville in after-dinner speeches. They and Ben Jonson were Neville's friends from the Mitre Club – the philosophical sister of the Mermaid Club (to which Neville's steward, Thomas Edmondes, belonged) – so it is hardly surprising that the real Shakespeare's identity could be kept within a very close and sympathetic circle. John Davies' poem to Shakespeare and Ben Jonson's poem to Sir Henry Neville are looked at again later in this book:

> *Some say (good Will) which I, in sport, do sing*
> *Had'st thou not plaid some Kingly parts in sport,*
> *Thou hadst bin a companion for a King;*
> *And, beene a King among the meaner sort.*
> *Some others raile' but raise as they thinke fit,*
> *Thou hast no rayling, but, a raigning Wit:*
> *And honesty thou sow'st, which they do reape;*
> *So to increase their Stocke which they do keepe.*
>
> *John Davies*

> **To Sir Henry Nevil**
> *Who now calls on thee, NEVIL, is a Muse,*
> *That serves nor fame, nor titles; but doth chuse*
> *Where vertue makes them both, and that's in thee:*
> *Where all is faire, beside thy pedigree.*
> *Thou art not one, seek'st miseries with hope,*
> *Wrestlest with dignities, or fain'st a scope*
> *Of seruice to the publique, when the end*
> *Is priuate gaine, which hath long guilt to friend.*
> *Thou rather striv'st the matter to possesse,*

And elements of honor, the[a]n the dresse;
To make thy lent life, good against the Fates:
    And first to know thine owne state, then the States.
To be the same in roote, thou art in height;
    And that thy soule should give thy flesh her weight.
Goe on, and doubt not, what posteritie,
    Now I haue sung thee thus, shall iudge of thee.
Thy deedes, vnto thy name, will prove new wombes,
    Whil'st others toyle for titles to their tombes.

                                     Ben Jonson

Chapter 3

The Neville Heritage

Family roots

Probably the most important single thing one can say about the real author of Shakespeare's works is that he was a Neville, a member of one of Britain's most influential, illustrious and powerful families, whose mark was set at the heart of the development of English history from the time of the Norman Conquest through the Tudor era. Although the family boasted of its links to Gilbert de Neville, steward to William the Conqueror, who had played a prominent role in the Norman victory at Hastings, it is more accurate to see the origins of its high status and fortunes in the career of Alan de Neville (d. *c.*1178), who lived about a century later.[1] Alan de Neville was Chief Forester under Henry II. The family rose as high officials under England's kings over the next 300 years, and became, above all, a major power in the north of England, rivalling the Percies (with whom the Nevilles eventually intermarried).

Eventually, they also intermarried with royalty: Sir Henry Neville was a descendant of John of Gaunt, 'time-honoured Lancaster'.[2] Neville's remote ancestor, Ralph, sixth Baron Neville of Raby and first Earl of Westmoreland, one of the greatest supporters of Henry IV in his successful attempt to gain the throne, married as his second wife Joan Beaufort, daughter of John of

Gaunt, Duke of Lancaster.[3] Neville was thus actually related to all the kings and most of their senior liegemen depicted in Shakespeare's history plays.

By a continuous series of other fortunate marriages with aristocrats, and continuing good luck in securing lucrative offices, the Nevilles became one of the richest and most prominent families in the country, producing a seemingly endless array of famous and powerful figures. A document in the Harleian Collection dating from 1652, when the power of the family was already long in decline, summarizes the extraordinary prominence of the Nevilles during the previous 500 years as follows:

of the most noble, and illustrious, and princely Family of the Nevills [sic], and of their progenitors and ancestors, there have been of the male line one Duke, which was of Bedford, one Marquis, which was of Montacute; fifteen Earls ... two Nevills Archbishops of York, two Nevills Bishops ... also a numberless company of Nevills (with their progenitors and ancestors) that have been Lords and Barons ... There have been one hundred Nevills that were Knights Bachellors [sic]; and divers Nevills Knights of the Noble Order of the Bath ... Of the House of Nevill in the female line ... there hath been one Nevill Queen of England. She [Anne Neville] was the first wife of Edward Plantagenet, Prince of Wales , the only son of King Henry the Sixth; and then secondly (being a widow), she was remarried to King Richard the Third ... There have been one Nevill Earl Marshall of England; three Nevills Lords High Admirals of the Sea ... There have been four Nevills Lord Chamberlains ... And from Lady Cecilia [Cecily] Nevill the Duchess of York, who was the mother of King Edward the Fourth, and to King Richard the Third, there have lineally descended seven Kings of England, two Queens of Scotland, two Queens of France, one Queen of Spain, and one Queen of Bohemia; and the aforementioned Princess Lady Cecilia, was a great aunt to Sir Henry Nevill, late Lord of Abergavenny ... and to Sir Henry Nevill, late of Billingbeare in Berkshire ... and she was a great-grandmother to King James [the First], the father of King Charles. And the like honour can not be said of any other English family.[4]

The most famous of all the Nevilles was probably Richard Neville, Earl of Warwick, 'the Kingmaker' (1428–71), often seen as the most powerful man in England in the mid-fifteenth century. Neville's younger brother Edward (d. 1476), created Baron of Bergavenny (later known as Abergavenny) was the great-great-grandfather of Sir Henry Neville, the author of

Shakespeare's works: in other words, he descended from a relatively minor, although still titled and wealthy, branch of the family.

No fewer than 48 Nevilles have biographical notices in the *Dictionary of National Biography,* all of whom seem to have been related. The Wars of the Roses, however, marked the apogee of the power and influence of the Nevilles, with many choosing the losing side in that seemingly interminable conflict.

Although diminished in power, the Nevilles entered the Tudor age with several peerages and a good deal of money. Yet high politics, even in early Tudor England, had distinct occupational hazards. Sir Henry Neville's grandfather Sir Edward (a brother of George Neville, third baron Bergavenny) was executed in January 1539 for conspiring with Lord Exeter to overthrow the Tudor dynasty, the so-called 'Courtenay conspiracy'. A boon companion of Henry VIII, Sir Edward, of Addington Park in Kent, was a notable courtier of the time who led a typically colourful life, which included several bouts of imprisonment and exile.[5] Nevertheless, coming from a highly literate household, and surrounded by constant reminders of the greatness of the Nevilles, it is clear that, as 'William Shakespeare', our Sir Henry Neville was prompted to write the history plays because of his family's key centuries-long role in English life.

Sir Henry, the author of Shakespeare's works, was the son of another Sir Henry Neville (hereafter to be referred to as 'Sir Henry I'). Sir Henry I, who was apparently born in 1520, was the son of Sir Edward Neville and Eleanor, daughter of Andrew Windsor, first Baron Windsor. His status in society was, however, not affected by his father's execution and attainder: he was the godson of King Henry VIII, and received an annual royal annuity of £20 which continued until at least 1553.[6] That Henry VIII was his godfather gave rise to a curious and persistent rumour that Sir Edward was in fact Henry VIII's illegitimate son.[7] This rumour is described by Duncan as 'patently false', and, indeed, it is plainly impossible to credit: Henry VIII was born in 1491, and while the date of Sir Edward's birth is unknown, it *is* known that he was knighted at Tournay in 1513, when Henry was only 22.[8] Yet Sir Edward bore a physical resemblance to Henry VIII (as did Sir Henry Neville) and received many favours from him. Neville, as 'Shakespeare', was well aware of this physical resemblance.

Sir Henry I was actually on good terms with Henry VIII, who died in 1547, leaving Sir Henry I £100 in his will; a document which Sir Henry I also witnessed. There are even indications that Queen Elizabeth may have believed that she and Sir Henry were related. In the mid-nineteenth century Lord Braybrooke, a descendant of Sir Henry, published the following claim in *Notes and Queries*, the monthly magazine:

> *Queen Elizabeth, in her first progress at Maidenhithe Bridge, being met by all the Nobility, Knights, and Esquires of Berks . . . coming just against Sir Henry Neville of Billingbear, made a stay, and laid her glove on his head, saying, 'I am glad to see thee,* Brother Henry.' *He, not pleased with the expression, swore she would make him seem a bastard, at which she laughed and passed on. [Emphasis in original.]*[9]

One stock-in-trade of today's anti-Stratfordians is the so-called 'Prince Tudor' theory, that the real author of Shakespeare's plays was actually the illegitimate son of Queen Elizabeth (by Leicester or some other). Incredibly, it is just possible that the real author of the plays believed it might be true; it may have influenced the tenor and direction of the extravagantly pro-Tudor viewpoint of *Richard III*. On the other hand, Neville might simply have written this particular play from a Tudor standpoint so that, should his authorship be discovered, it would counterbalance all the publicity he had given to the Nevilles in previous plays. More than likely, however, a principal message he wished to communicate throughout his history plays was that of kingship in crisis, as Neville was often called 'The English Tacitus' by his fellow Parliamentarians.[10]

Sir Henry I held a variety of offices under King Edward VI, and in the earlier part of Elizabeth's reign, such as Groom of the Bedchamber in 1546, Gentleman of the Bedchamber from before 1550 until 1553, and Master of the Harriers in 1552–55. He had also inherited considerable property in Berkshire, a holding expanded by a royal grant in 1551. He was knighted in October 1551.[11] Throughout his life and the life of his son, the centre of the family holdings was situated in Berkshire, at a stately home, Billingbear, near Waltham St Lawrence and about six miles south-west of Windsor, where our Sir Henry certainly spent much of his youth. Sir Henry I also owned other property in Berkshire around Culham, Warfield and Wargrave, as well as property in Yorkshire.[12]

On the death of his wife's uncle, Thomas Gresham, in 1578 he acquired property in Sussex left in trust for his son. In fact, as soon as his son returned from his continental tour, he took over the estate and ironworks he had been left in Mayfield in Sussex, south of Tunbridge Wells and a few miles south-east of Crowborough. Berkshire, however, was his father's chief domain, and Sir Henry I served in a wide variety of prominent local offices befitting a major Berkshire landowner and public official. He was joint Lord Lieutenant of Berkshire from 1559 until his death in 1593; High Sheriff of Berkshire in 1572–73; Steward of Mote Park in Windsor from 1557; Steward of Donnington and Bailiff of Crown Lands in Newbury, Berkshire (from 1562); High Steward of Reading and of New Windsor (both from 1588). Above all he was a long-serving Member of Parliament for Berkshire, a 'Knight of Shire' (officially given a knighthood in 1551) in the Parliaments elected from March 1553, serving for 40 years until his death in January 1593. He was also a local Justice of the Peace, trying (with other Justices) a wide variety of cases that may be of relevance to a life of 'Shakespeare', such as dealing with witches suspected of making wax figures of the Queen, trying to settle a dispute between clothiers and dyers at Reading, and combating unlawful hunting in Windsor Forest.[13] In 1578 he was required to search the house of a man named Trewchiled, keeper of the Park of Windsor, who was accused of harbouring a thief.[14] He was also parliamentary patron of Windsor borough, controlling the election of its MPs.

The High Steward of a borough was essentially a solicitor for the borough that chose him, furnishing advice and providing influence at the Court.[15] One of his official duties was also to muster men from his area for military service, and his son must have been present at such musterings, since he echoes just such an occasion in *2 Henry IV*, and was himself concerned to reform these 'outmoded' procedures when he took his seat in Parliament.

Sir Henry I also had a rather curious, but conceivably important, connection with theatre history. In June 1560 he leased the building which occupied the site of the old Blackfriars, surrendering it in 1568. Eight years later the site became the first Blackfriars Theatre, and much later still, it was used as Shakespeare's indoor 'other' theatre, in the City of London rather than across the Thames.[16] Whether Sir Henry I retained a continuing interest in this or any other playhouse, or whether this had any effect on the career of his son, remains unknown, but, potentially, these might have far-reaching consequences.

Sir Henry I was out of favour only once in his life, when the Catholic Queen Mary was on the throne (1553–58). Neville, a strong Protestant, was forced to travel abroad during this period. It should also be noted that Henry VIII apparently favoured him for a diplomatic career, for in March 1543 he was introduced to the French Ambassador.[17] This might well have been a factor either in inducing his son, our Sir Henry Neville, to accept this post nearly 60 years later, or a motive behind the rather curious decision of Queen Elizabeth I to appoint him as Ambassador to France in 1599–1600. Like his father, he was good at working in disguise, and his father had already undertaken secret missions abroad, which may indeed have led Elizabeth to trust his son with a diplomatic appointment.

The ability to work in disguise requires an ability to act. Sir Henry I could definitely act and showed his lighter side by devising and appearing in Court revels such as hobby-horse battles and 'saving the young maid at the tilt'. This sense of humour and acting ability were obviously qualities he passed on to his son, though our young Sir Henry kept his abilities in these directions more hidden, using them for more serious and professional dramatic work. Sir Henry I was also a good linguist and writer, his translation of Machiavelli's *Art of War* (1574) having been recently discovered. All in all, then, it could be said that our Henry inherited much of his father's spirit.

In appearance Sir Henry I was, unlike his son, a gaunt, thin-faced man with a long stringy beard, although he must clearly have been fuller of figure when younger in order to be thought kin to Henry VIII![18] He had reddish-brown hair, which his son inherited, and since he probably lived to be 73, a good age at the time, he also enjoyed better health than did his son.

Sir Henry I was married three times. His first wife, whom he married sometime between 1551 and 1555, was Winifred, the daughter of Hugh Loss of Whitchurch in Middlesex.[19] Little is known of her: she must have died before 1561 and they appear to have had no children.[20] But there is some mystery surrounding her, as three women are sculpted on the Neville tomb in Waltham St Lawrence Church, yet only two of them are named. By 1567 Neville had married his second wife, Elizabeth (d. 1573), the daughter of Sir John Gresham, and the mother of our Henry, and also of his brother Edward (b. 1567) and several daughters. However, he had obviously had some relationship with Elizabeth Gresham before this date, as two boys had been born to them by the recorded time of their marriage. Indeed, our young Sir Henry mentions in one letter that he has 11 male siblings. However, despite this assertion, the family and subsequent historians consistently name only three.

Five years after his second wife's death, Sir Henry I married his third wife, Elizabeth (d. 1621), daughter of Sir Nicholas Bacon, first baronet (*c.*1543–1624), and his wife Anne. Elizabeth was the widow of Sir Robert Doyley of Greenlands in Buckinghamshire. They had no children. She was the half-sister of Sir Francis Bacon (1561–1626) the celebrated lawyer who has often been credited with writing Shakespeare's works. The mother of William Cecil, first Earl of Exeter – the equivalent of the prime minister – was a Neville, and Sir Henry Killigrew, his future father-in-law, was also related to the Bacons.[21] It seems difficult to believe that our Sir Henry did not become friendly with his kinsman Sir Francis Bacon, who was probably no more than some 18 months older than he, a friendship of which there are obvious traces in the sequence of the plays and in other documents, such as the Northumberland Manuscript. Both were extraordinarily intelligent – although demonstrating very different kinds of intellectual ability and achievement – and were, in the early part of their careers (though not later) of fairly similar political loyalties. It is also very difficult to believe that Bacon did not know of his kinsman-by-marriage's literary works; indeed, this knowledge might well have saved our Sir Henry from the executioner at the time of the Essex rebellion in 1601. Certainly, in 1611, Sir Francis (then Solicitor General) intervened in a strange trial involving our Sir Henry's son, and his intervention essentially saved that same son from a scurrilous prosecution. That Sir Francis would do this for Sir Henry, despite the political differences which separated them by that time, certainly suggests a link between the two men that surmounted party politics.

It is, however, Sir Henry's second wife, the mother of our Sir Henry, who concerns us here.[22] She brought her son an inheritance, both genetic and financial, of quite a different kind. Elizabeth Gresham was the daughter of Sir John Gresham (*c.*1495–1556), a prominent London merchant who had been Lord Mayor of London in 1547. The Greshams came from Norfolk and their family fortune was founded by Sir John Gresham's grandfather, James, who moved to London around 1450 and adopted the grasshopper as the crest of his mercantile firm. James also moved to Holt, about three miles from his birthplace, and built an imposing manor house. By 1520 the Greshams were already among the leading merchants in London, trading especially with Antwerp and the Low Countries. As it expanded, the family firm added Bordeaux and Venice to their trade routes.[23]

The most famous member of this family was Sir Thomas Gresham (*c*.1519–79), Sir John's nephew, the celebrated founder of the Royal Exchange, and one of the best-known merchants of Elizabethan England. Sir Thomas was a relative of the founder of Gresham College, Holt, and the alleged originator of 'Gresham's Law', the famous economic maxim that 'bad money drives out good' – that is, that gold coins, being intrinsically valuable, will be hoarded by ordinary people if a government introduces coins made of base metal or paper money, although the phrase has wider connotations. In his will, he founded Gresham College in the City of London. Sir John's brother, Sir Richard Gresham (*c*.1485–1549) (the father of Sir Thomas), an extremely successful merchant, exchange dealer and property speculator, also Lord Mayor of London, was one of the richest men of his day, credited by historians as being worth £5.7 billion in today's currency.[24]

Sir Henry Neville

Our Sir Henry Neville, who inherited an estate and ordnance works from Sir Thomas Gresham, thus began life as a man whose lineage was comprised equally of both the old titled aristocracy and recent mercantile wealth, only a few generations old. In this, our Sir Henry Neville's background closely resembled that of the other candidate for the title of the greatest Englishman of the past millennium, Sir Winston Churchill. Indeed, Churchill was related to Neville through the Spencer connection. In our Sir Henry's family trees, primarily held now in Essex Record Office, the Spencer relationship has been stressed. Churchill's father, the Tory politician Lord Randolph Churchill, was the son of the Duke of Marlborough, but his mother, Jenny Jerome, was the daughter of Leonard Jerome, a millionaire New York stockbroker.

While Neville's maternal ancestors were successful London merchants, not only were they aware, to an unusual extent, of intellectual life, they also encouraged it. As noted, Sir Thomas Gresham was the initiator of Gresham College, London, founded in 1579 on the basis of a legacy in his will. It was established for the delivery of public lectures on divinity, music, astronomy, geometry, physics, law and rhetoric.[25] It was initially located at Sir Thomas's house in Broad Street, in the City of London, and then moved to a room above the Royal Exchange, and functioned as a kind of commercially oriented quasi-university (although it did not award degrees), similar to an

English polytechnic in the post-war period.[26] Our Sir Henry was a university student, then was overseas on his European tour when Gresham College was founded in 1579, and it is unlikely – although not impossible – that he had any hand in its establishment. The college's first lectures were not given until 1597, too late to have played any significant role in providing the materials from which 'Shakespeare' derived his early plays, although some Stratfordian historians, at a loss to explain the playwright's extraordinary erudition and access to sources, have suggested that he might have used its facilities in writing some of his works.[27] This seems implausible, although certainly the subject of its lectures strongly paralleled Neville's own interests. One is on firmer ground, however, in suggesting that this rather surprising bequest by a wealthy City merchant strongly implies that he was likely to encourage intellectual pursuits among his relatives, adding to the atmosphere of culture and learning which would have surrounded the young Neville at home and during his youth.

That a well-connected son of an illustrious and aristocratic family like the Nevilles could marry into a virtually *nouveau-riche* London merchant family is an important point worth stressing here, especially in view of the many suggestions that Shakespeare, in his plays, was defending 'feudalism'. This, of course, is a moot point, with an increasing number of scholars, such as Katherine Duncan-Jones of Oxford University and Carol Rutter of Warwick University, stressing the political nature of Shakespeare's works, along with the fact that kingship is nearly always portrayed in a state of crisis. (Even the triumphs of Henry V are negated by remarks in the Epilogue.)

It is important also to note that 'feudalism' in the continental European sense did not exist in England and had not existed since the earlier part of the Norman period.[28] Unlike on the Continent, England had no peasants or serfs; its aristocracy had no legal privileges (apart from sitting in the House of Lords and the right to trial by one's 'peers', as Essex was in 1601), nor was it owed any feudal obligations or payments by its underlings. In particular, and unlike the continental nobility, England's aristocrats were never exempted from paying any tax. Instead, England was already hall-marked by what Thomas Carlyle much later terms the 'cash-nexus society' in which all economic transactions were carried out for monetary payments or wages (within the middle and upper classes, that is). A titled man without a fortune was someone to be pitied and despised, and the English aristocracy was already in a constant, never-ending campaign to become and remain rich, and, if possible, to grow even richer, since ever more money was required for the innumerable ends of aristocratic life, from public display to providing dowries for one's daughters.

Because of this, few aristocrats ever turned down the prospect of marriage for themselves, or their sons or daughters, to a wealthy merchant or his offspring. Self-made men who acquired great wealth could, almost literally always, move into the ranks of the higher aristocracy or gentry, or see their children do so. There was virtually nothing in Elizabethan England of the continental sense of castle-like social class and ranks wherein 'trade' was despised. Indeed, the wealthy merchant classes were descended from younger sons of younger sons of the aristocracy. No aristocrat or wealthy tradesman agreed to allow his child to marry anyone whose pedigree he did not know to be 'gentile'. When our man made an exception to this strong rule, allowing one of his daughters to marry his manservant, his decision was literally the talk of the town. Letters on the subject passed to and fro between most of the courtiers of the time. (One automatically recalls Bassanio's marriage to the rich Portia in *The Merchant of Venice*. Neville's values were obviously occasionally at odds with some of his forebears.)

As England became a major international trading and mercantile power, the fortunes made by Elizabethan England's business tycoons became so large as almost to defy belief, such as the astonishing fortune of £500,000 – the equivalent of over £16 billion today – made by the Turkey merchant Sir John Spencer (d. 1610) or the £250,000 – the equivalent of over £8 billion today – earned by the famous diamond trader Sir Paul Pindar (*c*.1565–1650). Thus the marriage of the senior Sir Henry Neville to a wealthy heiress was nothing unusual, nor was the lifelong pursuit of money and riches by his son, who, for instance, became deeply involved in the second London Virginia Company and other trading companies. To be sure, there were limits to class-mixing, and few titled persons did not believe that God had not deliberately created them above the great mass of people in status. Common people and the middle classes almost invariably deferred to their social superiors, who, of course, dominated Court life, Parliament and local government administration. This paradoxical situation was perhaps responsible for the complex and dichotomous view of the aristocracy offered by Shakespeare in his plays, usually supporting their rule but also favouring, as circumstances change, their overthrow and supplanting. The plays often ridicule the ignorance of the common people but seldom criticize the merchants, clergymen and administrators who had managed to rise from their own, minor aristocratic ranks. Again, Neville's own complex value system will be seen to run along all these divergent lines.

We do not know when or where Sir Henry Neville was born. *The History of Parliament*, which includes biographies of all Members of Parliament of the Elizabethan period, gives his birth date as 1562, a view echoed by the Oxford University alumni register. The old *Dictionary of National Biography*, produced in the late nineteenth century, gives '1564?' as his year of birth, but its successor, the *Oxford Dictionary of National Biography*, which was published in 60 volumes in 2004, lists his birth date as '1561–62'. When Sir Henry matriculated at Merton College, Oxford, on 20 December 1577, his age was given as 15, meaning that he was born between December 1561 and December 1562, making 1562 the most likely year for his birth, although doubts have arisen due to the fact that he was apparently not baptized until May 1564, at St Anne's, Blackfriars. Sir Henry I, as well as his wife's family, owned properties near there and it would not have been unusual for his christening to have taken place there rather than at the family home at Billingbear in Berkshire. The gap of two years or so between his birth, as given in other, credible sources, and his baptism, is unusual, but any explanation is unlikely to be forthcoming at this stage.[29]

It may seem strange to us now that Neville could have gone to university at such a young age, but universities at that time often took on a joint role, acting in a capacity of what we would now call secondary boarding schools. The Earl of Southampton, for instance, entered Cambridge when he was 12 years old. This was not uncommon for the wealthy aristocracy, as the state had an eye for training such men to work abroad in the diplomatic service. For this they had to study modern languages and learn at least 41 different kinds of handwriting, corresponding with the various secretary, court and italic scripts used across Europe at the time. The facility to switch from one style of handwriting to another at will was greatly prized, as was the ability to disguise one's hand, this being particularly useful in certain circumstances thrust upon a state representative.[30] Manuals on the various and varying types of handwriting were available to buy in London, with the most famous of them having been produced in 1570 in Blackfriars, London.[31]

However, to become a Member of Parliament, it was necessary to have attained the age of at least 21 years, and few members were actually as young as that. Neville was first elected to Parliament as the member for New Windsor in 1584: if he was born in 1564, he would have only been 19 or 20 when first elected. While underage MPs were not unknown in Elizabethan England, it is plainly more likely that he was slightly older, around 21 or 22, when elected, thus further supporting 1562 as the year of his birth. He was therefore about two years older than William Shakespeare, the actor and theatre-sharer, and a year younger than his kinsman-by-marriage Sir Francis Bacon. He was born a generation or so after the English Reformation, at a time of upward economic expansion and – by and large – a national mood of euphoria and stability in Elizabethan England. He was 26 when the Armada was defeated and 41 when Queen Elizabeth finally died and was succeeded by James I. It is also self-evident that his dates – probably 1562–1615 – are almost identical with those of Shakespeare (1564–1616), and that – perhaps most importantly – the accepted chronology of Shakespeare's plays and other works can be accommodated by his dates. As we shall see, it is not just that they can merely be accommodated: the known facts of Neville's life consistently match the accepted chronology of Shakespeare's works in a way which is so precise, and so helpful in illuminating why the works of 'Shakespeare' were written, that they simply cannot be coincidental.

Nothing certain is known about Sir Henry Neville's childhood or education. As with other members of the English upper classes before the increase in public schools, he would probably have been educated at home, by a tutor, and almost certainly have made excellent use of his father's extensive library. The tutor or tutors were very likely to have been recent Oxford graduates. It is, however, quite likely that Neville also attended the school for aristocrats run by Burghley behind his house in the Strand, London. Burghley had several wards, and it is said that Henry and Burghley's own son, Robert, virtually grew up together, Burghley and Sir Henry I being friends and political associates. The Earl of Southampton became one of Burghley's wards and also studied at his school, and although this was after Neville's time, he still continued to call on the Cecils. In a later deposition, Neville was to say he had known the Earl 'as a boy at my old Lord Burghley's house', thus proving an early meeting between eventual patron and poet.[32]

Neville apparently flourished at Oxford, the nearest university to Billingbear, and the inference can be reasonably drawn that his tutors created a favourable atmosphere for university life, as well as preparing him so well that he quickly became one of the favourites of his Oxford tutor, the great Sir Henry Savile. The contrast between Neville's education and the rote learning which William Shakespeare almost certainly received at Stratford Grammar School was great. At village grammar schools, students were certainly beaten routinely for failure to parrot their lines and lessons in a satisfactory manner. In striking contrast, Henry Neville was evidently instilled with both a love of learning and very considerable erudition.

Shakespeare's education (if it ever took place) certainly ended when he was 12, the age at which his father lost all his money, and there is no evidence that Shakespeare of Stratford received any subsequent education of any kind. Henry Neville, in contrast, was an accomplished linguist and became familiar with the most advanced learning of the Renaissance throughout continental Europe. We know little about the course of his life prior to Oxford, but he presumably made many trips to London, where his mother's relatives lived in affluence and where his father was a Member of Parliament. He was certainly very familiar, as *The Merry Wives of Windsor* attests, with the environs of Billingbear, including Windsor, only six miles away, and its surrounding villages. Conceivably, Neville might have travelled further afield while still a youngster, even to the Continent, given the long-standing European linkages of so many of his family.

In 1573, when Neville was probably about 11, his mother died. This was perforce a crushing blow, which had unknown, but presumably very significant, consequences for his writings. It might have made him more introspective, perhaps occasioning an even wider and deeper reading in history and the classics, possibly even some experimentation with writing plays or other works. Neville's linguistic gifts and, presumably, his abilities at expression must have been evident at an early age, together with his real talent, demonstrated at Oxford, for mathematics, which is a strength he held in common with the poet, Sir Philip Sidney. The very first firm evidence we have about Neville's education occurred, however, on 20 December 1577, when he matriculated at Merton College, Oxford. A devastating outbreak of plague had erupted in Oxford shortly before, and he was lucky to survive. Other undergraduates left in fear of this, so Neville's love of learning must have been great for him to have stayed on.[33]

Oxford

Merton College, founded in 1264 by Walter de Merton, is one of the oldest Oxford colleges, and contains an outstanding library, founded in 1373.[34] (It is possible that one or more of Neville's significant tutors before matriculating at Oxford was connected with Merton: detailed examination of their records would be fruitful.) It was also strongly Protestant, and unquestionably helped to formulate, or reinforce, Neville's Protestant outlook. He clearly enjoyed his years at Merton: his two younger brothers followed him there, as did two of his own sons; a grandson became Assistant Warden of Merton in the mid-seventeenth century. Oxford, only about 40 miles away from Billingbear, was clearly preferable to England's other university, Cambridge, located over 100 miles away, to the north of London, and probably necessitating a journey through the arguably dangerous capital. By horseback or carriage, Oxford was probably less than a day's travel time from Billingbear; Neville probably journeyed back and forth by way of Reading and Wallingford. If Neville had attended Cambridge, his associates would of course have been very different. For instance, there he would have encountered his kinsman-by-marriage Francis Bacon and other members of his family, as well as the remnants of the best-known among the group of dramatists called 'The University Wits' – Marlowe, Greene and Nashe. While Oxford also produced its share of acknowledged dramatists such as John Lyly (*c.*1554–1606) and George Peele (*c.*1557–96), arguably the writers at Cambridge would have put a greater stamp on 'Shakespeare' than was the case. In particular, Neville would presumably have come into earlier and closer contact with Christopher Marlowe (1564–93), who was, until his premature death, Shakespeare's great rival as the finest Elizabethan dramatist. Nor is it likely that Neville would have made his four-year tour of the Continent, had he gone to Cambridge. There is no doubt that Sir Henry Savile, Neville's tutor at Oxford, was especially trusted to accompany Neville abroad because he was related to the Greshams, through the Pastons of Norfolk. Had Neville's choice of university been different, it is most unlikely that we would have the works of 'Shakespeare' as we know them.

Merton College in the late seventeenth century was widely regarded as the most intellectually distinguished of the Oxford colleges. It was also the one prone to admit more students from the merchant and middle classes than any other. Neville would certainly have read in a surprisingly wide range of subjects, ranging from astronomy, mathematics, classics and works of philosophy and logic to modern histories and languages. (Mathematics was compulsory for all first-year Oxford students, but Neville enjoyed it and would have opted for it anyway.) He would also have engaged in 'disputations', required by all students in their third and fourth years, which consisted, in effect, of debates in which the pros and cons of a proposition were debated at length, with a moderator summing up and pointing out the fallacies in the arguments of the debaters.[35] The education Neville received was so obviously vastly superior to that which can be documented for Shakespeare of Stratford that to draw a comparison between the two is ludicrous. And there was more.

Neville's tutor at Merton College, and probably the foremost intellectual influence on his life, was Sir Henry Savile (1549–1622), a Fellow of Merton College who became its Warden in 1585 and later became Provost of Eton College. Knighted in 1604, Savile was a staunch Protestant who was among the scholars who translated the King James version of the Bible.[36] In the 1590s Savile – like his protégé Henry Neville and others in Savile's circle – became a supporter of Essex; he was briefly imprisoned following the Essex rebellion. A Renaissance man in the literal sense, Savile translated Tacitus and spent much of his life producing an eight-volume edition of the works of the Church Father St John Chrystostum. In addition, he was a dedicated and talented student of mathematics and of the new sciences emerging from Europe, especially of astronomy. In 1619 (after Neville had died) Savile founded the famous Savilian Professorships of Geometry and of Astronomy at Oxford, stipulating – almost uniquely at the time – that professors were to undertake research. Savile himself held the first Chair of Geometry at Oxford. Savile was noted as well for his seriousness of demeanour. When a young scholar was recommended to him for a good wit he declared 'Out upon him ... give me a plodding student. If I would look for witts [*sic*] I would go to Newgate [Prison], there be the witts'.[37]

Savile apparently went out of his way to cultivate the young Henry Neville. In part this was because he was obviously and genuinely talented (and was praised by other scholars) and in part, one might surmise, because Savile made a point of cultivating the sons of the rich and powerful – provided they were talented – as Neville, the son of the Member of Parliament for the adjacent county, and the scion of one of England's most illustrious families, plainly was. A young man of Neville's background was surprisingly uncommon at Elizabethan Oxford, where most students did not emerge from the aristocracy or gentry but from the middle classes or from even lower points on the social scale. It has been estimated that about 2.5 per cent of 18-year-old males attended a university in the period around 1600, an incredibly high percentage, and probably higher than the equivalent figure in mid-Victorian England. Among the thirteen students who matriculated with Neville at Merton on 20 December 1577, eight identified themselves as 'plebians', that is, commoners lacking a coat-of-arms or other evidence of gentility.[38]

The European tour

Unquestionably the most important outcome of Neville's time at Oxford under Savile, and one which would literally change the course of English literature, was the extended tour of Europe undertaken by Savile and a handful of able, well-connected undergraduates chosen by him, which lasted from 1578 until 1582.[39] Apart from Neville, Savile took several other students of well-off background and promise with him: George Carew (later Sir George, d. 1612), later an MP, ambassador and judge; and Sir Philip Sidney's younger brother Robert (later first Earl of Leicester of a new creation, 1563–1629), a prominent MP, soldier and diplomat under James I. The party left Oxford on 3 April 1578 and returned some time in the spring of 1582.[40] Savile's ostensible reason for travelling was to gather manuscripts and newly published works for Merton's library, and also to meet with leading continental scholars. Four years is an extraordinary length of time for a leading Oxford don to be absent from the university, but Savile had obtained special permission to be away for three years (not four), and was granted an annual grant of £6.13.4 for each of his three years away.[41] Savile left a (near-indecipherable) common-place book of his travels for the years 1581–82 which survives at the Bodleian Library, but nothing in the way of a travel diary by Neville survives: if it did it would, of course, be a document of the highest significance.

The most relevant primary source of the tour we have to date is the diary kept by Arthur Throckmorton, who outlines some of the time he spent with the Neville group on the Continent and describes the usual modes of transport of the time, plus some of the inns at which they stayed.[42] Among other details, Throckmorton describes how he travelled through and from England, and how the Savile group was with him in Vienna and for part of his time in northern Italy. The Savile tour apparently first visited France, and then proceeded, in September 1580, to Nuremberg, where they visited the famous astronomer Johannes Praetorius at the Academy at Altdorf. It then proceeded to Breslau, Prague (in early 1581), Vienna (July 1581) and finally Italy, where the party stopped at Padua, Venice and Rome.[43] They returned home in the spring of 1582 after a second stay in Nuremberg. At Prague the party met the celebrated astronomer Tycho Brahe, as well as astronomers Thadeus Hajec and Paul Wittich.[44] Besides these men, Neville apparently spent six months with the great Hungarian humanist Andreas (or André) Dudith (1533–89).

Virtually unknown in the English-speaking world today, Dudith was 'educated in the Hungarian tradition of Erasmian humanism', lived for some years in England, where he was secretary to Cardinal Reginald Pole, and was made Bishop of Pecs around 1563.[45] Dudith was forced to resign a few years later when he married, became a Lutheran, and was condemned by the Catholic Church. He became one of the main European leaders of the 'New Learning', meeting or communicating with most of the leading intellectuals and scientists of his day, and building up a library of 5,000 printed books. In correspondence, he praised Neville for his *mathematical* ability: remarkably, the earliest surviving record we have of 'William Shakespeare' being praised for anything was for his proficiency at mathematics.[46] But this is not so surprising, when one thinks about it. The poet Sir Philip Sidney was known for his ability at mathematics, and nearer our own time we have Empson, a Cambridge Professor of Mathematics who changed tack in middle age and became a lecturer in poetics. Shakespeare's Sonnets bear similarities to mathematical and logic puzzles, so it does seem that poetry can bridge the fields of literature and science. Indeed, in Renaissance times, few such subject barriers were ever perceived, the marriage of mathematics and the arts leading to the great architectural and pictorial triumphs of Italy. One has only to think of Leonardo da Vinci to realise that subject barriers could do more to limit the mind rather than expanding it – and the man who was Shakespeare obviously had a mind approaching the level of da Vinci.

Dudith is best known to historians of science for his dispute about the comet of 1577, in which he rejected astrology and championed mathematical astronomy, and his example shows a totally unsuspected strand of continental humanism which was almost certainly a crucial element in the intellectual outlook of 'William Shakespeare'.[47]

Professor Peter Usher, who is Professor Emeritus of Astronomy and Astrophysics at Pennsylvania State University and has written widely on the subject of Shakespeare and the 'New Astronomy', demonstrated beyond doubt that Shakespeare had a profound knowledge of the latest astronomical subjects, including some of the findings of Galileo which did not become public knowledge until 1610 or later, after virtually all of Shakespeare's works were written.[48] Similarly, the mathematician Dr Steve Sohmer in his excellent book *Shakespeare's Mystery Play: The Opening of the Globe Theatre 1599*, explained the background to *Julius Caesar*, and clearly demonstrated how its author had an advanced knowledge of astronomy and of its associated subject – world time and date settings.[49] It is difficult to see any way in which the actor/theatre-sharer William Shakespeare could have known any of this, or why he would have taken the slightest interest in these developments. After 1578, however, Neville had a demonstrable and well-evidenced association with Europe's leading astronomers.

On this extended tour Savile, Neville and their companions also encountered other Englishmen. In France they met Arthur Throckmorton, the diarist, who was the son of Sir Nicholas, and a friend of Francis Bacon and Bacon's brother Anthony (1558–1601), who was operating a spy ring on the Continent. The precise date at which Neville finally returned to England remains unknown. Savile reached Oxford in late 1582, so it is likely that Neville accompanied him.[50] Neville was 20 or 21 when he returned, assuming that he did not interrupt his lengthy tour to visit his home. Undoubtedly, this tour must have had the most profound influence upon many of the works of 'William Shakespeare', more than half of which are set in continental Europe, and Italy in particular.

For orthodox biographers of Shakespeare there is an enormous problem in explaining not merely Shakespeare's repeated use of Europe as the locale for his plays, but his apparent first-hand knowledge of much of Europe, especially France and above all Italy, where so many of his plays take place. That Shakespeare had direct, eye-witness knowledge of Italy and its cities has been suggested by many historians and critics, especially and significantly by Italians. Dr Ernesto Grillo, for instance, an eminent Italian scholar of Shakespeare resident in Britain, stated that 'we are forced to conclude that Shakespeare must have visited Milan, Verona, Venice, Padua and Mantua'. Time and again Shakespeare's description of a place or geographical detail in Italy, often a detailed description, appears to experts to have necessarily been based on his own experience.

To take only one or two examples, *The Taming of the Shrew* (Act I, Sc. I, l. 42) states that someone is said to 'come ashore at Padua'. As Padua is an inland town, the reference seems curious. But Grillo discovered that in Shakespeare's time Lombardy was intersected by a network of rivers and canals which many travellers preferred to the roads, which were roughly made and infested with bandits. Padua was also connected with the Adriatic by a waterway.[51] In *The Merchant of Venice* (Act III, Sc. IV, ll. 53–4) Portia speaks of 'the traject ... the common ferry which trades to Venice'. This was the *traghetto* which took travellers from the mainland to the city.[52] In both the Quarto and Folio editions of the play, the word is misprinted as 'tranect', the compositors apparently never having heard of it. Since Shakespeare had to explain that the 'traject' was a ferry, he must not have expected his English audiences to have heard of it; indeed, in the nineteenth century Karl Elze, a German Shakespearean scholar, claimed that Shakespeare could not have read of the *traghetto* in any book.[53] Portia at the same time sends Balthazar to Padua in quest of legal aid for Antonio. Padua was then the leading Italian school of law, and only degrees granted at Padua were recognized as qualifications for Venetian lawyers.[54] In *The Winter's Tale* (Act V, Sc. II, ll. 93–8) Julio Romano is described as a 'rare Italian master' among sculptors. At one time, this was thought to be a mistake by Shakespeare as Romano was known only as a painter. It was subsequently discovered (from Vasari's

Lives, written in 1550, in Italian but long untranslated) that he was also a notable sculptor in plasterwork outside the elaborately decorated houses of the rich citizens of Milan, and is so described on his tomb.[55] Numerous other striking examples of what appears to be first-hand knowledge, added to the plays for no apparent reason, have been discovered by critics.

There is no *a priori* reason why Shakespeare of Stratford should not have visited Italy; the problem is that there is not a shred of evidence that he ever did. Historians have combed countless records, including the primitive passport records which survive at the Public Records Office, without finding even a hint that Shakespeare of Stratford ever left England. Plainly, if such evidence existed, it would be common knowledge, highlighted in every orthodox biography of the Bard. Nor is it clear when Shakespeare was supposed to have visited Italy: during the so-called 'lost years' (*c.*1582–89) he was presumably learning his trade as an actor in London, having a wife and three children to support. It is also frequently urged that during this time he was apprenticed to a solicitor, or a schoolmaster in the country. No early account of Shakespeare's life, even those such as John Aubrey's *Brief Life* account of 1681, written when persons who knew Shakespeare may still have been alive, mentions or even hints at his travelling abroad. Some orthodox historians, such as Sir E.K. Chambers, believe that he may have gone abroad in the period in 1593–94 when London's theatres were closed by the plague. However, apart from the fact that absolutely no evidence exists for this view (there is no evidence, for instance, that any theatre company travelled abroad at this time), Shakespeare apparently spent this time writing *Venus and Adonis* (published in April 1593), *The Rape of Lucretia* (published in May 1594) and possibly several of his plays. Furthermore, it was only the wealthy who could afford to travel abroad, the ferry to France costing the equivalent of £1,000 in today's money. Faced with the obvious difficulties, both in the lack of evidence and in the absence of any plausible opportunity for Shakespeare to have visited the Continent, nearly all recent biographers simply ignore the question, never examining or questioning how Shakespeare could have acquired the level of knowledge that he clearly possessed, nor why he chose to parade it in his plays.

The European tour had several other profound effects on Henry Neville. He became fluent in many European languages, and certainly acquired (or, via Savile, had access to) many continental books or manuscripts, as well, presumably, as developing a network of European book dealers and intellectual contacts.[56] Shakespeare's plays contain over 300 references to both classical and contemporary authors, many deriving from continental works which had not yet been translated into English. A number of his early plays, including *The Two Gentlemen of Verona* and *A Midsummer Night's Dream*, were heavily influenced by a work in Spanish by Jorge de Montemayor, *Diana Enemorada*, which was not published in English until 1598. *The Two Gentlemen* is normally thought to have been written in 1594–95 and *A Midsummer's Night* in 1595–96.[57] Henry Neville certainly knew Spanish (and was at one time being actively considered as Ambassador to Spain). There is no evidence that Shakespeare had the slightest knowledge of Spanish, any access to Spanish works, nor indeed any interest in them.

By 1582 or so, therefore, the two main strands in the early writings of 'William Shakespeare' – England's history and the rise and fall of its dynasties on the one hand and, on the other, dramatic (especially comical) situations set in France or (especially) Italy – were firmly in place. But we know little more than this about Sir Henry Neville's education. He was awarded an MA at Oxford in 1605, with James I attending his graduation ceremony. What Neville did to obtain this degree is not known, although King James obviously knew. The Jacobean courtier, diplomat and letter-writer, Dudley Carleton, casually remarks in one of his letters that King James was visiting Billingbear for help with his writing.[58] Such a throw-away remark in a private letter surely suggests that a certain circle knew of Neville's writing abilities, even though he published nothing under his own name. In another letter, Carleton refers to an episode from a Shakespeare play but calls its writer simply 'mine author' as if the recipient of the letter knows very well what Carleton is referring to.[59]

Knowledge of the law

More significantly for our knowledge of 'William Shakespeare', there is no evidence that he ever attended an Inn of Court, and he was never called to the bar. During the past 160 years many anti-Stratfordian historians have pointed out that Shakespeare's works show a deep and accurate knowledge of the law, and that, therefore, he must have had some kind of legal training. (The two best-known 'anti-Stratfordian' candidates are Sir Francis Bacon and Edward De Vere, seventeenth Earl of Oxford. Bacon was, of course, one of the greatest lawyers of his time and became Lord Chancellor; De Vere, although not a lawyer, did attend Gray's Inn.) Some orthodox biographers of Shakespeare, puzzled over the many legal references in his works, have suggested that he spent part of the 'lost years' (c.1582–89) as a lawyer's clerk. However, Shakespeare's signature has never been found on any legal document (of which many thousands survive) of the time in any legal capacity, which one might surely expect had he acted in this capacity. There is no evidence that Shakespeare trained as a lawyer, nor does any early biographical anecdote or tradition claim that he did. Moreover, if Shakespeare of Stratford was a trainee lawyer, it is difficult to see why he would have left the security of the law for the catchpenny insecurity facing a young actor in London, while, if he spent some years as an apprentice solicitor, he could not also readily have been an apprentice actor in London, a schoolmaster in the country and a traveller wandering around Europe, activities which he is also supposed to have packed into the 'lost years'. (Since there is no evidence from the Inns of Court records that William Shakespeare attended one of these academies for prospective barristers, if he did undertake any legal training, it must have been as a solicitor.)

While Shakespeare's knowledge of the law appears considerable to many experts, it must also be noted that many other legal authorities believe that he did not train as a lawyer. A summary of their views is that the weight of evidence from the plays does not clearly indicate that Shakespeare was a trained lawyer, as opposed to having a good working knowledge of some branches of the law with which affluent Elizabethans were likely to deal.[60] 'Shakespeare' did apparently have an excellent knowledge of the law of real property, and also, apparently, a first-hand knowledge of the local administration of justice, especially the county magistrates or Justices of the Peace.[61] William Shakespeare of Stratford might conceivably have had enough in the way of legal experience to have written the legal scenes, and demonstrated the legal knowledge, in his plays and other works, although his known legal activities were certainly on a small scale.

Shakespeare's father, John Shakespeare, had been a local Justice of the Peace and Bailiff (mayor) of Stratford, although, most strikingly, William Shakespeare himself held no legal or quasi-legal positions of any kind, despite the fact that he was far wealthier than his father and was officially regarded as a gentleman with a coat-of-arms. Given that William Shakespeare had been a major landowner in and around Stratford for at least ten years prior to his death, and had probably retired or semi-retired from London to Stratford seven years or so before his death, this is itself strange, especially in view of the legal knowledge demonstrated in his plays – that is, if he wrote the plays. Furthermore, none of his relatives become lawyers, and no pattern of legal careers can be traced in his family.

His situation stands in complete contrast to that of Sir Henry Neville, who, throughout his life, held a variety of legal and quasi-legal positions and engaged continuously in dealings in real property, conveyancing and businesses of various kinds. He became a Justice of the Peace around 1583 (when he was only about 21 years old), served as Steward of the Royal Manors of Donnington and Sonning and Bailiff of Crown Lands in Newbury from 1593, and was also High Steward of Wokingham.[62] As Justice of the Peace this Oxford-educated intellectual, immersed in learning, must have been a stark contrast to most of his fellow JPs, local landowners and superior tradesmen. As a Member of Parliament for virtually the whole of his adult life, he was engaged in the making of laws. Neville bought and sold lands on a considerable scale throughout his whole adult life, for instance selling his Sussex estates around 1598, engaged in ironmastery, and was a director of the London Virginia Company.[63] He certainly associated constantly with lawyers, including his kinsman-by-marriage Sir Francis Bacon. He had, in fact, exactly the kind of background – continuously immersed in legal matters, especially those concerning real estate and local government, but not a trained or practising lawyer – that one would expect from Shakespeare's works.

Apart from the law, Shakespeare's plays reveal an expertise with an enormously wide variety of other topics, ranging from falconry to gardening to heraldry, which are fully consistent with a man of Neville's background but are wholly inconsistent with a product of the provincial lower middle class such as Shakespeare. By the time Henry Neville was a young man in the 1580s, most of the pillars of Shakespeare's works would already be evident in his life and his activities.

Chapter 4

Becoming William Shakespeare, 1582–94

Although certainly not as dark as William Shakespeare's 'lost years', the period after Henry Neville returned from his continental sojourn with Henry Savile and several other Merton students is not especially well-documented. In particular, we can only surmise how Neville became 'William Shakespeare'. Nevertheless, although only supposition, some aspects of this process seem fairly clear.

There are several landmarks in Neville's public and private life in the 1580s for which good evidence exists. In 1583 he visited Scotland, in the company of the Earl of Essex and Sir Francis Walsingham (see p. 235). The visit of Essex and his party to Scotland, it should be noted, was described in a little-known epic poem in Latin by Richard Eedes entitled *Iter Boreale*. There, he is described as 'Neville, distinguished for his book-learning'. This is certainly the first published depiction of Sir Henry Neville: although only about 21 years old, his erudition struck observers as remarkable.

In November 1584 Neville was elected the Member of Parliament for New Windsor at the apparent age of only 22. Thereafter, for the rest of his life, with only one three-year break, he served as an MP. He was re-elected for New Windsor in 1586, and was then elected as MP for Sussex from 1589–93, for New Windsor from 1593–97, and for the Cornish borough of Liskeard from 1597, serving until the election of 1601. From 1601 until 1604, during which period he was held in the Tower of London for two years for his part in the Essex rebellion, he was, naturally, not a Member of Parliament, but, soon after his release, he was elected in 1604 for Berkshire and re-elected in 1614, serving until his death.[1] In all, Neville served in Parliament for 28 years, and for 15 of those he was a 'Knight of the Shire', a representative of one of the counties, generally regarded as more prestigious than election as a borough representative. Although a very notable MP in the 1600s, Neville was inconspicuous during his early period in Parliament during the 1580s: he neither spoke in the House nor served on any committee.[2] At this time, 'William Shakespeare' produced no eloquence at Westminster.

Although again elected as MP for New Windsor in 1589, Neville chose to sit for Sussex, where he had also been elected. This seemingly odd choice was occasioned by the fact that, at some stage between 1586 and 1588, he had moved out of Billingbear with his wife, Anne Killigrew, into a mansion at Mayfield, East Sussex, which he had inherited from Sir Thomas Gresham, his great uncle, in 1579.[3] The mansion had once belonged to Cardinal Wolsey, and then to Henry VIII before being purchased by Gresham in the mid-sixteenth century. Queen Elizabeth had visited it in 1571. The extensive landed estate which accompanied the mansion included considerable iron mines, already a lucrative business.[4] Images related to ironmastery, forges and the like are common in Shakespeare's works; probably a line such as 'Buy terms divine in selling hours of dross' ('dross' is the scum skimmed from the surface of molten metals), in the celebrated Sonnet 146, refers to Neville's experience as an ironmaster. In contrast, it is difficult to see any connection whatever between Shakespeare of Stratford and ironmastery. Among the major products of Neville's ironworks were cannons and armaments, which were sometimes exported, despite bans being placed on the export abroad of more than a certain tonnage of ordnance.[5]

The Killigrew connection

In December 1584 Neville had married Anne Killigrew, the daughter of Sir Henry Killigrew (c.1525–1603), of a wealthy, landed Cornish family. Killigrew was an MP (from 1553 to 1584) who led a varied career as a secret agent, courtier and diplomat. Killigrew, like his son-in-law, was well-educated and learned, with a keen interest in the classics, music and painting. Like Henry Neville, he was fluent in both Italian and French.[6] From before Elizabeth's succession until the end of her reign he was employed chiefly as a diplomat, serving as Ambassador to Scotland (then a separate country) in 1572–75. Immediately before this, in the early 1570s, he had been on a mission in France and had witnessed the St Bartholomew's Day Massacre of the Huguenots.[7] He was strongly pro-Protestant and had, at one stage, been military adviser to Lord Essex in the Netherlands. He continued to be employed by the Queen as a diplomatic adviser into his old age, being used on a mission to France for Elizabeth as late as 1591.[8] Generally, but not invariably, he enjoyed the favour of the Queen and held a number of lucrative positions, such as Teller of the Exchequer.

Killigrew also enjoyed the advantage of being related by marriage to Lord Burghley and to Sir Nicholas Bacon, the father of Sir Francis. His first wife (Neville's mother-in-law), Catherine Cooke (the daughter of Sir Anthony Cooke), who died in 1583, came from a remarkable family of four talented sisters; the others married, respectively, Sir William Cecil (Lord Burghley); Sir Nicholas Bacon; Sir Thomas Hoby, translator of the *Cortegiano* of Castiglione, which may have been used as part of the basis of some of Shakespeare's plays, and, after his death, Lord Russell, the son of the second Earl of Bedford. Catherine Cooke Killigrew is said to have known Latin, Greek and Hebrew, and to have published some of her translations.[9] Henry Killigrew's second wife was Jael de Peigne – a French Huguenot. She too was a linguist, and after settling in London she perfected her English well enough to form a circle of literary friends whom she invited to the Killigrew family house at Lothbury, where our Neville and his wife resided for much of every year during the first two-thirds of their married life. Presumably this was where Neville stayed when he made his early visits to the London theatre, although of course a wealthy relative of the Greshams would have had no trouble finding a place to live in London. According to one recent biographer, Killigrew 'got on well' with Neville, although this relationship came to an abrupt end with the Essex rebellion of 1601.[10] By his wife Neville had five sons and six daughters, most of whom survived to adulthood, and many of whom have living descendants today. Thus, from the mid-1580s the Neville household was first full of children and then, later, young people. While there is no reason to suppose that Sir Henry was anything but an affectionate husband and father (but bearing in mind that the plots of some of his plays, for instance King Lear, might be based in some measure on his domestic circumstances), it was also probably the case that he often wished to escape from this ever-growing brigade of offspring. Since that was the time before boarding schools were the norm for boys from wealthy households, it is not unreasonable to see Neville's adoption of playwriting as a kind of escape, although doubtless there were many other contributing factors.

In appearance Neville was a handsome, ruddy-complexioned, red-haired man who is depicted as serious and highly intelligent in the portraits of him which exist; in one painting he is wearing an enormous ruff, the apparel of men of high status in Elizabethan England. Probably Neville's most notable physical characteristic, however, was a tendency to put on weight, so that by the 1600s he was fat. He possibly looked like Henry VIII without Henry's grossness. Falstaff was a deliberate and central component of his persona, one of his main alter egos, and was apparently his nickname among his close friends such as Southampton. Neville suffered from gout and chronic arthritis, making him somewhat lame in later life. He also complained of deafness, which would appear to have been a family trait.

From Neville to Shakespeare

How Henry Neville came to be 'William Shakespeare' is a process which is unlikely to be fully resolved, unless (as is still possible) the identification of Neville as Shakespeare leads to major discoveries of hitherto unknown documents in unexpected sources. This topic might usefully be divided into four component questions, each of which is subject to a lesser or (more commonly) greater degree of surmise: Why did Neville decide to write plays? When did he begin? Why did he use a pseudonym? And what was the nature of his relationship with William Shakespeare, the Stratford-born actor?

Why write?

We simply do not know why Neville began to write, although some conjectures seem reasonable enough. Neville lived, with a growing family, principally at Mayfield, East Sussex, in the mid-1580s, a sojourn interrupted, one imagines, by visits to London (about 40 miles to the north), and to Billingbear (about 60 miles to the west). Although he was the county's MP, and became one of its Deputy Lieutenants in about 1591, he held fewer local offices and was not well known in the district. Indeed, his main friend in Mayfield appears to have been the local vicar, George Carleton, who was at Merton with Neville. Carleton had links with the Neville family, being a son of the Steward of the old Earl of Westmoreland, and shared Neville's interest in astronomy. Carleton was later to become Bishop of Chichester, following Harsnett (part of whose work is quoted briefly in *King Lear*); he was also destined to become Anne Neville's second husband, after the death of Sir Henry. Neville seems to have engineered Carleton's presence in Mayfield, since he was the sponsor for him to become vicar there. Curiously enough, Carleton began to bring out books of poetry in old age, once he had married the widow of Sir Henry Neville, that is.

As with his time at Billingbear, it is unclear how Sir Henry passed each day at Mayfield, apart from his iron-mining, ordnance-making (in which he was apparently closely involved at this time) and agricultural estates.[11] In addition, he might have gone frequently to London, and it is highly probable that he would have visited the local theatres, doubtless sitting in the expensive seats reserved for affluent playgoers. Travelling up to London from East Sussex Neville would presumably have noticed the Rose Theatre, opened in 1584, while his London homes in Lothbury and elsewhere were close to the Theatre, the Curtain and the Blackfriars Theatres. Perhaps he simply thought that he could have created better than what was on offer, seizing on the notion that two of the main intellectual and cultural influences in his life, his Neville ancestry and the exotic magic of his extended visit to the Continent, might well provide the material for successful drama. It is possible that Neville had, even earlier, experimented with writing dramatic juvenilia which was not produced, as *Edmund Ironside* is supposed by some, including E.B. Everitt and Eric Sams, to be by Shakespeare, although its style is 'unShakespearean'. Conceivably, Neville wrote the 'Ur-Hamlet' or other plays now either lost or revised into the versions we know. It is also quite probable that Neville wrote poetry at this time, and *The Phoenix and Turtle*, that mysterious and beautiful lyric poem which first appeared in 1601, was written in 1586, as E.A.J. Honigmann and others have recently argued.[12] We simply do not know why, although it is quite possible that Neville began to write because he was bored, was temporarily away from his normal haunts, and felt an intense creative urge.

When did the writing begin?

Around 1588 Neville began to take a more prominent role in Parliament, introducing a bill for the first time, one dealing with the assurance of a join-ture (a guarantee of a widow's inheritance) for his wife Anne. This was necessary owing to the complexities of his land purchases in East Sussex.[13] The bill went through a House Committee which included Sir Henry Savile and his step-kinsman Francis Bacon, and was passed early in 1589.[14] Although the late 1580s and early 1590s are a particular blank spot in Neville's life, it is likely that it was during this period that he began to write in earnest.

There is no reason to question the orthodox chronology of the plays of 'William Shakespeare', and at no point is there any awkwardness about explaining (or explaining away) any inconsistencies between Neville's life and the accepted chronology of the plays, as there is with the Earl of Oxford, and, indeed, with Shakespeare of Stratford himself. On the con-trary, as will be seen, the accepted chronology of the plays meshes extraordinarily well with everything that is known of Neville's life and career. It is thus likely, and there is no reason to doubt, that Neville, as 'Shakespeare', began his play-writing career in earnest around 1589–90, the commonly accepted dates for the appearance of Shakespeare's earliest plays. Neville was aged about 27 in 1589, somewhat old for a transcendently bril-liant author to write his first works, but Neville was also rich, the owner of an estate, an ironmaster, a Member of Parliament and a learned Oxford scholar. He had had no need to write plays for money, his income from other sources being vastly in excess of anything he could earn from being a London playwright. Neville's late start – Neville's life argues for a relatively 'late start' rather than what, for some reason, has been perceived as an 'early start' in 'Shakespeare's' writing career, the subject of so much dispute – was probably occasioned chiefly by the effort of will necessary for a wealthy MP and Oxford scholar to write plays at all, however strong the calling.

The defeat of the Spanish Armada, which was wrecked in storms off the Scottish and Irish coasts in August and September 1588, may well have been the essential factor that gave Neville the nerve and motivation to begin writing. It is quite possible, indeed likely, that the wave of patriotic fervour and pride which followed the English victory led Neville to embark on writing his first plays, which were, after all, triumphalist English histories in keeping with the mood of the time. It is also very difficult to believe that the appearance of the three parts of *Henry VI* and then of *Richard III* so soon after the defeat of the Armada was mere coincidence, although the link between the two events is, for some reason, not commonly made in biographies of Shakespeare. Given that Neville's earliest plays were about dynastic battles in which his ancestors were closely involved, and not about the Armada itself, it is reasonable to assume that he had been planning to write them for some time, and the mood of the hour stirred him to action.

Neville is virtually certain to have been the 'annotator' of the copy of Halle's *Chronicles* (as *The Union of the Two Noble and Illustre Famelies of Lancashire and Yorke*, by Edmund Halle (*c*.1498–1547) is commonly known) described by Alan Keen and Roger Lubbock in *The Annotator* (1954). Halle's work is thought to have been a more important source for Shakespeare's history plays even than Holinshed's *Chronicles*. The handwriting of the marginalia is almost certainly Neville's, while the book came from the library of Neville's son-in-law Sir Richard Worsley, whose wife inherited many of Neville's books after her father's death. Thus, Neville apparently did a good deal of research before embarking on the history plays.

Notes towards the history plays are also present in the two manuscript copies of *Leycester's Commonwealth* which Neville seems to have possessed. This was an anonymous book – printed in Antwerp and Paris in 1584, but banned in England – detailing the crimes and murders of the Earl of Leicester, Queen Elizabeth's favourite. However, after detailing Leicester's murders, the writer says that Henry Neville's father was heard to say that the same, wicked Earl was trying to sow dissent among the English aristocratic families, with the aim of provoking civil war again along the old dynastic lines. From all this confusion, Leicester, the writer says, hoped to gain a military victory and so become ruler himself. From this point in the manuscript, the writer goes on to detail the Wars of the Roses. The history of the Wars he produces is occasionally annotated in both copies – in what seems to be Neville's hand.

The book is now thought to have been written by Charles Paget, a double agent occasionally in the employ of Mary, Queen of Scots. Though this Paget was born a Catholic, he always opposed the extremists and hated the Spanish Inquisition. When Neville became Ambassador in France, he met the exiled Paget, whom he seemed already to know and whom he trusted so much that he employed him on various spying missions. This story will be told in full later in the book, but for the meantime it does seem that these two copies of *Leycester's Commonwealth* were also used by Neville as a source for his history plays. It is therefore possible that it was Paget who awakened Neville to the evils of civil war, thus leading Neville to determine to prevent such warfare ever breaking out again. With theatres being the only thing approaching mass media at the time, they were an obvious way to influence the population to reject any arguments over dynasties that might break out in a repeat of the bad old days. Neville would no doubt find it comfortingly symbolic that he, a Protestant, could work with the Catholic Paget towards such a laudable end.

It may seem surprising, on the surface, that Henry Neville, a Protestant whose Protestant father-in-law had fought with Leicester in the Lowlands, should be willing to collaborate with the Catholic Charles Paget in a work essentially against the Earl of Leicester. However, we would suggest that Neville's reason for collaborating was primarily personal. In 1583, Elizabeth sent the brother of Robert Dudley, Earl of Leicester, down to Mayfield to discipline Neville on his export of ordnance. Neville had probably been very careful only to export his cannons to Protestant countries, but still had what is now a well-documented argument with Ambrose Dudley, the then Earl of Warwick. As a result, Dudley appears to have returned to Elizabeth and complained about Neville's attitude. Elizabeth and Parliament took his complaint seriously, and Sir Walter Raleigh even stood up in Parliament and proclaimed that ordnance manufacturers who exported so many of their arms were a threat to the nation. This would have infuriated Neville, who would have put his undoubted scholastic and research abilities to work to find whatever he could against the Dudley family. He would have discovered their duplicity with Philip II of Spain, and much more about the true character of Robert Dudley than he had ever before suspected. All this was only one year before Paget's anonymously printed book damning the family came out on the Continent. So now Henry Neville, the committed Protestant, had at least two 'moderate' Catholic friends (Paget and the Earl of Southampton), which would explain how so many of his works look at issues from a much broader standpoint than the polarized writings of the times by other, more narrowly based authors. It also provides yet another reason for his wishing to begin work on literary creations that presented the anti-civil war message to the public. Even *Romeo and Juliet* may be included in this genre, the personal portrayal of two tragic, factionally divided lovers hitting the audience on an emotional level to add to the intellectual influence against civil war asserted by his history plays.

Why use a pseudonym?

Why Henry Neville wrote under a pseudonym is an easier question to answer than most of the others. Four reasons seem relevant to his decision. In the first place, he was an MP and the son of an MP, in 1589–90, a Knight of the Shire of Sussex, and gentlemen of this background, especially young gentlemen in their twenties, simply did not write stage plays in Elizabethan England. To be sure, some aristocrats, such as the Earl of Oxford, did write plays under their own names, but these were for private rather than public performance. Neville, with teaching the unity of the nation in mind, wished to write for the *public* stage, but his position as an MP and Knight of the Shire in a county where he had previously been almost unknown probably made his situation difficult and equivocal. Secondly, there was another Henry Neville (*c.*1575–1641), who was the son of the claimant to the Bergavenny peerage (and succeeded to it in 1622), and our Henry Neville, whose father was a cousin of the father of his namesake, may well not have wished to cause any confusion which could have arisen between the two men.

In the late 1580s the claim to the title of Baron Bergavenny was in dispute between the 'other' Henry Neville's father, Edward (*c.*1559–1622) and his cousin's daughter, Lady Fane, the dispute not being resolved (in Edward Neville's favour) until 1604.[15] That these two branches of the Nevilles were close is suggested by the fact that when our Henry Neville was elected MP for Sussex in late 1588, for the Parliament which convened in 1589, Edward Neville was selected to succeed him as MP for New Windsor, our Henry Neville's constituency since 1584.[16] Since this almost certainly occurred when Neville was writing his earliest plays, it would seem that he would surely have had no wish to muddy the waters by potentially embarrassing his kinsman.

Thirdly, it might have been the case that Neville wrote the early Sonnets and *Venus and Adonis* in order to try to persuade the Earl of Southampton to marry Burghley's granddaughter. Burghley had already asked one of his secretaries to attempt to write poetry with this end in mind; it is therefore highly likely that the next person he would turn to would be the son of his old friend, Henry Neville. Burghley had introduced young Neville to Court, and Neville was beholden to him; he was likely to do whatever Burghley requested of him. Burghley was a powerful man and obviously did not want his family stratagems and secrets publicized. There was no known connection between the Burghleys, William Shakespeare of Stratford and the Earl of Southampton. Publish *Venus and Adonis* with the attribution of 'William Shakespeare' and it would be open to many interpretations. However, had Neville's name been used, it would have helped the curious to put two and two together, because Neville was known as Burghley's protégé and Southampton's friend.

Finally, and perhaps most importantly, there is the fact that Neville's first plays were not merely depictions of some colourful aspects of England's history by a neutral writer of historical dramas, but accounts of the rise and fall of dynasties by a man named Neville who was writing in considerable measure about his own ancestors. In Neville's time the history plays had a very definite contemporary relevance, and might well be looked at very closely indeed for their partisanship, even for possible sedition. Neville might well be seen as advocating the claims of his own family to the throne, or at least failing to support the Tudor dynasty, or of commenting too directly, at least by implication, on the succession to Queen Elizabeth. *Richard II* appeared to sail very close to the wind, and the open identification of Neville as a dynastic partisan would have invited potential catastrophe. Once Neville married into the Killigrew family, kinsmen of the Cecils, this danger, already great, increased still further. Evidently, Neville thought that there was no point in inviting trouble when he could write under a pseudonym.

Why Shakespeare?

Just when Neville met William Shakespeare, and the exact nature of their collaboration, is, of course, perhaps the greatest mystery of all. It is quite possible that this did not happen until after the first few plays were written: the initial apparent reference to Shakespeare as a presumed playwright was, of course, in *Greene's Groatsworth of Wit*, placed on the Stationer's Register in December 1592.[17] There is no record of any performance of one of Shakespeare's plays prior to the period between February and June 1592, when *Harry the vj* (probably *I Henry VI*) was put on by Strange's Men (the basis of the Chamberlain's/King's Men, Shakespeare's enduring company), and there is no record of William Shakespeare as an actor prior to December 1594.[18] Since parts of the *Henry VI* trilogy were almost certainly written earlier, probably in 1589–90, it is at least arguable that Neville did not actually meet Shakespeare until about 1592, or at least did not engage him until then.

Although the precise nature of the initial circumstances of their association will presumably always remain unknown, we can nevertheless make some shrewd guesses about what quite probably happened. As extraordinary as this may seem, it appears that Neville and Shakespeare were distantly related; our evidence for this comes from the family trees and, secondarily, from Sir Edmund K. Chambers, among the greatest and most meticulous of twentieth-century Shakespeare scholars and the one least likely to engage in far-fetched speculation. Chambers knew nothing of Neville as a possible author, and was invariably dismissive of all alternative authorship claims. Yet in his *William Shakespeare: A Study of Facts and Problems* (1930), he points out that the Ardens, Shakespeare's mother's family, used the same coat-of-arms as the Beauchamps, Earls of Warwick. These arms are to be found in the church of Aston Cantlow, 'which was a manor of William Lord Beauchamp of Bergavenny, and descended through his grand-daughter to the Nevilles'.[19] Chambers then goes into a long, complex argument about the relationship of the Ardens to the Beauchamps, Earls of Warwick, with a family tree examining the relationship of Thomas Beauchamp, Earl of Warwick to Neville's immediate ancestor Lord Bergavenny.[20] If this is accurate and relevant, one can readily imagine what almost certainly happened: Mary Arden, Shakespeare's mother, and the rest of her family never let him forget that – in contrast to Shakespeare's petty tradesman father – they were related to the highest in the land (indeed, to royalty), and in particular to the illustrious Neville family. When Henry Neville was attending the theatre around 1589–91, with an eye to becoming a writer, but needing the cloak of anonymity, he must somehow have been introduced to the young aspiring actor from the provinces, who – either at once or when he was able to summon the courage – disclosed that they were, in fact, distant kinsmen. Rather than dismiss Shakespeare as an obvious opportunist, and his claims of kinship as an insult to the famous and powerful Neville family, Henry Neville probably realized that here was exactly what he had been looking for: a well-placed front man and factotum on the London stage. There were also other traceable links between Neville and Shakespeare, especially Neville's kinship with Thomas Russell (1570–1634), a wealthy Warwickshire landowner who was the overseer of Shakespeare's will. Sir Dudley Digges (1583–1639), Russell's half-brother, was a member of the council of the London Virginia Company, along with Neville, while his brother Leonard Digges (1588–1635), wrote commemorative verses in the First Folio to 'Shake-speare', the hyphenated version of Neville's pseudonym which was used by those apparently in the know. Besides, the anti-authoritarian overtones of the name probably suited Neville, who might well have been sympathetic with some aspects of Tacitus, the Republican, of whom his respected tutor, Savile, made a special study. There was also the curious coincidence that a certain William Speare had recently been buried in the churchyard of Waltham St Lawrence. All in all, the signs must have seemed to point in young Shakespeare's direction.

Sooner or later, once Neville and the man from Stratford became more confident of each other, the wealthy MP and Knight of the Shire made his extraordinary offer to the Midlands-born actor: become the ostensible author of my plays, and my directing operative in the theatre, and you will be well paid. The fact that they were distantly related probably made mutual loyalty easier to maintain, and, for the most part, it is unlikely that either man resented the agreement. We do not know how much Shakespeare was paid for his role, but it might have been, say, as much as £20 to £25 per play, bringing the overall sum he was paid during the 20 years of their collaboration to something like the 'thousand pounds' which Rowe, writing in 1709 and citing Sir William D'Avenant as his source, claimed that Southampton gave to Shakespeare.[21] This very welcome money also enabled Shakespeare to achieve his primary ambitions, to become one of the wealthiest men in Stratford-on-Avon, to become recognized as a gentleman with a coat-of-arms, and to found a dynasty – while the first two were achieved, the death of Shakespeare's son Hamnet in 1596 meant that the last of these, the creation of a dynasty, would take place only in the female line.

Shakespeare would also doubtless have been expected to clear the way for the staging of Neville's plays, to act as their producer-director, and to keep Neville fully informed about the personnel and technical aspects of his acting company. For this to work, presumably Neville and Shakespeare had to go over every play line by line; in Billingbear, we may surmise, or, very likely, in the family's London home at Lothbury.[22] While Shakespeare of Stratford was certainly incapable of writing any of the works which bear his name, for this arrangement to have worked he must have been intelligent, resourceful, keen to be upwardly mobile, and loyal to those who were loyal to him, while arguably duplicitous in a deeper sense. All of these qualities were obvious products of Shakespeare's meagre social background, as well, perhaps, as his very uneasy life as a possible Catholic recusant, in constant fear of a highly unpleasant fate if exposed. Indeed, one Edmund Neville of Stratford – contemporary to Shakespeare – was regarded by Elizabeth as a spy for the Spanish. Shakespeare's association with a powerful, committed Protestant must therefore have been a useful camouflage, and probably few regretted Neville's disgrace and imprisonment in 1601–03 more than Shakespeare.

We have no idea how Neville felt about the collaboration, but he was probably intrigued by his provincial actor 'cousin', and relieved that he, too, had found the ideal factotum. Apart from Shakespeare's useful professional role in the theatre, his purely provincial and parochial ambitions, and the fact that he totally eschewed any involvement in national or international politics or intrigue or partisan involvement, must have made him the perfect front man, whose very parochialism acted to disguise any question of an MP from an illustrious family commenting or campaigning in his plays about high politics, which it would be especially dangerous for a member of the ruling elite to do. Over the years Neville apparently also made other friends and contacts in the theatre, among them Ben Jonson and John Fletcher. Ben Jonson had been educated by William Camden, and Camden was a great friend of Henry Savile. (The wider question of just who knew that Neville was Shakespeare will be addressed in a subsequent chapter.) Neville might also have initially (or, indeed, later) paid for the costs of the production of his plays, and contributed financially in other ways to the costs of the Chamberlain's Company.

The plays

There is general agreement that Shakespeare's first three plays were the *Henry VI* trilogy, and that these had probably appeared some time between (at the outside) 1587 and 1592, when Greene's 'Shake-scene' reference was published. Much about them is in very considerable dispute, such as the order in which they were written and even the extent to which Shakespeare was their sole author. The date of 1589–90 for *I Henry VI* and 1590–91 for the latter two parts is, it seems, generally accepted as their most likely dates. They were not published until, respectively, 1623, 1594 and 1595, the latter two under different titles.[23] As noted, relatively little is known of Neville's life in the period 1588–92, other than that he had established himself at Mayfield, East Sussex, was an MP and Knight of the Shire for Sussex, and had a growing family. There is nothing in his life during this period which is inconsistent with his authorship of the plays. Neville had, as noted, certainly established his relationship with Shakespeare by 1592. The subject of these plays doubtless affected Neville's interest in his own family and in English history in this period generally, as evidenced by his annotations to Halle's *Chronicles*. One assumes that, initially, Shakespeare's company regarded these plays as the eccentricities of a rich gentleman who wished to remain anonymous, but came to realise that he was a good author, who had no trouble filling the theatre, and were not merely putting on his plays to satisfy a rich man's whims.

This conclusion would have become very evident with the appearance of *Richard III*, the very first of Neville's ever-memorable and immensely popular plays, which was probably written in 1592–93, or even earlier perhaps, in 1591. It may have been performed on 30 December 1593 (there is some doubt as to whether this performance was in fact *Richard III*, although it seems likely), and the consensus of virtually all scholars is that it dates from this period, and is the fourth part of a quartet about English history by Shakespeare, albeit one separated in time from the period of the reign of Henry VI, who was deposed in 1461 and murdered in 1471, while Richard III, formerly the Duke of Gloucester, who appears in *2* and *3 Henry VI*, came to the throne in 1483.[24] Nevertheless, these plays are often viewed as a sequence, with *Richard III* being markedly superior and vastly more memorable than the three parts of *Henry VI*, among the more obscure and least frequently performed of Shakespeare's plays.

Richard III obviously demonstrated that Neville had grown very considerably as a writer. It was the first of 'Shakespeare's' plays to be genuinely memorable for either its characters or its dialogue. Richard himself remains, of course, one of the greatest of all villains in any literary work, while historians have endlessly debated whether he did in fact murder the 'little princes in the Tower'. We can only speculate why Neville took such an extreme pro-Tudor position, although this was presumably linked in part to his political role. As described in note 25, there is an essay on Richard III dedicated to Sir Henry Neville. As the essay is signed 'Hen. W' this may have been written by Henry Wriothesley, Earl of Southampton. If so, it may be that Wriothesley thought Neville (as Shakespeare) had gone too far in denigrating one of his own ancestors in an attempt to secure Queen Elizabeth's favour by presenting her own grandfather, Henry VII, as the rightful King of England.

Upheaval and change

The year 1593 saw a number of changes in Neville's life which almost certainly affected his literary work. On 13 January of that year his father, Sir Henry I, died; he was buried at Waltham St Lawrence Church near Billingbear.[25] As a result, Henry Neville inherited Billingbear and his other Berkshire properties, beginning a process of moving back to Berkshire from East Sussex and, by 1597 or so, selling off all of his lands in that county.[26] Billingbear was a manor owned by the Bishop of Winchester and then by the Crown until 1549, when it was granted by King Edward VI to Sir Henry I. Around 1567 Sir Henry I built a large red-brick Tudor mansion where his son passed much of his youth. It is likely that most of the plays of 'William Shakespeare' were written there. By the eighteenth century Billingbear had no less than 365 rooms. It was eventually inherited by Sir Henry's descendant in the female line, Lord Braybrooke, who used it as his principal residence until the nineteenth century, when Audley End in Essex became the family's chief residence. Tragically, Billingbear burned to the ground in a devastating fire in 1924. The ruins were removed, and today nothing remains of it.[27] Almost as soon as Neville returned to Berkshire, and reflecting the standing of the Nevilles in that county, he was once more elected MP for New Windsor in the very brief Parliament which met for two months just after his father's death.[28] Neville spent the next few years in part in gaining control of several contested estates from his mother-in-law, Elizabeth, the daughter of Sir Nicholas Bacon.

From 1593, however, Neville was established again at Billingbear in Berkshire. It is also at just this time it would seem – so far as the chronology allows us to say this with assurance – that the nature of Shakespeare's work changed quite markedly, ushering in the period of his two long poems and of many of his Italianate comedies in place of the English histories. One can only speculate why Neville changed, and broadened, his oeuvre so markedly. The usual explanation for the appearance of Shakespeare's first long poem, *Venus and Adonis*, is that the London theatres were closed at the time owing to the plague, and Shakespeare was forced to turn to poetry instead. While this may well have been a factor, it is difficult to believe that the death of Neville's father did not also play a role. *Venus* was registered on 18 April 1593, three months after Sir Henry I's death, and Neville might well have regarded the writing of a play at such a time as unseemly and inappropriate. *Venus* is, of course, dedicated to the Earl of Southampton, and signed by 'William Shakespeare', proof that at least a small circle of Neville's friends were privy to the secret. Despite the Dedication's claim, *Venus and Adonis* was not 'the first heir of my invention', since it was preceded by at least four previous plays, although 'Shakespeare's' promise to 'honour' Southampton with 'some graver labour' might well have caught Neville's mood following his father's death and his relocation back to Berkshire.

The poems

By this time Neville had certainly known the Earl of Southampton for some years. When Henry Wriothesley, third Earl of Southampton (1573–1624) was eight, his father died, and he became the ward, first of Lord Howard of Effingham and then of Lord Burghley. Neville stated at his trial following the 1601 Essex rebellion that he had met Southampton at Burghley's house when he was living there as a ward. It is likely that this occurred in the mid-1580s, just after Neville's marriage to the daughter of Sir Henry Killigrew, Burghley's kinsman by marriage. From 1585 to 1589 Southampton was a student at St John's College, Cambridge, where he developed an interest in drama and literature. Although probably 11 years younger than Neville, it is likely that their common interest in literature cemented a deep friendship between them, productive of extravagant praise by Neville to Southampton, just at the time that Neville was becoming 'William Shakespeare'. This deep friendship continued for many years, despite the fact that Southampton testified against Neville at his trial in 1601, giving rise to many of Shakespeare's Sonnets in which a much-loved man is forgiven by the author for a serious transgression.

In contrast, there is not a shred of evidence of any kind to suggest that William Shakespeare of Stratford ever had dealings with the Earl of

Southampton: all attempts to discover any sort of link between the two, for instance in Southampton's surviving papers, have always failed. (As noted, there is no doubt that Southampton and Neville were friends and associates for many years.) Indeed, there is no reason to suppose that Southampton ever set eyes on the Stratford man, unless he saw him acting on the stage or was casually introduced to him by Neville or another mutual acquaintance.

It is conceivable, however, that Shakespeare did Neville one favour in the latter's authorship of *Venus and Adonis*, namely finding him a publisher, since Richard Field, the printer of this and 'Shakespeare's' two other poems, was also from Stratford and probably knew the actor; Field might also have known Neville as a London intellectual.[29] If Neville was spending most of his time at this stage taking over his father's estates in Berkshire and moving back from East Sussex, it is not unreasonable to suppose that he gave Shakespeare the task of finding a printer for his poem, or took his advice on using one with whom he (Shakespeare) was acquainted. It might be argued that Neville could have used the printer Ralph Newbury – his Berkshire neighbour – but this might well have led to the true identity of the author being discovered.[30] Also, questions would surely have been asked as to why Shakespeare would have chosen a printer from such a long way away.

There is general agreement that Field was an excellent choice: a careful, high quality printer, although he was not involved in producing any of the plays by 'Shakespeare'. It is interesting to note that after printing *Venus and Adonis* in 1593 and *The Rape of Lucrece* in 1594, Field's only other publication of a work by Shakespeare was in 1601, when *The Phoenix and Turtle* appeared, at a time when Neville was in prison, the implication being that he again used Shakespeare as an intermediary when he was otherwise occupied. Field may, however, have known Neville through his existing connection with Burghley, Neville's kinsman, and his circle. Besides, Field was apprenticed to Thomas Vautroullier – the writer of handwriting manuals – who had a shop at Blackfriars, therefore very close to Neville's father's property, where Neville was baptized and doubtless spent some of his formative years. Field must have continued to live there, because he was among those who petitioned against the opening of the later Theatre at Blackfriars.[31]

The following year, Neville produced the second of his longer poems, *The Rape of Lucrece*, which was registered on 9 May 1594 and presumably written in the preceding months in response to the popularity of *Venus and Adonis*. Again, the poem is dedicated to Southampton, 'to whom I wish long life still lengthened with all happinesse', sentiments echoed in similar language 15 years later in the Dedication to the Sonnets. In the Dedication to *Lucrece*, 'William Shakespeare' notes that 'the warrant I have of your Honourable disposition, not the worth of my untutored Lines makes it assured of acceptance'. Since Shakespeare had received no such 'warrant' for *Venus and Adonis*, and would receive no such warrant for *Lucrece*, Neville here is expressing his own sentiments, sentiments which would continue until 1609 and the Sonnets, long after Shakespeare, had he actually been the author, his admiration unrequited, would surely have given up. It is also likely that in these Dedications Neville was deliberately addressing Southampton in terms of abject obeisance as if he had been a baseborn man addressing an earl, employing Shakespeare's name as alleged Dedicatee precisely because he was a provincial actor of no high standing, as well as to disguise his own identity. It is, indeed, quite possible that both Neville and Southampton thought this situation comical: they were having a (rather unpleasant) joke at Shakespeare's expense.

The comedies

At around this time, Neville began writing his Italianate comedies. We may never know why – any more than orthodox Stratfordians can give a credible reason for Shakespeare to have done so – but it is possible that his return to Billingbear now gave him direct access to his father's large library, as well as to whatever books and manuscripts he had brought back from his extended sojourn on the Continent. Conceivably, he had simply left most of these in his old home during his years in Mayfield. In addition, Neville was now much closer to London, and was better able there to obtain the books he used as his sources. The young Neville couple also seem to have resided for long periods at Lothbury, father-in-law Killigrew's house, where there was also a sizeable collection of books and manuscripts. Plainly, Neville had internalized his Continental tour of the previous decade and wished to draw upon his exotic memories in plays. It is also possible that he visited the Continent again after 1582, although we have no record of any such trip before his appointment as Ambassador to France. It is arguable that his father's death, and his inheritance of Billingbear and other substantial properties, gave him the increased self-confidence he needed to branch out into new forms of dramatic creativity, possibly encouraged to turn from history to comedy by requests from the Strange/Chamberlain's Company for which he had written and where Shakespeare was in place.

Over the four years or so after 1593, on the generally accepted chronology of Shakespeare's plays, Neville wrote seven plays, all except two categorized as 'comedies', which were set in places he had visited in Italy. Most or all of these plays are based on a range of sources, often in foreign languages, which Neville might have found in the Billingbear library, collected on his continental journey, or read in London or, conceivably, Oxford. He was fluent in most major European languages, wealthy enough to obtain any books he wished, and would certainly have had a network of booksellers and literary informants throughout Europe. In contrast, explaining how Shakespeare of Stratford, an impoverished actor of whom there is no reason to suppose that he knew any living foreign language, came to obtain, read and absorb the extraordinary range of sources in the plays he allegedly wrote has inevitably consisted of highly unsatisfactory and implausible guesses.

This sequence of plays began with *Titus Andronicus*, generally dated to 1593–94: 'Shakespeare's' bizarre, perhaps repellent exercise in Grand Guignol, revolving around cannibalism and mutilation. One can only speculate why Neville started his Italianate sequence with such a work – which is frequently attributed wholly or partly to an author other than Shakespeare – although, as noted, appearance might indicate that, following his father's death, Neville broke from his familial restraint, or, perhaps, that he intended to produce a sensational drama, in another milieu, to rival *Richard III*.[32] However, *Titus* does have a theme persistent in Neville's works – the strumpeting of 'maiden virtue', which is echoed in Sonnet 66. The Nevilles, Killigrews, Cookes, Hobys and Sidneys were always much more sympathetic with women and their plight than many other noble families of the time, as well as being considerably more aware of their intellectual abilities.

The Two Gentlemen of Verona, one of 'Shakespeare's' least-known plays, probably also dates from this early period (or earlier still) and uses, indeed introduces, many of 'Shakespeare's' familiar conventions found in his later plays.[33] The Damon and Pythias-like theme of friendship might be intended by Neville to convey his friendship with Francis Bacon (or, conceivably, Southampton), although this is purely conjectural.

The next play, according to the accepted dating, was *The Comedy of Errors*, which we know was certainly produced at Gray's Inn on 28 December 1594. It is possible that this play was written earlier, but the consensus of opinion is that it was written just before its Gray's Inn performance.[34] As is well known, this performance ended in considerable chaos, and became known as the 'night of errors'.

There are two important aspects of the Gray's Inn performance of *The Comedy of Errors* which are often mentioned in anti-Stratfordian sources, especially those advocating the candidacy of Francis Bacon, but which are almost invariably passed over in silence by Shakespeare's orthodox biographers. First, the Gray's Inn performance, part of traditional Christmas revels there, was accompanied by six composed prose speeches. These were almost certainly written by Francis Bacon, as has been affirmed by many historians who categorically deny he wrote Shakespeare's works, including James Spedding and A.L. Rowse.[35] As noted, Neville and Bacon were step-kinsmen probably less than a year apart in age. *The Comedy of Errors* is about sets of separated twins, and Neville might well have been making a deliberate statement about their relationship in this play, possibly because of Bacon's recent and growing links with Essex (they are seen as having become close from 1592 onwards) and, through him, with Southampton (who had been formally introduced to Court by Essex) and others close to Neville, but possibly simply because at this stage they admired each other's great but very different types of intellect. Needless to say, no one has ever traced links of any kind between Bacon and Shakespeare of Stratford, and it is very difficult to envisage them collaborating on two components of a Gray's Inn Christmas revel, much less that Shakespeare would regard Bacon and himself as twins, a claim which Bacon, then a prominent Member of Parliament and a leading aspirant for high office, would plainly find intolerable.

Secondly, there is the interesting question of what the Lord Chamberlain's Men, of whom William Shakespeare the actor was certainly a member, was doing on the night *The Comedy of Errors* was being performed at Gray's Inn.[36] According to the Chamber Accounts, which give details of payments for entertainments performed at Court, at that very time they were ten miles down river at Greenwich Palace, playing before the Queen. Since *The Comedy of Errors* has 16 main parts, and the Chamberlain's Men probably consisted of no more than 12 actors, it seems difficult to believe that the company split in two. The entry in the Chambers Account actually mentions William Shakespeare by name (along with William Kempe and Richard Burbage) as acting at Greenwich on the same night as the Gray's Inn revels.[37] While it is not impossible that there was confusion in this entry about the precise date, it is much more likely that the entry was literally accurate and that, therefore, William Shakespeare is categorically known to have been elsewhere when one of his own plays was apparently being premiered. (It goes without saying that these embarrassing facts are consistently swept under the rug by most orthodox biographers of Shakespeare.) *Errors* was not registered until just before publication of the First Folio in 1623, and never published before the Folio's appearance, and there was thus no reason as such to regard the play as by Shakespeare before that date; Neville evidently wrote it for this special occasion and did not regard it as part of his stage oeuvre by 'William Shakespeare'. Significantly, too, the play was again performed (probably for the first time since the 'night of errors') before James I's Court at Christmas 1604, a year after Neville's release from the Tower and when he was still hoping for the King's favour.[38]

Neville also produced three other Italianate plays during this period: *The Taming of the Shrew*, first performed in June 1594, *The Two Gentlemen of Verona*, probably dating from 1594–95, and the celebrated *Romeo and Juliet*, believed to have been written in 1595–96 and first published in 1597. All clearly drew on Neville's Italian travels and are probably derived, in whole or in part, from continental sources he may have obtained on his trip or subsequently. Neville had found a popular genre which he fully exploited through Shakespeare and the Chamberlain's Company. He also set another comedy in France, *Love's Labour's Lost*, generally believed to date from 1594–95, although some scholars favour a slightly later date.[39] His father-in-law, Killigrew, had been at one time a diplomat in France and had witnessed the entertainment of Margaret of Valois, on which some of the play is said to be based. There is also an old document in the possession of the Earl of Abergavenny – Neville's kinsman – which speaks of French princesses visiting in the reign of Henry VIII.

Finally, another ever popular and famous play of similar ilk from this period is *A Midsummer Night's Dream*, set in ancient Greece, and usually dated to 1595–96.[40] This was the period when Neville was successfully taking his father's place as the owner of Billingbear and as an important local notable in Berkshire, and was also beginning to be seen as playing a more prominent national role. In April 1596 Neville was made a Deputy Lieutenant of Berkshire by its Lord Lieutenant, Lord Norreys, despite the fact that he had not yet received a knighthood, normally a prerequisite for being appointed.[41] He was also an active Justice of the Peace as well as an MP, and, nationally, had been formally introduced at Court, apparently by Sir Robert Cecil, Lord Burghley's son. With his 'channels' to the London stage well established, growing popularity (under a pseudonym) as a playwright and poet, a growing family and considerable personable wealth, this was the beginning of the period when Neville was probably at his happiest, a mood reflected in many of his lyric plays from this time.

Chapter 5

The Road to the Top, 1595–99

The next four years were probably among the most satisfying of Neville's life; they were certainly among the most productive. In this period, which ended with his appointment as Ambassador to France, he probably wrote eight plays. Many were in his history sequence, to which he apparently gave a more political edge as he seemingly became involved with the growing movement in support of the Earl of Essex. His plays became more profound, even his so-called comedies such as *The Merchant of Venice*, which was probably composed around 1596–97. In this period Neville also created his most popular character, Falstaff, and probably wrote most of his greatest patriotic play, *Henry V*.

Neville's political career took a number of unexpected turns during this period. In the parliamentary election of 1597, he found himself no longer an MP for New Windsor (as he had been since 1593) but elected for remote Liskeard in Cornwall.[1] Apparently, he attempted to challenge members of the well-established Norris and Knollys families for the Berkshire county seat, but was not strong enough, and hence was forced to accept a parliamentary seat in Cornwall. But the Killigrew family and Neville's brother-in-law Sir Jonathan Trelawney had electoral influence in Cornwall. Neville was close to Trelawney, who had married the sister of Neville's wife Anne Killigrew. He acted as an executor of Trelawney's will in 1604 and was guardian of Trelawney's two young sons.[2]

As High Steward of Liskeard, Trelawney had the right to choose the constituency's two MPs; a staunch Protestant, he opted for Neville – as well as for his own son – and Neville served as its MP in the 1597–1601 Parliament.[3] Robert Cecil was also anxious to have Neville, his cousin's husband, in Parliament in a safe seat. At this point, he regarded Neville as a dependable supporter of the government's policies, rather than a partisan of the charismatic Earl of Essex, with his increasingly more activist and pro-Protestant policies. At this stage Neville was undoubtedly playing both ends against the middle, appearing to be both a loyal supporter of Cecil and, in his plays (and, almost certainly, behind the scenes) an even greater partisan of Essex. Admittedly, there was, as yet, no overt contradiction between the two, since Essex was still emphatically the Queen's favourite. By 1597–98 Neville was more active in Parliament and was already writing to Robert Cecil with advice on foreign policy. By 1598 rumours that Neville was to be appointed to a major ambassadorship began to circulate.[4]

Support for Essex

Neville unquestionably saw himself at this time as on the high road to success, his important personal connections and rising reputation marking him out as very likely to fill the most senior positions of the next generation of national leaders – he was probably 33 years old in 1595 – perhaps reaching the highest of all positions, as his ancestors had done. But Neville, concerned to assert England's supremacy over the Catholic powers of the Continent, apparently also felt growing irritation at the extreme caution of the Cecils' policies and the failure of Queen Elizabeth to name a Protestant heir, which was to lead to personal catastrophe for him in 1601. He must certainly have had contacts with the Essex circle, which included his friend Lord Southampton, his mentor Henry Savile and other university academics, although no written documentation has yet to come to light. It is always possible that Neville destroyed any paper trail connecting him to the Earl of Essex, and indeed, it would have been wise for him to do so. His burgeoning attachment is clear enough, however, from his anonymously written plays. Similarly, his reluctance to jeopardize the esteem in which he was held in Court circles was evidently another significant reason for him to conceal his identity as a writer. While the fact that 'Shakespeare' was the author of the plays was certainly well known from the time of Robert

Greene, it is worth noting that around 1598 there is a definite upswing in public identification of Shakespeare as author of the plays, with Francis Meres' famous listing of the leading English playwrights (in his *Palladis Tamia: Wits Treasury*, registered in September 1598) naming 12 of 'Shakespeare's' plays, and with 'William Shakespeare' first explicitly named on the title page of a play (*Richard II*) as its author also in 1598. (No previous title page of a published play now known to have been written by 'Shakespeare', or any recording of it in the Stationers' Register, had named its author.) Neville was obviously taking even more pains than usual to keep secret his dramatic authorship, with its political message; with *Richard II*, which is actually about the justifiable deposition of an English monarch, he had to be particularly careful.

He wrote two comedies in this period. *The Merchant of Venice*, as noted, probably in 1596–97, and *The Merry Wives of Windsor*, also probably written around 1596–97, although a later date is possible.[5] *The Merry Wives* should more properly be considered with the other Falstaff plays, and will be discussed below.

The Merchant of Venice

Although classified as a comedy, *The Merchant of Venice* is, of course, a profoundly disturbing play, perhaps the earliest by 'Shakespeare' to introduce a theme of profundity, on a topic which has become so topical in the centuries since it appeared. During the past two centuries, much commentary has been forthcoming on whether the play is anti-Semitic, with opinion quite divided. Certainly Shylock is portrayed as a human being – unlike the cardboard depictions of the evil Jew in English literature up to that time – and Shakespeare's ultimate point appears to be that Jews are bad, but Christians are equally so; the best character in the play is Portia, who, as a female barrister, could not exist. (At least, Portia could not exist unless cross-dressing and disguise was occurring at the Inns of Court, in the same way as some nineteenth-century English women dressed as men in order to study medicine. Perhaps Sonnet 20 with its 'master-mistress' hints that such things may have occurred, as, perhaps, also do the many other cross-dressing women in Shakespeare's works.)

Up to this point 'Shakespeare' had written nothing like this, and *The Merchant* plainly marks a deepening in Neville's sensibility. How and why he decided to write on such a theme is unclear, but he would certainly have encountered Jews in Venice on his continental trip. In 1552 there were about 900 Jews in a total Venetian population of about 160,000; by 1655 the number of Jews had risen to about 4,800. According to one reference source, an incident detailing loans between Jews and Christians took place in 1597, a fact arguably relevant to the circumstances of the play.[7] How Shakespeare of Stratford could have known anything about the Jews of Italy is something best explained by orthodox Stratfordians: legally, no Jews could live in England between 1290 and 1656 (although some did), and there is no more reason to suppose that Shakespeare ever set eyes on a Jew than for supposing that he visited Italy. While some commentators have suggested that the so-called 'Dark Lady' of the Sonnets was Jewish, there is not a shred of evidence to support this claim. There is no evidence that any Jew secretly residing in England at this time had any connection with the theatre, while it is also worth making the point that since no Jew was legally resident in England between 1290 and 1656, none could have been engaged in money-lending, banking or commerce of any kind. These fields were invariably in the hands of British Protestants (or, occasionally, foreigners) such as Neville's own Gresham relatives.

It is also worth noting that the name 'Shylock' is unknown among Jews (or anyone else). The usual suggestion is that it derives from *shalach*, a word in Leviticus and Deuteronomy meaning 'cormorant', but Jews did not use this as a personal name, and there are no grounds for supposing that Shakespeare of Stratford knew any Hebrew, unless Stratford Grammar School was yet more wondrous than even orthodox Stratfordians regularly claim. It might not be irrelevant, however, to point out that there is a village called Shurlock Row in Berkshire, just over two miles north-east of Billingbear Park, which Neville would have known well. The coincidence is certainly striking.

Also worth noting is the fact that whoever wrote *The Merchant* knew that many Venetian Jews had previously lived in Frankfurt:

> SHYLOCK. ...*Why there, there, there, there! A diamond gone, cost me two thousand ducats in Frankfort! The curse never fell upon our nation till now; I never felt it till now ...*
>
> Act III, Sc. I

It is unlikely that anyone who had not visited Venice could have known this fact.

That it is problematic to regard Shakespeare of Stratford as the author of *The Merchant of Venice* is further illustrated by his relationship with one persecuted religious minority living in London with whom he actually had direct dealings. One of the very few facts about Shakespeare's life in London which we know with absolute certainty is that in the period around 1602–04 he lodged with one Christopher Mountjoy, a Huguenot tire-maker (a manufacturer of women's wig-like headdresses fashionable in society at the time) in Cripplegate ward just north of the City.

In 1604 an English apprentice, Stephen Bellot, married Mountjoy's daughter; in 1612 Bellot sued Mountjoy for failure to provide his daughter with a promised dowry. In the legal hearing which followed, William Shakespeare was called upon to give evidence. He deposed that he had indeed known the parties concerned, had persuaded Bellot to marry, but could remember nothing of the terms of the dowry. This is the sum total of what has become known as the Bellot–Mountjoy lawsuit: Shakespeare signed his deposition and exited the courtroom. Nothing more was heard of this matter for nearly three centuries. In 1909, however, the indefatigable American husband-and-wife team of Charles William (1865–1932) and Hilda Wallace rediscovered the previously unknown lawsuit at the Public Record Office. It included the sixth known signature of William Shakespeare and added one of the very few pieces of human interest known about Shakespeare of Stratford, whose private life is virtually a complete blank. (The Bellot-Mountjoy Lawsuit is almost the *only* new piece of information about William Shakespeare discovered in the whole of the twentieth century.) It cannot be emphasized too strongly that the lawsuit said absolutely nothing whatever about Shakespeare as an author.

The importance of this affair for our purposes lies in the fact that it is thus certain that William Shakespeare lodged in a *Huguenot* household. The Huguenots were French Protestants who had been tolerated for much of the sixteenth century: a successful and prosperous community of merchants and tradesmen. Living there, it seems inconceivable that he did not hear, on a frequent basis, many horror stories of the appalling persecution of the Huguenots in France, especially the infamous Massacre of St Bartholomew (23–24 August 1572), when thousands of French Protestants were slaughtered or fled abroad, among them the Mountjoys. Shakespeare's position would have closely paralleled that of an English author of the 1960s or 1970s who lived for two years in the household of German Jewish refugees in London. It is inconceivable that this author would not have heard innumerable harrowing accounts of Nazi persecution of the Jews, which would almost certainly have been used in the fiction or drama he wrote. Moreover, if Shakespeare of Stratford actually wrote the works attributed to him, we *know* that he was aware of, and sensitive to, the Jewish minority, and had written a play about them only five years or so earlier. Given Shakespeare's universal empathy, as well as the certain popularity and 'political correctness' which recounted the savage persecution of Protestants by foreign Catholics, it is surely strange that no part of the tribulations of the Mountjoys and other Huguenots figured in any work by Shakespeare.[8] Indeed, it is striking that French themes virtually disappear from Shakespeare's plays after 1602–04. Needless to say, orthodox Stratfordians have nothing to say about this incongruity, which strongly implies a major inconsistency in crediting Shakespeare of Stratford with the authorship of his works. Orthodox Stratfordians have, however, repeatedly suggested that the Bellot–Mountjoy affair *must* have influenced Shakespeare. Anthony Holden claimed that Shakespeare 'had probably known them [the Mountjoys] some years, as he had given their Huguenot name to the French herald in *Henry V*, written ... in 1599'.[9] But Shakespeare clearly stated in his evidence that he had known them since about 1602, not earlier. Similarly, some orthodox biographers of Shakespeare have claimed that the situation of acting as a kind of marriage broker for Stephen Bellot was used as an element of the plot of *All's Well that Ends Well* and *Measure for Measure*. Park Honan claimed that 'reluctant bachelors need to be nudged into marriage'.[10] But apart from the sheer banality of urging reluctant bachelors to marry as a dramatic device, Bellot's reluctance was based on the meagreness of the dowry, not on opposition to marriage *per se*. In his testimony given on oath ten years later, Shakespeare stated that he had trouble remembering very much whatever about the incident. This seems highly inconsistent with his allegedly having written two plays about this affair. In any case, the plots of both plays have been traced to works published much earlier, and have nothing to do with Stephen Bellot and Miss Mountjoy.

The events in *The Merchant of Venice* also present difficulties for Shakespeare's unorthodox biographers. Advocates of Edward De Vere, seventeenth Earl of Oxford, as the true author of Shakespeare's plays often point out that the original of 'Shylock' might have been one Michael Lok (*c.*1532–1615) a merchant and a governor of the Cathay Company, in which De Vere invested £3,000 in 1578–79 to finance one of Martin Frobisher's expeditions. The expedition went bankrupt, and Lok spent the rest of his life trying to repay the debt.[11] In their view, the '3,000 ducats' in the play refers to this investment. In fact, De Vere bought up £2,000 of Lok's own investment, adding to the £1,000 he had already invested.[12] There is no evidence of any kind that *The Merchant of Venice* was written before 1596–97, nearly 20 years later; in the interim De Vere had lost substantial sums – perhaps even more – in other, similar types of investments, in 1582 and 1584.[13] Since *The Merchant* is invariably seen as a response to the Roderigo Lopez affair (Lopez was executed in June 1594), it is difficult to see what it can have to do with a poor investment made by De Vere more than 16 years earlier. Finally, DeVere continued to employ Lok's nephew Henry Lok as his confidential agent up until his death in 1604.[14]

As noted, probably Neville's principal aim in writing *The Merchant* was to appear to defend, or at least give publicity to, the Earl of Essex for his role in the trial and execution of Roderigo Lopez (*c.*1525–94), the well-known Portuguese-born physician who had been appointed chief physician to Queen Elizabeth in 1586. Lopez, born a Jew, fell out with Essex, who was instrumental in obtaining Lopez's confession – under torture – that he had attempted to kill the Queen on behalf of Spain; in June 1594 he was hanged, drawn and quartered at Tyburn. Needless to say, he was innocent.[15] Essex's main object appeared to be to arouse the anti-Spanish (not necessarily anti-Semitic) prejudices of the London crowd in his favour. Although *The Merchant of Venice* is normally seen as a response to the Lopez affair – given its date, it must surely have been – Neville's purpose is rather ambiguous, perhaps mirroring his own mixed loyalties. It simultaneously appears to be an attack on Shylock as exhibiting 'Jewish' vices and a defence of him as a human being who is wronged. Shylock, moreover, is a money-lender, not a treasonous physician. While Shylock is depicted as a Jew, Lopez was an Iberian Catholic of Jewish ancestry, and hostility to him was certainly not wholly based on anti-Semitism.

Perhaps the main message to come out of *The Merchant*, however, is that business and friendship can be mixed together successfully. (This was a typically Nevillian stance in real life too.) Neville appears to be saying, therefore, that it is possible for Christians to be both friends and business partners, but that Jewish businessmen seem unable to mix the two. But it also gives the now, thankfully, outmoded message that Christians cannot therefore befriend Jewish men, even if they do business with them. The Jewish *woman* in the play, on the other hand, is quite another matter. She can be both a friend and a lover of Christians. Altogether, unpalatable as it may appear to our present day values, it seems that Neville was sending the message that the Christians should do all in their power to convert the Jews to Christianity, either by forcing them (as with Shylock) or by marrying them, as is the case with Jessica. In this case, Neville was not so much racist as religionist, which is perfectly in keeping with what we know of his character. Neville was 'a Christian inwardly' as his father-in-law said to him in a private letter. He even held Christian Bible readings in his residence in Paris while he was Ambassador there. All this may appear to be at odds with our overall assessment of Sir Henry, that he was progressive in spirit and intellect, but the past must not be judged in the context of today's knowledge and ideas. Neville was much nearer in time to Luther than we are now, and Luther's ideas were pervading Protestant Europe. Neville, having met continental philosophers and being such a good linguist, could not have failed to know Luther's works. But the point is that Luther wrote the most terrible things about Jews, and his recommended policy was what we would now call genocide. Though Christians today are rightfully ashamed to admit the fact, Luther actually wrote that all Jews should be killed and burned. Neville, a humanist and a Christian, must obviously have found this horrific and particularly disturbing, as Luther's teachings would have been far better known and more widely discussed in Elizabethan times than they are today. Neville would also undoubtedly have been told by his father about the wholesale slaughter and burning the late Queen Mary had perpetrated against Protestants, which must have aroused his disgust and pity. Viewed in its historical context, then, Neville's implied teaching in *The Merchant of Venice* – that the Jews should be pitied and converted, whether by force or by marriage – was hugely more enlightened than the then current European Protestant way of thinking.

In real life too, Neville was always concerned that the quality of mercy should be exercised wherever it was possible to combine this with justice, as was demonstrated by his forgiving and helpful attitude to a certain double-agent whom he perceived as being truly willing to make amends. John Chamberlain, the Court gossip and letter writer, remarked in a letter that

Neville was '. . . never the man to let anyone suffer where he could be of help' – very definitely an attitude evident in *The Merchant of Venice*. Neville, in his diplomatic letters to Robert Cecil, detailed the philosophical discussions he was having with King Henri IV of France. Henri, says Neville, agreed that Christians should convert men to their religion by good example rather than physical force. Shylock's speech about his treatment by Christians was obviously intended to make the Christian audience question whether they were always setting a good example in their everyday behaviour. In Christian thinking, pity is the quality that goes hand in hand with mercy, and 'Shakespeare's' play definitely makes us feel pity for the wrongs Shylock has endured, alongside the overt philosophical didacticism contained in Portia's speech on mercy. Protestants have traditionally been less concerned with ritual than Catholics but more concerned to examine the working of Christianity in everyday life. The plays of 'Shakespeare' generally exhibit this very Protestant ethic, and none more so than *The Merchant of Venice*.

We know nothing for certain of Shakespeare the actor's attitude to mercy and pity, but if we are to believe his contemporaries in the theatrical and literary world, then he was, indeed, quite unmerciful. He is often seen by biographers today as a ruthless money-lender and self-seeker. Neville, on the other hand, is constantly praised for his selflessness, and is remembered as such even by that most severe of critics and satirists, Ben Jonson, who wrote an epigram to him containing nothing but unstinting praise. Jonson knew Neville well, being in the Savile–Camden circle, and was also Neville's companion in the Mitre Club. Jonson had nothing to gain by writing this eulogy, as Neville was definitely out of favour with King James and other die-hard but wealthy absolutists when he wrote it, which lends even more credence to his words.

Neville also continued to write histories in this period. These were markedly different from his earlier English histories and exhibited separate characteristics. These later histories saw the introduction of memorable heroic characters, above all Prince Hal/Henry V, at their centre, in contrast to the rather discursive characterization of the earlier histories. Prince Hal definitely displays political qualities in line with those expressed by Machiavelli, who was not translated into English at the time, except by Neville's father, who, so far as we know, only had his work privately printed. Neville could have read Machiavelli in the original Italian anyway, while

Shakespeare would not have been able to, as modern languages were not on the curriculum of the grammar schools of the time. Yet Machiavelli is mentioned three times in Shakespeare's plays – in two of the *Henry VI* plays, and in *The Merry Wives of Windsor.*[16]

The Falstaff plays

In *Richard III* the history plays had assumed a more overtly political tone. But in totally marked contrast, the Henry IV and V plays also saw the introduction of 'Shakespeare's' most famous comic character, the loveable clown Sir John Falstaff. Both of these patterns seem to mirror trends in Neville's evolving career. As he became more deeply involved with Essex and his circle, Neville was clearly depicting the need for a charismatic hero, a 'man on horseback', to rescue England from the foreign peril and mediocrity of leadership at home. As Neville participated more and more in high political circles during a period, the late 1590s, when he himself increasingly appeared destined for a prominent place in such circles, the mood of personal optimism and self-esteem allowed him to bring to the fore an almost diametrically opposed element in his complex character, that of a buffoon and comic, in the form of Sir John Falstaff.

It seems likely that Falstaff was one side of Neville's own alter ego and an important autobiographical persona. Falstaff's name was, of course, originally Oldcastle, which was an obvious pun on Neville's name (from 'old castle' to 'new town', although 'ville' also itself has the implication of being a fortress). Neville, an increasingly fat man, was apparently soon well known to his inner circle of close friends as 'Falstaff'. This is certainly the source of the very mysterious reference in a postscript to a letter from Elizabeth Vernon, Countess of Southampton, to her husband Neville's great friend Lord Southampton, apparently written in June or July 1599, in which she states:

> *All the news I can send you that I thinke will make you merry is that I reade in a letter from London that Sir John Falstaffe is by his mrs. dame pintpot made father of a godly millers thumb, a boye thats all heade and a litel body – but this is a secret.*[17]

On 26 September 1599 Neville wrote a shorter diplomatic dispatch to Cecil than was usually his wont, his unhappy excuse being 'by reason of some domesticall Misfortune in the Losse of my Son lately born'.[18] Little is known of the physical appearance of Neville's wife Anne, but since her father, Sir Henry Killigrew, was known to have been a short man, it is at least plausible that she was short as well.[19] No one has ever satisfactorily explained this strange and possibly cruel reference. Shakespeare of Stratford had no children after 1585. He was not known to be fat, and – to reiterate a point which cannot be made too often – there is no reason whatever to suppose that Southampton, let alone Lady Southampton, ever set eyes on him, or why the birth of a possibly deformed baby in Stratford-on-Avon to the wife of an actor and theatre-sharer would have turned up as gossip in an affectionate private letter from a countess to an earl. Owing to the utter implausibility of matching this reference with Shakespeare of Stratford, a number of other possibilities have been suggested as the man nicknamed Falstaff. Henry Brooke, Lord Cobham, whose father William, Lord Cobham served briefly as Lord Chamberlain from 1596–97, was suggested by Sir E.K. Chambers. But, with typical honesty, Chambers admitted the serious difficulty inherent in this suggestion: 'he appears to have had no children'.[20] Nothing daunted, in 1949 Leslie Hotson echoed Chambers' verdict of 1930, noting that a 'miller's thumb' was 'at one time a common name for a small fish with a big head known also as a "cob" '. From 'cob' Hotson reached the conclusion that Cobham was indeed the man, despite the apparent impediment of being childless.[21] As usual, though, posit Neville and the mystery vanishes.

Just before the Falstaff plays, however, Neville probably wrote two other history dramas, both of which were very much more serious in their intent: *King Richard II* and *King John*. *Richard II* was almost certainly composed around 1595. Linguistic scholars have linked its high number of rhymed lines and other literary patterns with plays like *A Midsummer Night's Dream* written a short time prior to this.[22] Other recent contributors state unequivocally that 1595 was the date of its composition.[23] It was performed in December that year at the house of Sir Edward Hoby (1560–1617) in Canon Row, Westminster (Sir Robert Cecil was invited to see it). Hoby's mother was a sister of Neville's stepmother and must certainly have known Neville well: he was only two years older, educated at Trinity College, Oxford, and travelled on the Continent just before Neville did. Hoby married the daughter of Lord Hunsdon, the patron of the Lord Chamberlain's Company, and must almost certainly have provided additional links between Neville and the stage.[24] Hoby's father, Sir Thomas, had translated Castiglione's *Il Cortegiano* (*The Courtier*) into English in 1561, a work which apparently provided some of the dialogue in *Much Ado About Nothing*.

Richard II has always been linked with the beginnings of the rise of the Essex circle (and must have been seen as such by Neville, since he famously had it performed on the eve of the Essex rebellion in 1601).[25] Its theme, the lawful deposition of a king, was potentially incendiary, and it seems difficult to believe that Neville's growing attachment to Essex and his circle was not in some measure the reason why this particular play was written at this time. *Richard II* proved immensely popular, and Neville might well have introduced Falstaff in part to make his history sequence seem less overtly serious and subversively didactic. *King John* may have been written in embryonic format much earlier, since a play called *The Troublesome Reign of John King of England* was published anonymously in two parts in 1591. Neville followed the action of this play in *King John*, but rewrote it in a basic way. The question is when: it was certainly written before 1598, since it is mentioned in Meres's celebrated list, and most if not all of its commentators now believe that it was written in 1595–96, its language similar to that of *Richard II* and *The Merchant of Venice*.[26] Its strongly nationalistic tone probably shows a deepening of Neville's English patriotism, which were very evident when he was Ambassador to France a few years later.

Henry IV Part I (*1 Henry IV*) was the first of three plays featuring Falstaff (in *Henry V* he is famously mentioned as having died, 'babbling of green fields' in the best-known reading of these ambiguously printed lines. Coincidentally, Neville's own father may well have died with much the same thoughts. There is a clause in Sir Henry I's will that is often remarked upon for its unusual concern over country minutiae – he left his falcon to Charles Howard of Effingham (a Catholic) 'because the bird loves him'.) *1 Henry IV*, arguably Shakespeare's most satisfying single play, is generally believed to have been written in 1597–98. It was entered on the Stationers' Register in February 1598, just about the time rumours were circulating of Neville's likely appointment as Ambassador to France, probably the time when he was more expansive and optimistic than at any other period of his life.[27] Some authorities believe it might have been written a year or two earlier, in 1596.[28] Falstaff became immediately and enduringly popular, as perhaps did Prince Hal, although 'Shakespeare' soon took pains to end Hal's association with low company.

It would appear that 'Shakespeare's purest farce, *The Merry Wives of Windsor*, was written at this time, just after the first or both parts of *Henry IV*, and in order to cash in on the popularity of Falstaff. (*The Merry Wives* was formally registered in January 1602; it is just possible, although unlikely, that it was written when Neville was in the Tower; this possibility is discussed in the following chapter.) A 'tradition, now often repeated as if it were fact' has it that *The Merry Wives* was written at the request of Queen Elizabeth.[29] There is not a shred of evidence in favour of this 'tradition', which originated in a book by John Dennis published in 1702, although the first published edition of the play, which appeared shortly after it was registered in 1602, claims, on its verbose title-page, that it 'hath bene divers times Acted ... Both before her Majestie, and elsewhere'.[30] There is no real evidence for this claim, either, although, of course, the Queen might have seen *The Merry Wives* performed.

From these scanty facts Leslie Hotson, the well-known and respected Canadian-born Shakespearean scholar, devised the theory, now widely accepted, that *The Merry Wives* was in fact written for the Garter Feast at the Palace of Westminster in London on St George's Day, 23 April 1597, at which George Carey, Lord Hunsdon, was installed (with four others) as a Knight of the Garter, the highest order of knighthood. This possibility is examined in most recent discussions of the play, and has apparently been accepted as if it must certainly be true.[31] One important reason for the acceptance of this theory is that it is otherwise hard to account for why Shakespeare of Stratford set his only English comedy (with the exception of the introduction to *The Taming of the Shrew*) in Windsor, a town in which there is no reason to suppose that William Shakespeare ever set foot, let alone knew well, but which is intimately connected with the ceremonials surrounding the Knights of the Garter. In fact, this theory is highly implausible and highlights the inadequacy of the orthodox Stratfordian account of Shakespeare's life. *The Merry Wives of Windsor* is about Sir John Falstaff, a knight of the realm. He is depicted as a fat, lecherous buffoon, and probably a thief, who has written the same love letters to two married women and, as a result, is forced to hide in a trunk used for laundry, which is thrown into the Thames, and then to disguise himself as a witch; some of the play takes place in a hostelry called 'The Garter Inn' at Windsor.

Unless Shakespeare of Stratford had taken leave of his senses, or had an unaccountable wish to view the Tower of London from its inside, it is simply inconceivable that he could have written such a play for a stately occasion such as the Garter Feast. Such a scandalously inappropriate work would have been viewed as grossly insulting to everyone present, if not overtly seditious, and would surely have been remarked upon by many in the audience, probably with dire consequences for the Chamberlain's Men. No evidence exists for any such performance which, to reiterate, has been widely accepted largely to explain why the play is set in Windsor, a place with which Shakespeare of Stratford had no known connections.

With Neville as the author, however, the mystery vanishes. Billingbear was located only six miles from Windsor, and Neville, the local MP and the holder of many other local offices, must have visited the place countless times from his earliest days, and known intimately not merely the town itself but such places as 'Readins' [Reading] ... Maidenhead ... [and] Colebrook [Colnbrook]' mentioned in *The Merry Wives of Windsor*, Act IV, Sc. V. He would certainly have known the local legends such as those of Herne the Hunter, and presumably visited the original of 'The Garter Inn'. As with *1 Henry IV*, almost certainly Neville wrote *The Merry Wives of Windsor* when he was at his most expansive and optimistic, successful and on the road to greater success, with Court preference almost certainly promised. At such a moment he allowed the buffoon element in his character, his Falstaff persona, full rein. Doubtless Neville was also responding to the popular demand for another Falstaff comedy, even from royal sources, but it seems clear that he was primarily expressing his optimistic frame of mind at this time. Neville was ready enough to kill off Falstaff when he was called upon for high and serious office. It is difficult to believe that the premier of *The Merry Wives* took place at the Palace of Westminster, or anywhere other than in the Liberty of the Clink.

Neville's two final plays of this period, *2 Henry IV* and *Henry V*, were written next, almost certainly in connection with his appointment as Ambassador to France. Although Neville is often described in such accounts of his career as exist as a 'diplomat', this label is quite misleading. His only diplomatic experience consisted of the 15 months he spent as Ambassador to France, from May 1599 until his period of absence and subsequent return to England in September, 1600. He had no other diplomatic experience of any kind, and had never been employed by an English government in any known diplomatic capacity. The reason for his appointment thus remains rather mysterious. Neville had many ostensible qualifications for such an appointment: in 1599 he had served in Parliament for 15 years, was unquestionably able and intelligent, was a wealthy man and spoke fluent French as well as many other languages. Nevertheless, in the world of the Elizabethan courtier and politician these qualifications, although unusual, were far from unique. It appears likely that Neville's relationship to his father-in-law, Sir Henry Killigrew, and his friendship with Robert Cecil were the deciding factors. In addition, Neville's personal experience with matters of business and finance probably played a role in his appointment, given that many of the outstanding issues between England and France revolved around trade matters. Neville was, apparently, very reluctant to go, fearing (correctly) that the appointment would cost him a great deal of money, since only a portion of the enormous expenses of an ambassador were borne by the state. Much of the hostility he expressed in his surviving correspondence over his appointment might, however, be seen as feigned, since Neville was also clearly ambitious, and a successful diplomatic mission with a major power like France would almost certainly have led to further preferment by the government. Moreover, Neville was promised a knighthood when he was appointed. He had been known as 'Sir' since 1596, but this appears to have been from a knighthood given by Essex, probably for Neville's participation in that Earl's Cadiz campaign. He had also been created a Knight of Sussex. No official record of him being granted a Knighthood of the Garter, however, exists. Queen Elizabeth was notoriously niggardly in creating new titles and honours, so he would have been very lucky if she had fulfilled her promise. The Queen was looking for a new ambassador to France in 1597, and by the spring of 1598 Court gossips began to report that Neville was likely to be appointed.

During the period between his appointment and his journey to France as Ambassador, Neville, as Shakespeare, almost certainly wrote two of his best-known plays, *2 Henry IV* and much of *Henry V*, which were 'finished ... certainly before the end of 1598, perhaps well before', according to A.R. Humphreys in his 'Introduction' to the Arden edition (1966) of the play.[32] This verdict is echoed by all other authorities. Neville in all likelihood wrote this play just after his appointment became certain or virtually certain. The probable reasons for his writing it become clear once the course of its author's career is understood. *2 Henry IV*, his previous play, was one of Shakespeare's most popular and best-loved works. In Falstaff he created his most popular single character. Although a sequel was thus a strong possibility (one that became reality in *The Merry Wives of Windsor*), it need certainly not have taken the form it did, in *2 Henry IV*, marked by Falstaff's humiliation and banishment. Shakespeare's treatment of Falstaff in *2 Henry IV* would, in fact, seem to be the last possible way in which any rational author would build on the character's popularity. This was especially so in the case of the avaricious Shakespeare of Stratford: as a theatre-sharer, his profits depended directly on the size of the audience, and banishing the most popular character one has created hardly seems the best way to increase one's income. Rather than humiliate and banish Falstaff, surely it was economically rational and advantageous for William Shakespeare – if he was indeed the author – to have milked Falstaff for all he was worth in several more plays.

Nor did the play have to appear at that particular time. It seems likely that, first of all, Neville wished to use the same title as in *1 Henry IV*, given that the monarch he was about to negotiate with in France was also named Henry IV, that is Henry of Navarre (1553–1610), the former Protestant who changed religion and said famously that 'Paris is worth a Mass'. More importantly, in humiliating and banishing Falstaff – his most important alter ego – Neville was clearly announcing that any traces in his persona of buffoonery and irresponsibility were about to be totally replaced by the seriousness and gravitas required by an ambassador engaged in an important national mission. At the end of *2 Henry IV*, Neville presents some plainly autobiographical commentary about his mission. In Act V Sc. V, (the closing lines of the play) Prince John of Lancaster says:

> *I will lay odds that ere this year expire,*
> *we bear our civil swords and native fire*
> *as far as France. I heard a bird so sing,*
> *whose music, to my thinking, pleas'd the king.*

The final act of the play is followed by a prose Epilogue, which concludes:

> *One more word, I beseech you. If you be*
> *not too much cloyed with fat meat, our humble*
> *author will continue the story, with Sir John in it, and*

make you merry with fair Katharine of France; where,
for anything I know, Falstaff shall die of a sweat –
unless already a be killed with your hard opinions.
For Oldcastle died a martyr, and this is not
the man.

While this presages the French setting of *Henry V*, it also clearly refers to Neville's mission to France, shortly to be undertaken.

Very soon after *2 Henry IV* Neville wrote *Henry V*, which according to Gary Taylor in his 'Introduction' to the Oxford edition of the play 'must have been finished by May or early June of 1599'. Taylor notes that the well-known Chorus in Act V hails Essex's departure from London for Ireland on 27 March 1599. According to Taylor, the play 'can be firmly dated from January to June 1599. Early rather than late spring would fit best with what we can deduce of Shakespeare's other work at about this time.'[33] This dating fits in perfectly with what we know of Neville's activities in these months. Delaying his departure to Paris as Ambassador as long as he could, Neville left London for Dover in April 1599, arriving in France on 8 May and in Paris on 19 May.[34] It thus appears certain that he wrote *Henry V* chiefly in the first few months of 1599. This may seem like quick work, although Neville as 'Shakespeare' was certainly an extraordinarily rapid writer, and was probably both euphoric and also deeply concerned about the mission he was about to begin. That the references to Essex's departure in late March appear in Act V of the play argues that he was nearly finished with the work at that time. Self-evidently, for a newly appointed English Ambassador to France, about to commence an entirely (for him) novel set of difficult negotiations with the French King, to choose Henry V as the subject of a play was highly appropriate. Neville was doubtless thinking that he could replicate Henry V's military feats in the diplomatic sphere (or perhaps the analogy was meant ironically). The stirring English patriotism of *Henry V*, so potent that it was still used, in Laurence Olivier's famous film, as forceful propaganda almost 350 years later, was probably designed as much as anything to stiffen Neville's own spine for the hard task ahead. It might also have been designed as a kind of self-publicity exercise, to alert London's play-going public to the importance of Neville's mission, especially if the latter proved successful.

Knowing that Neville was 'Shakespeare' allows a reinterpretation of the motives for writing these two plays – *2 Henry IV* and *Henry V* – which makes them almost crystal clear. Contrast this – once again – with accepting Shakespeare of Stratford as the author. What conceivable motive could he have had for writing these two plays, one humiliating Falstaff and the other reliving England's greatest military triumph against France, at just this particular time, or in hailing Essex as a hero? Why banish Falstaff, his most popular character, for no apparent reason? The same lack of evident motive is found in considering the other authorship candidates. Only Neville's career can be meshed with this sequence of events, and it meshes perfectly.

Chapter 6

Ambassador to France,
1599–1600

S ir Henry Neville was in France, serving as Ambassador, between early
May 1599 and August 1600. It seems certain that he never visited
England during any of this period, since he often petitioned Cecil and the
Queen to allow him to return, without success.[1] In Paris, Neville was faced
with a number of overlapping, although related, responsibilities which made
his task particularly difficult. His most important duty was to attempt to
detach France from Spain, with which French ruling circles under King
Henri IV had increasingly become friendly. A previous conflict between
France and Spain had been ended by the Peace of Vervins in May 1598,
which drew France away from England and the Netherlands as anti-Spanish
powers.[2] Queen Elizabeth and the English government were not highly
regarded by the French Court at this time, and there seemed little chance
of recovering the enormous sum (over 1.3 million crowns, or £402,000)
given by England to France in pursuit of its former war with Spain.

This ill feeling was compounded by the apparently ever-increasing
power in France of the Jesuits and other pro-Catholic extremists, which
particularly grated on the pro-Protestant Neville. King Henri himself
was increasingly pro-Catholic, despite his former Protestantism. Neville
had also to decide the extent to which he ought, on England's behalf,
to encourage France to fight with other European powers (or with

Spain itself) and thus turn away from conflict with England. The most promising potential conflict was between France and Savoy (an ally of Spain) over the Marquesate of Saluces, a province seized in 1583 by the Duke of Savoy. As well as this, Neville also had to deal with a separate, long-running trade war between English and French merchants, in which the English harassed French shipping and vice versa.[3] The issues with which Neville had to deal were thus serious, very complex and vexatious; they were also compounded by the distracting presence of the Earl of Essex in Ireland and by the chronic shortage of funds in the Elizabethan treasury. It took anything from four days to a week or so for messages to reach London from Paris, although, as Ambassador, Neville had access to a dedicated, secure express messenger service.[4] He thus had to take a great deal on himself in the way of major decisions without knowing whether they would be approved by the English Court.

Neville arrived in Paris on 8 May 1599, and lost no time in holding his first audience with Henri IV, which took place at Moret a few days later. Eight days after this he held a second audience with the King at Fontainebleau. These meetings were held immediately because Henri IV was about to set out on a tour of the French provinces.[5] At Moret, Neville was 'first feted and dined by the King's cousin, Marshal Biron'.[6] A character of this name had appeared in *Love's Labour's Lost,* and it is possible that Neville had already previously met Biron and Henri IV. Indeed, Biron had stayed at Neville senior's home in Blackfriars. What is more, while staying there he witnessed an incident that is featured in the play itself. Biron had hunted with the Queen, accompanied on horseback by her ladies at Windsor, and Sir Henry I was the Queen's hunting companion and tutor. During the hunt, Sir Henry had instructed Queen Elizabeth in the shooting of a young deer, and it is surely this incident which is recorded in the play:

> *PRINCESS. . . . Then, forester, my friend, where is the bush*
> *That we must stand and play the murderer in?*
> *FORESTER. Hereby, upon the edge of yonder coppice;*
> *A stand where you may make the fairest shoot.*
> *PRINCESS. I thank my beauty, I am fair that shoot,*
> *And thereupon thou speak'st the fairest shoot . . .*

PRINCESS. *See, see! My beauty will be saved by merit.*
   O heresy in fair, fit for these days!
   A giving hand, though foul, shall have fair praise.
   But come, the bow – now mercy goes to kill,
   And shooting well is then accounted ill.
   Thus will I save my credit in the shoot,
   Not wounding, pity would not let me do't;
   If wounding, then it was to show my skill,
   That more for praise than purpose meant to kill.
   And out of question so it is sometimes,
   Glory grows guilty of detested crimes,
   When, for fame's sake, for praise, an outward part,
   We bend to that the working of the heart,
   As I for praise alone now seek to spill
   The poor deer's blood, that my heart means no ill . . .
COSTARD. *I have a letter from Monsieur Berowne [Biron] to one Lady*
   Rosaline.

Act IV, Sc. I

It is thus tempting to assume that the forester in this exchange was none other than our Sir Henry's father, one of whose roles was indeed that of forester to a large area of Windsor Park. On top of all this, in the text of the play, the 'Princess' is often referred to as the 'Queen', which seems to suggest that the character's name had been changed in the dramatis personae but that the text itself had not been extensively revised in line with this change, thus making it even more likely that the 'Princess' of the play was originally based on Queen Elizabeth herself. As this play seems only ever to have been given private performances at the time, the allusions did not have to be so carefully monitored as would have been necessary had it been originally intended for the public stage.

Diplomatic problems

Initially, Neville and the French King got on well at their meeting, as if they had indeed met before (perhaps during Neville's earlier European tour), although Henri's procrastination was increasingly irksome. Neville sent home vivid accounts of his dealings with the King, which were apparently widely noted at Court. He held a third meeting with Henri on 8 July, a fourth in September, and a fifth in January 1600, by which time relations between the two had notably soured, Henri actually dismissing Neville abruptly at their fifth meeting after sharp words passed between the two.[7] Neville's meetings with the King thereafter came sporadically (he had two meetings in February 1600), and he had to content himself with meetings with the King's advisers. Neville came to regard Henri as untrustworthy. He increasingly feared Catholic plots against England and the succession to the English throne, and attempted to seek aid for French Huguenots.[8]

Increasingly, too, Neville was extremely discontented by a variety of adverse acts and pressures which he saw as aimed against him, including the willingness of Robert Cecil to use the French Ambassador in London as his negotiating partner rather than Neville; discourtesies shown to him by other ambassadors; and the extraordinary amount of money he was required to spend – he said £4,000 – on entertainment and other expenses.

Neville visited Boulogne to hold talks with Spanish commissioners for six weeks in April and May 1600; as it turned out he never actually met with them owing to a dispute over precedence.[9] The Spanish noblemen sent by the King of Spain said they felt it would demean them to accept an untitled Englishman as the first speaker in the conference. They also brought in many laughable arguments in favour of Spain and its dynasties being the greatest and most respected in the world. The truth, Neville suspected however, was really that these Spanish noblemen were not politically educated like himself and thus were actually afraid to enter into negotiations with him. Indeed, Neville's reputation as a clever disputer may have preceded him from France. He had sent many fully detailed accounts of his arguments there to Robert Cecil back in England, and their standard of logic and eloquence match the speeches in his plays. This must have both annoyed and disquieted his French opponents, who would doubtless have warned their Spanish friends to be very wary of Sir Henry Neville's disputational skills.

Increasingly frustrated and bitter over the difficulties, if not overt failure, of his diplomatic mission, Neville repeatedly petitioned Cecil and the Queen to return to England. This request was continuously denied until late July 1600, when he was granted permission to return to England for one month. On 2 August 1600 Neville landed at Dover, thoroughly weary of diplomacy, and reached London on 6 August.

While he was in France, Neville, as 'William Shakespeare', probably wrote at least two plays: *As You Like It* and *Twelfth Night*. He might also have written *Much Ado About Nothing* in this period, although one could argue that it was written much earlier and is most probably the *Love's Labour's Won* mentioned by Meres in 1598. Its theme of men returning from the war rather accords with the triumphal return of military officers after the defeat of the Armada. (*Julius Caesar* was probably completed before he went to France, as it was performed at the Globe in September, 1599.)

Time for writing?

Even for the greatest author in history, writing two or three plays as an Ambassador is asking quite a lot. Thus, before we consider these works individually, we must ponder how such a work rate was feasible: could the English Ambassador to France realistically have written any plays at all in those 15 months? This question might be divided into two separate matters for consideration: whether in France Neville had the time and the means to write these plays, and whether he could have sent them back to London in a way which facilitated their production.

As Ambassador, Neville certainly had the time to write plays. He met with the French King only half a dozen times in 17 months, and, apart from this, his official duties seemed to consist of meeting with other French officials, writing letters and memoranda back to London, and entertaining, activities which probably entailed meeting local notables and attempting to gain information from them. The rest of his time appeared to be his own, and, indeed, as at Billingbear, just how he filled it is something of a mystery. Paris in 1600 should not be confused with the 'city of light', the world capital of culture and fashion, which it only became in about 1750, a world metropolis with countless tourist attractions, intellectual salons and a magnetic *demi-monde*. In 1600 Paris had a population of about 300,000 – about one-third greater than London's population at that time – but, unlike London, it was almost universally condemned and feared by visitors, with one writer in 1594 describing Paris as 'a den of wild beasts, a citadel of Spaniards, Walloons, and Neapolitans'.[10] Unlike London, Paris experienced little in the way of a cultural renaissance at this time, but was dominated by a superstitious, almost medieval Catholic Church notorious for its bigotry and persecution, especially against the Protestant Huguenots.

Probably the best-known French intellectual of this time was Michel de Montaigne (1533–92), whose *Essays* are often believed to have influenced the later works of Shakespeare. Montaigne lived most of his life in or near Bordeaux, not Paris. His *Essays* were first published in French in 1580 and a complete, expanded edition published in French in 1595. They are often credited with having influenced *Hamlet* (as well as *The Tempest* of 1611–12). *Hamlet* was certainly written in 1601–02, and was first performed not later than July 1602. An English translation (by John Florio) of Montaigne's *Essays* did not appear, however, until 1603. Orthodox biographers get around this difficulty by such suggestions as 'Shakespeare may have read Florio's translation in manuscript'.[11] There is, needless to say, no evidence that Shakespeare ever heard of Florio, or Florio of Shakespeare.[12] Neville, however, an avid reader and scholar, and fluent in French, was in France for 15 months a few years after the publication of Montaigne's *Essays*, and just before he wrote *Hamlet*. It is also unlikely that Neville, as Ambassador, had many of the other time-consuming duties of modern ambassadors in major capitals, especially the endless round of ceremonial occasions, diplomatic functions and national day celebrations, which occupy foreign envoys today. Indeed, the snobbish French aristocracy of the time refused to meet him because he was not a titled lord. Neville also had a personal staff with him, including his secretary, the highly competent Ralph Winwood (1563–1617). It seems clear that Neville could certainly have written plays at this juncture; indeed, he might well have had less to occupy his time in Paris than in England where he had to manage his estates and attend to family matters, as well as performing his official functions as Member of Parliament and county official.

As Ambassador, too, Neville, as noted, had access to a confidential, express system of messengers, which could deliver documents and letters from Paris to London in about a week. There is no reason why plays or other literary works could not have been sent by Neville via his usual chan- nels in the theatre, although whether they were is, as we shall see, arguable. As a wealthy man, Neville could certainly have employed scribes and secre- taries when writing his plays in Paris. On either count, it is certainly reasonable to conclude that Neville had more than enough time to write the plays he did.

As with every other aspect of the authorship debate, exactly the same question might be posed of Shakespeare of Stratford: could he have written three or four plays in this period, despite the fact that he was both an actor and theatre-sharer in London and also had a family, a new home (New Place was probably purchased in 1597) and increasing business interests in Stratford? Such documentary evidence as exists shows that Shakespeare was active in both places in 1598–1600, although he was probably chiefly living in Bankside, London.[13] Arguably, Shakespeare had more to preoccupy him, with greater logistical difficulties in having two households and two business venues, but with many fewer resources than Neville had in Paris at this time. The question might also be asked why Shakespeare of Stratford, if he wrote the plays, wrote just these at this particular time; of course, despite centuries of research no answer can be given to this question.

Julius Caesar

The play which Neville wrote before going to France was probably *Julius Caesar*. Shakespeare's *Julius Caesar* was probably seen by Thomas Platter, a Swiss visitor to London, on 21 September 1599. He wrote:

> *After lunch on September 21st, at about two o'clock, I and my party crossed the river, and there in the house with the thatched roof we saw an excellent performance of the tragedy of the first Emperor Julius Caesar with about fifteen characters; after the play, according to their custom, they did a most elegant and curious dance, two dressed in men's clothes, and two in women's.*[14]

There is some doubt that this was Shakespeare's play, performed at the Globe, although the weight of evidence strongly supports the view that it was.[15] (On the other hand, it should be noted that the rival Admiral's Company had also performed a play about Caesar in 1594–95.) Platter does not remark on either the theatre being new or the actors being unsure of their lines, although it is often supposed that Shakespeare's *Julius Caesar* was performed as perhaps the first play acted at the new Globe Theatre. Ben Jonson, however, remarked that Shakespeare the actor made some of his lines seem ridiculous, and they are lines that a foreign visitor would probably not notice as being odd. Jonson quotes something Shakespeare the actor said from *Julius Caesar* which is not actually in the lines of the play, viz. 'Caesar doth not wrong without cause'. The actual lines were:

Know, Caesar doth not wrong, nor without cause
Will he be satisfied.

Act III, Sc. I

Stratfordians have been at pains to show that Ben Jonson was talking about the *writer* when he said this, but that a writer of 'Shakespeare's' stature should make such a mistake is most unlikely. The wrong lines also do not scan. Jonson himself had probably been constrained to confuse the issue whenever he might write about 'Shakespeare's' works.

Thus the evidence seems to point to the actors having little time to learn their roles before the actual performance, which would suggest that Platter was probably referring to Neville's *Julius Caesar*, the first performance at the new Globe Theatre. Perhaps Neville's reluctance to take up his post in France was not so feigned after all. He would obviously have preferred to have an elevated post in the English state at such a time.

Other evidence also points to this time, the autumn of 1599, as the date for the first performance of the play. Neville thus must have completed the play by the summer of 1599; in view of the time constraints, he must almost certainly have begun it before leaving for Paris, probably for performance at the opening of the new Globe Theatre. It was, in any case, an ideal play to have completed in Paris. Most of it is based on Sir Thomas North's translations of Plutarch's *Lives*, which appeared in two editions, in 1579 and 1595 respectively. As Ambassador, Neville could certainly have taken a number of books with him as part of his baggage and effects, but he could not have transported a library. This made it unlikely for him to have continued writing plays which required a plethora of obscure works as their sources; English history was probably out for that reason while Neville was abroad. But Julius Caesar was, of course, one of the most famous men in history, and it would have been just as easy to find works on him, if needed, in Paris as in London. Additionally, the play might have been intended to warn the Essex conspirators against drastic action, at that stage, at least. Neville was, in the middle of 1599, very much in favour with Elizabeth's Cecilian government, and in no mood for sedition.

As You Like It

Neville's next play was probably *As You Like It*, which is generally thought to have been written in 1599–1600. It is often grouped stylistically with

Twelfth Night and *Much Ado About Nothing,* and was registered – as we will discuss below – on 4 August 1600. *As You Like It* is not included in Francis Meres' list of Shakespeare's plays, but its song (Act V, Sc. III) 'It was a lover and his lass' was printed in a book by Thomas Morley in 1600. Morley was married to a maidservant of Elizabeth Bacon Neville, Sir Henry's step-mother, and was apparently living at Billingbear at this time. If so, it seems difficult to believe that Neville and Morley did not know each other.[16] The play concerns a usurper of the French throne, and is set in the 'Forest of Arden', which is usually interpreted as a reference to the Ardennes in north-west France, rather than to the Warwickshire Arden woods or to Shakespeare's mother's family. As Park Honan has noted, the Arden woods in Warwickshire were being deforested and enclosed; they were the home of vagrants rather than of aristocrats.[17] Given that Neville was then in France, the reason for its French setting is thus obvious.

Some clue as to the date when *As You Like It* was written might well be provided from a letter Neville wrote to Cecil in December 1599, in which he registered his wish that, rather than continue the arduous work of Ambassador, he wished to 'be a hermit in Ashridge or the forest, and do penance for the faults committed here', which very much echoes the char-acter of the exiled Jacques in that play.[18] 'Touchstone' is the curious name of the clown in *As You Like It* – curious, that is, until one realizes that a touchstone was a kind of basalt used for testing the difference between gold and base metals. We know that Neville 'had skill in this' as there is, in the Berkshire Record Office, a letter from his land agent in Yorkshire, saying as much, when he tells Neville that there is touchstone present on his land there:

> *I have sent you a touch of a stone, or rather a mynerall gotten att Lun, and I thinke there is of itt in the ground at Lunwood, you have skill in affirmtidge of it, for I have none. And now, resting to be disposed by you wherin I am ever also remembring my best service to the good ladie att billinbear and the gentle-women, not forgetting my kindest commendacions to youre self, I conclude.*
>
> *Your ever assured loving frend and kinsman,*
> *Ric: Beaumont*   *Whittley, this 9 of march 1600*[19]

Twelfth Night

The third play written by Neville at this time was *Twelfth Night,* which was certainly completed by 1602, when (on 2 February) it was performed at the Middle Temple.[20] Much internal evidence suggests that it was written around 1600 and performed at Whitehall in 1600, although it is not included among the four plays registered in August 1600 – but this is perfectly possible if it was then meant for the Queen and her private audience only. Its plot is the usual Shakespearean comedy situation, with a shipwreck, misidentification, a twin brother and sister, and includes a Falstaff-like character in Sir Toby Belch, arguably showing hasty writing by Neville. Although Neville almost certainly began *Twelfth Night* in France, it was probably originally intended for a performance at Candlemas (2 February) 1601, six months after Neville returned to England.

Then it seems as if Neville was inspired to finish it earlier and to add other topical elements to the play. Although this was based on two earlier works – one Italian and the other by an English soldier who had served in the Lowlands – it may well be that Ralph Winwood inspired some extra ingredients. This he seems to have done unwittingly, by telling Neville the story of Don Virginio Orsino.

It has often been attested by Dr Leslie Hotson and other scholars that this play was probably written to entertain that Italian nobleman. The main argument *against* this assumption has always been that no one had any hint of the Venetian Orsino's visit until two weeks before he actually arrived. Certainly, Shakespeare the actor could not have known of it. However, Neville was one of the very few who had prior knowledge of Orsino's projected stay in London. He was indeed informed of it by Winwood in a letter dated 20 November, 1600. And it is even possible that some of Neville's unofficial intelligence agents had told him of the possibility of the nobleman's visit *before* this date. But assuming that he knew by 20 November, and that the play was perhaps not performed exactly on Twelfth Night (6 January) but after 20 January (as Neville only mentioned it on 29 January), this still gave Neville at least two months in which to complete the play he had probably already begun as a celebration for his return home.

It would also not be surprising if Neville's mind had been full of shipwrecks and exiles well before this date, and that the name of 'Orsino' was added as a special compliment, once he knew the date of the nobleman's arrival. It would have been no difficult matter for him to have filled in one or two relevant details concerning the real Orsino's background, after reading Winwood's narration of Orsino's own difficulties. Winwood tells of Henri's presentation of gifts to three Italian princes at his Court, including

> *Virginio ... and Antonio, to each of them a Jewell to wear in their Hatts: ... Don Virginio made shew to depart with the Galleys, but afterwards came disguised to Avignon. He hath a purpose to pass through France, and I understand into England and the Low Countries, in which Places he doth desire to pass his time, during the time of this Pope; against whom, as he hath (as he pretendeth) just Cause of Discontents, so for a Disgrace which he lately at Florence did offer to Cardinall Aldorbrandino, he is willing to retire himself; knowing how unequall a Match he is to contest, either with the Malice of the one, or the Power of the other.*[21]

The parallels between the fate of Orsino's father and Viola's brother and his friend, Antonio, in *Twelfth Night* cannot be missed.

> SEBASTIAN. ... *I am bound to the Count Orsino's court. Farewell.*
> *Exit*
> ANTONIO. *The gentleness of all the gods go with thee!*
> *I have many enemies in Orsino's court,*
> *Else would I very shortly see thee there.*
> *But come what may, I do adore thee so*
> *That danger shall seem sport, and I will go.*
>
> *Act II, Sc. I*

And Sebastian finally marries a girl (Olivia) he does not know, just like Paulo had done in Winwood's telling of Orsino's family story. The theme of disguise too would have struck a chord with Neville who, as he told Cecil in a diplomatic dispatch from France, went in disguise to the King of Spain's funeral, as casually as if it had been a usual tactic of his. In *Twelfth Night* Viola disguises as Cesario.

Into the same soup-pot of a play, the writer also placed Robert Greene (the man who had criticized 'Shakespeare's' writing) in the character of Sir Toby Belch, and Sir William Knollys (as Malvolio). He may even have mentally set the play at the home of Thomas Posthumous Hoby, his kinsman by marriage, who sued some drunken revellers at his home for disturbance of the peace. Indeed, the name 'Posthumous' was also to turn up again in

Cymbeline. William Knollys had made a fool of himself at Court by chasing Mary (Mal) Fitton. He was by that time a man in his fifties, while she was a beautiful, 17-year-old maid-of-honour to the Queen. Hence the name 'Malvolio' (I want Mal). She was in love with William Herbert, the young Earl of Pembroke, who later became patron of the First Folio of Shakespeare's plays. Knollys had also been one of the commissioners at Boulogne, and it began to be rumoured that he was going around the Court blaming Neville for the failure of the Treaty. Thus the true writer of the plays had reason to vilify Knollys on stage. Mal Fitton had been accused by the Queen of disguising as a boy and going through the streets at night in order to meet Herbert, her lover, so Viola's disguise would have been seen as no novelty for those in the Court who knew the truth. But by the time Neville wrote the play, Mal had already been disgraced:

> SIR TOBY. . . . *Are they like to take dust, like Mistress Mall's picture?*
>
> Act I, Sc. III

Clearly, Neville has to remind the Court audience of times past, in order to discredit what Knollys is saying about him at this moment.

For the cognoscenti, then, *Twelfth Night* is indeed a bitter comedy. Certainly, the portrayal of Knollys, alias Malvolio, as a madman perhaps goes too far in its tormenting, when viewed with modern eyes. However, Neville was a desperate man. He felt that Knollys' slanders could have given Elizabeth an excuse to force him to return to France and 'put things right'. Henry therefore felt justified in using any tactic to prevent this. As already noted, 'Mistress Mall's' name was really 'Mary'. In the play, it is Maria who writes a letter asking Malvolio to wear yellow cross-gartering on his tights. One wonders if the real-life 'Mary' tried to put a stop to Knollys' attentions by writing him a letter asking him to dye his beard red, for this is what Knollys did, with disastrous and comic consequences. In the play itself there is also a reference to the colour of Malvolio's beard, so the assumption that Maria has been given the character of Mal Fitton, and that Knollys is Malvolio, is as good as proven:

> MARIA. *I will drop in his way some obscure epistles of love;*
> *wherein, by the colour of his beard, the shape of his leg, the*
> *manner of his gait, the expressure of his eye, forehead, and*
> *complexion, he shall find himself most feelingly personated.*
>
> Act II, Sc. III

The yellow cross-gartering may well have been meant to remind courtiers of Knollys' ridiculous red-orange beard, which made him a laughing stock at Court. How Neville must have enjoyed his revenge: it must have been difficult for Knollys to find anyone willing to listen to his accusations against Neville. Henry had things to do in London and Berkshire, and things to write, whereas he had enemies in France and had even been issued oblique threats. Above all, he wished to remain with his wife and children. His ridiculing of Knollys was therefore a weapon in his campaign to stay in England.

Thus does Knollys' inclusion in *Twelfth Night* become smoking-gun evidence for Neville's authorship of the plays. In addition to the fact that it was Neville who had privileged knowledge concerning the arrival of Virginio Orsino, who other than Neville had an interest in reminding the Court of Knollys' past madness?

Neville was supposed to return to France after a month in England, but delayed in order to treat his deafness and attend to his personal affairs. Following his arrest for taking part in the Essex rebellion, Neville wrote in his own account of his actions during the rebellion that 'I fully proposed to have set forward [back to France] upon the Thursday after Candlemass day at the farthest . . .' It is thus possible that Neville was present at the first performance of *Twelfth Night*.[22]

As noted, Neville received permission to return to England, after nearly a year and a half away, in July 1600. He arrived at Dover on 2 August and in London on 6 August. *On 4 August 1600* there appeared in the Stationers' Register a listing of four plays 'to be staied': *As You Like It, Henry V, Every Man in His Humour* (written by Ben Jonson) and *Much Ado About Nothing*. It is very unclear why this entry appeared, by whom it was written, or for what purpose.[23] The normal interpretation, which has been widely discussed, is that either the Lord Chamberlain's Company, or Shakespeare himself, wished to forestall piracy; another interpretation is that it indicated that formal entry in the Register 'was to be held over for a while, rather than publication prevented altogether'.[24] With our knowledge of Neville as the author and of his movements, it is now possible to shed more light on this entry. Evidently, when Neville learned that he would at last be returning home, he sent word to his channels in the theatre either to register plays which he had already written and previously sent across, or which he was bringing with him. Word of this must have reached London just as Neville was setting out, and he found, on his return, that his channels had done as he asked. Possibly – indeed, probably – Neville intended to discuss these plays with the Chamberlain's Men soon after arriving, and perhaps he actually did that, although he was very fully occupied. If so, this sheds a good deal of new light on 'Shakespeare's' techniques, which must have included a discussion of the plays with at least some of the actors.

But these entries remain puzzling: why was *Julius Caesar* not included? Since it had almost certainly already been performed the previous year, does this mean the other plays had yet to be premiered? Why was *Henry V* there? Had Neville hurriedly taken it to France before it was ever performed? Quite probably: it was again entered in the Stationers' Register on 14 August and printed in its first Quarto form at some date in 1600.[25] Why was Ben Jonson's play registered at the same time? Was he in on the authorship secret at this date? Quite probably he was. Above all, the tallying of these dates with Neville's itinerary is so extraordinary that it simply cannot be coincidental, while we know of no plausible connection with anything in the life of Shakespeare of Stratford.

Chapter 7

The Catastrophe, 1601–03

A lthough he had been only partially successful in his admittedly difficult role of Ambassador to France, when Neville returned to London on 6 August 1600 he was, to the outside world at least, at the height of his status and influence, a man still in his thirties who appeared destined for a memorable career in the service of the government. As 'William Shakespeare' he had already written about 22 plays, among them such masterpieces as *The Merchant of Venice* and *Julius Caesar,* although at that stage his ultimate status as the greatest of all writers appeared problematical. Within a brief period of time, however, his status both as a public figure and as a secret writer were to undergo total and drastic transformations. Almost overnight, his career and future promise collapsed and he was faced with the worst public and private catastrophe of his life. This experience, however, deepened Neville the writer, engendering the greatest of all works in our literature.

The Essex rebellion

The circumstances of Henry Neville's involvement with the Essex conspiracy remain controversial, with a strong likelihood that it was more extensive than he admitted following his arrest. Something, however, must first be said of what the Essex rebellion was and why it was the seminal event for so many late Elizabethan public figures. Robert Devereux, second Earl of Essex (1566–1601) succeeded to the earldom at the age of ten, and by the mid-1580s had accompanied his stepfather, the Earl of Leicester, in the military campaign in the Netherlands, notably the Battle of Zutphen, Although 33 years younger than Queen Elizabeth, after Leicester's death in 1588 he succeeded him as the Queen's latest favourite. Relations between Elizabeth and Essex, an ambitious and argumentative but charismatic young man, were unusually electric, marked by a long series of quarrels starting with his marriage in 1590 to the widow of Sir Philip Sidney. As with some of her previous favourites, the Queen consistently forgave Essex many insults and offences, with the earl benefiting financially from a long-term monopoly which he enjoyed on sweet wines. Essex also acquired an exaggerated reputation as a skilful military leader, and in 1591–92 commanded the forces which were sent to help France's King Henri IV against the Catholic League in Normandy.

Additionally, during the mid-1590s Essex built up an important political faction consisting largely of anti-Cecil 'outsiders', among them (despite his Protestantism) some Catholic and poorer nobles and veterans of his Irish campaign. Sir Francis Bacon was originally a follower of Essex, but deserted his cause by about 1597. Essex was probably most responsible for the arrest in 1594 and eventual execution of Roderigo Lopez, the Queen's Jewish Portuguese-born physician, for allegedly assisting Spain; if Lopez was 'Shylock', it appears likely that Neville was among Essex's supporters at the time. Essex became increasingly arrogant, which culminated in a notorious scene in 1598 in which Essex burst into the Queen's private chambers and drew his sword in anger at her insulting remarks. Naturally, he would ordinarily have been sent straight to the Tower, but instead, after a reconciliation, was given command of an army in Ireland to put down the rebel Irish leader Hugh O'Neill, Earl of Tyrone.

In Ireland, Essex proved a mediocre military leader, but he created many battlefield knights, as he was entitled to do. On Essex's return to London in September 1599 the Queen finally ordered his arrest, although he managed to remain free. From 1600 he was increasingly engaged in a treasonable series of activities leading to overt rebellion, the aim of which was to capture the Queen, displace the Cecils, and guarantee a Protestant succession to the throne under King James VI of Scotland after Elizabeth's death. Essex, who was by all accounts an amazingly attractive and charismatic man to his supporters, managed to gather behind him a wide range of adherents, including the Earl of Southampton. (Some even maintained that Essex's eventual aim was to be king himself.)

The 'Essex rebellion' took place in early February 1601, but failed dismally. Essex was put on trial for treason on 19 February and beheaded on 25 February. He had been involved in the arts and literature, acting as patron to Essex's Men, a provincial company of actors founded by his father around 1572.[1]

There are several reasons why Henry Neville would be attracted to Essex and his faction, and also several why he would not. In the mid- to late 1590s Neville was clearly on the upward path of favour, but he was never appointed to a truly major position, and his role as Ambassador to France was arduous, expensive and of mixed success. The Essex faction, as will be seen, recognized Neville's talent, and clearly intimated that he might succeed Robert Cecil as Secretary of State, appealing both to Neville's obvious ambition and, perhaps, some kind of restoration of the Nevilles to national pre-eminence. On the other hand, Neville had been given high office by Cecil and the Queen (though certainly not the kind of office he had wanted); he was related to Cecil by marriage and also to Sir Henry Killigrew, a senior Cecil/Court insider.

We shall probably never fully know what tipped Neville into engaging in the rebellion. On a personal level, he must have thought that the prospect of returning to France (a country and culture he had grown to dislike) was a worse prospect than remaining in England and taking the chance of gaining quick promotion to high office. But probably, above everything else, there was his central desire to ensure a Protestant succession to the throne after the death of the Queen (who was 67 years old in 1600 and visibly ageing), in the person of James VI of Scotland. Neville had extensive contacts with Scottish emissaries while in Paris, where he was described (not wholly accurately) by one unnamed observer as 'a puritan and entirely Scottish . . . he confers much with the Scottish ambassador'.[2] This motive appears, as well, to have been behind the active participation of Southampton, Neville's great friend, among the Essex rebels.

We do not really know what Neville's own attitude towards Essex as a leader and charismatic figure actually was; perhaps the author of the Sonnets found a commanding male authority figure highly attractive, although Essex and Neville do not appear to have had much in the way of direct contact until just before the rebellion. But appearances can be deceptive, and sensitive correspondence can be destroyed. We do know that Neville was a close friend of Anthony Bacon, Essex's factotum. We also know that, according to Chamberlain, it was the Earl of Essex who finally persuaded Neville to take the French ambassadorship, not because he thought this a fit office for Neville but because he, Essex, needed a new representative over there because his current one had decided to return to England. It can also be seen from Neville's diplomatic correspondence with Cecil and with his own secretary, Ralph Winwood, that he was constantly concerned about the Earl of Essex's progress in Ireland, and also concerned that the French should not perceive any friction between Essex and Cecil. Some historians have claimed that he was the Henry Neville knighted by Essex at Cadiz, in which case he would have owed him loyalty. In addition to all this, it is hard to believe that Essex would offer high office under his 'new regime' to a man he hardly knew. In all, the absence of surviving correspondence between the two men looks strange enough to have been engineered.

The succession question

The divisions engendered in late Elizabethan society, especially among the elites and those who reflected their viewpoint, can hardly be exaggerated. Although today we invariably view Elizabeth I as 'Gloriana', the uniquely popular and powerful female ruler of a triumphant England of an age to which she gave her name, in fact the Queen, during the last years of her reign, was widely viewed as a dismal figure, who was living on borrowed time, and who was a figurehead for the Cecils and other powerful courtiers. More than anything else, the lack of an assured and certain successor caused widespread unease as well as opening the floodgates of intrigue. It was by no means certain that the Protestant James VI of Scotland would succeed: many feared that the Catholic Infanta of Spain might receive the Queen's 'dying voice' as her successor. Indeed, anything might happen, even the succession of an outsider with some remote claims to the throne such as the Earl of Essex, no more implausible a possibility than Henry Tudor had been a century earlier. Open discussion of the succession was forbidden by law. Nor was it certain how much longer the Queen might live: she had been born in 1533, and thus might well live into the 1610s or even later.

Neville, though primarily against civil war, had a broad enough outlook to accept that there were occasions on which a bad monarch could be replaced if they were guilty of misgovernment – as witnessed by his play *Richard II*. The potential danger Elizabeth was causing the realm by her ill-advised law against discussing the succession might well have led to Neville mentally labelling her as guilty of just such misgovernment. He would have done what he did primarily out of a sense of 'common good to all' therefore, like Brutus. But he nevertheless recognized the potential dangers. Those who reported what he said when Essex told him of his plans declared that Neville first called them 'rash', and then, with Shakespearean menace and double-meaning, said, 'It is in the number of those things that are never praised till performed'. But what spurred these educated men to such rash action? We think that by playing down Neville's role in the rebellion, historians may also have wrongly labelled the conspirators as mere hotheads. If Neville was their intended political leader, should their rebellion succeed, then they were simply forced into precipitate action because Neville was under significant and daily-increasing pressure from the Queen to return to France. As the entry on Neville says in the recently published *Oxford Dictionary of National Biography*, Neville is a much more important figure than it appears on the surface.

Support for Essex

The charisma and controversy generated by the figure of Essex also extended into the world of the London theatre. In 1935, an American professor, Robert Boies Sharpe, published an unjustly neglected but extremely important work entitled *The Real War of the Theatres*.[3] Sharpe argued that the two main London theatre companies of the time, the Chamberlain's Men and the Admiral's Men, in fact had clearly defined political allegiances, with the Chamberlain's Men supporting Essex and his circle, the Admiral's Men the pro-Cecil 'establishment'. The audiences at the Chamberlain's Men's performances may have been drawn from a younger, rowdier element than those put on by the Admiral's Men.[4] If Sharpe's view is tenable, Neville might have found this theatrical connection another mode of entry into the pro-Essex partisans, as well as another reason to keep his identity a secret.

When Neville arrived in London on 6 August 1600 he found a note waiting for him from Henry Cuffe (1563–1601), an old academic friend of his. Cuffe, from Somerset, matriculated at Trinity College, Oxford, in 1578, and, like Neville, was a protégé of Sir Henry Savile. Cuffe spent his adult life at Oxford and held the position of Professor of Greek there from 1590 to 1596; as well, he was a proctor of the university. Rather oddly, perhaps, he then fell under the spell of the Earl of Essex, becoming his secretary and accompanying him on military expeditions to Cadiz and Ireland. In 1600 Cuffe produced his only book, *The Differences of the Ages of Man's Life* (perhaps a hint towards Jacques' famous speech in *As You Like It)*. He participated, in 1592, in a debate at Neville's alma mater, Merton College, Oxford, attended by the Queen and presided over by Savile. Its topic was 'the usefulness of civil dissent to the state'.[5] Cuffe had also been secretary to Neville's relative Anthony Bacon, who had built up a pro-Essex intelligence network. In addition, he was a friend of Southampton, and of growing influence, in an ever more reckless way, on Essex himself.[6] In his note, Cuffe requested a meeting with Neville, obviously to discuss any action by Essex and Neville's potential role in it.

Neville prevaricated, visiting Billingbear for the first time in over a year and also continuing his duties as Ambassador – a post he still officially held – through his secretary Sir Ralph Winwood, who had remained in France.[7] It is also virtually certain that he made contact with his London theatre associates, as one must infer from the Stationers' Register entry of 4 August. *Much Ado About Nothing* was also formally entered on the Stationers' Register on 23 August 1600, while a Quarto version of *Henry V* was published some time in 1600, and was formally entered on that register on 14 August of the same year. Significantly, Neville spent much of August and the first part of September in London, and it is difficult to believe that the theatre did not occupy part of his time there.[8] He also did his best to be relieved of his ambassadorial post, persistently and visibly requesting that his resignation be accepted.[9] Despite his wishes, however, the Queen requested that he return to France as quickly as possible – Neville had already overstayed the month's leave he had been granted – and began to become seriously annoyed at his unauthorized delay, which continued into 1601.[10]

Neville was kept fully informed about Essex, writing of his activities to Winwood and, moreover, had held a secret meeting with Essex and Cuffe in late October 1600 at Essex's home of Ewelme in Oxfordshire, about ten miles from Billingbear. Neville left discreetly by the back gate, and kept the meeting a secret.[11] Neville also had many meetings with Cuffe. Essex had, meantime, moved to a more extreme position, becoming convinced that Robert Cecil intended Elizabeth's successor to be not the Protestant James

VI of Scotland but the Catholic Infanta of Spain, who also had a claim to the throne. The possibility of a Catholic succeeding to the throne probably did more than anything else to attract the support of staunch Protestants such as Neville to Essex's cause, although Essex's charismatic persona was also arguably a major factor.[12] In January 1601 Neville met several times with Essex's principal associates, and apparently became convinced that a possible pro-Catholic conspiracy existed, following a physical attack on Lord Southampton by Lord Grey on 9 January 1601.[13]

Although Neville was still the Ambassador to France, he felt that his advice regarding France was increasingly being ignored by Cecil and the Queen. Neville finally agreed formally to meet the leaders of the Essex faction on Candlemas Day (2 February) 1601 at Drury House, in London, where Southampton and another pro-Essex leader, Sir Charles Danvers, were living. In his defence during his subsequent trial, Neville claimed to have seen Essex, Southampton, Danvers and Sir Christopher Blount drive by on the Strand in Essex's coach and that, recognizing them and halting the coach, he spoke to Lord Southampton for the first time since the latter was a child ward at Lord Burghley's house.[14] This claim was almost certainly disingenuous; Essex and Southampton had just, unexpectedly, named Neville as a conspirator and Neville was literally in grave peril of his life. Southampton indeed described these men – including Neville – as his 'best friends', which would hardly have been the case if Neville had not seen him in the past ten years. If Neville dedicated two poems to Southampton and addressed many of the Sonnets to him, plainly they must have met. Moreover, all of these men were Members of Parliament at the same time as Neville himself was an MP – Blount and Danvers in the Commons, Essex and Southampton in the Lords, making it almost inconceivable that they had not met.

So flimsy was Neville's claim, in fact, he was lucky that the prosecution did not pursue it, which leads one to wonder why they did not. In all probability, they had been advised by Cecil not to do so. Cecil might well have known about Neville's writing, especially as the Earl of Southampton had been one of his father's wards and was now patron to the great poet. (As discussed earlier, it was probably Cecil's father who instigated the poems to Southampton.) Neville then had a lengthy, formal meeting with the leaders of the Essex group, at which they stated their goals as merely wishing to improve relations between the Queen and Essex in the interests of

Protestantism. During his discussions, it was repeatedly hinted to Neville that, should Essex and his supporters replaced the Cecils, Neville would become Secretary of State in lieu of Robert Cecil.[15]

Neville held subsequent meetings with Cuffe 'a day or two later', that is, on 3 or 4 February 1601. He was not, however, present at the large meeting at Drury House at which the rebellion was plotted, shortly before the uprising that took place on 8 February 1601.[16] *On 7 February, five days after Neville's meeting with the Essex conspirators*, there occurred the well-known but hitherto utterly inexplicable performance of *Richard II* at the Globe Theatre, a day before the rebellion and at the specific request of the conspirators.

Richard II

Richard II is, of course, about the justifiable deposition of an English king. There has been some discussion about whether this performance was of Shakespeare's *Richard II,* or of a version of a work by Sir John Hayward (*c*.1560–1627) who, in 1599, published a prose history of the life of King Henry IV, dedicated to Essex, which also deals with the deposition of Richard II. As Chambers argued convincingly many years ago, however, the play must have been Shakespeare's: it was given by the Chamberlain's Men, Shakespeare's acting company; and the request to perform the play was received dubiously by the company on the grounds that it was 'so old and so long out of use' that it could not be quickly put on *(Richard II* dates from 1595).[17] The play might have been performed as many as 40 times before the rebellion – so claimed the Queen – but the limited time-frame means that this is most unlikely.[18] Moreover, and even more to the point, Hayward's was a *prose* work, published in 1599: *The First Part of the Life and Raigne of King Henry IV*. It could thus not have been 'performed' by the Chamberlain's Men. (It was, however, dedicated to Essex, which got its author into serious trouble after the Essex rebellion.) While the Chamberlain's Men were under some suspicion after the rebellion (although they escaped any penalty), the author of the play was never penalized in any way. If its author was Shakespeare of Stratford, this is exceedingly odd – indeed, almost inexplicable, given his apparent lack of friends in high places. Neville, however, was shortly arrested and tried for treason; a reasonable inference is that those who knew of his authorship, such as Francis Bacon (one of the government prosecutors) and Southampton did not wish to give away the secret, which would probably have meant a certain death sentence for Neville. Once again, the dating is remarkable and must, surely, be more than coincidence. Presumably Neville, with his recent theatre contacts, had the 'brainstorm' to put on *Richard II* (already a favourite play of the Earl of Essex) but took particular care not to be seen to be involved in any way. This would strongly imply that his involvement with the Essex conspirators and their very serious aims was, at this stage, considerable, certainly much greater than he allowed in his court testimony. As will be discussed shortly, the performance of *The Mousetrap*, the play-within-a-play in *Hamlet*, is surely based on the author's own sense of guilt and, possibly, self-importance, over the performance of *Richard II* on the eve of the rebellion. Once again, it is very difficult to perceive any connection between Shakespeare of Stratford and the Essex conspirators; hence the staging of *Richard II* remains (for Stratfordians) mysterious and inexplicable. William Shakespeare of Stratford invariably kept as low a profile as possible in England's political intrigues of the time, realizing full well the fate that might well await a provincial actor with no powerful friends, and a possible secret Roman Catholic, who meddled in high affairs of state, let alone treasonably.

Failure and the aftermath

Neville was still in active, apparently normal, communication with Cecil about diplomatic matters when the Essex rebellion took place on 8 February 1601, and, indeed, was at Court on the day of the rising.[19] The rebellion failed dismally, although with a better strategy Essex might well have succeeded in seizing both the Queen and Cecil and becoming ruler of England. On 19 February Essex and Southampton, along with the main conspirators, were arrested and, after a trial, sentenced to death, as were Essex's main followers such as Cuffe (who was hanged, drawn and quartered). Southampton was sentenced to death for treason, but reprieved and sent to the Tower of London, where he remained (near Neville) until the accession of James I in 1603.[20] On 21 February 1621, at his trial and during a frank exposition of the rebellion and those who took part in it, Essex, backed by Southampton, named Sir Henry Neville, 'whom no man did suspect', as one of the participants in the first Drury House meeting.[21] Neville, probably expecting the worst, was by this time hastening back to France, completely reversing his former policy of procrastination, before returning to his ambassadorial duties. The warrant for his arrest from Cecil reached the authorities when Neville was at Dover. As Duncan put it, 'Sir Henry obviously sensed that he had been discovered. Upon being stopped . . . he leaped to his horse and, abandoning his wife, his children, and his servants, rode off to court [in London] with two . . . men in pursuit to guarantee that he did not vary from his course'.[22] In London, Neville was placed under arrest at the Lord Admiral's house in Chelsea, where he proceeded to draft a series of lengthy and apparently honest accounts of his role in the rebellion which, needless to say, comprehensively minimized and whitewashed it. Lady Neville's father, Sir Henry Killigrew, was so enraged by his son-in-law's apparent treason that 'he would not permit her in his house' until ordered to take in his daughter and grandchildren by the Privy Council.[23] It seems abundantly clear that Neville's role was greater than he asserted while, no doubt, all of Neville's Shakespearean gifts were used to provide an account which would spare his life.

In May 1601 Neville was sent to the Tower of London, dismissed from his offices, and fined the extraordinary sum of £10,000. Only with difficulty did he avoid being beheaded. Following numerous pleas to Cecil and to the Queen (who was almost unyielding), Neville's fine was reduced to £5,000, payable in annual instalments of £1,000 each. It would appear that Neville had paid about £3,000 by the time of his release in April 1603, at the accession of James I. Neville and Southampton were the only Essex plotters who were neither executed nor freed. Neville could not fathom why he was punished so severely while many of Essex's closer collaborators were pardoned, and it is also difficult for us to see why Neville suffered from such protracted imprisonment. Perhaps it was feared that, as Ambassador, he was part of an international conspiracy; perhaps Elizabeth or Cecil had an inkling of Neville's role as the author of *Richard II*; we simply do not know for sure. However, we do know that Cecil saw a performance of *Richard II* at Hoby's London house shortly after it was written. Both Cecil and Hoby were relatives of Sir Henry Neville through his marriage to Anne Killigrew.

For Neville, it should be noted, life in the Tower was probably fairly comfortable. He could and did write – writing many letters and memoranda to Cecil and others and keeping the Tower Notebook. He was also able to receive visitors and enjoyed conjugal visiting rights. In a nearby cell was his old friend Southampton, who also lived as if he were in the equivalent today of a good hotel rather than in a prison, judging by the famous portrait depicting him in the Tower with his pet cat. However, Neville and Southampton remained prisoners in the Tower for 23 months until, on 10 April 1603 they were released, pardoned and restored to all their titles and property. Although the surroundings were probably bearable, Neville obviously daily feared exposure as the writer of that 'seditious play', and many of his notes in his Tower Notebook are concerned with preparing a case detailing the legality of Richard II's deposition.

Almost certainly, Neville had had long-standing secret dealings with James in the interest of making him King after Elizabeth's death, and James recognized Neville and Southampton as among his staunchest supporters in England. Neville had very high hopes of James, expecting to be given senior office; *Henry VIII,* perhaps eventually intended as a coronation pageant, was completed with this now in mind. Yet nothing was forthcoming and Neville received no offices or favours from James 1, and by 1603–04 he was again a disappointed man.

The catastrophe of 1601–03 changed Neville in marked and obvious ways. He became more Protestant and religious, more pessimistic, perhaps more politically radical, and probably more cynical. Yet it is indeed an ill wind which blows no good, for this terrible experience also altered the course of English literature. As a result, out went the light Italianate comedies and triumphalist histories, and in their place came the great and immortal tragedies and the so-called 'problem plays'. Only, perhaps, at the very end of Neville's career, with *The Tempest,* was some kind of homeostatic balance restored to Neville's temperament. It is, however, no exaggeration to say that the Essex debacle transformed Sir Henry Neville from a very good Elizabethan author to the greatest writer in history, the icon and fountainhead of English-language authors.

The Essex rebellion and other authorship candidates

One might also consider here the likely effects of the Essex conspiracy and rebellion on William Shakespeare of Stratford as well as its effects on Edward De Vere, seventeenth Earl of Oxford, and Sir Francis Bacon, the two leading authorship 'candidates' among those who cannot credit the

Stratford man with writing the plays. As noted, there is simply no traceable connection between Shakespeare of Stratford and Essex and his circle: although the Chamberlain's Men probably performed *Richard II*, Shakespeare was not arrested or even questioned. Shakespeare had purchased New Place, the second largest house in Stratford, in May 1597 for the not inconsiderable sum of £60, and was described in the deed of purchase as *'generosus'*, a gentleman. In March 1600 he sued a local yeoman in Bedfordshire for the recovery of a £7 debt. In October 1600, Shakespeare was officially brought to the attention of the Court of the Bishop of Winchester (whose jurisdiction included the Southwark area south of the Thames) for non-payment of taxes. An inference is that he had recently left the area, presumably moving almost full-time to Stratford. In March 1601 a shepherd to the Hathaway family died and left a will recording that Shakespeare and his wife owed him 40 shillings. In May 1601 Shakespeare paid £320 – an enormous sum – for 107 acres of arable land near Stratford, and also purchased a cottage and garden opposite New Place.[24] Despite centuries of diligent searching in every conceivable source, no other records of Shakespeare's activities at this time have ever been traced, not even records of him as an actor, although he was almost certainly still a sharer (part-owner and manager) in the Globe Theatre. The evident inference from all this is that Shakespeare was chiefly living in Stratford, probably returning to London only to deal with important theatre business – such as, presumably, liaising with Neville about his plays – although Neville's period overseas as a diplomat presumably made Shakespeare's presence in London required less frequently. There is thus no reason to suppose that Shakespeare had any connection with Essex or, for that matter, with any political intrigues of any kind, activities which not only contradict everything we know of Shakespeare's life, but also support his evident and well-documented concern to transform himself, slowly but surely, into a leading Stratford gentleman and landowner.

There is, thus, not only no reason to suppose that Shakespeare was involved in the Essex rebellion, but no reason to suppose that his work was made more profound by it, or by any known event which occurred at this time, although this is exactly what happened. The normal explanation for this new profundity in his works is Shakespeare's grief for the death of his only son Hamnet (1585–96), who had died at the age of 11. But the break in Shakespeare's works appears clearly to have come at this time, not five years earlier when his son died. In the interim, Shakespeare had written the Falstaff plays, hardly the obvious products of an author in mourning. No good explanation has yet been offered as to why Shakespeare of Stratford now chose to write *Hamlet*.

Nor can the events of this period readily be meshed into the lives of the two leading anti-Stratfordian authorship candidates, Oxford or Bacon. Bacon was one of the chief government prosecutors against Essex, while De Vere was the foreman of the jury of peers – members of the House of Lords – which condemned Essex and Southampton to death for treason for his role in the Essex rebellion. Partisans of De Vere as 'Shakespeare', who almost always regard Southampton (accurately) as 'Mr. W.H.' of the Sonnets, as well as the dedicatee of Shakespeare's two early poems, normally pass over this regrettable fact in silence. If Oxford was as close to Southampton as his partisans urge, how could he vote to condemn Southampton to death? Absolutely nothing survives in any of De Vere's papers to indicate that he had any favourable feelings towards Essex or Southampton; according to his recent biographer, Professor Alan Nelson, Oxford 'had expressed bitterness against Essex in a postscript to a letter of 20 October 1595', but does not mention him further. He had no traceable dealings of any kind with Southampton after the ill-fated attempt by Burghley to have Southampton marry Oxford's daughter (and Burghley's granddaughter) in 1590.[25] De Vere also had no traceable connection of any kind with William Shakespeare. Nothing exists in any of De Vere's papers to connect him with Shakespeare, while contemporaries such as Francis Meres (and others), when drawing up lists of prominent authors of their time, refer to them as two distinct individuals.[26] Oxford's surviving poems (none of the plays he wrote survives) show talent rather than genius and are obviously not by Shakespeare, lacking the extreme complexity invariably found in his works.[27]

Oxford had no traceable relations of any kind with Sir Henry Neville, who was 12 years his junior and moved in very different circles. The only place these circles could have overlapped was occasionally – and then only by chance – at Burghley's house in the Strand, because Oxford was Burghley's son-in-law. De Vere was educated at Cambridge rather than Oxford; his notoriously violent and quarrelsome personality – he apparently killed one of Burghley's servants and later killed another man in a duel – was very different from that of the scholarly, introspective family man Neville;

and De Vere's two companies of actors, Oxford's Boys and (from 1580) Oxford's Men, who played at the Blackfriar's Theatre and elsewhere, had no connection with the Chamberlain's Men, Shakespeare's company. Bacon's connection with Shakespeare is stronger, via the so-called Northumberland Manuscript in which the names of Bacon, Shakespeare and Neville all appear; and was, as has been repeatedly noted, Neville's kinsman by marriage. However, Bacon wrote no surviving poetry or drama, and the ponderous style of his famous essays and legal writing is radically different from anything Shakespeare ever wrote.

Hamlet

In the Tower, and with abundant leisure time, Neville continued to write plays, disturbed as he must have been. He certainly wrote three plays and possibly as many as five while in custody, showing from the first the transformation which had altered the nature and direction of his art. From the depths of his despair, humiliation, regret and vexation, Neville now produced his greatest work, the most famous work in English and perhaps in any language, namely *Hamlet*. It seems as certain as it is possible to be about this subject, in view of our present knowledge, that Neville wrote *Hamlet* in the winter of 1601–02 while incarcerated in the Tower, and that it concerns the Essex rebellion and Neville's response to it. *Hamlet* is about Essex and his rebellion and Neville's response to the terrible events which had befallen him because of it. Almost certainly – given the dualities and multiplicities of identity which are so characteristic a part of its author's writing style – *Hamlet* was meant to be a blending of Essex and Neville himself; Gertrude is probably Queen Elizabeth, in the dichotomy between her legitimate rule, but also her increasingly and frustratingly unwise conduct of government; her new husband, Claudius, is no doubt Essex's 'wicked' stepfather, the Earl of Leicester who (claims the writer of *Leicester's Commonwealth*) had murdered Essex's father and married his mother. Polonius is certainly Burghley, with a component of Sir Henry Killigrew; Laertes is Robert Cecil; and Fortinbras, King of Norway, of whom Hamlet (Act V, Sc. II, ll. 360–1) says 'I do prophesy th'election lights/On Fortinbras – he has my dying voice', is plainly King James I (James VI of Scotland).

Given that we now know when, why, and by whom *Hamlet* was written, this much is clear. As noted, too, the performance of *The Mousetrap* is plainly a recollection of the performance of *Richard II* just before the rebel-lion. The identities of some of the characters in *Hamlet* do remain quite ambiguous, however: was Ophelia meant to be Lady Neville? Possibly, though the rest of the freebooting Killigrew family in Cornwall and in London seems to have produced nothing but strong women, the sole exception being Anne's sensitive and empathetic sister, Dorothy. Abandoned by her first, reckless husband, and then left a young widow by his death, Neville took on the care of her two children. There still exists a lovely and self-deprecating letter from her to Sir Henry; she is concerned about her father, and equally concerned about Neville's gouty leg, so perhaps this gentle lady was the main model for Ophelia. Perhaps also Ophelia is a distant remembrance of Neville's youth – the vulnerable and mistreated Anne Cecil, old Burghley's favourite daughter, who had the great misfortune to fall in love with and marry the cruel and tempestuous Earl of Oxford. Horatio, Hamlet's close friend, may well be Southampton, while Rosenkrantz and Guildenstern are probably Charles Paget and his fellow-spy, Thomas Morgan. As mentioned earlier, Neville knew Paget and used his spying abilities in France but, for the earlier part of his career, Paget had always worked in conjunction with Morgan.

Of course, the names of Rosenkrantz and Guildenstern have their origin in Tycho Brahe's ancestors. Tycho Brahe sent an engraving of himself to Henry Savile's brother Thomas, the presentation of which was accompanied by a request, begging Thomas Savile to be so kind as to print copies of it and distribute them among 'the friends' in England. Neville was assuredly in this category, and so would have received a print of this engraving, which included the names and arms of Rosenkrantz and Guildenstern on its border. No one, however, has attempted to explain how such a picture and such knowledge could ever have reached William Shakespeare in Stratford or, indeed, any of the other authorship candidates.

Obviously Neville, who was, after all, probably a prisoner in the Tower convicted of treason when the play was written, and who still faced the possibility of execution, could not and would not draw *exact* parallels in writing the play, and in particular had to disguise the identity of the monarch and the reasons for Hamlet's hostility to him, but the entire nature and meaning of the play now seem quite apparent. Hamlet's celebrated delay presumably mirrors the difficulties experienced by Neville in commit-ting himself to rebellion, and it is notable that Neville does not directly address the question of treason and the legal and ethical difficulties this arouses in any traitor. Doubtless there is an element here of whitewashing himself through ambiguity of plot. The famous soliloquies are clearly Neville's existentialistic response to the plight in which he found himself: he must certainly have contemplated suicide. The largest and most impressive portrait of Neville now in existence has him, like Hamlet, dressed in black, and this was painted just before he left for France. His sad and empathetic eyes haunt everyone who sees it. It seems, then, melancholy had taken its place in his soul just before the tragedy of Essex. These new depths of expression continued as an important component in his subsequent plays.

Hamlet was entered in the Stationers' Register on 26 July 1602 as 'lately acted' by the Lord Chamberlain's Company. There is no reason to doubt the chronological accuracy of this entry, which strongly suggests that the play was written during the winter of 1601–02. A German play called *Der Bestrafte Brudermord*, often believed to be a form of the 'Ur-Hamlet' version of the play which had been performed as early as the late 1580s, and known to have been staged in Dresden in 1626, differs from Shakespeare's version in many respects. The opening scene, set on the parapet of a castle probably not dissimilar to the Tower of London, is, of course, in Shakespeare's version 'bitter cold', but in the possibly earlier version is 'not so cold' as it was.[28] It is difficult to believe that the chilled temperature did not represent the meteorological and physical environment in which Neville found himself when he began the play. There was thus, apparently, a gap of over a year between *Twelfth Night* and *Hamlet,* exactly what one might have expected of Neville as the author, given his trial and imprisonment, which would obviously have precluded writing plays until a modicum of his balance and sanity returned.

A number of other questions about the dating of Shakespeare's *Hamlet* has been widely debated. Irrefutably, there was a so-called 'Ur-Hamlet' which was seen on the London stage as early as 1589 and certainly the mid-1590s. At least two witnesses have quoted the Ghost's 'Hamlet, revenge' as one of its memorable lines, although no such line exists in Shakespeare's *Hamlet*.[29] The relationship of this 'Ur-Hamlet' to Neville's play is obscure: he is unlikely to have been the author (it is often attributed to Thomas Kyd) but he certainly knew about it and used it as the basis of his *Hamlet* once he grasped its relevance to his situation. 'So all my best is dressing old words new', as he says in Sonnet 76. Using an old but apparently well-known play as a shell and disguise to express his opinion of the treasonable and politically dangerous Essex rebellion was a clever move by Neville, exactly what one might expect of him under the circumstances.

A number of commentators on *Hamlet*, such as Harold Jenkins, have dated it somewhat earlier than 1601–02, in Jenkins' case to 1599–1600.[30] This verdict is based chiefly on an undated note written in a copy of Chaucer by Gabriel Harvey which apparently dates the play to before Essex's execution, since it seems to refer to him in the present tense. Jenkins argues, on what seems very little evidence, that *Hamlet* 'reached the stage in or shortly before 1600' and then 'had the topicalities about players [i.e. child actors] grafted on to it the next year'.[31] Given the play's manifest relationship with the Essex rebellion, this seems far-fetched, and it is indisputable that the play was registered in July 1602 as 'lately acted', not two or even three years earlier. There thus seems no reason to doubt that it was completed in the first half of 1602. However, it must also be remembered that the banned *Leycester's Commonwealth,* featuring Leicester's poisoning and murderous stepfather, had been around since 1584. Even though it was banned in England, several manuscript copies have been found in various aristocratic libraries. There was obviously a network through which those with sufficient persistence and interest could view its shocking contents, and Belleforest's French version of *Hamlet* itself had been obtainable since 1576. Obviously, it was open to any educated dramatist to see concurrences between the two stories, though of course it is difficult to see how Shakespeare of Stratford, who had never learnt French and did not move in the circles where *Leycester's Commonwealth* would be available to him, could have had any access to these texts.

A further point which is often made by orthodox biographers in furtherance of the view that *Hamlet* was written by William Shakespeare of Stratford is that Shakespeare's only son was named 'Hamnet Shakespeare'. This might seem like telling evidence until it is realized that the boy was certainly named for Hamnett (or Hamlet) Sadler (d. 1624), a baker in High Street, Stratford, who was, apparently, the boy's godfather and who was left 26 shillings 8 pence in Shakespeare's will.[32] The son was born in 1585, three or four years before Shakespeare wrote anything. As noted, a so-called 'Ur-Hamlet', which was almost certainly not written by Shakespeare (whoever he was), was already on the London stage at the time. The similarity of 'Hamnet' and *Hamlet* is an odd coincidence, and nothing more.

Other 'Tower' plays

Neville also almost certainly wrote at least two other plays while imprisoned in the Tower: *Troilus and Cressida* and *All's Well That Ends Well*. It is possible that he wrote *Othello* at this time as well, and, conceivably, *The Merry Wives of Windsor,* although this last possibility is far less likely than the others. *Troilus* was registered on 7 February 1603, just before the Queen's death but when her end appeared to be imminent, although the play's text was not published until the Quarto version of 1609. Most authorities believe that it was written in 1602, for the entry in the Stationers' Register says that it was registered 'as yt is acted by my lo: Chamberlens Men'.[33] There seems no reason to question their verdict. In the Tower Neville would surely not wish to write on English history, and was probably in no mood for comedy. A classical drama, based on well-known classical texts, was likely to have been exactly what he would have written next; he may have seen the rivalry between England and France in the fight between the Trojans and Greeks. *Troilus* is hallmarked by 'scepticism about all forms of chivalric idealism . . . a satirical, anti-heroic burlesque', and is dominated by a peculiar sense of the passage of time and performed in what would now be termed 'real time'. [34]

These characteristics were doubtless products of Neville's detainment in the Tower. The famous disquisition (Act I, Sc. III, ll.75–137) by Ulysses about the importance of 'degree, priority, and place . . . Take but degree away, untune that string, and hark what discord follows' might well be Neville trying to prove (presumably to Cecil and the Queen), ingenuously or not, that he was no revolutionary, or that he repented of his role in the rebellion. On the other hand, it might also have been a plea to the Queen for an orderly transition to a Protestant heir without suspense or chaos. The depiction of Achilles in *Troilus* is sometimes interpreted as a commentary on Essex. It is possible that *Hamlet* was seen at the time as a thinly veiled portrayal of the Essex rebellion, and Neville might well have thought it wise to disguise his commentary on the current affairs of his day by masking it with classical forms and sentiments which the authorities could hardly criticize. Since the play was printed in 1609 with a Prologue or Epistle stating that it had never been performed in public, many have suggested that it was first put on for a private showing, at, for instance, one of the Inns of Court. This, too, makes sense: Neville would be happy for the legitimacy which he might have seen such a performance as giving to him, a traitor and a prisoner, while being happy that any dangerous political sentiments were being voiced at a private performance rather than in a public theatre.

The anonymous Prologue or Epistle to the 1609 printing of *Troilus*, which claims that the play was 'never stal'd with the Stage, never clapper-clawd with the palmes of the vulger' also states that the play was printed because of its 'grand possessors will', without identifying who the 'grand possessors' (or 'possessor') might have been, or why an ordinary Shakespeare play, seemingly no different from any other, might be in the hands of a 'grand possessor'. Orthodox biographers and critics have little or nothing to say about this curious expression.[35] It would clearly indicate that the 'grand possessor(s)' was (or were) still alive, and a member of the English elite, both of which were certainly true of Neville in 1609, when he was a knight and one of the acknowledged leaders of Parliament. In contrast to orthodox biographers, anti-Stratfordians have seized upon it as evidence that Shakespeare, who, by no stretch of the imagination could be described as a 'grand possessor', could not be its author, and the writer of the Epistle was well aware of this fact. In particular, advocates of Edward De Vere as the actual author have repeatedly claimed that the heading of this 'Epistle' is a reference to their candidate. The heading reads: 'A never writer, to an ever reader. Newes.' Oxfordians claim that this is a pun on 'De Vere'. While this interpretation is superficially attractive, the Epistle makes it clear that the 'grand possessor(s)' was still alive, while De Vere had died five years earlier in 1604. (Oxford's only son, the eighteenth Earl, was born in 1593, and was thus only 15 or 16 in 1609.) The heading might be a pun, but it is more likely simply to be a facetious reference to the author of the Epistle as someone who has published nothing, addressed to readers who are likely to read virtually everything. And the 'Never' writer is much more likely to be Neville, on two counts. First, Neville's name could be spelt Nevel, and often was. Secondly, Neville had never published anything under his own name. The 'ever reader' may well refer to Puritans in general, since they could *read* this play because it had never been performed – 'clapper-clawd with palmes of the vulger' being a typically Puritan description of what occurred in the theatre. The style of the Epistle therefore echoes the kind of satire popular at the Inns of Court, and it is for this reason that F.E. Halliday and other scholars think it almost certain to have been written by Richard Martin, sometime Prince d'Amour of the Middle Temple.[36] Is it mere coincidence, one wonders, that Richard Martin became a member of the Mitre Club along with Neville, and that a hand-written treatise by Richard Martin is to be found alongside Neville's notebooks in the Lincolnshire Record Office? Mere coincidence too that Martin was a shareholder in the Virginia Company, and ultimately a settler there?

The first edition of *Troilus and Cressida*, published early in 1609, states that the work was 'imprinted by G. Eld for R. Bonian and H. Walley'. George Eld (or Elde) (d. 1624) was an established printer in Fleet Street who also printed the Sonnets in the same year. It is thus possible that Eld was the author of the Epistle, although the second 1609 edition of *Troilus* – later in 1609 – containing the Epistle does not name its printer.

While it is thus likely that the heading of the Epistle is a weak, facetious salutation rather than a pun intended to convey secret authorship, it is still evidently possible that it is a pun which has been misunderstood until now. If the heading is intended to read 'A neville writer . . .' – which seems just as likely as a pun on Oxford's name – then the Epistle might well have been written by Neville himself, in what would constitute presumably the only edition of a Shakespeare play brought out by the author in his lifetime. As will be seen when the Sonnets are discussed in a later part of this work, the celebrated Dedication of the Sonnets ('To the onlie begetter . . .') was almost certainly written by Neville himself. It is thus not unreasonable to suppose that he might also have written the Epistle at the front of *Troilus*. Against this, however, it must be said that the Epistle does not read as if it was written by Shakespeare, while its fulsome praise of the author of *Troilus*, 'showing such a dexterity and power of wit' does not seem likely to have emanated from Neville's own pen, unless he was having some fun.[37] All in all, then, the best suggestion is probably still that it was Richard Martin's work, not written while he was Prince d'Amour in 1598 (as Leslie Hotson theorized, necessitating an awkward re-dating of the play) but in the early seventeenth century, after he got to know Neville through the Mitre Club and the Virginia Company.

The dating *of All's Well that Ends Well*, also attributed to the 1601–03 period, is quite problematical, as there is no mention of the play before the First Folio. Since the eighteenth century, some have argued that the play is a retitled version of *Love Labors Wonne*, a Shakespearean play mentioned in Meres' famous enumeration of 1598.[38] Most recent commentators, however, have dated the play to around the same time as *Hamlet*, reflecting the late-nineteenth-century view that much of the play was written in the 'supple sinewy, dramatic verse of the *Hamlet* period'. It is also generally believed that the part of the Clown was designed for Robert Armin, who replaced Kempe as the Chamberlain's Company's chief clown in 1599. Many commentators have also drawn attention to the links between *All's Well* and *Measure for Measure,* probably the first play Neville wrote following his release from custody in 1603. '*Measure for Measure* and *All's Well* are obvious twins', Hunter has stated.[39] The title *All's Well that Ends Well* might quite conceivably have been added once Neville knew, or became fairly confident, that he was soon to be freed. One might also speculate that Neville, fully occupied after his release, put the play aside so that nothing was seen of it until publication of the First Folio, and more accurately recorded his emotions after gaining his freedom in *Measure for Measure*.

Two other plays might also have been written while Neville was in the Tower. *Othello*, the second of Neville's great tragedies, has been dated by some commentators, including Alfred Hart and E.A.J. Honigman, to 1601–02, although it is more commonly believed to have been written in 1604. Its black mood of betrayal means that it might well have been written by Neville in the Tower, just after *Hamlet* (or, indeed, before) – there is nothing anomalous in this. *Othello* may also contain yet another aspect of the Essex theme. The character of Iago seems very similar to that of the treacherous husband of Lady Essex's maidservant, whose name was John Daniel. The Countess of Essex (Frances Walsingham and the widow of Sir Philip Sidney) entrusted some of the Earl's letters to him. This Daniel then employed a master of miniature writing, one Peter Bales, to copy these letters, but Bales' suspicions were aroused and Daniel was ultimately tried in the Star Chamber, pilloried and given a life sentence. Daniel may well also have been the 'suborn'd informer' (blackmailer) of Sonnet 125, as the Countess had to sell her jewels to redeem these letters. (One wonders if they contained any information that might have provided a paper trail between Neville and Essex, since Daniel was set free by King James just after Neville himself, which would make complete sense of Sonnet 125 talking of the canopy in the same stanza as the blackmailer.) Neville knew Walsingham, and the Nevilles were always great friends of the Sidneys. Here was yet another link, then, between Sir Henry Neville and the Earl of Essex.

Furthermore, *The Merry Wives of Windsor* is sometimes also dated from 1601–02; it was certainly first entered in the Stationers' Register on 18 January 1602.[40] Conceivably, Neville wished to escape his misery with ribald, subversive, slapstick comedy, although facing the prospect of being hanged, drawn and quartered at worst, indefinitely imprisoned in the Tower at best, is not an obvious frame of mind in which to produce slapstick comedy, or even a play possibly tinged with nostalgia for Billingbear, as *The Merry Wives* might be. It is also just possible that Neville wrote *The Merry Wives* at this time to move the Queen to compassion for his case: this hypothesis, of course, assumes that Elizabeth knew that he was the author, an assumption for which there is no evidence, while, if she was aware of Neville's authorship, she must also have known that he wrote *Richard II*, performed for the rebellion. All in all, although a post-1601 date for *The Merry Wives* is possible, it seems much more plausible that it was written in Neville's happier, more expansive period around 1597.

The Sonnets

Perhaps even more importantly, Neville certainly also wrote some of his Sonnets while imprisoned. The celebrated Sonnet 29, 'when in disgrace with Fortune and men's eyes ...', was manifestly and assuredly written while he was in the Tower, and evidently addressed to Southampton, his much-admired prison companion. Sonnet 30, 'When to sessions of sweet silent thought ...', which follows it, was also likely to have been written at around the same time, for the same reason. Why these were published in 1609 among earlier Sonnets in the collection, rather than towards the end – assuming that many were written in the 1590s, as seems likely – is unclear; Neville, if he arranged the Sonnet order, might simply have been disguising the circumstances in which they were composed. (It is possible that the Sonnets were published in – very roughly – reverse chronological order, a possibility which will be considered when the Sonnets are discussed in more detail. However, we must remember that Neville was keen on numbers, and there are many symbolic numberings in the sonnet sequence, so this too may be a clue to their ordering.)

Many of the Sonnets were probably written between 1601 and 1603 while Neville was imprisoned, and were chiefly written with Southampton in mind. It is possible that, while confined to prison, Neville had some kind of homosexual relationship with Southampton, although Neville, with 11 children, was obviously heterosexual under normal circumstances. A more plausible view, however, is that they simply reflect the extravagant respect and admiration Neville had always felt for Southampton, and was common in flowery verse of the time. Neville, in his letters, never had any problem in using the word 'love' or telling a man that he loved him. It is therefore quite probable that 'love' was used in relation to people (of either sex) while 'like' was more usually used for abstract nouns or concepts. Quite possibly, Southampton had boosted Neville's depressed and conceivably suicidal spirits, and he simply wished to acknowledge this.

Several of the Sonnets which Neville unquestionably wrote in the Tower in 1601–03 speak of the catastrophe which had befallen him. Apart from Sonnets 29 and 30, the author's 'disgrace' is prominently mentioned in at least five sonnets, as well as his 'brand', the 'vulgar scandal stamped upon my brow' (112), 'public honour and proud titles boast, / Whilst I whom fortune of such triumph bars' (25), and so on. Orthodox Stratfordians, needless to say, cannot explain these heart-felt confessions, which do not appear to relate to anything in Shakespeare's known life. In many of the Sonnets, too, the poet specifically forgives the addressee for some serious offence he has caused to the poet, such as 'Nor can thy shame give physic to my grief; / Though thou repent, yet I have still the loss' (34) and 'No more be grieved at that which thou hast done: / Roses have thorns and silver fountains mud' (35). It was Southampton whose testimony at Neville's trial provided confirmation for Essex's original, highly unexpected claim that Neville, the respected Ambassador to France, was involved in treasonable conspiracy, as a result of which he was imprisoned in the Tower for life, ironically along with Southampton himself. Once again, there is no known situation in Shakespeare's life which corresponds to this (nor, for that matter, in the careers of any other authorship candidate). Some commentators have supposed this might refer to Shakespeare's supposed relations with Southampton, to whom his two long poems were dedicated – Shakespeare noted in his second poem, *The Rape of Lucrece* (1594) that 'the warrant I have of your Honourable disposition ... makes it assured of acceptance' – followed by no further mention of Southampton in Shakespeare's works. This is sometimes taken to mean that Shakespeare originally secured the support of Southampton, but was then cast off, and it is this to which he refers in the Sonnets. As has been said before, however, there is no evidence that Southampton had ever given him any 'warrant' of his 'disposition', or, indeed, had ever set eyes upon him; and nothing in any document of Southampton's refers directly or indirectly to Shakespeare, or suggests that he ever acted as Shakespeare's patron. Furthermore, if the Sonnets were dedicated to Southampton in 1609, as seems very likely, Shakespeare, if he were the author, must once more have found favour with the then-powerful Southampton, and, again, no evidence exists that he did.

The Tower Notebook

Towards the end of his stay in the Tower, Neville kept a miscellaneous commonplace book, known as the Tower Notebook (1602). After Neville's death it was inherited by his daughter-in-law, Lady Worsley, and remained in the Worsley family until about 1954, when it was given to the Lincolnshire Record Office (where the later family owned land). The Notebook may be an extremely important literary document. In it, Neville wrote the stage directions for a pageant coronation, which were subsequently used in 1613 in Shakespeare's *Henry VIII*, a play of which there is no evidence until then. In the Notebook, Neville also hints at his hopes to 'bear the canopy' at the coronation, hopes which might have been dashed, for he either regrets or records the event ('Were 't ought to me I bore the canopy ...') in Sonnet 125. Neville plainly expected great things of James I after the passing of the old Queen – probably high office, certainly clear evidence of honour and esteem. He was indeed freed and restored to his titles and property in 1603 (along with Southampton), but in all other respects he was to be sorely disappointed.[41]

Chapter 8

Freedom and Disappointment, 1603–08

It has been widely noted, with surprise, that William Shakespeare was one of the few well-known poets of his time who failed to produce a tearful elegy and tribute to her memory when Queen Elizabeth finally died in March 1603. From him there was only a virtually audible silence, a silence so striking that it was commented upon by Henry Chettle:

> *Nor doth the silver tongued Melicert*
> *Drop from his honeyed muse one*
> *sable tear*
> *To mourn her death that graced*
> *his desert.*
> *And to his lays opened her Royal ear.*
> *Shepherd, remember our Elizabeth,*
> *And sing her Rape, done by that*
> *Tarquin, Death.*[1]

By repute at least, Shakespeare was one of Queen Elizabeth's favourite play-wrights, making his silence all the stranger.[2] Moreover, if Shakespeare of Stratford was indeed the author of *Richard II*, performed just before the Essex rebellion, he must surely have been keen to prove, by literary tribute, that he had only admiration for the deceased monarch.

Since Queen Elizabeth was responsible for Sir Henry Neville's incarceration in the Tower, one may be sure that his only response to her death was that it was far too long delayed. The Queen's death, and the accession to the English throne of James I, must have been greeted by Neville with joy and elation. Neville certainly expressed his real feelings in the much-debated Sonnet 107, which manifestly refers to Queen Elizabeth's death and the period immediately following it, and which was, therefore, almost certainly written in 1603 or 1604:

> ... *Supposed as forfeit to a confined doom.*
> *The mortal moon hath her eclipse endured,*
> *And the sad augurs mock their own presage,*
> *Incertainties now crown themselves assured,*
> *And peace proclaims olives of endless age* ...

Here Neville certainly appears to be saying 'Thank God she's dead'. The remark about 'supposed as forfeit to a confined doom' is obviously autobiographical, just as the rest of the poem almost certainly relates to his continuing relations with Southampton.[3]

James I's succession

With James on the throne, Neville clearly expected that his release from the Tower in March 1603, and restoration to his former places and wealth – along with Southampton, released and restored to favour at the same time – would be the harbinger of further preferment, possibly to the very highest offices of government. A widespread expectation existed that this was, indeed, likely: the Venetian Ambassador reported to his government that the new King had 'destined great rewards to the Earl of Southampton and Sir Henry Neville'.[4] Unfortunately, such was not the case. Neville did indeed play a considerable political role during the next decade or so, but was never given any official position. For whatever reason, the new King appeared seriously to mistrust him, perhaps fearing that a conspirator against one monarch could readily turn against another. King James had almost lost his life in the Gowrie conspiracy of August 1600 (a complex affair, the alleged plot of which might have been invented by James himself); he was unlikely to look kindly upon proven plotters such as Neville. In addition, Neville had acquired a reputation in some circles, possibly exaggerated, as a pro-Puritan and a rather fanatical Protestant.[5] Although James was generally in favour of this stance, he was also anxious not to appear too aggressively pro-Protestant, and might have had the same doubts about the wisdom of Neville's perceived leanings as Cecil apparently had.[6] Probably the most striking example of James' mistrust of Neville (and his associates) came in late June 1604. Rumours came to the King's attention that a plot had been hatched aimed at some of the monarch's Scottish friends and perhaps at James himself. James ordered guards to surround his quarters and his heir, Prince Henry, to remain at home. He then ordered the arrest and interrogation of Neville, Southampton, Sir Maurice Berkeley, Sir William Lee and Henry, Lord Danvers (later Earl of Danby).[7] Both the precise charges against them and the identity of their accusers remains unknown, although the general view is that the arrests were brought about by English Catholics who feared a strongly pro-Protestant faction.[8] The five men were released, rather shaken, after an overnight stay in prison, but Neville must have known that the King could easily be persuaded to mistrust him and that there were few prospects for an early promotion.

Upon his release from the Tower, Neville appears to have gone at once to Billingbear – which he had hardly visited for four years – and remained chiefly at his house for some time. According to Duncan, Neville realized that high appointment was not imminent, and 'retired to the countryside, where, by the winter of 1603–04, he had begun to sulk'.[9] His absence from Court life was widely noted by his friends in public life such as Sir Ralph Winwood, who had succeeded him as Ambassador to France.[10] He seems to have moved round from one country house to another. But by February 1604, Neville had obviously been forced to abandon Billingbear for a while. He wrote to his friend Ralph Winwood:

> *Soon after I had written unto you from my own House at Shellingford, I removed to my other House, and within a few Days after one of my Servants fell sick of the Plague and died, and two other were sick of it, but recovered.*
>
> *By this evill Accident I was driven to forsake my House, and to disperse my Family, and my self made unfit for any Company, and especially for the Court, and this was the Cause why I received not your second Letter till it was almost Christmas, and which made me also so backward to answer it, which I pray you excuse.*

> *Now having received a third Letter from you by your Servant Moor, I cannot but let you know how thankfully I take your kind Remembrance of me and how willing I would be to make it appear more than in Words, if in your absence you would make any use of me. I know you have many Friends of whose Affection you may be assured, but none more desirous to approve his Love than I am, therefore if you will have me think you esteem it, I pray you use it, and use it freely.*[11]

And now Henry makes it quite plain that he has been content to stay in the country and write, even during and after the terrible danger of infection that surrounded him:

> *But I am out of my proper Orb when I enter into State Matters; I will there-fore leave these Considerations to those to whom they appertain, and think of my husbandry in the Country, which puts me often in mind of that Beatitude which Horace so much commends. Yet I do not so wean my self from these Thoughts, but I will be always glad of your Letters, and to understand by them how the World goeth with you there; for I concur with you, that he must be very senseless, that doth not discerne how necessary your Conversation there [in France] is for our Estate.*
>
> *I will hold you no longer at this time, but conclude, wishing you all Happiness and Contentment in your Imployment, and my self often with you*
> *. . .*

The 'Beatitude which Horace so much commends' is staying in the country and writing. Nothing could be clearer: Neville's life and art ran an uncannily similar course to that of Horace, which Neville must have recognized, and as the following extract from the 1974 edition of the *Encyclopaedia Brittanica* demonstrates:

> *Horace's fame rests chiefly upon the likable person revealed in his works. Autobiographical touches proliferate in his poetry: he seems to tell far more about himself, his character, his development, and his way of life than any other great poet of antiquity, and this, combined with the fact that he lived in one of the best documented periods of Roman history, creates the illusion that a good deal is known about him. Yet his autobiographical 'disclosures' are not realistic but literary, a feature of his technique for creating an intimate atmosphere. What he tells about himself is part of the work of art he is creating; even his beliefs are impossible to pin down with any certainty, since apparent declara-*

tions of them are often no more than devices to create a mood or theme. Horace claimed that criticism in his poetry was for the good of society. As time went on he became convinced that the good poet must first be a good man and useful to the community as educator and civilizer.

It is startling that everything written above applies so exactly to Neville. It is as if Henry consciously set out to emulate all these aspects of the outlook and works of Horace. As such, he would have seen his role in life mainly as being an 'educator and civilizer', and considered his plays to be a means to those ends. Through the medium of pleasurable entertainment, the dramas carried their many messages, prime among which being that humans, as thinking animals, have a god-given responsibility to weigh their thoughts and actions with great care. If this can be said to be a very Puritan ideal, then it is expressed in anything but a Puritanical manner, conceivably with the aim of making its message all the more transmittable to the as-yet unthinking masses.

Measure for Measure

Thus, now estranged once again from Billingbear, with his head full of infection, feeling that he was insecure, under-used, and, in all likelihood, temporarily separated from his family, whom he feared might otherwise catch the infection, Neville probably wrote the first of his post-Tower plays, *Measure for Measure*. No wonder it was such a dark comedy. The play was performed (at Court) on 26 December 1604, although its premier is widely believed to have taken place earlier in the same year.[12] Most commentators believe that the exchange between Mistress Overdone and Pompey (Act I, Sc. II) refers to the proclamation by the King on 16 September 1604 calling for the demolition of houses in suburban London.[13]

The connections between Neville and this play abound in a way which has never been seen before in any other authorship contender. The 'inside experience' of prison is obvious. Isabella's pleadings with Angelo for her brother's release mirror the letters written by Anne, Neville's wife, to the Queen and Sir Robert Cecil during Neville's incarceration.[14] In addition to all this, Neville had stayed in Vienna in 1581 during his European tour. Dudith (the Hungarian humanist philosopher who met Neville in Breslau) had given young Henry and his group introductions to some of the very highest officials in that town, while Savile already knew Hugo Blotius. He was one of the city's residents who seemed to share Savile's humanist yet somewhat Calvinist way of thinking. It has been difficult for scholars to tie up *Measure for Measure* with anything approaching Shakespeare's experience. The most they can do is say that the Duke is some sort of glorification of James I's wisdom as a ruler. However, with the identification of the author as Sir Henry Neville, much more can be deduced. The play is set in Vienna, and the ban on extra-marital relations, which forms the backbone to the drama, was part of Blotius's Calvinistic beliefs. Dudith and Savile indeed together introduced the young protégés to a wide Viennese intellectual circle, which makes it highly likely that a writer who was able to include special knowledge of the city and its intellectuals in his work came from Savile's exclusive little group. Blotius considered himself a reformer and peacemaker, and had set up the first public library in Austria. Yet, being a Calvinist, he was doubtless over-strict in some matters. Who but someone with first-hand knowledge of these facts could have invented the complex character of the Duke in that play? And who was better placed than a member of Savile's circle to be able to set such a play in that particular city?

Neville obviously had an enormous amount to do after his release from the Tower, especially in securing the return of his confiscated property and in restoring his position as a political leader. In the general election which took place at the beginning of 1604 (the Parliament elected at the time met for the first time on 19 March of that year) Neville was elected both for Lewes in Sussex and for the more important county seat of Berkshire. He took his seat as a Knight of the Shire for Berkshire.[15] This must have happened after he had begun his play, a situation which would also explain the extensive discussions in it comparing political action with personal morality. He was also seriously considered for the post of Speaker of the House.[16] In the country at large – as opposed to the Court – Essex was viewed as a martyr and his supporters as popular heroes.[17] To add to this, Neville had, as well, all the normal affairs of a still substantial landowner to attend to, burdens which had piled up since 1599, and no doubt wished to spend time with his large family.

Even allowing for his phenomenal rate of output, it is not surprising that probably over a year elapsed before he wrote another play; the interval is probably just what one might expect. Neville also had to re-establish his working links with Shakespeare and his troupe. Indeed, it was not a foregone conclusion that he would write anything again. On 19 May 1603, the Lord Chamberlain's Men secured the patronage of the King, and were thenceforth known as the King's Men, performing often at court over the next few years.[18] The King took a keen interest in drama, and shortly thereafter demanded eight performances from the company.[19] There is little reason to suppose that James I knew anything about the true authorship of the plays of 'Shakespeare' – or cared for that matter – but doubtless Neville had, as under Elizabeth, to take the King's interest in drama into account when writing, and to weigh his words and their implications with great care.[20] While presumably *Macbeth* was written with the King's homeland firmly in mind, it is worth noting that there were no more English history plays after *Henry V* until *Henry VIII* appeared in 1613. Neville obviously thought it politic not to complete whatever he had written in the Tower of this play until much later.

As has been already noted, *Measure for Measure* contains clear and obvious references to Neville's life just before 1604. Bearing in mind that Neville had been Ambassador to France, came within an inch of being beheaded, was fined £5,000 and probably paid £3,000 in all during the period he was imprisoned, suffered from gout and lameness, and had just been in contact with the Plague, consider these lines near the opening of the play (Act I, Sc. II, ll.35–6):

LUCIO. *Behold, behold where Madam Mitigation comes! I have purchased as many diseases under her roof as come to –*
SECOND GENTLEMAN. *To what, I pray?*
LUCIO. *Judge.*
SECOND GENTLEMAN. *To three thousand dolours a year.*
FIRST GENTLEMAN. *Ay, and more.*
LUCIO. *A French crown more.*
FIRST GENTLEMAN. *Thou art always figuring diseases in me, but thou art full of error – I am sound.*
LUCIO. *Nay, not as one would say, healthy, but so sound as things that are hollow – thy bones are hollow – impiety has made a feast of thee.*
FIRST GENTLEMAN. *How now, which of your hips has the most profound sciatica?*
MISTRESS OVERDONE. *Well, well: there's one yonder arrested and carried to prison was worth five thousand of you all.*

> SECOND GENTLEMAN. *Who's that, I pray thee?*
> MISTRESS OVERDONE. *Marry, sir, that's Claudio, Signior Claudio.*
> FIRST GENTLEMAN. *Claudio to Prison? 'Tis not so.*
> MISTRESS OVERDONE. *Nay, but I know 'tis so. I saw him arrested, saw him carried away; and, which is more, within these three days his head to be chopped off!*

Measure for Measure is often seen as the first of the so-called 'problem plays': dark and ambiguous comedies. Its theme of punishment for sexual misbehaviour, besides echoing his meetings with Blotius in Vienna, also seems clearly to have been chosen by Neville as a means of indirectly airing the moral issues raised by his own predicament – political misbehaviour – while disguising his real subject. At the same time, questions were being raised in the English Parliament concerning the problem of 'bastard children' being thrust onto the care of the parish in which they were born. Neville's (as it were) topological approach to a theme – in mathematics, the study of bodies whose elements remain constant when their shapes are altered – is a familiar and often recurring device in the works of a man who was keeping his identity a secret and whose difficulties, increasingly political, had to be disguised, so that his real dilemma is discussed by reference to a seemingly unrelated theme. The title *Measure for Measure* alludes to Matthew, 7, 1–2: 'Judge not ... with what measure you mete, it shall be measured to you again': the theme of mercy tempering justice must have been a constant preoccupation for Neville at this time. The play's attack on extreme Puritanism should perhaps be read as an attack on the arbitrary punishment of high-minded political rebels.

It has long been an accepted view among Shakespearean critics that there is a major 'problem' with *Measure for Measure*: it appears to be 'strange ... a play of undeniable but somehow evasive peculiarities'.[21] The play *seems* to be a product of some major upheaval and crisis in Shakespeare's life, but there is, as ever, nothing in the known facts of the life of Shakespeare of Stratford which might account for such a crisis or upheaval at the time. Much ink has been spilled in attempting to identify the reasons for what has been termed the 'broken-hearted bard' of 1604, when *Measure for Measure* was written, but no attempt to account for the mood of the play has ever been successful.[22] In the twentieth century, such endeavours were generally abandoned – providing any link with the known facts of Shakespeare of

1. John of Gaunt, Duke of Lancaster: Neville's ancestor and the wise statesman in *Richard II*. Like Neville, John of Gaunt was a political visionary who was ignored because his open nature and outspoken ideas made absolutist monarchs uncomfortable. Private collection/The Bridgeman Art Library, London

2. Richard Neville, Earl of Warwick, the 'Kingmaker': Neville's ancestor and hero of the *Henry VI* plays. Bodleian Library, University of Oxford, MS. Top. Glouc. D. 2, fol. 36v

3. Billingbear Park (1738) by Jan Griffier. © English Heritage Photo Library

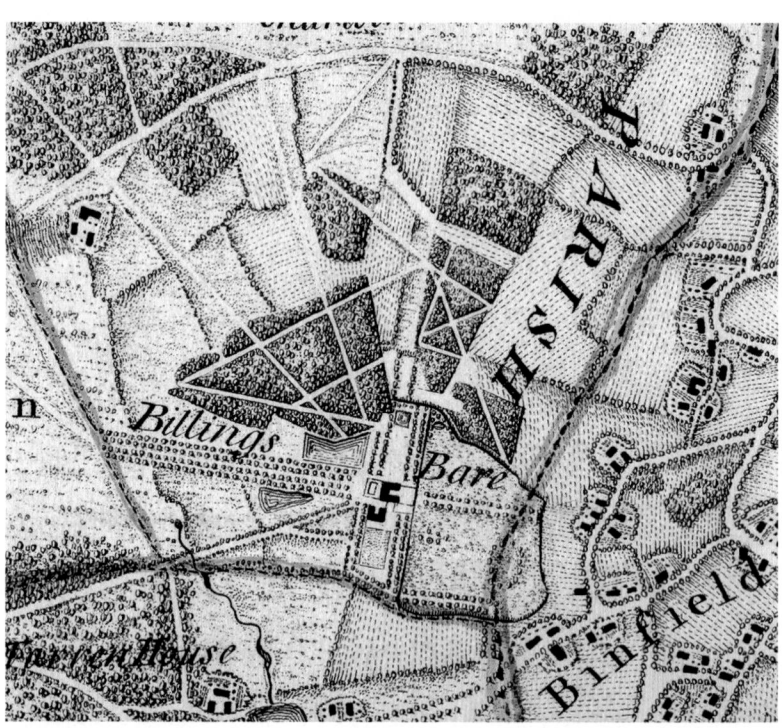

4. Billingbear Estate, from Rocque's map of Berkshire, 1761. Berkshire Record Office

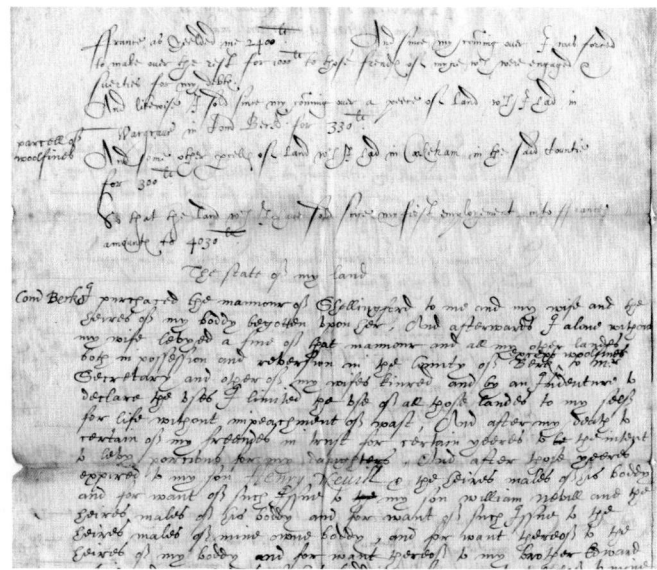

5. In this document, Sir Henry Neville is listing the income he obtains from his various properties, so that Queen Elizabeth might be able to collect these ongoing rents to pay his fine, which was imposed on him after his involvement in the Essex rebellion. Note how he changes from 'court' hand at the top of the page to 'secretary' hand lower down. Berkshire Record Office

6. Portrait of Sir Henry Neville by Marcus Gheerarts (often anglicized to Garret). © English Heritage, National Monuments Record

7. Portrait of Lady Anne Neville, née Killigrew, *c*.1606. Anne came from a long line of intelligent, educated women on her mother's side, and from rich, free-spirited Cornish buccaneers on her father's. © English Heritage, National Monuments Record

8. Audley End House: the eventual home of the Nevilles' descendents, the Lords Braybrooke. The entrance hall to the house contains pictures of Lords William and Philip Herbert, the 'Incomparable pair of Brethren' who were patrons of the First Folio of Shakespeare's works. Their portraits face Neville's diagonally, their prescribed positions having been maintained by the family following their removal from Billingbear House. John Bethell/The Bridgeman Art Library, London

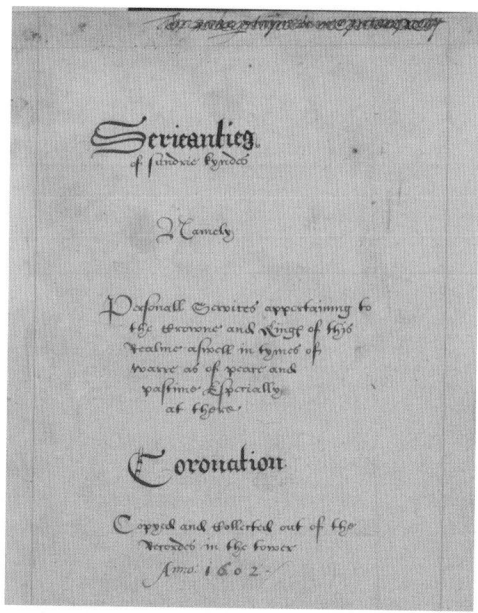

9. Title page of the Tower Notebook. Lincolnshire Archives

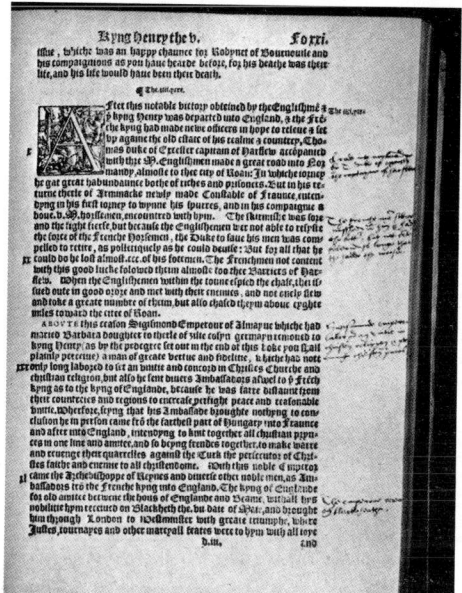

10. A page from the annotated copy of Halle's *Chronicles* bought by Alan Keen from an auction near the home of the Earl of Yarborough, owner of the Worsley papers. As will be seen from the following plate, the slope of the writing and many of its generic features resemble those found in the annotations of the Tower Notebook.

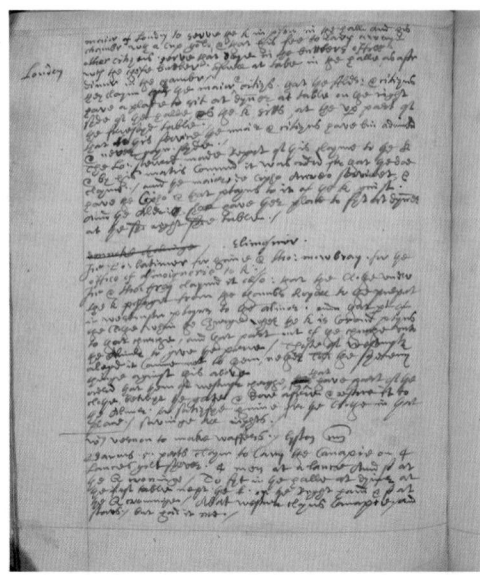

11. The 'Anne Boleyn Coronation' page from the Tower Notebook. The annotator's handwriting shares several features with that of the annotator of Halle's *Chronicles*. Lincolnshire Archives

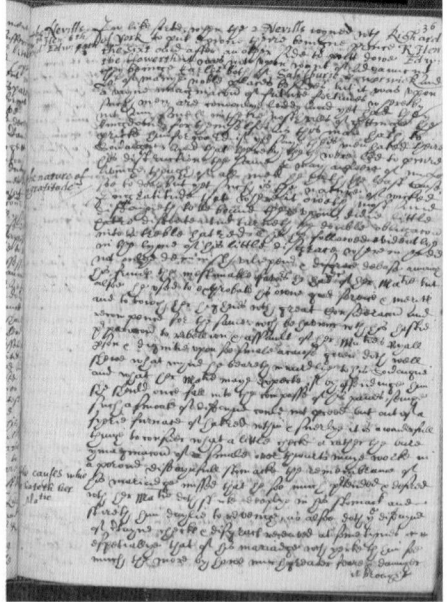

12. A page from *Leycester's Commonwealth* in the Worsley collection, now housed in the Lincolnshire Record Office. The name 'Neville' is emboldened and/or commented upon every time it appears in the text, as can be seen on the first line and marginal note at the top of this extract. Lincolnshire Archives

13. The original cover page of the Northumberland Manuscript.

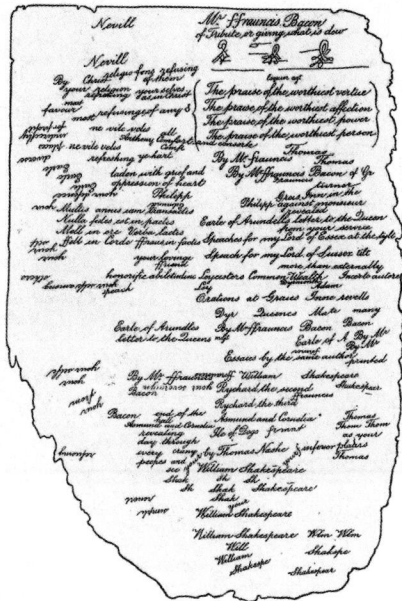

14. A nineteenth-century transcription of the Northumberland Manuscript.

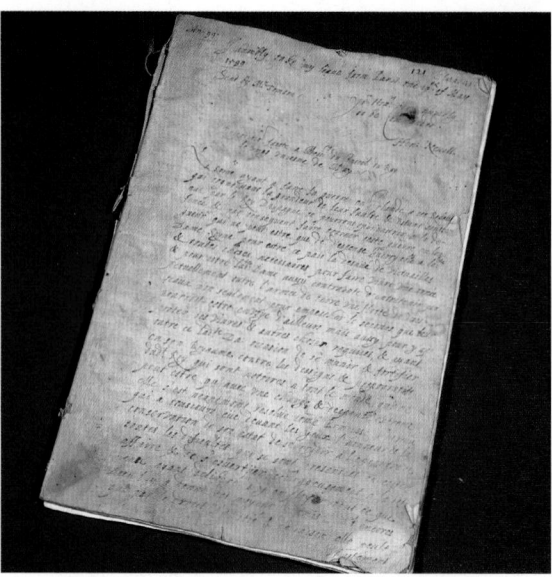

15. An example of Sir Henry Neville's italic hand, from his personal diplomatic notebook. The National Archives, Kew

16. A full-length portrait of Sir Henry Neville, thought to be by Marcus Gheerarts. A strange device of rings is depicted in the left-hand corner. The top ring seems to represent the sun, containing the face of a roaring lion, while the lower ring may represent the moon. The Greek inscription below is still undergoing analysis by Greek scholars, as the third word contains some non-standard lettering. The first two words are translated as 'everywhere without. . .' © English Heritage NMR, The Private Collection of Lord Braybrooke, Audley End House, Essex

Stratford's life simply defeated the critics. Once more, however, situating *Measure for Measure* in the life and career of Sir Henry Neville illuminates its meaning in terms of a response to his imprisonment and release, and the deep moral and personal issues raised by these events.

Re-entry into politics

In politics, although Neville was forced, over the next few years, to feel his way, he succeeded in making his mark. Back in Parliament, he served on numerous committees in the House of Commons, and gradually gained a reputation for supporting the 'popular' side (as it became known) on controversial matters.[23] This shift, to what might now be described as an ideologically based position, took place over several years, and was probably not fully in place until about 1607–08, when Neville emerged as a politician with distinctive principles. Perhaps he had hitherto shown only the occasional sign that could have led the casual observer to believe that one day he might take up this almost radical stance. During his earlier days in Parliament, for instance, he had sat on various committees which were generally concerned with reforms; for example, the Committee to stop 'irksome and outmodish' recruitment to fight (one is reminded of the farcical recruitment scene in *2 Henry IV*), the committee on monopolies, and those concerned with poor relief and horse stealing, together with one on 'abuses committed by the lewd and licentious soldiery'.[24] Altogether, Henry had thus indeed been concerned with reform and was evidently known as a very approachable man by the workers on his Billingbear estate.[25]

In general, however, Neville's position under James I entailed opposition to the extension of the executive powers of the King, especially when this was accompanied by the royal usurpation of funds without specific parliamentary authority, an issue which was to prove fundamental over the next few decades in fomenting the English Civil War. King James's increasingly outspoken descriptions of himself and his role as near-absolute, enunciated even before he came to the throne in works such as *Basilikon Doron* (1599), aroused very considerable parliamentary hostility, in which Neville was soon recognized as a leader. Neville was, however, a moderate, keen to return to a balanced view of the traditional constitution; although in some respects a radical, he was probably neither a proto-republican nor proto-Cromwellian. He also supported free trade and, despite his wealthy mercantile relatives, opposed the trade monopolies granted to London merchants.[26] Instead of legal monopolies, he consistently favoured the creation of joint stock companies such as the East India Company, whose shares were cheap and available for anyone to buy.[27]

Neville became increasingly involved in joint stock trading companies, especially the second London Virginia Company, with profound consequences – as unlikely as this would seem at first glance – for English literature. He was also rather badly in need of money, a fact which constrained many of his actions over the next few years. He had spent, by his own account, £4,000 as Ambassador to France, and had paid £3,000 in fines during his imprisonment, a total equivalent of some £7 million today. His 11 children were rapidly growing up, and he had a social and political role to fulfil. By 1605 or 1606, however, Neville had been consistently disappointed in his political ambitions, having been passed over for a number of posts, for example the Ambassadorship to Spain, a position to which, rumour had it in December 1605, he was about to be appointed.[28] There was also gossip that he might actually succeed Robert Cecil (who was created Viscount Cranborne in 1604 and Earl of Salisbury in 1605) as Secretary of State, but this, too, came to nothing, as did other rumours of senior appointment.

Neville was also increasingly active as an advocate of a vigorously anti-Spanish and pro-Protestant foreign policy.[29] He increasingly took the view that toleration of Catholics in England would lead to their domination of the country, and appears to have been genuinely shocked at the Guy Fawkes conspiracy. He became something of a fixture on parliamentary committees which produced anti-Catholic proposals, such as a requirement that all Catholics take an oath of loyalty.[30] However, he also tempered his reaction with feeling for the innocent Catholics, saying that he and other Parliamentarians were working out how to qualify 'in execution' some of the harsher strictures imposed against the Catholics by the King.[31] What we do not know is how any of this affected his personal relations with William Shakespeare. It is frequently and increasingly argued that Shakespeare was a Catholic recusant, a proposition for which there is evidence both for and against.[32] It is likely that Neville neither knew nor cared about Shakespeare's religious convictions. On the other hand, what little we do know about the professional and personal life of Shakespeare of Stratford at this time suggests that, from about 1604–05 he spent most of each year in Stratford rather than in London, and it is possible that Neville and Shakespeare had a falling out, perhaps a major one, at this juncture. Conceivably Shakespeare, increasingly wealthy and rooted in Stratford, and habitually keen to avoid a visible political profile, wanted as little as possible to do with the just-released traitor Neville; or perhaps after the Guy Fawkes plot of 1605, Shakespeare, if indeed a secret Catholic, thought it wise to make himself scarce in London. Conceivably both motives were at work.

For whatever reason, the only plays generally dated from the period 1604–1613 with Shakespeare named on their title pages (if published separately), or in the Stationers' Register, were *King Lear*, registered in November 1607 and published in Quarto form in 1608, and *Coriolanus*, believed to have been published in 1609.[33] It is also possible that Neville wanted little to do with the secret Catholic Shakespeare, especially if, as has been suggested by a number of Shakespeare's recent biographers, he had connections with some of the Guy Fawkes conspirators, for example Robert Catesby, who was born in a town just north of Stratford.[34] It is also possible that Neville became increasingly friendly with other members of the King's Men rather than Shakespeare, especially with the erudite Robert Armin, who had joined the Chamberlain's Men between 1599 and 1603.[35] Again, there is no conclusive evidence on this question.

Also at this time, in Parliament Neville was siding visibly with those who advocated free trade between England and Scotland, and the naturalization of Scots born after 1601 as English subjects from birth.[36] However, Neville also opposed the apparent favouritism shown to the Scots by James I and in March 1607 gave a speech in Parliament attacking the prospect of a formal union between England and Scotland until the Scottish government renounced any close friendship with France.[37] Obviously, this preoccupation with Scotland formed a major part of the background to *Macbeth,* while the political trends of the time strongly affected the tenor of his dramatic works. By 1608–10 Neville had evolved a highly visible reputation as one of the main progenitors of the so-called 'popular party' in the House of Commons, strongly pro-Protestant, seeking parliamentary checks on the powers of the monarch, and supportive of free trade and the rights of independent merchants over closed trading monopolies.

The tragedies

During the years 1604–08, Neville, as 'William Shakespeare', probably wrote three of his greatest tragedies, *Macbeth*, *King Lear* and *Anthony and Cleopatra*; and three other tragedies, *Timon of Athens*, *Coriolanus* and *Pericles, Prince of Tyre*. As noted, there has long been a consensus among commentators that the nature of Shakespeare's writing changed around 1601, an evolution which continued to the end of his writing career. This change can clearly be linked with Neville's imprisonment and, after 1603, with the process of his increasing disenchantment with James I and his evolving political position. That Shakespeare's later works, up to and including *The Tempest*, reflect the same evolving political and religious stance as that of Neville has been argued by many commentators, despite the fact that they knew nothing of Neville as 'Shakespeare'. For instance, in her *Shakespeare and the Politics of Protestant England*, Donna Hamilton notes Shakespeare's apparent 'oppositionist' politics at this time, as evidenced in his plays, and his 'alignment with the new Protestant consensus'.[38] Other scholars have noted Shakespeare's position at this time as 'one rejecting tyranny and warning against its basis in absolutism'.[39] Obviously, one should not expect these plays to be political documents – 'Shakespeare' was producing entertainment, not political tracts. Neville was still intent on keeping his secret; as an increasingly visible and influential Member of Parliament he had to be even more careful than in the 1590s, and he still hoped for royal appointment to senior office. However, there is a clear link between Neville's career and his writings. In contrast, it is difficult to see why Shakespeare of Stratford, if the author, would wish to engage in any political commentary at all, and his apparent behaviour in spending increasing amounts of time in Stratford suggests that he was keen to eschew the limelight or controversy. As a leading member of the King's Men, one would assume that 'oppositionist' plays were the last sort which Shakespeare, if the author, would write. As usual, there is no good fit between the known life of Shakespeare of Stratford and the evolution of his plays, while there is an obvious and clear-cut match between Neville's life and the plays.

· *Macbeth* was probably written in 1606, although it is possible that an earlier version was penned when Neville was in the Tower, as the play contains apparent allusions to the Gowrie conspiracy of the previous year.[40] Chambers tentatively dated the play to 'late in 1605 or early in 1606', and this has been broadly accepted by most scholars.[41] A slightly later date, after June 1606 or even as late as 1607, has been suggested by recent authorities.[42] The play was evidently written to express Neville's simultaneous feelings of expectation and disappointment from the Scottish monarch; by 1606 it must have become apparent that the latter mood outweighed the former. The scenario and atmosphere of the play must have derived from Neville's visit in about 1583 to many of the places depicted in the play. It might also be relevant to note that Neville, through his ancestors the Barons Bergavenny, was descended from the eighth king of Dalriada in Scotland 'in the shape of the line of Anglo-Scottish thanes and mormaers who held sway on the English–Scottish borders long before the original Nevilles even arrived in England [from Normandy]'.[43] Neville was himself descended from King Duncan and from a close relative of Macbeth, a fact of which the historically minded author could hardly have been unaware. He seems to be saying that his Scottish lineage was as good as the King's, and that the King ought not to forget this fact. But this play also attempts to present the ancestry of King James VI of Scotland (James I of England) in a respectable light, differentiating it from the bad associations which the old Elizabethan Englishmen had been brought up to believe about that country. Neville had actually visited James in Scotland, and had long promoted his cause to obtain the throne of England.

Many Scots also claim that whoever wrote the play must have had first-hand knowledge of Scotland. For instance, on visiting Macbeth's castle at Inverness, Duncan and Banquo remark that the air is suddenly milder there:

> DUNCAN. *This castle hath a pleasant seat; the air*
>   *Nimbly and sweetly recommends itself*
>   *Unto our gentle senses.*
> BANQUO. *This guest of summer,*
>   *The temple-haunting martlet, does approve*
>   *By his loved mansionry that the heaven's breath*
>   *Smells wooingly here. No jutty, frieze,*
>   *Buttress, nor coign of vantage, but this bird*
>   *Hath made his pendant bed and procreant cradle;*
>   *Where they most breed and haunt, I have observed*
>   *The air is delicate.*

Act I, Sc. VI

This mildness is totally unexpected for anyone travelling from further south. One would expect the atmosphere to grow colder, but, for several reasons of changing wind directions, plus the effect of the Gulf Stream, the opposite is true; but this fact was not documented at the time. (It is also typical of a Neville to notice birds – his father even made a specific point of mentioning his falcon in his will, while over the centuries Neville's descendants kept birds which they had stuffed because they could not bear to part with them when they died.) Added to this, the English ambassadorial contingent always stayed at Glamis Castle.[44] Glamis was not truly the home of Macbeth, so only a writer who had stayed there would have bothered to have transported his character to the wrong place. Neville knew Glamis, and obviously it is always easier for a writer to set the scene in a place he knows.

King Lear was probably the last of the four great tragedies, and appears to have been written just after *Macbeth*. It was entered in the Stationers' Register on 26 November 1607 'as it was played before the King's Majesty at Whitehall upon St. Stephen's Night at Christmas last'.[45] One of the most profound and difficult of all the plays, one can only offer suggestions as to what the play might mean: perhaps a commentary on the increasingly unwise policies of James I; perhaps a commentary on Neville's own family of 11 children, whose adolescence and youth, and their eventual succession to his property, must have been of growing concern to him at this time. Significantly, according to Duncan, by 1608 Neville was 'having serious financial difficulties', caused in part by his having 'three daughters[46] who needed husbands and dowries'.[47] It is just possible that this situation was, for him, vexatious enough to influence the choice of *Lear* as a play. *King Lear* was based in large part upon an anonymous play, *King Leir*, first registered in 1594, whose plot centred around King Leir and his three daughters. Unlike *King Lear*, however, this play ends happily. Neville may have been inspired by a production of the old play which took place in 1605. The political message in *King Lear* is also in line with Neville's thinking – as a privileged man, King Lear should not have abdicated but carried on with his responsibilities, right to the end. Or, had he lost his strength and wits, then he should also have lost the right to have any say about the future of his kingdom. Worst of all, Lear split the kingdom, thereby leaving the obvious opportunity for Civil War, which was what Neville himself dreaded most. His history plays and *Romeo and Juliet* had spelled out the same basic message from so many points of view. Now, in line with his 'debate' in *Measure for Measure* concerning the effect of private morality on public policy, Neville was spelling out the dangers of a divided ruling family, whose position dictated that their domestic troubles would inevitably have macrocosmic consequences. The inescapable message seems to be that no one is made fit to rule by birth alone: a king must not only reign in name but be a philosopher too. If he is not, then not only should he cease to rule, he should automatically lose the right to will his kingdom to his own nominees, for if he is not a philosopher, then his choice will inevitably be flawed, the national consequences of which will be dire.

On a personal level, the famous Annesley connection with King Lear's theme of madness (mentioned by Charlotte Stopes and A.L. Rowse among others), could be quite probable, once Neville is in the equation. Cordell Annesley was the daughter of Brian Annesley, a Kentish landowner. Her two sisters wanted their father certified insane in order to inherit his estate. Cordell, however, wrote to Robert Cecil in an attempt to prevent this. In 1608, Cordell married the widower of the dowager Countess of Southampton. Cordell was therefore married to Southampton's father, a fact which placed Sir Henry Neville in an excellent position to know about the case. Seen in this light, the naming of Cordelia in *King Lear* is again a pointer to the true writer, who must have been in constant touch with the circle who knew of the Annesley case. Indeed, a husband of one of the other two Annesley sisters was married to Baron William Sandys, who took part in the Essex rebellion.

In the five years or so before 1608–09, Neville probably also wrote four other plays: *Timon of Athens, Anthony and Cleopatra, Coriolanus* and *Pericles, Prince of Tyre*. While his rate of production may well seem extraordinary – as of course it was – Neville generally wrote only one play per year during the post-1603 period, only half as many as he had done prior to 1601, when he managed to write two new plays each year. This diminution was, one supposes, chiefly caused by Neville's increasing parliamentary duties as well as, perhaps, his anxieties and ill-health. *Timon of Athens*, which 'enjoys the dubious distinction of being perhaps the least popular play in the Shakespearean canon', was probably written before *King Lear*.[48] Many commentators regard it as an unfinished play, possibly written in collaboration with Thomas Middleton.[49] It is a particularly bitter play, concerned with bankruptcy and misanthropy, which clearly matched Neville's mood when it is generally supposed to have been written, in 1604–05. And Timon is even put under house arrest – just as Neville was for some time after he had been accused of complicity with the Earl of Essex. At this time, it had become apparent to Neville that – in contrast to Southampton, who had received some gifts of land from King James as compensation for his wrongful imprisonment – he would receive nothing for what he had suffered.[50]

Anthony and Cleopatra was recorded on the Stationers' Register on 20 May 1608, but might have been written slightly earlier, in 1606 or 1607.[51] The play appears to signal a return to something like a more heroic classical mood, reminiscent of *Julius Caesar*. It is possible that the play was conceived before 1601. The story line, however, has certain affinities with the saga of Essex and Elizabeth, and thus might be another disguised commentary on those traumatic events. The play's use of language and metaphor shows Neville at his most inspired; presumably he was in the process of recovering from his deepest post-release gloom and disappointment.

The third of Neville's plays from this period was *Coriolanus*, another Roman tragedy, often dated to around 1608, although it is unusually difficult to date with confidence.[52] One well-known orthodox dating links it with the death of Shakespeare's mother in September 1608. Other authorities place the likely date in the spring or early summer of 1608.[53] It is worth noting that in May 1608 Robert Cecil (by then the Earl of Salisbury) assumed complete control of English public affairs, becoming Lord Treasurer as well as Secretary of State, a move which attracted widespread envy. While Neville wrote to Winwood, perhaps ironically, that it was the most popular move the King had ever made, and presumably hoped to benefit from the move, it is difficult to believe that *Coriolanus*, if indeed written just after Cecil's assumption of the Treasury, did not at least to a certain extent have this event in mind.[54] The protagonist of the play, a Roman general originally named Caius Marius, is offered the consulship, but his arrogance and contempt for the common people so infuriates them that he is banished. It is also very difficult to see why William Shakespeare, chiefly resident in Stratford, would possibly wish to comment on English high politics in this manner, while it is easy to see why Neville would wish to do so. R.B. Parker's 'Introduction' to *Coriolanus* stresses the Jacobean political circumstances under which the play was written, with the themes of the House of Commons' struggle against James's absolutism in many areas of contention, such as the question of who had the right to decide disputed elections.[55] Parker points out that the very rhetoric used by the Commons was Roman in origin. It was at this time that Neville became known as the English Tacitus. *Coriolanus*, then, is a product of a politician in the centre of all these debates, and Neville was the very hub.

Pericles, Prince of Tyre, is another rather obscure Roman play, classified as a comedy. It was written around the same time as *Coriolanus*, probably between January 1606 and November 1608.[56] It was entered into the Stationers' Register in May 1608, and printed in a Quarto version, 'by William Shakespeare', in 1609.[57] Despite this, it was not included in the First Folio. While universally regarded as authentically Shakespearean, many authorities believe that it was either a collaboration with someone else, or represents a Shakespearean revision of an older play.[58] The plot is complex and meandering, but contains many apparent parallels to *The Comedy of Errors*, written more than a decade earlier. *Pericles* – arguably like others among his late plays – may show Neville as preoccupied by other things, and merely going through the motions rather than producing another supreme masterpiece. It seems incontestable that Neville's mind and heart were increasingly focused elsewhere at this time. However, plays he wrote around this time also have at their heart a kind of neo-platonic philosophy. Perhaps Neville was tiring of the everyday parliamentary squabbles and trying to step back and look at more eternal values.

Chapter 9

Towards Closure:
the Last Plays, the Sonnets
and the Parliamentary
'Undertaker', 1609–15

The last six years of Neville's life marked the period when he was most active in English political life, and very nearly succeeded in gaining the high political office which had always eluded him. Yet, as before, he was doomed to political disappointment, and, as before, constantly felt the need for more money. As a result, he became increasingly involved with a number of major business ventures, especially the second London Virginia Company.

By 1610 he had also become the major shareholder in the New River Company – a project to divert rivers in order to bring a water supply to North London. He seemed to have entirely given up on gaining direct royal assistance by this time. Neville was obviously a clever schemer, though, for instead of asking the King directly for help, he and the more 'progressive' earls now presented James with commercial projects from which he, the King, could also benefit. James therefore eventually gave a royal charter to the Virginia Company.

These new tactics marked a definite change in Neville's approach to King James. In the early years of James' reign Neville had written to his friend, the Earl of Southampton, to ask him if he could persuade the King to give him some financial 'amenity' to compensate for the losses he had suffered under Queen Elizabeth's reign.[1] Neville obviously felt he had been unjustly treated. All during his embassy in France, he had surrounded himself with Scottish contacts and had tried to protect their and James's interests. He had been to see James in Scotland in 1583, alongside the Earl of Essex, and he felt that his friend Essex had paid the ultimate price for trying to promote James's interests from that time onwards, while he, Neville, had suffered an agonizing time in the Tower and had had to pay substantial fines. Southampton had received lands from the King to mark his loyalty and suffering, while he, Neville, had received nothing. Of course, it may be that James had private reasons to suspect that Neville might have imposed very strict constitutional conditions on his reign in England, had Neville been the parliamentary leader following a successful rebellion. He had, after all, shown himself to be out of sympathy with James's conception of an absolute monarch ruling by the Divine Right of Kings.

But still Neville continued to feel badly done by. It seems the only compensation he received from James's hand following Southampton's intercession was a small 'fee farm' in the shape of being allowed to collect one-twelfth of all the importation tax on indigo – the dye used in ink, amongst other things.[2] This may have been a sarcastic gesture on James's part, suggesting that the King may have either known or suspected Neville's secret authorship of Shakespeare's works.[3] There is probably an echo of Neville's bitterness in the lamenting Sonnet 111 (perhaps representing I,I, I), obviously addressed to Southampton at this time:

> O, for my sake do you with Fortune chide,
> The guilty goddess of my harmful deeds,
> That did not better for my life provide
> Than public means which public manners breeds.
> Thence comes it that my name receives a brand,
> And almost thence my nature is subdued
> To what it works in, like the dyer's hand.
> Pity me then, and wish I were renewed,
> Whilst like a willing patient I will drink

> *Potions of eisel 'gainst my strong infection;*
> *No bitterness that I will bitter think,*
> *Nor double penance to correct correction.*
> *Pity me then, dear friend, and I assure ye*
> *Even that your pity is enough to cure me.*

The tone of this sonnet is so similar to that of his letter to Southampton that Neville's – the dyer's – hand can be seen in both. In addition to this, in that very letter, Neville proclaimed that everyone who knows him well knows that all he has done in life has been devoted to that earl's service – the same claim as that made in his Dedication to *Lucrece*:

> *What I have done is yours; what I have to do is yours; being part in all I have, devoted yours. Were my worth greater, my duty would show greater; meantime, as it is, it is bound to your lordship, to whom I wish long life still lengthened with all happiness.*

Thus, during these later, difficult and financially troubled years, Neville wrote his final plays, including *The Tempest*, and also published the immortal Sonnets. Ill, disappointed, and in relatively straightened circumstances, he can have had no inkling of the extraordinary posthumous fate which awaited him: to remain virtually unknown while, under the pseudonym of his stage factotum, to become the world's most famous and influential writer.

In the years prior to about 1610, Neville had gained a reputation as one of the major leaders of the 'popular party' in Parliament, who were opposed to granting very major funding to the King without parliamentary scrutiny and approval.[4] As was noted at the time, his stance was among the factors which cost him a realistic chance of achieving the high government office to which many expected him to be appointed.[5] During this period Neville gained a reputation as at least a moderate radical, to the extent that he was included in a biographical dictionary of seventeenth-century British radicals published in the 1980s.[6] He was also, for eight years, one of the members of the council of the London Virginia Company. As 'William Shakespeare', however, his writing career drew to a close, ending several years before his death in 1615.

During this period Neville probably wrote *Cymbeline* and *The Winter's Tale*, the last of his 'romances' (these are sometimes included among his 'problem plays'), as well as *The Tempest*, his farewell to the theatre, and two 'encore' plays probably dating after *The Tempest*, namely *Henry VIII* and *The Two Noble Kinsmen*, which he is generally believed to have co-authored with John Fletcher. This period also saw the publication of Shakespeare's Sonnets in 1609, and the publication in the same year of *Troilus and Cressida*, usually supposed to have been written earlier.

Neville's two 'romances', normally included with Shakespeare's comedies, dated to this period were *Cymbeline* and *The Winter's Tale*. With its very elaborate plot and 'its multiple happy endings [snatched] from the jaws of several disasters', *Cymbeline* contains the standard Shakespearean formulaic devices such as a wager about charity, a trick to gain access to a woman's bedroom, disguises, Roman generals, and revelations of the identities – in short, the lot.[7] Its date has been a matter of conjecture, with 1609 now generally accepted. Simon Forman, the astrologer and physician, recorded seeing *Cymbeline* around April or May 1611. It is believed that some of its plot, although not set in Scotland, might derive from a section of Holinshed's *Chronicles* concerning Scotland, which have led some commentators to suggest that it was written about the time of *Macbeth* in 1606.[8] Stylistically and in other ways, however, it seems clearly to belong to the period of *Anthony and Cleopatra* and *The Winter's Tale*; its somewhat hackneyed apparatus the product of Neville's preoccupation with parliamentary matters and his own personal finances at this time. Chambers' suggestion of 1609–10 as its 'date of production' seems plausible, with the play's theme of a Roman army meeting defeat in Britain perhaps reflecting Neville's heightened mood of nationalism at the time.[9]

However, there are also some strange pointers in *Cymbeline* – an altogether strange and symbolic play – which overlap with Neville's own life and relatives. For instance, the name itself could even be read as a convolution of Cym [cf. Welsh cwm] beli ne, 'born in the valley of Beli' (or Bell). Beli was the Celtic god from whom Billingbear (Neville's home) got its name. His home was indeed in the valley of the White Horse of Uffington. This white horse is carved onto the hillside and was itself the sign of Beli. Then there is the character of Posthumous. This is not the most usual of names but was one given to the youngest of the Hoby sons, who now lived at Bisham Abbey – the Neville's ancestral home. Bisham was only two miles from Billingbear, and the Hobys and Killigrews were related; Richard Neville, Earl of Warwick, is buried at Bisham Abbey.

Neville's last 'romance' – omitting, for a moment, *The Tempest* – was *The Winter's Tale*, with yet another involved plot about royal children raised secretly and with a happy ending. Many of the names of its characters are derived from North's 1603 translation of Plutarch, while the play was seen in performance at the Globe by Simon Forman on 15 May 1611.[10] From other internal evidence, *The Winter's Tale* is normally thought to have been written in 1610 or 1611.[11] A date 'early in 1611' was also suggested by Chambers.[12] It was thus probably written shortly before *The Tempest*, which was almost certainly intended as Neville's farewell to his career as a playwright; the title of *The Winter's Tale* was already a proverbial phrase, a 'winter's tale' being a long story told 'to while away a winter evening'.[13] Neville was presumably signalling here, as in *The Tempest*, that his career as a playwright was drawing to a close; at the time, he was preoccupied with politics.

Within *The Winter's Tale*, however, we again have pointers to a connection with Sir Henry. After Neville had returned from France, his secretary, Winwood, had deputized for him there and had sent Neville texts of the entertainments performed at the wedding in Florence, by proxy, of Henri IV and Catherine de Medici. What Winwood had not said was that the entertainment consisted of a performance of Peri's *Orfeo* and Caccini's *Euridice* (the earliest known operas). Of course it was not like the entertainment at home, as he said, and as it was so new, he did not know how to term this particular art form. However, he must have described the performances well to Neville, and the play he wrote under their influence, *The Winter's Tale*, contains a great number of songs and much music and dancing.

Neville cleverly leaves a hint within the play for those on his trail. Hermione's statue is said to have been crafted by the sculptor Giulio Romano. In fact, the words used to describe the work and the supposed artist are very strange:

> *a piece many years in doing and*
> *now newly performed by that rare Italian master, Julio*
> *Romano, who, had he himself eternity and could put breath*
> *into his work, would beguile Nature of her custom, so perfectly*
> *he is her ape.*
>
> *Act V, Sc. II*

This is a statue we are talking about, and yet the writer speaks of the work being 'newly *performed*'. It is strange too that Giulio Romano was not a sculptor. There was a minor painter of that name, and that painter also occasionally sculpted stucco characters on the outsides of grand houses in Italian cities, which Neville would have seen, but for any contemporary Italian the name would be thought to refer to the composer, Giulio Romano, otherwise known as Caccini. It is as if Neville sees the new art form – opera – as a synthesis of all the arts. The now lost *Cardenio*, written with Fletcher, was also reputedly a synthesis of words and music more exquisitely beautiful than had ever been seen in England to that date.

Neville's two most important literary achievements at this time, however, were the publication of the Sonnets and the authorship of *The Tempest*. The circumstances of the two are closely linked and revolve in part around the same venture in which he was engaged.

The Sonnets

Although much about the circumstances of the Sonnets is likely to remain a mystery – the identity of the 'dark lady' and of the 'rival poet' may never be conclusively resolved – we believe that very considerable new light can be cast on every aspect of the Sonnets, especially the mystery of the celebrated Dedication and what it might mean. On the basis that Neville is the author, it is also realistic to postulate a literary influence on the Sonnets quite apart from any implied personal meaning. Neville's father was a leaseholder of quite a large portion of the Blackfriars property, in which building the famous theatre was situated.[14] Our Sir Henry was baptized at St Anne's, Blackfriars, and there is also much subsequent evidence to show that his father and mother lived there for a large part of their married life. (After all, Billingbear was still under construction at the time, so it is perfectly feasible that Sir Henry senior would not have wished to be present there during the busiest times of the building taking shape.) It is significant, therefore, that the writer John Lyly (who had been awarded an MA at Oxford in 1575) was associated with Blackfriars Theatre for a time – significant because Lyly wrote a prose work, *Euphues*, describing a parallel love triangle to that found in the Sonnets. What is more, the name of the 'dark lady' in that story was Lucilla who, after splitting up two friends, ultimately becomes a prostitute. In his book *Mr. W.H.*, Leslie Hotson finds many literary allusions in Shakespeare's Sonnet sequence to a woman whose name must be Lucy. Hotson then takes this Lucy to mean, perhaps, the Black Luce who was a famous prostitute in Clerkenwell during Shakespeare's lifetime, but the clever Sir Henry Neville was 'book-learned'[15] and would certainly have not missed a chance of making this literary-plus-real-life allusion. So the 'dark lady' may even have been a private literary and London joke between the Earl of Southampton (Neville's 'champion' and the most likely dedicatee of the Sonnets), Neville and other London literati.[16]

To understand why the Sonnets were published when they were and what Neville's motives were in having *Shake-speare's Sonnets* published at that particular time, a few key dates should be kept in mind:

20 May 1609 – *Shake-speare's Sonnets* recorded on the Stationers' Register.

23 May 1609 – King James officially grants the charter of the second London Virginia Company.

With these two dates must be grouped another that may be highly relevant to understand the Sonnets:

2 May 1609 – Sir Henry Neville's eldest son, also named Henry Neville, marries Elizabeth, daughter of Sir John Smythe [or Smith] at St Margaret's Lothbury Church.

The celebrated Dedication to the Sonnets, which must form the starting point of any discussion of their meaning, has probably engendered more debate than any short passage in English literature:

> *TO.THE.ONLIE.BEGETTER.OF*
> *THESE.INSVING.SONNETS.*
> *Mr.W.H.ALL.HAPPINESSE.*
> *AND.THAT.ETERNITIE.*
> *PROMISED.*
> *BY.*
> *OVR.EVERLIVING.POET.*
> *WISHETH.*
> *THE.WELL-WISHING.*
> *ADVENTVRER.IN.*
> *SETTING.*
> *FORTH.*
>
> *T.T.*

This Dedication contains so many anomalies and mysteries that one hardly knows where to begin the discussion. 'T.T.' is universally accepted to be Thomas Thorpe, the book's publisher (but not its printer, George Eld (or Elde), who had also printed *Troilus and Cressida* in 1609). Endless debate, however, has been occasioned by the identity of the dedicatee, 'Mr. W.H.', by the meaning of 'onlie begetter' and of 'our everliving poet', by the precise relationship of Shakespeare to the circumstance of its publication (did he supervise the Sonnets' publication, or even know about it?), and by a dozen other questions which flow from the Dedication's general strangeness and elusive nature.

Perhaps the best way to begin is to ask why the book's *publisher* has written its dedication. Since when does the *publisher* of a book of poems (or any other work) write the dedication to that book? Are not all dedications written by their authors?[17] Indeed they are, and we would like to suggest that the Sonnets' Dedication was not written by Thomas Thorpe but by the author of the Sonnets, Sir Henry Neville. Since Neville was engaged in keeping his authorship a secret from the public, there is nothing strange in his adopting, when signing the Dedication as if from Thomas Thorpe, the pseudonym of an actual living man, just as he had been doing during the previous 20 years or so in adopting as his pseudonym the name of another actual living man, the Stratford actor and theatre-sharer, William Shakespeare.[18]

In our opinion – and in the opinion of the majority of commentators on the Sonnets since the early nineteenth century – 'Mr. W.H.', the dedicatee of the work, was certainly Southampton, and, indeed, positing another dedicatee makes little sense. Many, conceivably most, of the Sonnets were written by Neville to Southampton during their joint imprisonment in the Tower in 1601–03. During the years just before the publication of the Sonnets, they were close friends and close political allies. As will shortly be discussed, they were both members of the council of the second London Virginia Company. Southampton is the only person whom Neville would have regarded as the 'onlie begetter' of the Sonnets; the term 'begetter' meant chiefly in the sense of 'inspirer'. 'Mr. W.H.' must have been Neville's affectionate nickname for Southampton. Indeed, while they were in the Tower, Sir Henry and the Earl of Southampton were stripped of their titles, so it is highly likely that they would have referred to each other as Mr. H.N and Mr. H.W. Or, even more likely, as both of their first names were

'Henry', that Neville might have reversed his friend's initials so that there was no confusion as to which Henry was which. The phrase in the Dedication wishing the dedicatee 'all happiness' is of course an echo of Shakespeare's Dedication of *The Rape of Lucrece* to Southampton, which concludes by wishing him 'long life still lengthened with all happiness'.

Nor can there be the slightest doubt of the reason for the publication of *Shake-speare's Sonnets* at just that time. It was, quite plainly, occasioned by the granting of a royal charter, three days after the official registration of the work, to the second London Virginia Company, of whose council, as noted, both Southampton and Neville were members and major participants. Indeed, A.L. Rowse notes that the company's affairs were mainly run from Sir Thomas Smythe's house in Philpot Lane, and it was Sir Thomas' grand-daughter, Elizabeth, who married Neville's son.[19]

Neville was pinning his battered financial expectations in part on the success of the venture. This is the manifest reason why the Dedication ends so curiously with 'the well-wishing adventurer in setting forth'. If one supposes that the normal explanation of the Sonnets' Dedication is true – it was written by the publisher, Thomas Thorpe, probably to Southampton – what could conceivably be meant by this phrase? Why would the issuing of the Sonnets volume be described in this way? An 'adventurer' in English commercial law was an investor in a major commercial enterprise involving risk such as a chartered company like the London Virginia Company. (The term 'venture capital' contains a contemporary echo of this term.) Investors in the second London Virginia Company were repeatedly described in its royal charter as 'adventurers'. In contrast, Thorpe was a professional publisher who had been involved in the appearance of dozens if not hundreds of books. Every work he published was a 'setting forth' by an 'adventurer', so why should *Shake-speare's Sonnets* receive special mention or note? The Sonnets volume was produced, moreover, as a tiny pamphlet, only 13 copies of which are known to survive today; only one person, Edward Alleyn, ever mentioned purchasing *Shake-speare's Sonnets* at the time in any written record which survives. Its price was only five pence.[20]

No one knows how many copies of the Sonnets were actually printed, but it is difficult to see how the total number could have exceeded 200 or so, an estimate which, if anything, is probably generous.[21] Its publication 'apparently met with total silence', and no further edition of the work was published until John Benson brought out a rearranged and bowdlerized edition (substituting 'her' for 'him' throughout) in 1640.[22] Its publication by Thorpe in 1609 was simply too inconsequential and routine a publication for its publisher to describe himself as an 'adventurer' in bringing it out. Such a term might realistically have been applied to the syndicate of publishers which produced the First Folio in 1623, a major and very expensive work which sold for £1, 40 times as much as a Quarto volume and 48 times as much as *Shake-speare's Sonnets*, who were taking an enormous commercial risk in producing such a costly work. The 'adventure' referred to in the Dedication has nothing to do with the volume of Sonnets but with the great trading company being launched on almost the same day. So there is little scope for an alternative meaning other than that it was an 'adventurer' in the Virginia Company who wrote the Sonnets and was now wishing his fellow-adventurer, friend and dedicatee 'All happinesse'.

The American adventure

The first London Virginia Company was established in April 1606 with the aim of publicizing a colony of Englishmen in the area between 34° and 41° north. In May 1607 it founded the famous colony at Jamestown, Virginia, headed by Captain John Smith. Sir Henry Neville was a member of the council of this company. He also provided wood from his estate to help build the ships that sailed on various commercial enterprises.[23]

The Jamestown colony almost came to grief, with only 35 of the original 120 English settlers surviving the colony's first seven months of existence. Nevertheless, the Jamestown colony saw such iconic moments in American history as the marriage of the Indian princess Pocahontas to the colonist John Rolfe. In July 1619, after Neville's death, the first representative assembly in the western hemisphere was convened at Jamestown Church, the foundation point of American representative democracy. Also in that year, the first African slaves in North America arrived at Jamestown, beginning America's long racial ordeal and creating the circumstances which eventually resulted in the American Civil War. In 1609 the charter of the original company was varied to allow individual persons to subscribe relatively small sums to join the company as 'adventurers', thus greatly enlarging the financial base. It was also given the right to appoint its own governors, and certain other new rights. The Letters Patent of the

Company, allowing individual subscribers to join, was issued by the King 'sometime prior to 17 February 1609'; subscribers were probably allowed to join in January 1609.[24] Subscribers' lists were kept open until May 1609 and, as noted, the King officially granted the second London Virginia Company its charter on 23 May 1609.[25] A total of 659 individuals subscribed to the company as investors or 'adventurers', of whom 21 were peers and 96 were knights, the rest being mainly 'esquires', citizens of London and merchants.[26] The minimum cost of subscribing as an 'adventurer' was £12, although 230 had paid £37 10s. or more. Southampton was the third of eight earls to sign and Neville the fifth of the 96 knights, strongly suggesting that they were early and enthusiastic supporters of the venture, probably joining in January or early February 1609.

It is very important to note who was *not* an 'adventurer' in the second London Virginia Company. One man who was not among the 659 subscribers was Thomas Thorpe, although he had, three days prior to the royal promulgation of the company's charter, ostensibly described himself as an 'adventurer', a term which, given its date, he must surely have known was being ubiquitously applied to the hundreds of subscribers in the Virginia Company, and was a wholly inappropriate way of describing the publisher of a small volume of sonnets. Even more importantly, William Shakespeare was not among the company's 659 subscribers, although by 1609, now among the richest men in Stratford, he could obviously have afforded the £12 fee. (Had he been, this fact would of course be prominently rehearsed in every orthodox Stratfordian biography.)

The mystery of the Sonnets

It seems likely that Neville expected the success of the Virginia Company to restore much of the fortune he had lost during the previous ten years. Early in 1609 he pleaded with Robert Cecil (by then Lord Salisbury) to request that the King reimburse one-half of the £4,000 he had spent as Ambassador to France. Without Salisbury's 'charitable office' he claimed that he would 'sink beneath the burden of his debts'.[27] There is no evidence that he was ever paid anything by Salisbury. The second London Virginia Company thus arose as a potential godsend. We have no way of knowing what, precisely, Neville was thinking, but it is possible that Southampton 'got him in on the ground floor', so to speak, with every expectation of making substantial profits, or that both Southampton and Neville became key figures in the company at the same time, each sharing with the other their expectation of profits. Neville had been a member of the council of the earlier London Virginia Company from 1607, and its reconstitution with a vastly greater investors' base must have been welcomed by him.[28] Again we obviously cannot be sure, but the Sonnets were probably intended as a 'thanks-offering' offering by Neville to Southampton to mark a likely upturn in his financial fortunes and perhaps in the financial fortunes of both, and the probable ending of Neville's long period of depression and disappointment. 'Mr. W.H.' *must* be Southampton, since many of the Sonnets were written to him by Neville, in the Tower; the initials cannot have been, for instance, those of William Herbert, Earl of Pembroke (1580–1630), later one of the joint dedicatees of the First Folio, who could not possibly have been the 'begetter' of any of them. Others who have been suggested as 'Mr. W.H.', such as the Oxfordian candidate, a Mr William Hall supposedly resident in Oxford's parish, are purely speculative and lacking in any plausibility. In what sense was any such man the 'only begetter' of the Sonnets, and how did he come to be involved in their publication? If Edward De Vere was the actual author of Shakespeare's works, surely the Sonnets were the property of De Vere's heir, his only son the eighteenth Earl of Oxford, not of 'William Hall', even if he had some relationship to De Vere, a proposition for which no evidence exists.

The Sonnets are mysterious in part because they do not seem to form a coherent, unified whole, but are composed of apparently unrelated groups of poems on different themes. The first 13 (or 17) Sonnets appear to be addressed to a much-admired young man – the so-called 'fair youth', who is enjoined by the poet to marry and have children. Who this young man could be, and why the poet is so concerned that he marry and have children, has also been the subject of endless speculation.[29] The most common explanation of this sequence is that they were written by the young Shakespeare around 1589, possibly as a commission, and addressed to the young man Southampton at the time of his proposed marriage to Elizabeth De Vere, Oxford's daughter and Burghley's granddaughter. As is well known, Southampton, who was 16, was so little smitten by 14-year-old Elizabeth De Vere that he was willing to pay a fine of no less than £5,000 to avoid the match, and later married Elizabeth the daughter of Sir John Vernon, a Shropshire squire and Essex's cousin. This explanation might be true, although there are strong considerations against it: Shakespeare's dedication of his two poems to Southampton came four or five years later, and there is no evidence, even on the suppositions of orthodox Stratfordians, that he had any connection with Southampton as early as 1589–90. There is no reason to suppose that William Shakespeare would have been regarded as a poet worthy of a commission of this kind in 1589–90 – he had, after all, written no poetry at this time and was only about 25 years old. Furthermore, there is no evidence that anyone who might have wished to commission this series of match-making Sonnets, such as Lord Burghley or Southampton's mother (sometimes supposed to be the commissioner) did so or, indeed, had ever heard of William Shakespeare in 1589–90. Finally, if these Sonnets were indeed the relics of an unsuccessful, costly attempt at match-making on behalf of Southampton, it is difficult to think of any poems less likely to be included in a collection of sonnets *dedicated to* Southampton 20 years later. Their inclusion would surely be regarded by Southampton as painful and gauche in the highest degree, and insulting to his wife. The publication of these 13 (or 17) Sonnets as the first in the collection, moreover, meant that Southampton, if he saw *Shake-speare's Sonnets*, could hardly have avoided noticing them.

It is certainly possible, however, that Neville was commissioned to write these Sonnets for the young Southampton. Neville knew the young Southampton when he was a ward of Lord Burghley; as a member of the English upper classes, the scion of an illustrious noble family, who had been elected to Parliament in 1584, there would have been nothing anomalous in his writing such poems on commission from Southampton's mother or from Burghley himself, although there is no evidence that he did. Since in 1609 Southampton and Neville were close friends, political allies, and, in effect, business partners, the younger man might well have regarded the publication of these old Sonnets, so many years later, as a well-intended joke rather than as an unwelcome and impudent reminder of the distant past, responding in quite a different way to their publication than he would have done had the actor William Shakespeare been their author. Burghley had indeed already commissioned his personal secretary to write a poem encouraging Southampton to marry, so Burghley was obviously trying to keep his secret ambitions for his granddaughter within his own close circle. One of his best and most trusted friends at the time was Sir Henry Neville senior, and, to judge by his extant letters, he was a good writer. The young Sir

Henry, his son, had already been noted as being 'book-learned' so it is quite within the bounds of possibility that Burghley turned to Sir Henry senior and junior to come up with a better set of verses than his secretary had done. It is, however, unthinkable that he would have commissioned a lowly stranger, such as the young Shakespeare, to undertake the task. Burghley would also have been aware of the growing friendship between the young Earl of Southampton and Sir Henry Neville, so that poems written by him would be more likely to influence the young boy.

There is, however, another entirely different explanation for the first 13 (or 17) Sonnets, which may well account for them as well as the traditional supposition that they were intended to induce Southampton to marry. On 2 May 1609, less than three weeks before *Shake-speare's Sonnets* were registered, Neville's eldest son, also named Henry Neville (*c*.1586–*c*.1629) was married at St Margaret's Lothbury Church in the City of London to Elizabeth, the daughter of Sir John Smythe [or Smith] of Ostenhanger, Kent. Although we have no direct evidence on this matter, it can hardly be doubted that Neville would have welcomed this match as a godsend of good fortune similar in magnitude to the riches foreshadowed by the second London Virginia Company; Sir John Smythe was the sole surviving son of Sir Thomas Smythe (*c*.1558–1625), an enormously wealthy City of London merchant who had been instrumental in obtaining the charter of the second London Virginia Company, and was involved in a vast range of other important mercantile ventures.[30] He had been a participant in the Essex rebellion, and, like Neville had actually spent some time in the Tower, and was heavily fined before being released. Unlike Neville, he enjoyed the favour of James I and was appointed by the new King to a range of lucrative offices.[31] His son John, of Ostenhanger in Kent, was also a wealthy knight, who was married to a sister of the Earl of Warwick, a distant relative of Neville's. Sir John's daughter obviously came with a substantial dowry and the prospect of a large inheritance for herself and her offspring. From Neville's viewpoint, especially in his financially strapped personal situation, it was difficult to imagine a more potentially advantageous situation, which also brought with it the likelihood of being brought into the City's inner financial and mercantile circles.

Suppose, then, that the Sonnets addressed to the 'fair youth' were actually written late in 1608 or early in 1609, *to Neville's son and heir*, as an inducement for him to marry? This would account for the intensity – indeed near-desperation – of the tone of these sonnets, widely remarked upon by many critics and commentators. Such lines as 'You had a father, let your son say so' (Sonnet 13), and 'make thee another self for love of me' (Sonnet 10) appear to be so personal that it is really very difficult to imagine another plausible context in which they were written; written from father to son, however, they make perfect sense. That they were published at the opening of *Shake-speare's Sonnets* was thus entirely appropriate: Neville's celebration of his eldest son's advantageous marriage. It might seem unusual for someone to write poetry to enjoin his own son to marry, but everything about Sir Henry Neville was unusual, and penning sonnets might well have seemed a highly appropriate way of tipping a wavering son into matrimony. Suppose, moreover, that it was Southampton, well aware of the situation, who recommended that Neville compose and address some of his marvellous sonnets to his son, which he did with the desired effect? Perhaps Southampton recommended this course late in 1608 or early in 1609, when Neville also told him that he intended to publish a volume of his sonnets. The marriage in fact took place in May and produced a line of descendants. The coincidence of dates between the wedding, the launch of the second London Virginia Company, and the publication of *Shake-speare's Sonnets* is so remarkable that it surely requires an explanation.[32]

Much else about the Sonnets and the Dedication still remains mysterious and may always remain so. The phrase in the Dedication about 'our ever-living poet', it is often pointed out, was normally applied only to the dead or to God. For this reason, Oxfordians are fond of noting that it could apply to De Vere, who died in 1604. In all likelihood, and constrained by what he could say in the Dedication, it was suggesting that his career as a poet was now over, just as, the following year, he apparently declared in *The Tempest* that his career as a playwright was over. We do not know who the 'dark lady' was, although Neville's wife, Anne Killigrew Neville, was Cornish and was therefore presumably dark-haired: the 'secret' here might be no more than this. And it is known that the free-booting Cornish side of the Killigrew family was full of strong, unladylike ladies. We do not know who the 'rival poet' was, or what Neville had in mind here. We do not know if Neville and Southampton had a homosexual relationship. Since both were emphatically heterosexual, this is highly improbable, except in the context of their Tower imprisonment.

Whether the Sonnets were printed in some kind of deliberate sequence is also unclear. If the first 13 or 17 Sonnets were written by Neville *last*, in late 1608 or early 1609, and *if* the next 40 Sonnets or more were largely written by Neville in the Tower and addressed to Southampton, it is arguable that *Shake-speare's Sonnets* were printed in reverse chronological order, at least in a general way. Although many commentators believe that the Sonnets were all or nearly all written in the 1590s, it seems apparent that up to half or more were actually written after 1601.[33] It is also possible that quite a lot of 'symbolic numbering' is undertaken in the Sonnets. Neville was a mathematician, and numbers would have fascinated him in every way. Within the miscellaneous poems collected as *The Passionate Pilgrim*, number 8 refers to the addressee's musical ability. It is our guess that both this and Sonnet 128 were written by Neville to his wife, and both include the number 8, which refers to the octave:

> *If music and sweet poetry agree,*
> *As they must needs, the sister and the brother,*
> *Then must the love be great 'twixt thee and me,*
> *Because thou lovest the one, and I the other.*
> *Dowland to thee is dear, whose heavenly touch*
> *Upon the lute doth ravish human sense;*
> *Spenser to me, whose deep conceit is such*
> *As, passing all conceit, needs no defence.*
> *Thou lovest to hear the sweet melodious sound*
> *That Phoebus' lute, the queen of music, makes;*
> *And I in deep delight am chiefly drown'd*
> *When as himself to singing he betakes.*
> *One god is god of both, as poets feign;*
> *One knight loves both, and both in thee remain.*
>
> *The Passionate Pilgrim, poem no. 8*

> *How oft, when thou, my music, music play'st*
> *Upon that blessed wood whose motion sounds*
> *With thy sweet fingers when thou gently sway'st*
> *The wiry concord that mine ear confounds,*
> *Do I envy those jacks that nimble leap*
> *To kiss the tender inward of thy hand,*
> *Whilst my poor lips, which should that harvest reap,*
> *At the wood's boldness by thee blushing stand.*
> *To be so tickled they would change their state*

And situation with those dancing chips
O'er whom thy fingers walk with gentle gait,
Making dead wood more blest than living lips.
Since saucy jacks so happy are in this,
Give them thy fingers, me thy lips, to kiss.

Sonnet 128

In a similar way, Sonnet 18 'Shall I compare thee to a summer's day' may well have been written to Anne on the occasion of her eighteenth birthday, while the 17 early Sonnets could have marked the age Southampton (or perhaps, even, Neville's son) had reached by the time he completed that cycle. The date of birth of Neville's eldest son is not altogether certain, but as he is generally taken to be his oldest child, it was possibly around 1586. If this is the case, then he was exactly 17 years old when his father was freed from the Tower.

The sophistication and precision of so many of the Sonnets implies that they were written at a time when Neville had a good deal of leisure time, as he certainly did when imprisoned for treason. The volume itself, *Shake-speare's Sonnets*, is notorious for its many typographical errors, suggesting that it was hurriedly produced by Neville. Conceivably, he distributed copies as gifts to his friends, while only a component of the small print run was sold in the normal way, which would account for its rareness and complete lack of contemporary renown. The work was certainly authorized by Neville, and most clearly had been published with his approval.

As printed, *Shake-speare's Sonnets* also contained, after the sonnet sequence, another poem, *A Lover's Complaint*, occupying the final 11 pages of the book.[34] For many years it was believed to have been written by another author, but the recent weight of critical opinion is that it was indeed written by 'Shakespeare'.[35] Indeed, since Neville certainly knew and approved of the volume of Sonnets, it must have been included in the work with his authority, although it is not encompassed in the Dedication, which refers specifically to 'these ensuing sonnets'. The form of *A Lover's Complaint* is not unlike *Lucrece*, and previous critics have dated it to the 1590s, but more recent commentators have found resemblances to *All's Well that Ends Well* and to *Measure for Measure*, written in 1602–04, as well as to the late *Cymbeline*.[36] Perhaps it was written in the Tower, or just before the publication of the Sonnets, to remind Southampton of his long association with Neville.[37]

The Tempest

That the London Virginia Company had become a central obsession to Neville was shown a year or two after the publication of *Shake-speare's Sonnets* with the appearance of *The Tempest*, almost certainly his last substantial play. *The Tempest* is now almost invariably dated to late 1610 or 1611: it was first performed at Court in November 1611, and the date of 1611 has seemed 'reasonable' to Chambers and most other scholars.[38] This date – late 1610 or 1611 – is seemingly set in stone by the fact that much of it apparently derived from three sources which appeared late in 1610 which discussed the famous shipwreck of the *Sea-Venture*, one of nine ships which had set out in June 1609 to settle Virginia under the auspices of the London Virginia Company. It was wrecked on Bermuda, where the survivors managed to build another ship, and to reach Jamestown, Virginia, in May 1610.[39] News of what had occurred reached England in September 1610, causing a great sensation. A spate of reports and commentaries were soon written, most famously *A True Repository of the Wrecke and Redemption of Sir Thomas Gates*, by one of the survivors, James Strachey, often known as the 'Strachey Letter'. Strachey's account was dated 15 July 1610 and remained in manuscript form until it was published many years later, in 1625.[40] In manuscript form, it was, however, 'circulated to the Council' of the London Virginia Company of which Neville was a prominent member.[41] Two other contemporary works are seen by most authorities as having been used in *The Tempest*: Sylvester Jourdain's *A Discovery of the Bermudas*, which appeared in October 1609 before word of the shipwreck had reached England, and another work apparently compiled by the Virginia Company itself, *A True Declaration of the Estate of the Colonie in Virginia*, published in November 1610.[42]

Ordinarily, the contemporary sources on which a Shakespearean play such as *The Tempest* was based are of interest only to specialist scholars, but in this case there are two reasons for these sources being of very great relevance to the authorship question; indeed, arguably central to it. The first is that if *The Tempest* was indeed based on sources which were written in 1609–10 and which, by necessity, could not have appeared earlier, then *The*

Tempest must have been written by someone who was alive at the time. This would *ipso facto* rule out Edward De Vere, the seventeenth Earl of Oxford, who died in 1604. As this fact must also presumably rule out Oxford as the author of any of Shakespeare's works, the dating of *The Tempest* is, therefore, of the utmost concern to Oxfordians. The originator of the Oxfordian theory, Thomas Looney, attempted to get around this objection by arguing that the play was actually written by someone else, but more recent Oxfordians, aware of the unconvincing special pleading in this strategy, have attempted to show that *The Tempest* was in fact written much earlier than 1610.[43] The weight of evidence, however, that the author of *The Tempest* was plainly and indisputably influenced by the 1610–11 works about the Bermuda shipwreck is surely so overwhelming as to be irrefutable.[44] Before the rise of Oxfordianism there was a theory, advanced by a few commentators, that the play was written earlier; this is now rejected by virtually every authority, although of course the play might well be based in part on travel works and dramas written before 1609.[45]

The Strachey Letter

There is also an equally important debate about the sources used in *The Tempest*, and one over which orthodox Stratfordians invariably flounder – the question of how William Shakespeare gained access to the manuscript version of the Strachey Letter. This has never been satisfactorily explained, and the dubiety of efforts by orthodox Stratfordian biographers to account for it clearly shows the weakness of their case. To reiterate, William Shakespeare of Stratford, the actor and theatre-sharer, was not an investor in the second London Virginia Company, although he could certainly have afforded the purchase of a share, while many hundreds of men in all likelihood no richer than Shakespeare did in fact purchase shares in the company. There is, in fact, no evidence that he had anything to do with the Virginia Company or took the slightest interest in its activities. The few documents which exist about Shakespeare's business life in 1609–11 show him to have been in Stratford, where he was engaged in adding to his wealth by the purchase or lease of land; there he also engaged in lawsuits and paid local taxes. The Strachey Letter was a confidential, lengthy manuscript of some 20,000 words, which remained unpublished until 1625, and was addressed to an unnamed 'Excellent Lady' who was familiar with the Virginia Company.

(This address could surely also have been a coded way of referring to the officers of the Virginia Company, 'Virginia' being a lady's name.) It was circulated to the Virginia Company's directors, but was otherwise regarded as confidential. So how did William Shakespeare get to read it, or come to use it in a play?

Orthodox Stratfordians have always credited his knowledge of the Strachey Letter to the 'multiple connections' which allegedly existed between Shakespeare and members of the Virginia Company. The evidence for these 'connections' is, however, at best slight, and at worst, frankly laughable. They are never direct and unequivocal, and always entail multiple suppositions which obviously violate Ockham's Razor, the injunction that it is wrong 'to multiply entities without necessity' – i.e., it is illogical to posit a complex explanation for something when there is no real evidence for any of the legs of the explanation.

One of the most frequently suggested of these possible sources was via Dudley Digges (1583–1639), an MP who was a member of the council of the Virginia Company and who was also the stepson of Thomas Russell (1570–1634), a Warwickshire landowner who in 1616 was appointed an overseer of Shakespeare's will. Russell did not live in Stratford itself but in Alderminster, four miles south of Stratford.[46] Leslie Hotson pointed out, in all seriousness, that Digges had visited Russell in late 1610 to attend to some business matters and 'might have brought along a manuscript of Strachey's letter'.[47] Of course, this is not impossible, merely improbable in the highest degree: why on earth would Digges bring along a handwritten 20,000-word confidential manuscript (at 200 words to the page, that's 100 manuscript pages) on a journey to a provincial town three days' travel away, probably made on horseback or in a primitive carriage, on a business visit to his stepfather, and why on earth would he let Shakespeare read it? Would he really allow a well-known and prolific playwright see and copy out a confidential document relating to a major London chartered company, knowing that it was likely to end up being used in a play?

Other suppositions about the source of Shakespeare's knowledge of the letter are similarly tenuous: for example, the family physician of Sir Henry Rainsford, another member of the Virginia Company council, was Dr John Hall, Shakespeare's son-in-law (who was a leading Puritan with no interest in the theatre, and was not an investor in the Virginia Company), and so on – always invariably based on far-fetched speculation lacking actual evidence.[48]

To make matters worse, Strachey himself was a theatre-sharer, but in the wrong company: the Children of the Queen's Revels, a major rival to the King's Men.[49] Of course, one can demonstrate many apparent linkages between Shakespeare and members of the London Virginia Company, but no *direct* linkages, and no plausible explanation as to why any member of its council would allow Shakespeare, who was unwilling to invest even £12 in the venture, to see a confidential document about the company or allow him to copy it out and use it in a play. Given that there were 659 known investors in the company, such supposed links could probably be made with every middle-class man in England. Strikingly, however, there are no known direct links, since Shakespeare of Stratford took no interest in the London Virginia Company. Posit Sir Henry Neville as the author and none of these far-fetched suppositions is necessary; on the contrary, since the Strachey Letter was circulated to the members of the Virginia Company's council, there is direct evidence that he had access to the letter.

Final works

The Tempest was written during a period when Neville had a higher profile in national politics than at any previous time. The play is often seen as Shakespeare's farewell to the theatre – 'But this rough magic / I here abjure ... I'll break my Staff, Bury it certain fathoms in the earth, / And deeper than ever did plummet sound / I'll drown my book.' (Act V, Sc. I, ll. 50–6) – and it does seem likely that Neville did intend it as a farewell to the theatre, just as the previous year his Dedication to the Sonnets may well have been intended as his farewell to poetry. Only a few works, probably co-authored, came after *The Tempest. Henry VIII* (sometimes known as *All is True*), parts of which were certainly written in 1602–03, was first performed at The Globe in June 1613, when the theatre famously burned down in a fire started by a canon fired in Act I, Scene IV of the play. John Fletcher (1579–1625) is usually regarded as Shakespeare's co-author.[50] By 1613, Neville's animosity towards Queen Elizabeth had presumably diminished, and her baptism is depicted in the play's final scene, along with Cranmer's prediction that her reign and that of her successor would be glorious. *The Two Noble Kinsmen* was probably also written in collaboration with John Fletcher, and is normally dated to 1613–14, at the very end of Neville's career.

A 1614 play by Ben Jonson, *Bartholomew Fair*, apparently contains a reference to *The Two Noble Kinsmen*.[51] That it was co-authored with Fletcher is attested by its entry in the Stationers' Register, not made until April 1634.[52] Shakespeare and Fletcher are also believed to have collaborated on a play, *Cardenio* (or Cardenno), which was performed by the King's Men in May and July 1613.[53] It was evidently based on a story in Cervantes' *Don Quixote*. The play is now lost, although another play published in 1728, *Double Falsehood: or, The Distressed Lovers*, and still extant, probably represents a rewritten version of the original play.[54]

Political involvement and business ventures

In these years, Neville was heavily and directly involved in English politics at the highest level. Increasingly critical of both Cecil (Lord Salisbury) and the King, in November 1610 he was one of 'the thirty' MPs, as they were known, who conferred with King James about supply and other matters of difference between the Sovereign and Parliament. The King specifically asked Neville, regarded as one of the leaders of Parliament, to summarize their differences, which he did by stating that 'whene your Majesty's expense groweth by the Commonwealth we are bound to maintain it, otherwise not', and enumerated other grievances as well.[55] In 1611 many rumours circulated that Neville would succeed the ailing Cecil as Secretary of State. The following year Neville offered to act as 'undertaker' – organiser of parliamentary business for the King in the House of Commons – provided that James refrained from inflammatory remarks, sought parliamentary approval for funding, and instituted discreet consultation between the Crown and a committee of Parliament. Neville had the support of many moderate reformers in Parliament, especially his great friend Southampton, who was one of the leaders of this group in the Lords. At this time too, Neville was becoming increasingly friendly with William Herbert, Earl of Pembroke, who also supported Neville's policies, and who eventually became a patron of the First Folio of Shakespeare's works. Indeed, they had always had a point of contact through Sir Robert Sidney – Neville's old travelling companion during the continental tour – as Sidney was Pembroke's uncle.

Probably because of his known antipathy to the King and his privileges, James I did not look to Neville for his new Secretary of State, but instead turned to his friend and former secretary in France, the more reliable Sir

Ralph Winwood.[56] By 1613–14, Neville's last realistic hopes for high office and senior appointment had passed. Had Neville been appointed, and his advice followed, it is possible that the course of events leading to the English Civil War and Cromwell's Protectorate might have been averted. Increasingly desperate for money, Neville also pursued other business ventures, especially the Muscovy Company, and was also part of an attempt to open an overland route to the Far East across Asia for trading purposes. The longed-for success of the London Virginia Company did not materialize with the speed he and the other 'venturers' had hoped or expected, and *The Tempest* is evidence of how bitterly Neville felt its setbacks. Although Neville's eldest son had indeed married well, as had several of his daughters, he still felt the constant need for money, and had, essentially, never recouped what he had lost between 1599 and 1603. The second London Virginia Company not only did not result in the Golconda of wealth its investors had hoped for, but incurred debts of £1,000 by 1612. It was not until a decade or two later, after Neville's death, that it became profitable.

Neville was also increasingly ill, and his failure to produce any new plays on his own after *The Tempest* is evidence of this, as well as his high-profile political involvement. As noted, however, he did continue to collaborate with the younger John Fletcher, and was a prominent member of the Mitre Club, a group chiefly composed of lawyers, poets and the few 'progressive' aristocrats. They met at the Mitre and Mermaid Taverns near St Paul's. The Mitre in Bread Street also included prominent intellectuals: Jonson, Fletcher, Francis Beaumont and John Donne.[57] It is just possible that William Shakespeare was also a member of the Mermaid Club, since the landlord of the Mermaid Tavern was William Johnson, who acted as trustee for Shakespeare when he bought the Blackfriars Gatehouse in March 1613, a strange undertaking which has been the subject of much speculation, since it was a known Catholic haunt.[58] However, Shakespeare was not a member of the more intellectual Mitre Club.

As is so often the case with Shakespeare of Stratford's dealings, Shakespeare's purchase of a lease on the Blackfriars Gatehouse is murky and complex. Whether Neville had any hand in this purchase, perhaps using his old factotum as his agent, is unknowable. Nor is there any direct evidence that Shakespeare was a member of the Mermaid Club, which is entirely in keeping with the Stratford man's continuing lack of known intellectual or courtly connections.

Early in 1615, apparently aware that the end was in sight, Neville made his estates over to his children.[59] In 1614 he had been granted a lucrative patent to prosecute spoilers of forest lands, but his patent was 'crushed' – one assumes on royal orders – and he complained that 'all his hopes [were] at an end'.[60] According to John Chamberlain, a prominent society gossip of the time, Neville was suffering from jaundice, scurvy and dropsy (oedema, or abnormal water retention). Neville died on 10 July 1615, probably aged only 53.[61] It was scurvy – a disease caused by a Vitamin C deficiency – which killed him, according to Chamberlain, who also claimed that Neville's disappointment at being passed over for Secretary of State also badly affected his health.[62] He died without knowing, or suspecting, that he would eventually be regarded as the greatest Englishman of the past thousand years.

Chapter 10

Life after Death: the First Folio and the Apotheosis of Shakespeare

Sir Henry Neville died in 1615 and life went on. Around 1619 his widow remarried George Carleton, Bishop of Chichester (*c.*1557–1628). Carleton had been at Oxford at the same time as Neville, and had also been a student of Sir Henry Savile. Although originally at St Edmund's Hall, in 1580 he was admitted to Merton College while Neville was still a student there.[1] Carleton was a friend and admirer of Neville and, in 1603, wrote a Latin work praising Neville, *Heroici Characteres*. Carleton's first clerical position had been as Vicar of Mayfield, Sussex, from 1589 to 1605.[2] Like Neville, he had suffered from being passed over for preferment until he was made Bishop of Llandaff, in Wales, in 1617 and Bishop of Chichester in 1619. He was a noted religious writer and theologian.[3] It is impossible to say what he really knew of his wife's first husband's secret life as an author, and although it is doubtful whether he took an interest in the theatre, his friends wrote of him as a merry, witty gentleman who seemed to be quite different in real life from the strictly Puritanical image he portrayed in his religious tracts.

Neville's surviving children generally married well, and his best-known grandchild was certainly his namesake Henry Neville (1620–94), a very prominent radical politician and writer of the Cromwellian and post-Cromwellian period, who was the first to translate Machiavelli into English.[4] Originally a member of Cromwell's cabinet, he became disaffected with the Protector and retired to Berkshire, where he wrote the famous *Isle of Pines* (1668), described as a 'libertine fantasy', about one George Pine, shipwrecked with four women – conceivably influenced in part by *The Tempest* – and *Plato Redivivus* (1680).[5] Of course, genius is seldom really hereditary and there is almost always an inevitable regression to the mean in the course of a few generations among the offspring of enormously talented people, and the appearance of these two Henry Nevilles in three generations is arguably noteworthy. While William Shakespeare left no surviving descendants after the death of his only granddaughter, Elizabeth Hall, Lady Barnard, in 1670, Shakespeare's daughter, Susanna, who died in 1649, was described on her gravestone in Stratford Church (on no known evidence) as 'witty above her sexe' and, moreover, 'wise to salvation'.[6] Nevertheless, William Shakespeare left collateral descendants, the offspring of his sister Joan Hart (1569–1646), who survive to this day. Something is known of their careers. Even bearing in mind the inevitable regression to the mean, their occupations are startling. Joan Hart's grandson George (d. 1702) was a tailor; his son Shakespeare Hart (d. 1747) was a plumber; his son William Shakespeare Hart (d. 1750) was a glazier. Two descendants of the next generation are known, John Hart (d. 1800) a chairmaker 'who apparently claimed to have Shakespeare's Bible', and Thomas Hart (d. 1800) a butcher.[7] So far as is known, none ever became a solicitor, a vicar, a physician, or even a 'schoolmaster in the country', and none wrote a thing.

We are, however, left with many mysteries. Who knew of Neville's secret in his lifetime? Why was it not revealed at the time, or since? Above all, why was the First Folio published, when it was, as emphatically being the work of William Shakespeare? While it is unlikely that these mysteries will ever be completely resolved, we believe that we have gone a long way towards answering some of them. For instance, there were still other aristocratic Sir Henry Nevilles alive at the time the First Folio was published, so it is likely that the then patrons and publishers would not have wished there to be any confusion concerning these men.

It seems likely that a number of published sources in Neville's lifetime came close to giving the secret away. One of the most important was the poem 'To Our English Terence Mr. Will: Shake-speare' by John Davies of Hereford (*c*.1565–1618), a poet and author who knew Sir Francis Bacon and was also a member of the Mitre Club along with Neville. It is one of the many epigrams in Davies' *Scourge of Folly*, published in 1610–11, which contains brief poems on the personalities of his day, and reads:

Some say (good Will) which I, in sport, do sing
Had'st thou not plaid some Kingly parts in sport,
Thou hadst bin a companion for a King;
And, beene a King among the meaner sort.
Some others raile' but raise as they thinke fit,
Thou hast no rayling, but, a raigning Wit:
And honesty thou sow'st, which they do reape;
So to increase their Stocke which they do keepe.

This poem is, plainly, very mysterious, and has given rise to much discussion, since it is one of the very few sources written by an apparently well-informed contemporary of Shakespeare's during his lifetime which evidently has something important to say about the man. But, even apart from its ambiguity per se, its contents do not seem to be relevant to the known life of Shakespeare, or to any of the other authorship candidates. In what sense was Shakespeare a 'companion for a King'? What 'King'? Shakespeare, moreover, did not play 'Kingly parts in sport' but as a professional actor, was paid to perform. The poem has rightly been described by the arch-Stratfordian Sir E.K. Chambers as 'cryptic' and 'obscure', and is often omitted from biographies of Shakespeare, despite the apparently important information about the man.[8] Davies' poem, however, ambiguous as it is, seems to be relevant to Sir Henry Neville. A decade earlier, he 'had[st]' indeed been a 'companion for a King', when he was Ambassador to France and was well known in England for his friendship with King Henri IV. By 1610–11 moreover, Neville was widely seen as 'King among the meaner sort', as one of the most important leaders of the 'popular party' in Parliament, a reputation which, again, was generally and widely known. Indeed, apart from his imprisonment in the Tower – most unlikely to be emphasized by Davies in an affectionate poem – they were essentially the *only* things for which Neville would have been widely known.

The poem's title, 'To Our English Terence', is also rather odd. Terence was a famous Roman author of comedies. Shakespeare wrote comedies, but also famous tragedies, histories and poetry, and it seems curious to compare him with an author known only for his comedies. But Elizabethans also knew Terence as an author accused of having written some comedies 'bearing Terence[s] name [but which] were written by worthy Scipio and Laelius'.[9] In other words, Terence was known to have given his name to works actually written by others, in just the same was as 'Mr. Will: Shakespeare'.[10]

A more basic question is why no one, in Shakespeare's lifetime, openly raised the authorship question, or overtly claimed that someone else wrote the plays. The first point to be made here is that, while no one overtly raised the question of the author's identity during Shakespeare's lifetime, it is also the case that no one clearly and unequivocally identified the Stratford man, the actor and theatre-sharer, as the author of the plays. Contemporaries who mentioned the plays, such as Francis Meres, simply stated that 'William Shakespeare' (or Shake-speare) was their author, since that was the name on the title page or the name commonly given as that of the author. This was never accompanied, at any point in Shakespeare's lifetime, by any linkage of the Stratford man as an author to the works attributed to him. There are no known anecdotes, letters, or biographical material of any kind from Shakespeare's lifetime which unequivocally state that the man who was born in Stratford in 1564 and died there in 1616 wrote the plays, or provide any information about him as an author.[11] As we have seen, in the case of John Davies of Hereford, the few references to Shakespeare as a writer in his lifetime, by men who probably knew him and seem to have something interesting to say about him as a man, seem completely inconsistent with what we know of Shakespeare's biography.

It must also be borne clearly in mind that Shakespeare did not become 'Shakespeare' until generations later, that is, the British national poet and fountainhead of Western literature. It is now normal to date his apotheosis and deification to the mid–late eighteenth century, especially to the famous Stratford Jubilee of 1769 – actually held five years after the 200th anniversary of his birth – which was masterminded by David Garrick, the great actor.[12] The slowness of the pace at which the deification of Shakespeare proceeded, and the tardiness of the assemblage of what biographical information exists about the Stratford man, are surely the most striking features of this process. The first biography of Shakespeare of Stratford, no more than 40 pages long, did not appear until 1709, written by Nicholas Rowe as a preface to a new edition of Shakespeare's works.[13] By then, of course, for several decades at least there had been no one alive who had known either Shakespeare or Neville; Shakespeare's last direct descendant, Lady Barnard, had died in 1670. Shakespeare's famous will, with its celebrated bequest to Anne Hathaway of the 'second best bed', was not seen by any writer or scholar until 1747 and not published anywhere until 1763.[14] No one ever attempted to produce a viable, well-researched chronological account of the order in which the plays were written until Edward Malone did so in 1778.[15]

During his lifetime – and notwithstanding Shakespeare's contention in Sonnet 55 that 'neither marble nor the gilded monuments / of princes shall outlive this powerful rhyme' – Neville had no real reason to suppose that his plays would be performed or even remembered ten years after his death. Dozens of new plays were premiered every year in London, and talented new authors were appearing constantly. He could not imagine that the drama and poetry of his time would be of much greater interest to posterity than the sermons of theologians or even the works of contemporary philosophers. He could not foresee that this would single-handedly replace the Greek and Latin classics, or that the English language would eventually grow to universal significance with the rise of England's daughter nation across the Atlantic, which he had played a considerable part in founding, eventually to become the *lingua franca* of the whole world, replacing both Latin and all modern languages. Had Neville's contemporaries been aware of any of this, plainly they would have taken a keen interest in the author of Shakespeare's works, but none was.

The work which gave the whole world its dominant view of William Shakespeare as unquestionably the author of the works bearing his name was, as we have seen, the First Folio, recorded on the Stationers' Register on 8 November 1623, eight years after Neville's death and seven years after Shakespeare's. The First Folio was a gigantic collected edition, 908 pages long, containing 36 of Shakespeare's plays, 18 of which were previously unpublished. The First Folio, of course, opens with the famous commendatory verse by Ben Jonson and others, and the celebrated Droeshout portrait. Given that the plays in the First Folio were clearly attributed to the Stratford man, described as the 'Sweet Swan of Avon', and, moreover, that he is described in the introductory matter by two of his fellow actors in the Chamberlain's/King's Company, John Heminge and Henry Condell, as 'so worthy a friend', the First Folio presents almost irrefutable evidence that he must have written the plays which bear his name.

If one accepts that Sir Henry Neville wrote Shakespeare's works, it follows that the attribution by the creators of the First Folio to Shakespeare of Stratford must be fraudulent. Most historians and scholars would naturally be very uneasy with such a claim, involving an apparently deliberate effort at fabrication which might be described as a conspiracy, but it must be true. There must be an explanation of how and why the First Folio appeared in the form it did, with its direct crediting of William Shakespeare as its author. In light of what we know, there are three major questions which must be posed about the First Folio: why was Neville not credited with the authorship of the works it contains, by whom was it organized, and why was it produced when it was? While no definitive answer can be given to these questions, we believe that a good deal of progress can be made in that direction.

Organization of the First Folio

The question of who organized the production of the First Folio in the form it took can be answered with much greater certainty. It seems clear to us that Ben Jonson, who wrote most of the introductory material, was the crucial driving force behind the First Folio, and there is a strong likelihood, amounting to a near certainty, that he was paid to do so by Neville's family. Jonson had known and admired Neville, having met him at the Mitre Club, or possibly even before, as Jonson was educated by Camden and Camden was a close friend of Sir Henry Savile.[16] We know from the collected State Papers that Neville was avidly collecting funds at one point 'to make a Christian out of a young Cockney', which suggests that Neville was always on the lookout for talent among the poorer citizens of London. At some stage late in Neville's career, Jonson wrote a 16-line poem in praise of Neville, contrasting his virtue with his lack of honours. When Jonson wrote it is not known – it was published in Jonson's *Epigrammes* in 1616 as part of his collected *Works* – although Duncan describes it (erroneously, since it is written in the present tense) as 'an epitaph'.[17]

To Sir Henry Nevil

Who now calls on thee, NEVIL, is a Muse,
  That serves nor fame, nor titles; but doth chuse
Where vertue makes them both, and that's in thee:
  Where all is faire, beside thy pedigree.
Thou art not one, seek'st miseries with hope,
  Wrestlest with dignities, or fain'st a scope
Of seruice to the publique, when the end
  Is priuate gaine, which hath long guilt to friend.
Thou rather striv'st the matter to possesse,
  And elements of honor, the[a]n the dresse;
To make thy lent life, good against the Fates:
  And first to know thine owne state, then the States.
To be the same in roote, thou art in height;
  And that thy soule should give thy flesh her weight.
Goe on, and doubt not, what posteritie,
  Now I haue sung thee thus, shall iudge of thee.
Thy deedes, vnto thy name, will prove new wombes,
  Whil'st others toyle for titles to their tombes.

Jonson's lines here, 'Goe on, and doubt not, what posteritie, / Now I haue sung thee thus, shall iudge of thee ...' are slightly curious. Why should Jonson's lines in a short poem, published as one of 133 'epigrams', immortalize Neville's 'deedes' for 'posteritie'? Neville was a well-known public figure in his day, and a member of an illustrious family. Was there already more to this than meets the eye? 'To be the same in roote, thou art in height' also suggests that there was just as much of Neville that no one saw as there was 'above ground', and Neville was a big man. The word 'titles' may also very well have a double meaning. Added to this, if the first two lines are simply re-punctuated they could read:

Who now calls on thee? NEVIL is a muse
That serves nor fame nor titles ...

With the word 'titles' being reiterated in the last line, we are led to believe it is important. (Jonson's term for a poet was most often 'muse', so 'Nevil is a muse' means, in Jonsonian parlance, 'Nevil is a poet'.)

The First Folio was apparently begun after the failure of a venture by the printers William Jaggard and Thomas Paine in 1619 to print most of Shakespeare's plays. The initials 'T.P.' appear as the printer of six plays, five of which have false dates. It is often thought that Paine's efforts sparked a much more conscientious one to collect and publish all of Shakespeare's plays in one collected volume a few years later.[18] The only substantial previous collection of plays by a single author was Ben Jonson's *Works* (which included most of his poetry and masques), published in 1616. The printing of the First Folio probably began around April 1621 and took over two years to complete, with *Troilus and Cressida* the last part of the Folio to be printed, apparently not completed until early December 1623.[19] Jonson certainly wrote two parts of the preliminary material, the (possibly facetious) poem 'To the Reader' on the Droeshout portrait of Shakespeare, and the famous long tribute 'To the Memory of My Beloved, the Author Mr. William Shakespeare: And What He Hath Left Us'.[20] It is believed by many researchers that he was the driving force behind most or all of the preliminary material, including that ostensibly written by Heminge and Condell.[21]

When Jonson wrote his portion of the preliminaries is of great importance. We do not know when these were written, although they were almost certainly among the last part of the First Folio to be printed, just as one might expect. According to Greg, the preliminaries were printed in 'late November 1623'.[22] This was also the view of Charlton Hinman, the great expert on the printing of the First Folio, who stated that the preliminaries were 'in all likelihood produced more or less immediately after *Cymbeline*', which was set in print between April and early November 1623 and 'probably before the end of October [1623]'.[23] Although we simply do not know, Jonson presumably composed his poetic tributes to Shakespeare in the First Folio just before this, probably after reading the whole oeuvre, probably for the first time, and being genuinely awed by it.

In the years immediately preceding the writing of the First Folio preliminaries, Jonson was extremely hard up, and 'casting about for new sources of money'.[24] 'In 1621 there is evidence that he was struggling, not too well, with real financial difficulty', and had to borrow £36, a large sum, from a London citizen named John Hull.[25] Although a few of his plays were performed over the next few years, by the autumn of 1623 his situation had apparently changed quite drastically. On 20 October 1623 Jonson appeared in the Court of Chancery to give evidence about the settlement of the estate of Sir Walter Raleigh's widow. He described himself and place of residence as 'Benjamin Jonson of Gresham College of London, gent.'.[26] In other words, *at the very time – or immediately after – when, in all likelihood, Ben Jonson wrote the preliminaries to the First Folio, he was resident at, and probably employed by, the college founded and endowed by, and named for, Neville's great uncle*. All biographers of Ben Jonson have been puzzled by how and why he came to be at Gresham College, a place with which he had no previous connection. He had certainly not been appointed to any of the six professorships there, in the fields of astronomy, physic, divinity, geometry, law, music and rhetoric. Only one of these, in rhetoric, could conceivably have been held by Jonson. All of Gresham College's professors were Oxford and Cambridge graduates.[27] 'Rhetoric' apparently encompassed the art of literary composition, and Jonson would, in Rosaline Miles' words 'have made an able deputy to the Professor of Rhetoric', while 'the use of deputies was common at this time'.[28] Jonson was, of course, not a university graduate, but had received an honorary degree from Oxford University in July 1619.[29] (Interestingly, the award of Jonson's MA was proposed by the Earl of Pembroke, Jonson's patron and the Chancellor of the University, to whom the First Folio was jointly dedicated.) Jonson was also well known for his knowledge of the classics and was regarded as the first Poet Laureate, although the title did not yet formally exist. On the other hand, he was also a famous playwright and the author of such poems as 'Drink to Me Only With Thine Eyes', and the two universities had certainly produced dozens of less controversial graduates who would, presumably, have been keen to act as deputy to a professor at what was, after all, the only institution of higher learning in the arts in London (omitting the entirely legal world of the Inns of Court). There is simply no further evidence on how or why Jonson came to be at Gresham College at this point.[30] One theory, that Jonson was simply using Gresham College as a temporary residence following a disastrous fire in his lodgings, has been mooted by some historians, but the fire occurred in November 1623, after he was resident in the College.[31]

Appointments to chairs at Gresham College were vested by Sir Thomas Gresham's will in the Mercer's Company. We know little or nothing about how more junior appointments were made. It was well known, however, that the Nevilles – Sir Henry's father and mother and their immediate family – enjoyed a privileged position under Sir Thomas Gresham's will. According to Vanessa Harding, Gresham was 'close to' his niece Elizabeth Neville (our man's mother) 'regarding her as his "heir apparent" after his son Richard's death'.[32] Gresham left her children cash legacies in his will and the reversion of his country estates.[33] Sir Henry Neville I, our man's father, was the chief mourner at Gresham's funeral.[34] Our Sir Henry was the eldest son of Gresham's chief mourner; it is difficult to believe that *his* children could not, had they so wished, have influenced Gresham College to appoint the Poet Laureate to a junior, but prestigious, position; they could, of course, have paid him more directly as well. There is no direct evidence for any of this, but the coincidence of date and place is so extraordinary – Ben Jonson was apparently employed at Gresham College for the first and only time just when the preliminaries to the First Folio were apparently being written – that it is simply very difficult to believe there was not more in the appointment than meets the eye. Gresham College was, as well, located about a quarter mile from the Jaggard's printing-house in the Barbican area, where the First Folio was printed.[35]

The sequence of events

Based on this landmark, we can make some plausible surmises about the likely sequence of events. It is quite possible that Neville discussed the posthumous fate of his works with his inner circle of friends during his lifetime, including Fletcher, Beaumont and Jonson, swearing them to keep his identity a secret even after his death. Around 1615 Francis Beaumont wrote a well-known poem 'to Mr B.J.' [Ben Jonson] in which he stated

> *And from all Learning keep these lines as clear*
> *As Shakespeare's best are, which our heirs shall hear*
> *Preachers apt to their auditors to show*
> *How far sometimes a mortal man may go*
> *By dim light of Nature . . .*[36]

Why would 'preachers' be 'apt' to tell their listeners anything about Shakespeare, much less than that he went far 'by dim light of Nature'? And does this not contradict the notion that Stratford Grammar School provided him with all he needed in the way of learning and erudition? Just after this, the same poem asks that its lines be 'as free / As he, whose text was, god made all that is, / I mean to speak: what do you think of his / state, who hath now the last that he could make / in white and Orange tawny on his back / at Windsor?'[37] This could, of course, refer to the recently deceased Neville if the poem was written, as Chambers apparently believes, just after 1615. Neville's coat-of-arms was a white cross on an orange (or 'tawny' in heraldic terminology) ground, so a flag with these arms may well have draped his coffin.[38] In 1621 came Jonson's first remarks, in conversation with William Drummond, during Jonson's visit to Hawthornden in December 1618 to January 1619, that 'Shakespeare wanted art' and had claimed that Bohemia had a sea coast.[39]

In 1621 as well, Sir Richard Worsley, the husband of Frances Neville, Sir Henry's second eldest and apparently favourite daughter, died suddenly. It is possible that it was at this stage that Lady Frances Worsley, probably in conjuncture with her elder brother Henry, her father's son and heir, first toyed with the idea of a collected edition of Neville's works as 'William Shakespeare'. Perhaps they were spurred on by the inadequate Pavier edition. Since Sir Richard and Lady Worsley are known to have inherited some of Sir Henry Neville's crucial books, it is also reasonable to believe that they also held copies of those plays of Neville's which had never been published; this would account for how they mysteriously became available for the First Folio. Possibly earlier, in 1620, they had completed the preliminary task of enlisting the survivors of the King's Company, including Heminge and Condell, probably bringing in Ben Jonson in 1622, paying him directly and securing him a post at Gresham College to supervise the editorial work and write the encomia to William Shakespeare. Jonson's task was certainly to secure forever the legend of William Shakespeare as author, which he did skilfully, although, as has often been pointed out, his poetic tributes to Shakespeare were curiously ambiguous. He famously claimed that Shakespeare 'had[st] small Latin and less Greek', although whoever wrote Shakespeare's works was, unarguably, profoundly learned. (But the line '. . . and though thou hadst small Latin and less Greek' should really be read differently from its present-day meaning. In seventeenth-century English, this could just as well mean '. . . and even if you had have had small Latin and less Greek . . .') Jonson also described him as the 'Sweet Swan of Avon', but native swans in Britain are mute, so this might well be a subtle hint that we are not speaking of a true writer here. The famous portrait of Shakespeare by Droeshout is so absurdly amateurish as to be laughable, as Jonson broadly hinted in his short poem accompanying it. It is difficult to believe that its inclusion was not meant facetiously.

There is, as well, the question of explaining who paid for the First Folio. Ostensibly, its production was headed by John Heminge (1566–1630) and Henry Condell (1576–1627), two of Shakespeare's fellow actors in the King's Company, whom the Stratford man remembered with legacies in his 1616 will. Yet there is no evidence just who provided the enormous sum of money, which necessarily had to be paid in advance, for the production of the First Folio. The price of the First Folio is almost always stated to have been one pound, an astronomical amount at the time, the equivalent of £1,000 or more today.[40] The number of copies actually printed of the First Folio is normally estimated at about 1,000, although another recent estimate is that about 750 copies were printed.[41] In 1909 Alfred W. Pollock stated that the First Folio would not be commercially attractive unless 'something approaching 1,000 copies were sold'.[42] Something over 200 copies of the First Folio survive today.[43] A production of this magnitude – in which sales equivalent to at least £250,000 today were necessary just to break even – certainly required a guarantee of several hundred pounds in advance by a small group of wealthy men or a consortium of publishers whose commitment to the success of the venture rode roughshod over their caution and better judgement. It requires an effort of will to recall that Shakespeare was not the national poet in 1623, and that the great majority of educated persons, those who could afford to spend the equivalent of £1,000 on a single book, would probably never have heard of William Shakespeare. There would at the time have been absolutely no rational reason to suppose that any more than a tiny minority of even the well-educated and affluent would be interested in purchasing a volume with 18 previously unpublished Shakespeare plays. Indeed, there was much snobbery concerning the reading of plays by the 'educated classes'. Thomas Bodley refused to have 'printed plays' in his famous library, the Bodleian, though he would allow manuscript versions, especially if those manuscripts had been written by men associated with the university. (But, of course, 'Shakespeare' was not associated with Oxford.) However, Bodley's personal wishes were overruled by a 1611 agreement between the Bodleian Library itself and the Stationers' Company. The Library agreed to house one copy of every book printed under their watchful eyes, which meant that the Bodleian was automatically sent a copy of the First Folio.[44]

Although the First Folio appeared to sell well, the second edition of the work, the so-called Second Folio, was not printed until 1632, nine years later.[45] A Third Folio was not printed until 1663, although the intervening time of Puritans may have played a part in this.[46] On the other hand, there is no reason to suppose that those with a keen interest in the theatre – who could even remember Shakespeare's early plays, written 30 years before – would have the means to spend a fortune on purchasing the First Folio, any more than bohemian literary enthusiasts would have had the means at any other time. While both Condell and Heminge are said to have been comparatively wealthy, it seems likely that the considerable funds necessary to produce the First Folio came from Neville's own family, with, perhaps, a small group of his wealthy admirers. William Herbert's ancestral home was Wilton House in Wiltshire, so it would not have been difficult for Frances to have had the papers taken over from the Isle of Wight to the mainland by rowing boat and then have them transferred by land for the relatively short journey to Wilton House, had the Earl of Pembroke wished to coordinate things initially from his own home. William Herbert had become a friend and political supporter of Neville, so it would not be surprising if he had taken an active part in the preparation of the manuscripts, especially bearing in mind that his mother was Mary Sidney, who had edited her brother's works and seen them through to publication.

But the dedication of the First Folio to the brothers William Herbert, third Earl of Pembroke (1580–1630) and Philip Herbert, first Earl of Montgomery and fourth Earl of Pembroke (1584–1650) is also curious, if we view Shakespeare as the author. Neither had anything whatever to do with Shakespeare or his Company; the notion that William Shakespeare had been a member of 'Pembroke's Men', a minor playing company of the 1590s, before joining the Chamberlain's Men, is purely speculative, while the patron of this company was the second Earl of Pembroke, the father of the two brothers, who died in 1601. More relevant is the fact that, in 1623, Pembroke was the Chancellor of Oxford University, while his younger brother was a royal favourite and Gentleman of the Bedchamber. Pembroke, as Chancellor of Oxford, was an entirely suitable dedicatee for the works of an eminent product of Merton College, while dedicating the work as well to a royal favourite could do no harm. It seems likely that Ben Jonson, also by then an MA of Oxford, dreamed up the dedication.

The authorship secret

This raises the question of who, besides Neville's family and Ben Jonson, knew the authorship secret. Certainly the facts were known to a small group which must have encompassed Southampton, Sir Francis Bacon, the other writers of the dedicatory verses at the beginning of the First Folio, and the surviving members of the King's Company. Beyond this it is impossible to go, just as it is impossible to know the extent to which men like Southampton and Bacon were involved in its production. The fact that the First Folio contains none of Shakespeare's poetry suggests that Southampton, the dedicatee of the two long poems, and, certainly, of the Sonnets, might well have vetoed their inclusion. The so-called Spanish marriage crisis of February–October 1623, when Prince Charles unsuccessfully visited Spain with the Duke of Buckingham to arrange a marriage with the Catholic Infanta, leading to universal joy in Protestant England, might also conceivably have had a significant effect in determining that the political implications of the plays had at all costs to be deflected.[47] Having decided that Neville could not be named as the actual author, the creators of the First Folio evidently decided to gild the lily by crediting the work to a dead, inconsequential, provincial former actor and property owner, a man without any political profile who had hardly been visible as an individual person during his lifetime, and about whom virtually nothing was known. As was pointed out in the first part of this book, there is no evidence that Shakespeare's surviving family in Stratford was ever approached by the editors of the First Folio to provide materials, and no evidence that they, or anyone else in or near Stratford, actually bought a copy when the work was first published as a tribute to the local genius.

The extent to which the rest of the Stratford evidence – the Latin inscription near Shakespeare's grave, the much-debated bust, and so on – were a deliberate part of this process, is simply unknowable at present. The Latin inscription on Shakespeare's Stratford monument, for example, that compares him to Socrates, Nestor (an elder statesman) and Virgil would be highly appropriate on the tomb of Sir Henry Neville, but by no stretch of the imagination could plausibly be applied to the Stratford man. In what sense, for instance, was William Shakespeare an elder statesman? He never held any office of any kind, and deliberately eschewed all political involvement. As Diana Price has shrewdly noted, there is nothing on the Stratford monument to indicate that Shakespeare was a dramatist.[48]

What, then, remains of William Shakespeare? His dates of birth and death were almost identical to Neville's, which in itself accounts for much of the confusion over the authorship, and the willingness of the majority to believe that a man utterly without the requisite qualifications, of whom virtually nothing whatever of relevance to his alleged career as an author can be traced despite centuries of research, actually wrote the greatest works of the world's literature. Shakespeare was Neville's front man and factotum, in all likelihood the equivalent of the producer-director of his plays on the stage, who was regarded as sufficiently insignificant to be credited with writing his plays after both men were dead, just as Shakespeare's name had been associated with them during his lifetime. No evidence of any kind is known to us that anyone besides Sir Henry Neville (and the known and admitted collaborators in his last plays, like John Fletcher) had any role in writing Shakespeare's works. The seventeenth Earl of Oxford, who died in 1604, could not have written Shakespeare's works, and no plausible evidence exists that he did. Although J. Thomas Looney first proposed the Oxfordian theory in 1920, no one has found any real evidence to support it. The Baconians were much closer to the truth, and Sir Francis Bacon certainly must have known of his kinsman-by-marriage's authorship, although Bacon did not write Shakespeare's works. No evidence of any kind exists that any of the many other authorship candidates, such as Christopher Marlowe, wrote any of Shakespeare's works. In complete contrast, with Sir Henry Neville there is apparently direct evidence and a biography which matches the chronology and evolution of Shakespeare's works at every point.

Indeed – as many readers have doubtless asked themselves – the salient question is why no one has ever thought that Neville might be 'Shakespeare', amidst the dozens of suggested authorship candidates over the past 150 years. There is no clear answer to this. Neville unquestionably had a genius for being seen but not noticed. No one has ever asked why his name is on the Northumberland Manuscript, or what his relationship might have been with Southampton, his fellow-prisoner in the Tower. No one has ever before been struck by the coincidence in the dates of Neville and Shakespeare, or by Neville's involvement in the Essex rebellion as making a plausible turning-point in the evolution of the writings of William Shakespeare. Additional evidence lay unnoticed in remote parts of England. Neville is usually described, inaccurately, as a 'diplomat' and is known to historians chiefly for his parliamentary role under James I. He published no literary works under his own name. He was a 'least likely person' worthy of a great classical detective story, although some of the clues were there to be seen.

Bearing in mind his role in founding the English settlement in America, Sir Henry Neville may be seen as one of the six or eight most influential men in history, who arguably did more than any other individual to lay the foundations of the world-wide hegemony of the English-speaking peoples. For 400 years two of the statements which Neville made about himself in the Sonnets have indeed been valid, both that,

Not marble, nor the gilded monuments
Of princes, shall outlive this powerful Rhyme,

But also that,

Every word almost doth tell my name ...

Justice has belatedly been done at last to this great man and, henceforth, only the first of these will continue to be true.

Chapter 11

Documentary Evidence: Analyses and Shakespearean Parallels

The Tower Notebook

Sir Henry Neville's Notebook of 'Extracts Copied and collected out of the Recordes in the Tower Ann: 1602' has been briefly described here in Chapter 2. Its connections to the play of *Henry VIII* were also summarized. However, there are even more links between Neville and the theme and dramatis personae of that play. These links will of course be more comprehensible now that the story of Sir Henry's life has been told. But the best way to understand the circumstances behind the writing of the play is to review Henry's and the country's situation in the year when the Notebook was written, 1602.

Until Elizabeth died in 1603, not many people bothered to research the records kept in the Tower of London regarding coronation protocols, such as much of the Tower Notebook outlines. Elizabeth had reigned for a long time, so most of the English population had never heard of, let alone witnessed, a coronation. Added to this, Queen Elizabeth herself had passed a law making it illegal for anyone to discuss the succession, so coronation protocols would have been a rather dangerous area of study for a researcher to undertake in 1602, while she was still alive. (Queen Elizabeth died on 24 March, 1603. The old calendar used at the time did not usually change the year until 25 March, meaning that 1603 could only be mentioned *after* that date.) However, it would obviously have been quite impossible for a researcher to have collected the material now in the Tower Notebook, and the annotator to have written his own additions, in the space of one single day. It is therefore certain that this Notebook was compiled well before Queen Elizabeth's death, so there can be no possibility that its compiler undertook the research in order to find protocols for King James I's coronation. Such an action would definitely have lain the compiler open to a charge of treason. As the title to the Notebook proclaims, then, its researcher must have undertaken his task for the purpose of 'pastime'. 'Pastime' means entertainment rather than reality, so on this count too the coronation ceremonies outlined in the Notebook were not described and annotated with a view to a real-life coronation, which is another important factor leading one to suppose the notes could well have been early background sketches for some form of entertainment, such as a play.

In English coronation ceremonies, various Lords were and are allowed their allotted duties from generation to generation – duties that go with the inheritance of their title.[1] The compiler of the Notebook has put these together and then annotated and footnoted the material he has gathered, and it is my contention that Henry Neville was both the compiler and the annotator. To the best of anyone's knowledge, the Tower Notebook has not been attributed to Neville's ownership for centuries, even though it was found together with other manuscripts (also unattributed) which are associated with Sir Henry, his scribe, one of his friends, and his general concerns around this time. It may have missed being attributed to him simply because it was moved far from its former home by Sir Henry's remote nineteenth-century descendants who had little idea of its origins. But once the connection between owner and annotator are revealed, the Notebook becomes a piece in the jigsaw puzzle that finally comes together to reveal the true author of Shakespeare's works. This is because of the parallels between the Notebook sketches and the play of *Henry VIII*, though the sketches are dated as 1602 – 11 years before that play was finally performed.

Neville was imprisoned in the Tower of London itself at the time the Notebook was written. He would have been allowed to pay a researcher to take notes in the library, and it is quite probable that the man who was his scribe and clerk in France – John Packer – undertook this task. Neville had long complained of gout, which affects the hands, so a scribe must have been something of a necessity for him. Dr Geoffrey Parnell, Keeper of Tower History at the Royal Armouries HM Tower of London, asserts that it must have been a rich man (such as was Neville) who undertook the research, since hiring such a researcher and paying for the use of the Tower Library was expensive.[2]

The role of the Cinque Port Barons is stressed both in the Notebook and in the play of *Henry VIII*. Their role in supporting the canopy at English coronations has now been superseded but it certainly existed throughout medieval and early modern times. The official website of the Cinque Ports still records that fact, and they base it on Coronation Rolls kept since ancient times. These Rolls detailed the usual offices that were and often still are traditionally undertaken by those inheriting certain titles.[3] Noblemen sometimes copied them out, so that there are various records of these traditionally appointed roles in several record offices throughout England.[4] During Neville's lifetime, documents written in Old French and detailing these ceremonies were obviously kept in the Tower of London, and it was passages from these that were copied into the Tower Notebook.

By the time James I's coronation was being organized in 1603, many other researchers must also have investigated these records too, as the Coronation Protocols were then discussed among statesmen of the times, as is recorded in the Calendar of State Papers Domestic: James I, 1603–1610 (1857):

> *July 24.*
> *Wesminster.   76. Proceedings before Charles Earl of Nottingham, Grand Seneschal, and the other Commissioners to receive claims for offices at the Coronation. The claims preferred were as follows:–*
> *Edward Earl Oxford, High Chamberlain, to dress the King on the morning of the Coronation. Also to serve him with basin and ewer to wash at dinner. The latter claim was allowed; the former referred ...*
> *... Thomas Lord Burleigh, on behalf of Dorothy, his wife, Sir Thos. Snagg, and William Gostwick, as seised of the Barony of Bedford, to be Almoner; Lord Burleigh admitted.*
> ***Barons of the Cinque Ports to carry the canopy over the King; admitted.***

Dean and Chapter of Westminster to instruct the King in the ceremonies, and
to assist the Archbishop in the service; admitted ...
The following claims were left unexamined, viz.:–
Lord Mayor and Citizens of London, to be Butlers to the King and Queen. Sir
Stephen Soame, as seised of Haydon, in Essex, to hold the basin and ewer ...
Wm. Clopton, as seised of Liston, Essex, to make and serve the wafers.[5]

As can be seen from the extract above, many of the offices described in
these papers are also mentioned in the Annotation page (see p.45) of the
Tower Notebook, with the Cinque Port Barons' bearing of the canopy
being foregrounded.

However, it is nevertheless clear that although the offices described are
identical, the personnel named for these offices differ. (Titles are inherited,
but sometimes through the female line, or else because the family dies out,
causing the monarch to invest a relative with that title. This means that sur-
names can change through the ages, yet the title itself, or its recognized
equivalent, still qualifies its holder to carry out a particular, traditional ceremonial office.) It is therefore obvious that the Annotation page from The
Tower Notebook is not describing James's coronation. As discussed in
Chapter 2, the personnel named are those who were present at the coronation of Anne Boleyn – as in Act IV, Scene I of *Henry VIII*. First, the John,
Lord Latimer mentioned at the beginning of the second section of the
Annotated page (see p.45) was in fact John Neville, third Lord Latimer,
who was a companion of Henry VIII. Then in the third section of the page
there is the phrase 'Wm. Vernon to make the wafers' (p.45). James and
Richard Vernon were gentlemen in waiting to the young Princess Elizabeth,
daughter of Anne Boleyn. Anne Boleyn was already pregnant when Henry
married her, so 'Wm. Vernon' may well have been James's and Richard's
relative. Most probably, they hailed from the Yorkshire Vernons. In 1545,
one William Vernon had a daughter, Joan, who married Henry Savile,
Sheriff of Yorkshire, whose descendant and namesake – Sir Henry Savile of
Merton College, Oxford – became such a firm friend of Sir Henry Neville.
Once again, Neville is naming people with whom he has a family connection – the Nevilles and Saviles, besides being friends, were related through
the Pastons. The Lord Grey who was to be the almoner (see transcription,
p.45) was indeed almoner at Anne Boleyn's wedding.[6] (The man who had
inherited that title in 1603 certainly did not play any role in James's

coronation, as he had been sent to the Tower accused of plotting against the King.)[7]

Neville cleverly chose the theme of Anne Boleyn's (Elizabeth's mother's) coronation, so that it could appear to be a play written in honour of the birth of Elizabeth herself. Perhaps he felt that if he were discovered as being the writer of Elizabeth's most hated play, *Richard II*, then he could show how he was now about to redress the 'wrong' by writing a play in the Queen's praise. Thus *Henry VIII* – with its inclusion of Anne Boleyn's coronation scene – was probably intended to please a Tudor monarch, so who better to praise than that monarch's Tudor father and mother? The play therefore ends with a huge celebration of Elizabeth's birth:

> *This royal infant – heaven still move about her! –*
> *Though in her cradle, yet now promises*
> *Upon this land a thousand thousand blessings,*
> *Which time shall bring to ripeness. She shall be*
> *– But few now living can behold that goodness –*
> *A pattern to all princes living with her,*
> *And all that shall succeed. Saba was never*
> *More covetous of wisdom and fair virtue*
> *Than this pure soul shall be. All princely graces*
> *That mould up such a mighty piece as this is,*
> *With all the virtues that attend the good,*
> *Shall still be doubled on her. Truth shall nurse her,*
> *Holy and heavenly thoughts still counsel her;*
> *She shall be loved and feared; her own shall bless her;*
> *Her foes shake like a field of beaten corn,*
> *And hang their heads with sorrow: good grows with her.*
> *In her days every man shall eat in safety*
> *Under his own vine what he plants, and sing*
> *The merry songs of peace to all his neighbours.*
> *God shall be truly known, and those about her*
> *From her shall read the perfect ways of honour,*
> *And by those claim their greatness, not by blood.*

Act V, Sc. V

Extravagant praise indeed, and not at all like the William Shakespeare of Stratford who never bothered to mark Elizabeth's passing with a tribute of even one small elegy. Neville, confined in the Tower at the time when he was planning this play, would certainly have had a vested interest in writing such flattering phrases while the Queen was still alive, in 1602. However, that interest disappeared after her death. But by the time the play was first performed in 1613, there was another monarch on the throne. Necessary revision would have to take place, and it could well be that this necessary revision dictated there should also be praise for the monarch who followed such a 'paragon of virtue' as Elizabeth. So, at the end of Cranmer's flattering speech in Act V, Scene V of the play, Elizabeth's successor is referred to as 'Star-like': ·

So shall she [Queen Elizabeth] leave her blessedness to one –
When heaven shall call her from this cloud of darkness –
Who from the sacred ashes of her honour
Shall star-like rise, as great in fame as she was,
And so stand fix'd. Peace, plenty, love, truth, terror,
That were the servants to this chosen infant,
Shall then be his, and like a vine grow to him;

Thus, Neville had left himself the possibility of adding those lines, should another monarch be reigning by the time he was released from the Tower. He was then sure to please him or her too with this play. And Neville had concentrated on the same points in his Notebook, as those which were finally used in the play.

As has been demonstrated, therefore, there are pointers on the Notebook page in question which make it possible to state beyond doubt that the annotator's notes are indeed referring to the coronation of Anne Boleyn. But of course, it is also noticeable that a Neville (John Neville, Lord Latimer) is foregrounded here, making it even more likely that these annotations were written by Neville, and that he had originally chosen this member of the Neville 'clan' to feature in this play, in just the same way as he had chosen Nevilles to feature in his former history plays. These include the Earl of Warwick in *2 Henry IV*, and Richard, Earl of Warwick, the Kingmaker, in the *Henry VI* sequence; the Earl of Salisbury, who again featured in more than one of the plays; the Earl of Westmoreland (Ralph de Neville) in *1* and *2 Henry IV*, *3 Henry VI* and *Henry V*; Edward Neville, Earl of Abergavenny (Sir Henry's grandfather) in *Henry VIII*; plus numerous others whose mothers were Nevilles, including Richard III himself. Richard

II married a Neville, and Richard III also married Anne (who was Anne Neville). Joan Beaufort, daughter of John of Gaunt (in *Richard II*) married Ralph de Neville, Earl of Westmoreland. As Sir Henry was also directly descended from the Plantagenet King, Edward III, the Plantagenets were his relatives too, including Henry V himself.

What made Sir Henry change his mind about including John Neville, Lord Latimer, in his play of *Henry VIII* is not altogether clear, for John Neville does not feature in the version of the play that was eventually performed. Perhaps, if Elizabeth did indeed know he was the writer, then there would have been no problem in placing that Neville in the play if it had been performed during her lifetime, as John Neville was a friend of her father. However, as it was performed long after she had died, Neville may have decided to change certain aspects of the play. Instead of Lord Latimer – the friend of Henry VIII – being the 'featured Neville', we have Neville's grandfather, Edward Neville, Earl of Abergavenny, the once friend of King Henry who later led a movement against him and was executed for treason. There would have been less of a problem in mentioning his grandfather's rebellious role against the Tudors, now that a Stuart was on the throne of England.

Perhaps, then, Neville wrote only part of *Henry VIII* during his time in the Tower and then abandoned it when Queen Elizabeth died, only to review it again at a point in his career when it might have been advantageous to him to remind King James of his (Neville's) one-time support of him personally and of his continuing belief in his dynasty's succession, despite the fact that he was opposing many of King James' ideas in Parliament. James was a great believer in the Divine Right of Kings, which made him feel he could rule without Parliament. Henry had spent time opposing this absolutist point of view; but on Robert Cecil's death, Neville started to try and ingratiate himself with the King, hoping that his royal favour might be turned in his (Neville's) direction after all. Neville hoped to gain Cecil's old post, that of Secretary of State, for himself.

Neville had indeed supported James's succession to the throne of England. His 'outward honouring'[8] of James had probably been demonstrated by his carrying of the canopy at his coronation, and this is one feature of the play which did remain from the Tower Notebook early sketch. (James's coronation was a somewhat curtailed affair due to the plague then raging in London,[9] but it nevertheless included the main parts of the ceremony, including the carrying of the canopy, as can be seen from the State records of the time.[10])

The inclusion of the Cinque Port Barons' carrying of the canopy remained firmly in the play we know today. But that tradition has since changed, which is probably why Neville was not associated sooner with the canopy carrying present both in the play and in Sonnet 125. There was such a squabbling amongst the Cinque Port Barons about who should hold the canopy at the coronation of George IV in 1821 that the tradition was abandoned. But it was still in force in James's time. In 1613, when the play was first performed, Neville needed to remind the King of how he had once honoured him. Shakespeare of Stratford could never have been considered for this privilege, so strict are the rules governing those who serve anywhere near royalty, and especially those who bear the canopy.

Neville also appears to have had a copy of Halle's *Chronicles* which he annotated. Many of Halle's details find their way into the play in expanded form, but here, on this Annotation page of the Notebook (transcribed on p.45), we have the product of Neville's own mind, working on ideas originally conceived by Halle's historical accounts of the coronations of Henry VIII and, later, that of Anne Boleyn. It is as if the annotator is fusing together elements in each and at the very beginning of mapping out his new pageant play. The notes found in the Tower Notebook therefore now flesh out the stage directions given in *Henry VIII* itself – directions which are much more explicit than in any of the other plays (not surprisingly, as their writer, Henry Neville, was now in the Tower and so could not pass them on by word of mouth).

Some other annotations in the Tower Notebook also point to Neville being its owner. They hint at astronomical calculations he may have performed to see if the timing of previous coronations and holding of Parliaments was sometimes due to the alignment of certain planets – which is what some of the historical documents he had to hand seemed to suggest. Neville had studied astronomy at university and would have been very interested in such things: 'This I find not trew' he adds proudly, after carrying out his own observations and historical research. The annotator also mentions Grafton's writings on the medieval monarchs – a source long thought to have been used by 'Shake-speare'.[11]

However, if we now take a look at other elements in *Henry VIII* we immediately find details in the play which overlap with Neville's own situation. In Act I, Scene I, Buckingham and Norfolk discuss Henry VIII's glorious appearance in his famous 'Field of the Cloth of Gold' meeting with the King of France. The meeting took place "Twixt Guynes and Arde' – where Neville had been just before returning from France. Buckingham then explains how he was his 'chamber's prisoner' for two years, just as Neville had been:

> BUCKINGHAM. An untimely ague
> Stayed me a prisoner in my chamber, when
> Those suns of glory, those two lights of men,
> Met in the vale of Andren.
> NORFOLK. 'Twixt Guynes and Arde.
> I was then present, saw them salute on horseback,
> Beheld them, when they lighted, how they clung
> In their embracement as they grew together;
> Which had they, what four throned ones could have weighed
> Such a compounded one?
> BUCKINGHAM. All the whole time
> I was my chamber's prisoner.
> NORFOLK. Then you lost
> The view of earthly glory: men might say,
> Till this time, pomp was single, but now married
> To one above itself. Each following day
> Became the next day's master . . .
>
> Act I, Sc. I

The heroic speech from the scaffold is also reserved for the man already marked out in the first scene as our Sir Henry's alter ego, the Duke of Buckingham:

> BUCKINGHAM. All good people,
> You that thus far have come to pity me,
> Hear what I say, and then go home and lose me.
> I have this day received a traitor's judgment,
> And by that name must die; yet, heaven bear witness,
> And if I have a conscience, let it sink me,
> Even as the axe falls, if I be not faithful!
> The law I bear no malice for my death,

'T has done upon the premises but justice;
But those that sought it I could wish more Christians:
Be what they will, I heartily forgive 'em;
Yet let 'em look they glory not in mischief,
Nor build their evils on the graves of great men,
For then my guiltless blood must cry against 'em.
For further life in this world I ne'er hope,
Nor will I sue, although the king have mercies
More than I dare make faults. You few that loved me,
And dare be bold to weep for Buckingham,
His noble friends and fellows, whom to leave
Is only bitter to him, only dying,
Go with me, like good angels, to my end,
And as the long divorce of steel falls on me,
Make of your prayers one sweet sacrifice . . .

Act II, Sc. I

Knowing Neville's own escape from the 'long divorce of steel' after his involvement in the Essex rebellion, this could be the very speech he imagined himself declaiming from the block.

Elsewhere in the Notebook, Neville tries to justify Bolingbroke's usurpation of King Richard II by showing that primary sources themselves stated that a king could be deposed if he seriously mismanaged the country. Once again, Neville was hedging his bets: if he were ever identified as the writer of *Richard II* – the play that Elizabeth thought so seditious; the play that had been performed 40 times on the eve of the Essex rebellion, in the hope of inciting the masses – then he would be able to claim that he had done no more than repeat what was already said in the primary sources. Neville himself had played a role in the Essex rebellion: he was gathering together evidence that might one day save his life.

Consequently, Neville could obviously not state his name openly in the Tower Notebook. But let us look at evidence pointing to his ownership of the Notebook. First, the Notebook emanated from the estate of his own daughter and son-in-law. Secondly, the Tower Notebook was found bundled together with other works also annotated by Neville, and with a letter on a subject about which he had been in correspondence.

But how had all this forgotten ownership come about? Briefly, Neville's second daughter married Sir Richard Worsley of Appuldurcombe House, Isle of Wight (see the Worsley family tree illustrated on p.xxii). After their marriage Neville is known to have visited them frequently. It must have been on one of these visits that he left the Notebook and the other documents with his daughter. Indeed, the letter found with the documents was written at a sensitive point in his career, when he was vying for the position of Secretary of State after Robert Cecil's death, so it would not be surprising if he had left them there in order to hide them. Without careful management, his political career could have come crashing round his ears yet again at this time, and some of these documents had once been officially banned, so he would not have wished them to be found in his possession. Perhaps he also wanted his daughter and son-in-law to give them to their own children, when times changed. He could not possibly have foreseen the tragedy that was to overtake the family: Sir Richard Worsley, his favourite son-in-law, was to die after catching smallpox while visiting sick people on his estate. His little daughter ran to greet him when he returned home from that visit, so she caught smallpox and died too. Sir Henry Neville's daughter, Frances, married again, but her son by her marriage to Sir Richard was not told the secret of the papers because his father died when his son was so young and a new father, Jerome Brett, who had Royalist sympathies, took his place. Frances must have considered it wise on the eve of the Civil War that her son should not know that his grandfather was a Parliamentarian whose secret works gave an insight into the working of the minds of those in power, and went to the heart of the nature of monarchy itself.

Yet one of Sir Henry's grandsons knew about his grandfather's ideas and ideals, even if he perhaps did not know that his grandfather was the true Shakespeare. He was the son of our Sir Henry's eldest son, and was also called Henry Neville. A Parliamentarian, just like his grandfather, he too became a writer, one of his most famous prose works being *Plato Redivivus: A Dialogue concerning Government* ... very much in the style of *Leycester's Commonwealth*. In it, the young Sir Henry tells of his grandfather's struggle to persuade King James I to rule with Parliament and not act like a despot, predicting that, unless James is willing to become a constitutional monarch, civil war will break out yet again, although this time it would not be based on family feuds but on political ideals. Prophetic words indeed, and just what we might expect from the true writer behind those very political history plays attributed to William Shakespeare.

The male line of the Worsleys finally died out in 1805, and the last Worsley niece inherited everything. She married Charles Anderson Pelham, first Baron Yarborough, and took some of her inheritance to her husband's home in Brocklesby Park, Linconshire. It is probable that neither the niece nor her husband knew the origins of the Tower Notebook, nor anything about the other manuscripts bundled together with it, so that they were forgotten, being deposited in the Lincoln Record Office only in the 1950s. In 1855 the Appuldurcombe estate was sold, probably resulting in a further dispersal of documents throughout the world.

Documents discovered together with the Tower Notebook

The most important manuscripts in the Lincolnshire Worsley collection, aside from the Tower Notebook, must be the two copies of *Leycester's Commonwealth*, one of which is written in italic handwriting, the other in Elizabethan secretary script. This work had been banned by Queen Elizabeth because it related the misdeeds of the Earl of Leicester, her favourite and, possibly, her lover. It was published anonymously in 1584 in Antwerp and Paris.

No matter what anyone thought of its contents, it has to be acknowledged that *Leycester's Commonwealth* is well written, and that its style and themes would have interested 'Shake-speare'. It begins by telling how ambitious the Earl of Leicester really was, even including his alleged poisoning and murdering in order to get closer to the Queen. It was already rumoured that he had killed his first wife, Amy Robsart, and known that he generally treated the women in his life pretty badly. After Amy's death, he married the widowed mother of the Earl of Essex, and it was rumoured that he had poisoned her husband in order to marry her. (Shades of *Hamlet*, indeed!) Though young Essex generally found Leicester quite a good stepfather (on the surface), he could never quite overcome the feeling that he may once have fallen victim to one of his alleged poisoning attempts. Indeed, Essex was later to blame his somewhat erratic behaviour on this 'fact'.

The two versions of the *Commonwealth* are written in a dialogue form. Even the poisoning scene in *Hamlet* is precursed in the *Commonwealth*, which also refers to Polydore Vergil's *Chronicles*, yet another source long thought to have been used by 'Shakespeare' and, incidentally, by Halle, whose *Chronicles* were also used by Shakespeare.[12]

Eventually, however, *Leycester's Commonwealth* begins to dwell on the Earl of Leicester's political ambitions: it openly states that he is trying to sow trouble between aristocratic families, hoping once again to begin the dynastic wars (which were the basis of the Wars of the Roses.) Out of all the resultant muddle, the document claims, Leicester could then proclaim himself the new monarch. The writer of the *Commonwealth* also says that old Sir Henry Neville senior – our man's father – saw through Leicester's plans.

This same writer then proceeds to document the Wars of the Roses, portraying the Neville family strongly and, usually, sympathetically. Within these two copies[13] found in the Lincolnshire Record Office (see Plate 13), the name Neville is emboldened every time it appears, which is itself suggestive of a Neville having owned them. But the chief object of Shakespearean interest in these manuscripts lies, once again, in the annotations. Within the margins of the book, at many points in its history of the Wars, there are annotated remarks commenting upon the very incidents used in the history plays attributed to William Shakespeare. Even the occasional remark such as 'ambition' and 'cruelty' is suggestive of the annotator summing up a personality. Altogether, it seems probable that the annotator is planning the characterization of the personalities on whom he is commenting. And the annotator – who emboldens his own name every time it appears – was probably the owner of this copy of the *Commonwealth*.

The evidence leading towards the supposition that Sir Henry Neville owned the copy is, admittedly, circumstantial, but when these circumstances are added together they produce a great total weight. The main circumstances can be listed:

- The name *Neville* is emboldened throughout one of the copies.
- These papers are known as 'The Worsley Papers' and they were all in the possession of the descendants of Sir Henry Neville's daughter, Lady Frances Worsley.
- They were discovered as a direct result of specifically searching for any possible unknown remnant of Sir Henry's papers.
- They tie in with Sir Henry's known political and aristocratic interests.

- There is a *Treatise on the Royal Mint*[14] by Sir Richard Martin – a friend of Sir Henry Neville. It was bundled together with the Tower Notebook and the two copies of *Leycester's Commonwealth*. This Treatise was written out by one of Sir Henry Neville's main scribes – John Packer, who had also been his scribe in France,[15] so it seems as if he loaned him to his friend, Richard Martin, and then received a free copy of Martin's treatise in return.

- Besides being Neville's secretary and scribe, Packer was also a great friend of Sir Richard Worsley, Frances Neville's husband.[16]

- Packer eventually became a secretary and scribe for a number of King James's favourites,[17] so in all likelihood he was a trustworthy and careful workman. This being the case, he probably carefully catalogued, filed and archived his masters' papers. As he was a friend of Sir Richard Worsley, and as the Worsley Papers included a treatise written out by him, it is highly probable that Packer passed on any archived notebooks, letters, etc., in his possession after Sir Henry's death to the members of Sir Henry's family whom he knew best – i.e. his friends, Sir Richard and Lady Frances Worsley.

- If this was the case, it may even have been Packer who passed on the Tower Notebook to the Worsleys too.

- A copy of *Leycester's Commonwealth* is mentioned on the Northumberland Manuscript, but this book was never found along with some of the works mentioned on this paper too. Neville's name heads the Northumberland Manuscript (as briefly described in Chapter 2 and detailed later in this chapter) so it is logical to assume that he was the owner of the books listed on that page. It may well be, therefore, that the copies of the *Commonwealth* which finally came into the possession of his daughter were the ones mentioned on the Northumberland Manuscript itself.

It may also be significant that William Herbert, the Earl of Pembroke – patron of the First Folio of Shakespeare's Works in 1623 – was seen defending Packer's interests, at a time when Packer seemed to be still a frequent visitor on the Isle of Wight.[18] In fact, there are more extant letters from Pembroke to the Lord Lieutenant of the Isle of Wight than from that same Earl to any other single venue. Oglander mentions Sir Richard Worsley's and his own friendship with that Earl, and one or two of the letters from Pembroke mention Lady Worsley and/or her new husband, Colonel Jeremy [or Jerome] Brett.

The annotations in *Leycester's Commonwealth* are so closely allied with the subjects dealt with in the history plays themselves that they recall another incident in which a famous annotator was discovered. This topic has again been touched on in Chapter 2, but there are some extra incidents which may also be quite telling. As mentioned, there is a book actually entitled *The Annotator,* which was published in 1954. The writer, Alan Keen, was an antiquarian book dealer who bought a copy of Halle's *Chronicles* at an auction in York. The book had been rebound in the eighteenth or nineteenth centuries but turned out to be an early sixteenth-century imprint. It was annotated, and the annotations bore such a close relationship to the concerns within Shakespeare's history plays that Keen reasoned Shakespeare might have been the annotator. However, try as he would to trace its origins, he did not find any tangible connection between Shakespeare and the *Chronicles*, mainly – as we can see now – hampered by two misconceptions: 1) that the book had originally been housed in the north of England and 2) that it had once been in the possession of Shakespeare of Stratford.

True, the book had once been owned by a northern gentleman named Newport, whose daughter had been a patroness of the arts, and especially of John Donne, but Keen never could discover a connection between Donne and the Stratford man or, indeed, between the Stratford man and any intellectual. (However, the Duke of Rutland possesses a document inviting his ancestors to a party at which Sir Henry Neville, John Donne and Inigo Jones will be present and jointly entertain,[19] so there is a documented connection between John Donne and Sir Henry Neville.)

Keen frankly admitted that all his leads had come to a dead end. Then, one day, another antiquarian bookseller pointed out that he too had bought a book very like Keen's, which also had a similar 'library mark' inside. Keen's book bore the letters Eed, while his friend's bore those of App, together with the name, Robert Worsley.

Now on a quest to discover the identity of Robert Worsley, Keen found a family of that name in Lancashire, but was again unable to discover a direct connection with Shakespeare. However, as can be seen from our own work, the Robert Worsley in question happens to have lived many miles south of that county; in fact he was the grandson of Neville's son-in-law, Sir Richard Worsley, who lived at Appuldurcombe House on the Isle of Wight (hence the App of the library mark.)

It seems, then, that Keen's copy of Halle's *Chronicles* may eventually have been passed up to the Earl of Yarborough, who had taken over everything that belonged to his wife, the nineteenth-century heiress of the Isle of Wight Worsleys, when the male line died out. It was beginning to look very much as if a later Earl of Yarborough may have cleared out and auctioned some of his possessions, not realizing their importance. It was looking as if Keen's and his friend's books began their itinerant life by being sold off along with the rest of the Appuldurcombe estate in 1855.

But was the former Earl of Yarborough so careless? Or is there perhaps another explanation for Keen's book being separated from its companion documents, and so not being formally catalogued by the Earl or his descendants? The man who helped the Earl of Yarborough to catalogue the Appuldurcombe collection in 1834 was a William Allason, who had a bookshop in New Bond Street, London. He was something of a specialist publisher, having Gibbon's *Decline and Fall of the Roman Empire* reprinted, and covering the volumes in calf and cardboard, with inside marbled end papers – just the same as appears in both Keen's discovery and in the Lincolnshire Record Office Worsley collection. Did Allason perhaps borrow the Appledurcombe book of Halle's *Chronicles* in order to copy out its text and so have it reprinted? There was at one time a slight suggestion of this, but more research now needs to be carried out in order to verify whether Allason did in fact bring out a new edition of the *Chronicles*. What is definitely known is that C.J. Stewart, Allason's assistant, who had a bookshop in the Strand, spent much of his time in Yorkshire, cataloguing books for Mary Curer Bell, friend and neighbour of the Brontës.

Keen had even consulted a handwriting expert who had found three different forms among the handwriting in the annotations of Halle's *Chronicles,* and yet the specialist still considered they were from the same, single hand. The expert supposed that this might be because they were written by a very young man who had not yet settled on a style, but this diagnosis does not tie in with the obvious semantic maturity of the annotator's remarks. No, one answer to this particular puzzle could be Neville's love of continually varying his writing styles, and of using scribes. There are documents scribbled by Neville, with scrawl and abbreviations which look very like the scribbled sections of the Northumberland Manuscript (an analysis of which follows later in this chapter). Even in some of his later papers and notes, Neville changes from one style to another. He was trained for the diplomatic service and both he and his father had appeared in disguise abroad; so if one is going to disguise in every aspect of one's life, then why exclude disguising one's handwriting? And to be able to do that effectively, it is surely necessary to keep in practice.

So, altogether, the rebound, annotated books and notes, and Keen's annotated book, were probably all originally deposited as one whole collection with the true author's daughter and son-in-law. When the son-in-law's family estate was abandoned, nearly 200 years later, the books were moved to their new home in Lincolnshire. Now, with their origins unrecognized, only Henry's notes and annotations remained to give the game away. Finally confirming Neville's own wish to remain a secret writer during his lifetime, he emboldens the word 'all' in 'Lye in **all,** then' – an annotation he makes in the margin of the Tower Notebook – after discovering that a law passed in Elizabeth's reign gave the Archbishop of Canterbury the right to vet all books, including plays.[20] Knowing that the 1602 Archbishop avidly pursued this right[21] – and even more avidly set out to find the true author of an anonymous work – Henry obviously decided he must continue to use a pseudonym. This same Archbishop had also been greatly disturbed by the Essex rebellion, so any work attributed to Neville (Essex's choice for the leader of Parliament under his new regime) would find itself automatically banned by him. Now that the documents' true origins have again come to light they can at last illuminate the Shakespeare enigma and disguise.

One candidate for the authorship of *Leycester's Commonwealth* was Charles Paget – a spy working in Walsingham's service. (Another author sometimes mentioned is Robert Parsons – a Catholic priest who sometimes wrote under the pseudonym of Dolman, but he is a less likely candidate, as the writer of the *Commonwealth* is concerned about the danger and disrepute the Earl of Leicester is bringing on the Queen. Paget always professed to be a moderate Catholic and loyal to Elizabeth, whereas Parsons was a hard-liner who wished to replace Elizabeth by a Catholic monarch.)

Many connections between Paget and Henry Neville existed even before they met again in France, including the fact that they were together in Scotland in 1583, one year before *Leycester's Commonwealth* was written. And the connection between Paget and Neville turns out to be important from many points of view, while the connection between Neville and Scotland is a crucial pointer to his authorship of the plays of Shakespeare. Scotland was at this time a foreign country. Few Englishmen travelled there, and even then they were usually on official business. Anyone visiting the country had to have a passport. William Shakespeare is never known to have possessed a passport and is thought never to have travelled abroad. Yet there most certainly exists a connection between Scotland and the plays. The whole theme of *A Midsummer Night's Dream* is more Scottish than English: there was a strong Scandinavian influence in Scotland, and it is the Scandinavians and (in past years) the Scots who celebrated the pagan midsummer most extravagantly. Documentary proof exists to testify that Neville was in Scotland before this play was written. The same document also talks of Neville as 'book-learned'.

The document that proves all this was written by one Richard Eed (or Eedes) – the very word written inside the book Alan Keen bought. Eedes was Neville's fellow Oxford scholar who wrote a Latin epic poem, *Iter Boreale*, in which he spoke of Neville returning from Scotland in company with the Ambassador to Scotland, Sir Francis Walsingham (Elizabeth's spymaster) and the Earl of Essex:

> *Ut dominum Walsinghamum comitentur in urbem.*
> *Hic ut praeriperet reverendus episcopus omnem*
> *Gratiam, in Aurora clam se subduxerat, inque*
> *Finibus extremis, pluvialibus obvius Austris . . .*
> *Accedunt istis, queis purpura fulget et aurum*
> *Mildmaius, doctusque libros tractare Nevillus*

> *So he was the earlier to meet Walsingham, though our group was much more welcome in his sight . . . Our number was great, but that of those who composed the Lord Ambassador's [of Scotland] retinue was even greater. Foremost among them was the Earl of Essex, then the two Wardens of the border country, Lord Scrope and fierce Foster . . . Joined to them were others in resplendent purple and gold, Mildmay, Neville, distinguished for his book-learning*[22]

The year that this happened was 1583 – the year in which Neville returned from his continental tour, and also the year before *Leycester's Commonwealth* was published. The man who wrote the epic poem mentioning Neville returning from Scotland was Richard Eedes. Mere coincidence does not usually stretch this far: Eedes varied his name just like other writers of the time, one version therefore being Eed – the very letters found on the front page of Keen's copy of Halle's *Chronicles*.

But who was Richard Eedes? Why should he and Neville have struck up such an acquaintance that Richard would possibly give him his copy of Halle's *Chronicles* and also mention him in his poem? To begin with, both were tutees and friends of Henry Savile who, though older than Neville, remained his life-long friend. They sometimes researched and worked together, and Savile became an executor of Neville's will. It is thus quite likely that Neville and Eedes shared common interests. Eedes and another Oxford writer, Gager, are mentioned by Francis Meres – an Oxford man himself – in 1598. Until we see Neville as the true 'Shakespeare' it is indeed difficult to explain how the Stratford man ever gained a mention in *Palladis Tamia*, that 1598 work by Meres, who otherwise mentions only Oxford and Cambridge men, including Edward De Vere, the Earl of Oxford:

> *These are our best for Tragedie, the Lorde Bukhurst, Doctor Leg of Cambridge, Doctor Edes of Oxforde ...*
>
> *The best for Comedy amongst us bee, Edward Earle of Oxforde, Doctor Gager of Oxforde, Maister Rowley once a rare Scholler of learned Pembroke Hall in Cambridge, Maister Edwardes one of her Maiesties Chappell, eloquent and wittie John Lilly, Lodge, Gascoyne, Greene, Shakespeare, Thomas Nash, Thomas Heywood ...*

A product of the Westminster School, Eedes matriculated from Christ Church in 1571. He was a distinguished academic who was appointed Canon of the fourth stall of Christ Church in 1586. In the same year he was made Chaplain to Queen Elizabeth and created Doctor of Divinity in 1589. He died in 1604. Earlier that same year, he had been numbered among the Oxford group who were appointed to prepare the King James version of the Bible, under Savile's leadership. Eedes was a playwright as well as an author of occasional verse. On the strength of his lost play *Caesar Interfectus*, Meres included him in his list of 'our best for Tragedie' in that same *Palladis Tamia*. His *Caesar* seems to have been staged on the same occasion as the first performance of William Gager's *Meleager*, in 1582, and Gager was also from Oxford and also mentioned in Meres's work. The pity is that only the epilogue of the play survives – such a relatively early example would have been of great interest for the development of the Elizabethan history play, and has even been suggested to have been a source for 'Shakespeare's' *Julius Caesar*. It therefore makes great sense to see Neville mentioned alongside these writers (under his pseudonym of 'Shakespeare'). Eedes is careful to say that Neville was renowned for his 'book-learning'. It is unthinkable that one given this epithet at such a young age should have left no published written works.

The Northumberland Manuscript

The Northumberland Manuscript is known among Shakespeare scholars, but its true meaning and place in the jigsaw of the writer's life has been overlooked. Of course, it is far easier to speak with hindsight: the discovery of Neville as the real Shakespeare has permitted a totally fresh perspective on the Northumberland Manuscript, for Henry Neville's name stands at the top left-hand corner of that very document. In fact, the only reason his name's presence there has either been missed or given only a passing reference is because far more famous names appear in the manuscript. These famous names have, therefore, relegated Neville to a back seat – which is precisely the position in history he has occupied for far too long. However, scholarly researchers can be forgiven – there is no doubt that Neville himself engineered his own shadowy existence:

> *Lye in **all**, then*
>
> *Annotation found in the Tower Notebook*

The following passages from Shakespeare's Sonnets appear, with hindsight, to confirm the true writer's wish to hide his identity:

> *Your name from hence immortal life shall have,*
> *Though I, once gone, to all the world must die;*
>
> *Sonnet 81*

> *Among a number one is reckoned none.*
> *Then in the number let me pass untold,*
>
> *Sonnet 136*

> *Do not so much as my poor name rehearse;*
> *But let your love even with my life decay.*
> *Lest the wise world should look into your moan,*
> *And mock you with me after I am gone.*
>
> *Sonnet 71*

O lest the world should task you to recite,
What merit lived in me that you should love
After my death (dear love) forget me quite,
For you in me can nothing worthy prove.
Unless you would devise some virtuous lie,
To do more for me than mine own desert,
And hang more praise upon deceased I,
Than niggard truth would willingly impart:
O lest your true love may seem false in this,
That you for love speak well of me untrue,
My name be buried where my body is,
And live no more to shame nor me, nor you.

Sonnet 72

(It is a sad fact that Neville was drained, depressed and disappointed towards the end of his life, which makes the above lines even more poignant.)

So now the Northumberland Manuscript can be re-examined in the light of the newly discovered identification of Henry Neville, the man whose name appears prominently on it, but who did not intend his name to be remembered. The document was, after all, meant for private use, not for public display. The so-called 'Northumberland Manuscript' is merely a scrap of torn paper that seems to be part of the cover of a folder used to hold or catalogue some sixteenth-century literary works. It was discovered in the London home of an Earl of Northumberland in 1846, and the fact that it contains the names of sixteenth-century writers and includes titles of works makes it an intriguing rarity. During Neville's lifetime, the Earl of Norhumberland was a friend of Charles Paget, the possible author of *Leycester's Commonwealth,* who is known to have stayed at his home in Sussex and then accompanied his two sons to France. So at last there is an explanation of how this Northumberland Manuscript came into the possession of the descendants of that Earl: Neville and Paget were probably lending books to each other, and perhaps even working on the Wars of the Roses research together. *Leycester's Commonwealth* is actually referred to in the Northumberland Manuscript, yet a copy of it was not included inside the package that this scrappy cover wrapped. It is probable, therefore, that Neville's copy of the *Commonwealth*, which was omitted, was one of those that has turned up in the possession of the Earls of Yarborough, and now lies in the Lincolnshire Record Office.

The Northumberland Manuscript, therefore, seems to be a mixture of a list of books and a scribble pad. Besides Henry Neville, Francis Bacon is prominently mentioned in the manuscript, and the words 'William Shakespeare' have been scribbled several times at its foot.

This latter scribbling has been the cause of all the controversy. Was someone practising Shakespeare's signature? Is there a known writer mentioned on the page who has just begun to invent a pseudonym? In whose handwriting is the sheet composed? These are questions asked frequently by those examining the document. To modern eyes, the most famous name on the paper is that of Francis Bacon, so it has been in his direction that much scholarly attention has been turned.

No researcher till now seems to have bothered to investigate the less famous name in the top left-hand corner – Sir Henry Neville's – even though it appears at the head of the manuscript, and is accompanied by a poem and his family motto. If this were not enough proof that the manuscript were his, there is the added fact that Sir Henry's particular life and outlook coincide with the themes of Shakespeare's plays in a way which Bacon's do not. With this new identity there is even an explanation for the sudden change from comedy to dark tragedy in the plays of Shakespeare at around 1600–01, a factor missing from the life of every other authorship candidate. Here, therefore, with the Northumberland Manuscript, is a parallel case to that of Poe's 'Purloined Letter': a piece of evidence that has been staring us in the face for centuries yet whose true significance has been overlooked.

So Neville's name is at the head of the manuscript – and Neville's various styles of handwriting, even down to the strange, shorthand scribble seen among some of his known papers, is as varied as that found all over the Northumberland document. (Educated men used different styles of handwriting for different purposes during this era. The 'secretary hand' is the quick form of writing seen in Plates 10–11, while the italic hand was becoming favoured for important, public documents in which the writer did not wish his meaning to be mistaken. Add to this the fact that most wealthy men also called upon the services of more than one scribe, and handwriting becomes a somewhat unreliable point of evidence for authorship at this time. Circumstantial, contextual, derivational and chronological factors are far more persuasive.) But throughout the manuscript, the names of 'ffrauncis Bacon', Spenser, Marlowe, Peele, Nashe, Greene and Jonson are separately mentioned. They obviously refer to the works by these authors which Neville had in his collection. Then there is a scribbled variation of line 1,086 from Shakespeare's early poem, *Lucrece:*

revealing
day through
every cranny
peepes and
see
Shak

the only difference is that the word 'spies' used in the original poem is replaced by 'peepes' in the manuscript; and, obviously, 'Shak' is added at the end. The name Shakespeare in full, and 'William Shakespeare', together with abbreviations such as S, Wlm, Sh and Mr. also occur frequently. Other suggestive jottings have tended to make researchers associate the document with Francis Bacon; for instance, the words 'Anthony all comfort and con-sorte' are said to appear, according to the nineteenth-century transcriber. However, on looking at the original document itself, the word is not 'Anthony' but 'Anthem'. There was an Elizabethan church anthem, 'All comfort and consort'. Once again, nineteenth-century secondary sources have confused the issue.

The strange word 'Honorificabilitudine' also appears on the manuscript. 'Honorificabilitudinitatibus' is a word that appears in *Love's Labour's Lost*. This same word appears around a medieval goblet owned by the family of Woodforde from Leicestershire, while the name 'John Woodforde' appears at the end of a letter at the back of one of the copies of *Leycester's Commonwealth*. In that latter document, the name Woodforde is also fol-lowed by scribblings very similar to those which appear at the head of the Northumberland Manuscript. The Woodfordes and the Nevilles had inter-married. Clearly, connections leading back to Sir Henry Neville are present in all these documents, even if we do not yet know the exact feelings of kinship and friendship that drew Sir Henry to use all these associations in his secret works.

The date when the manuscript was written is not certain. Yet the evi-dence given by the listing of known works of the time suggests that it is not

later than the reign of Elizabeth I, i.e. before 1603. In fact, the whole manuscript appears to contain a list of works once kept in a box or on a
particular shelf of a library, and if this is indeed partly a list of contents it
shows that it held a copy of Bacon's *Essays*. The first edition of these
appeared in 1597, but they were circulated in manuscript several years
earlier. Sir Francis, in his 'Epistle Dedicatorie' to the first edition, dated 30
January 1597, says

> ... *I helde it best discreation to publish them my selfe as they passed long agoe
> from my pen.*

Even Sir Francis' own words here are somewhat ambiguous: does he mean
that he did not want anyone else publishing them because he wrote them a
long time ago? Perhaps, but another interpretation would surely be that
someone else completed or edited the essays for him, but that someone
wanted them 'discreetly' published under Francis' name only, rather than
taken to a publisher who would have asked questions about their authorship. As Neville's stepmother was Francis Bacon's half-sister, it is easy to see
how he would have obtained early access to these essays.

The plays of *Rychard II* and *Rychard III* are also included in the list of
contents. These were first printed in 1597 too, and sold at sixpence each,
though the true writer would obviously have known the work earlier than
that. It seems, therefore, reasonable to conclude that the Northumberland
Manuscript was written not later than January 1597. Other works written
before this date are also listed: the Earl of Sussex's speech, spoken in 1596,
and the Letter of Sir Philip Sydney to Queen Elizabeth, written about 1580.
The stinging political pamphlet, *Leycester's Commonwealth*, also listed on the
Northumberland Manuscript, was printed secretly on the Continent (in
Antwerp and Paris) in 1584.

The whole of the Northumberland Manuscript is written and over-
written. It consists of several different styles of handwriting, and of quite a
lot of barely decipherable scribblings. It seems to have become something of
a jotting pad, as some of the words and phrases appear upside down. Several
handwriting experts have attempted to identify the hand used, but all say
they cannot come to any very satisfactory conclusion. Several have said that
it bears a resemblance to the poet Sir John Davies' hand. In fact Sir John
Davies wrote a poem about Sir Henry Neville. And Davies', Neville's and
Bacon's secretary script (the quick handwriting of the day) bear a striking

resemblance to each other. In the case of Bacon and Neville, it is even poss-ible that they had the same early tutor, being related and also close in age.

No one has ever before claimed to discover handwriting that matches the 'scribblings', however, but there are examples of 'quick note-taking' among Neville's writings which resemble the Northumberland's 'cryptic script'.[23] Sir Henry delighted in using several different handwriting styles, which was quite common at the time.

But all of the above was written further down the manuscript than that which logically announces its ownership – the name and rhyme written at the top left-hand corner. Convention dictates that this is where we should begin our reading. Neville's signature is at the very top left, thus announcing its origins, followed by the rhyme incorporating his family motto (Ne vile velis):

> *Nevill, Nevill, Ne vile velis*
> *Multis annis iam transactis*
> *Nulla fides est in pactis*
> *Mell in ore Verba lactis*
> *ffell in Corde ffraus in factis*

Roughly translated, this means 'Nevill, Nevill, no vile intentions, / Many years have I transacted, / No faith in the agreement, / Honey in mouth and milky words, / Cunning in heart and false in practice.' (Hardly the con-tented courtier, our Henry. Hardly the sentiments of someone who has nothing to complain about, or nothing to hide!)

The fact that Neville was a special friend of Robert Sidney, younger brother of Sir Phillip, whose letter and other connections, e.g. 'Phillip against Monsieur', are mentioned in the Northumberland document, rein-forces the inference that the Northumberland Manuscript is Neville's document. It follows that it was therefore he who was practising Shakespeare's signature. But the very quotation from *Lucrece* hints at the fear of discovery: 'Revealing day through every cranny peepes / and see Shak' (as the lines appear on the Manuscript). The original stanza from *Lucrece* that inspired the quotation reads:

> *Revealing day through every cranny spies,*
> *And seems to point her out where she sits weeping;*
> *To whom she sobbing speaks: 'O eye of eyes,*

Why pry'st thou through my window? Leave thy peeping;
Mock with thy tickling beams eyes that are sleeping;
Brand not my forehead with thy piercing light,
For day hath nought to do what's done by night.'

Other documentary evidence

At this point we can see unmistakable, documentary links between Shakespeare, Neville and the fear of discovery. A more complete picture of what is probably happening is thus revealing itself. Neville has a known, 'daytime' role in Court and Parliament, but by 'night' he writes, secretly.

A letter found in Lambeth Palace goes quite a long way towards confirming this theory. Known as the Tenison Manuscript, it is written by one Rodolphe Bradley to Anthony Bacon:

> *Your gracious speeches be the words of a faithfull friende, and not of a courtiour*
> *who hath Mel in ore et verba lactis, sed fel in corde et fraus in factis.*

Neville was known to be a good friend of Anthony Bacon. Besides being related to him through his stepmother, Neville took pains to visit him in France and also would have worked with him in the service of their mutual commander, the Earl of Essex, because that Earl organized a group of his closest followers in the running of a kind of semi-official intelligence service. (This was a role Essex undertook after the death of his father-in-law, Sir Francis Walsingham – the man known as Elizabeth's spy master.) Some researchers have tried to suggest that Bradley (quoted above) was here referring to Francis Bacon as being the writer of Anthony's speeches, but this does not accord with the semantics of the letter: if Bradley had been referring to Francis he would have called him Anthony's brother, not his friend. Added to this, there is of course the overwhelming evidence of the quotation from Neville's own family-motto poem, in that same letter. After looking closely even into his *known* life, Neville emerges as a respected orator who also assisted others with their writing, but who was constantly admonishing everyone to keep his opinions and sympathies secret. In one of his letters to the Earl of Southampton, he says that 'every man who knows me well' knows that he has devoted his life to that Earl's service; but they certainly did have to know him well to have knowledge of this fact. He certainly did not wish 'revealing day' to spy upon him.

One may therefore conclude that his 'service' to the Earl consisted of writing, as he indeed states obliquely in a letter to Southampton.[24] Rudolph Bradley was probably someone who knew or suspected Henry's secret hand at work in more than one document. He hints at Neville's loyalty in friendship; and in so many letters Neville will often tell his addressee that he loves him. Neville celebrated friendship, definitely seeing it as kin to love, which echoes the loyalty and friendship expressed in the Sonnets.

All this now begs the question as to whether there existed also a close friendship between Sir Henry Neville and Sir Francis Bacon. Neville was careful not to leave many 'crannies' through which others could 'peep' at his personal life, so the precise relationship between him and Francis is difficult to pinpoint. But there are surrounding facts that enable the researcher to speculate on something approaching a firm basis. Neville's stepmother would surely have introduced her stepson to her half-brother. The young Henry and Francis were roughly the same age – around 12 years old when Sir Henry senior married Elizabeth Doyley, née Bacon. Yet there appear to be no letters or record of a friendship between Francis Bacon and Henry Neville on a personal basis, and Neville in later years belonged to the Mitre Club and found his friends there, whereas this was far too radical a society for Bacon. However, parliamentary records of the time show that they were often present in the Lower House together, and in the early days they would have been mutual friends of the Earl of Essex. It was during these early days that the *Comedy of Errors* was written and, as discussed in Chapter 4, it seems likely there was a connection between the writings of Francis and Henry on this occasion, just as the Northumberland Manuscript appears to suggest.

The only way we know that our Sir Henry got along well with Anthony Bacon – Francis' elder brother – is that Anthony made arrangements to see Neville and his group while they were touring the Continent. Certainly, though, after the death of his father, Henry Neville had some acrimonious correspondence with his stepmother concerning their inheritance of his father's land. It therefore seems that the situation between him and the Bacons was only truly comfortable when it came to his friendship with Anthony.

However, Sir Francis and Sir Henry shared scientific and business interests, so it is likely that they shared an 'intellectual companionship'. They also were both adherents of the Earl of Essex, in the early days, and both involved with learning the diplomatic codes and ciphers that Earl needed when he took over from Walsingham as the main manager of 'international intelligencers' (i.e. 'spies'). But in the end they must have split irrevocably over the Essex rebellion: Sir Francis utterly deserted Essex, his patron, and it was through his compilation of evidence that Essex was finally condemned to death. Neville, however, demonstrated that he lived on a different emotional plane from Bacon. He followed Essex to the bitter end; and this was typical of the warm Henry. Whenever contemporaries wrote of Sir Henry, they spoke of him as 'that noble knight' and were constantly sending him their 'love' and the love of his friends. When they spoke of Sir Francis, they spoke with respect; they were in awe of his intellect, but not so many truly liked him as a man.

Neville was characterized by a warmth of nature and depth of feeling, coupled with a tremendous intellectual concept of politics and state affairs. Through his care for all classes of men, coupled with his firmly rooted scholarship, Neville gained a popular parliamentary following that Francis never achieved. When it came to politics, Francis was something of an absolute monarchist, with little feeling for those who did not agree. Sir Henry, on the other hand, was a progressive thinker. Again, during the reign of King James I, he and Francis worked together on many parliamentary committees, but the personal advice they sent to the King was directly opposite to each other, Francis advising the King to be firm with all those who opposed him, while Henry told James he should take up a position of negotiation, suggesting some definite political strategies. From all this, therefore, it is probable that they attempted to work together in the early days, when their families were connected by marriage, and that a friendship continued between Sir Henry and Anthony Bacon. (Anthony simply disappeared after Essex's downfall. He, like Henry, had stayed loyal to the Earl, so his disappearance was probably necessary for his survival.) However, because of the dangerous times, it is probable that most of any correspondence between Anthony Bacon and the Nevilles has been well hidden or else destroyed.

Altogether, Neville's warmth combined with intellectuality are qualities found in the plays. That some of the philosophy within the plays sometimes suggests a Baconian point of view is not surprising, given the intellectual interests and kinship Francis and Neville shared. But it is overwhelmingly Neville's ancestry, feelings and interests that are found within the works of 'Shakespeare'. Bacon and the other contenders may, of course, also have made a direct or indirect contribution to the plays, and thanks and respect are due to all those who have, through following their own line of research, kept the authorship debate alive. It is indeed the efforts of the Baconians, Marlovians and Oxfordians in their ongoing research which have uncovered manuscripts that also relate to Neville. Indeed, Neville's circle included most of these men. 'Sir Henry Neville reconciles all' his friend John Chamberlain was to write of him, and this is now shown to have been as true of his secret writing as it was in every other area of his life.

There now remains another small piece of evidence which, for all its sketchiness, finds an echo elsewhere in this work. The historian Neil Cuddy discovered a letter from Henry Howard, Earl of Northampton, referring to 'Harry Neville' as the Earl of Southampton's 'Dear Damon'.[25] The Earl appeared to be referring to the play *Damon and Pythias* by Richard Edwards, and this fact is significant from several points of view. Damon and Pythias were two friends who had become the subject of an earlier play. They were ancient Greeks who were followers of Pythagoras and also promoted the art of the theatre. They remained friends despite political and other forces attempting to separate them. Straight away this gives us the multiple links we would expect from discovering Neville as Shakespeare: friendship is the greatest theme in the Sonnets, and now we know that Neville was a personal friend of the Earl of Southampton (long supposed as one of the addressees in the Sonnets) and that they were both interested in popularizing the theatre amongst the upper classes, otherwise it would be difficult to explain why the Earl chose this particular pet name for him.

But finally, many seekers after Shakespeare have been conditioned for at least a century to expect that the true author would somewhere embed his true name in his works. Elizabethans always loved acrostics and anagrams, so where is Neville's name? Unfortunately, such theories of encoding were brought into disrepute by the ridiculous lengths to which some researchers took their ideas, claiming that almost every line 'Shakespeare' wrote was a code. However, there is no denying the Elizabethan penchant for the occasional conundrum, though they were much more subtle about it than some 'theorists' have maintained. There are indeed many possible encodings of 'Neville' in the works, with its variations of Nevil, Nevill and Nevel – all of which were used by his family and others – but it is of course hard to say whether all these were intentional, since his name contains phonemes (i.e. sound syllables) common in other words too. But, even taking all this into account, it has been mentioned by such scholars as Katherine Duncan-Jones, among many others, that there is some strange wording in Sonnet

121, with much stress upon the words 'vile' and 'evil', with their similar phonemes in 'level' and 'bevel':

> *'Tis better to be **vile** than **vile** esteem'd,*
> *When not to be receives reproach of being,*
> *And the just pleasure lost, which is so deem'd*
> *Not by our feeling, but by others' seeing.*
> *For why should others' false adulterate eyes*
> *Give salutation to my sportive blood?*
> *Or on my frailties why are frailer spies,*
> *Which in their wills count bad what I think good?*
> *No, I am that I am; and they that **level***
> *At my abuses, reckon up their own:*
> *I may be straight, though they themselves be **bevel**;*
> *By their rank thoughts my deeds must not be shown;*
> > *Unless this general **evil** they maintain, –*
> > *All men are bad, and in their badness reign.*

In this angry sonnet, with such repeated 'evil' phonemes, we may indeed be meant to perceive Neville's name, for it is a poem that could so easily have been written by him in response to his prosecution for involvement with the Essex affair. He is stabbing at all those who believe anyone who seeks to change a reigning regime is automatically 'evil', even though they might only wish to replace it with something better, less corrupt, and so improve everyone's lot. Social improvement was indeed Neville's aim in life, and he felt comfortable with himself for forwarding that role.

The end of Neville's life is certainly better documented than the beginning, and some of it does indeed give witness to his interest in writing and in plays. He was, for instance, a friend of Sir Thomas Overbury – the writer who was also the secretary of James' favourite, Sir Robert Carr. Indeed, when Overbury died, Neville lost hope of effective contact with the King, though Carr genuinely liked him and offered him the alternative post of Lord Treasurer, after he was passed over for the post of Secretary of State. However, even in his manner of refusing this post, Neville spoke with a dramatic metaphor: 'I have not performed in politics for so long in order to accept a role for which I have never rehearsed'.[26]

As time went by, Neville had hopes of one or two more fee-farms, but these were always dashed by jealous rivals. Yet despite not having access to the amount of money ideally needed to support the arts, Neville still kept up his interest in plays, as witnessed by a stationer's note appended to the play *A King and No King* by Beaumont and Fletcher:

TO THE RIGHT WORSHIPFUL AND WORTHY

KNIGHT SIR HENRY NEVILL
Worthy Sir

I present, or rather return unto your view, that which formerly hath been received from you, hereby affecting what you did desire. To commend the work in my unlearned method, were rather to detract from it than to give it any lustre. It sufficeth it hath your worship's approbation and patronage, to the commendation of the authors, and encouragement of their further labours; and thus wholly committing myself and it to your worship's dispose, I rest, ever ready to do you service, not only in the like, but in what I may.

THOMAS WALKLEY

Although this was only printed in 1619, it was obviously produced well before that date, as it speaks of the authors still living. Beaumont died in 1616, and he started collaborating with Fletcher only in 1607, so Neville must have reviewed the play between around 1609 and his death in 1615. He had little money to spare for anything outside the needs of his own large family, so the writers must have sent him their work because they respected his literary judgement. And it is no coincidence that 'Shakespeare' collaborated with Fletcher on his last two plays, *The Two Noble Kinsmen* and the lost *Cardenio*. Neville, therefore, must have been very adept at keeping the political and literary sides of his life separate: it was by these means that he has so long escaped discovery. It is heartening to think that, even while he was at his lowest political ebb, he still had the confidence of literary men, and was indeed still writing.

However, Neville never lost his commercial acumen either. As late as 1614 we find him mapping out a trade route between England and India, envisaging a passage through Persia, up the Volga then overland to the Baltic States and into Archangel, where English ships were habitually moored.[27] (This route had been the one used by the old Vikings, so one wonders if Neville heard of it when he visited Denmark.) Sir Francis Bacon pronounced Neville as an impossible dreamer for devising this plan, but surely this ability to dream and envisage spatial projects is the trademark of a playwright.

Finally, Chamberlain writes sadly of a further deterioration in Neville's health in February, 1615:

> *[he] hath at this instant three dangerous diseases upon him, this is the jaundice, the scurvy, and the dropsy, which have brought him to a very weak case and will utterly overthrow him if he find not present remedy.*

In April Neville made his will, and by 10 July he was dead. For some unknown reason, his son and namesake never engraved on the family tomb the epitaph he had left him. Perhaps it was because the aftermath of the severe head injuries he had received some six years earlier had had more effect on young Sir Henry than the family wanted the world to know. The young man had been violently arrested in Cornwall on suspicion of piracy. In this particular case, however, blood did indeed prove thicker than water – Sir Francis Bacon, by then Attorney General, intervened in young Henry's trial and effectively came to the conclusion that Jean Gandon, the Frenchman who had accused him, had stolen the goods himself, and not lost them at young Henry Neville's hands, as he claimed. How Neville's son came to be known by Gandon – a merchant navy captain – while he was studying in France was never explained; once again it seems that country had been just an unlucky place for the family to visit. Or perhaps young Henry had indeed secretly had dealings with his free-booting Cornish, piratical relatives by marriage, the Killigrews. With such a large family, it must have been difficult for Sir Henry to keep an eye on all of them. Poor Neville had thus faced private as well as public adversity: a sense of tragedy must have filled his later life as well as his later plays.

What a long way had Neville's political views now progressed since those earliest 'dynastic' plays of his. Perhaps it was the very act of researching and writing them that helped him to realize that such a system could not last. He had looked into the very heart of feudal society and found it wanting. The feudal age had now well and truly ended; Neville, the personification of the Renaissance, had been instrumental in its passing. Now, despite his illnesses and political disappointments, however, Neville must have kept an outwardly brave face on things, as he was due to give an after-dinner talk on the day he died. Only after his strangely private funeral did the waiting audience hear of his death. Only his close family was allowed to mourn his passing.

Among his truest friends was James Whitlocke. He was later to be knighted and become an eminent judge. Whitlocke had attended the Merchant Taylor School, where he had been tutored by Richard Mulcaster, who had also taught such writers as Spenser, Kyd and Thomas Lodge. It is also known from Whitlocke's own writing that he (Whitlocke) was always interested in plays and acting:

> *I was brought up at school under Mr. Mulcaster, in the famous school of the Merchantaylors in London ... Yeerly he presented sum playes to the court, in which his scholers wear only actors, and I one among them, and by that meanes taughte them good behaviour and audacitye.*[28]

It therefore becomes highly significant that this same James Whitlocke was the political companion who paid Neville the most appropriate tribute at his death:

> *he was the most sufficient man for understanding of state business that was in this Kingdom, ... and a very good scholar and a stout man, but was as ignobly and unworthily handled as ever gentleman was ...*[29]

Yes, indeed, Neville had been underestimated, underused and underappreciated. He was too advanced a philosopher for the age in which he lived. To the outward world, therefore, he has for centuries been labelled as just another country squire who never left behind him much to be remembered. Such historians and researchers have, like some of his contemporaries, mistaken his visionary complexity for muddled thinking. It has often been said that the composer Richard Wagner was 'a beautiful sunset mistaken for a dawn'. The exact opposite could surely be said of 'William Shakespeare' – he represents a tortured dawn that has been mistaken for a beautiful sunset. He portrays the feudal system generally in tatters, and also the tragedy of the personal feud in *Romeo and Juliet*. But the new alliances and friendships made through trade and a just legal system (as portrayed in *The Merchant of Venice*, for instance) become the herald of a new dawn. As a man, their true writer, Neville, knew that breaking the strings of the old monarchical system would be a painful process, so he tried instead to retune them as gradually and gently as possible. That the dying system would not allow him to do this was none of his fault.

Neville clearly wished to carry over some of the best ideals of the medieval knight – honour, patronage, protection of the poor, benevolent leadership, even-handed justice and bravery – into the newly emerging socio-economic system. (Such were the chivalric codes embedded in Shakespeare's earlier plays too.) The trouble was that so many knights were themselves abandoning these ideals in favour of personal gratification. Perhaps, indeed, the ideals had only ever truly existed in the old romances. Inevitably, therefore, Neville was left unable to prevent the death-throes of feudalism becoming a war-ridden, agonizing experience, despite his best efforts.

So, as he surely was 'Shakespeare', in the end it was those with literary connections who were best able to assess Sir Henry's worth. Prime among these was Ben Jonson, who was to spend the next eight years helping to collate 'Shakespeare's' plays into a book. Jonson recognized Neville's worth as a poet and a man who had lent his life to another, and to the world. And Jonson left a cryptic epigram addressed to 'Sir Henry Nevil' – an epigram that reads more like an epitaph, and whose significance will be discussed further in the appendix on Shakespeare's commendatory verses:

> *Who now calls on thee, Nevil, is a muse,*
> *That serves nor fame, nor titles; but doth choose*
> *Where virtue makes them both, and that's in thee:*
> *Where all is fair, beside thy pedigree.*
> *Thou art not one, seek'st miseries with hope,*
> *Wrestlest with dignities, or feign'st a scope*
> *Of service to the public, when the end*
> *Is private gain, which hath long guilt to friend.*
> *Thou rather striv'st the matter to possess,*
> *And elements of honour, than the dress;*
> *To make thy lent life, good against the Fates:*
> *And first to know thine own state, then the State's.*
> *To be the same in root, thou art in height;*
> *And that thy soul should give thy flesh her weight.*
> *Go on, and doubt not, what posterity,*
> *Now I have sung thee thus, shall judge of thee.*
> *Thy deed, unto thy name, will prove new wombs*
> *Whilst others toil for titles to their tombs.*

This should now surely be placed alongside Mark Anthony's oration on the dead Brutus:

This was the noblest Roman of them all.
All the conspirators, save only he,
Did that they did in envy of great Caesar;
He only, in a general honest thought
And common good to all, made one of them.
His life was gentle, and the elements
So mix'd in him that Nature might stand up
And say to all the world, 'This was a man!'

Julius Caesar, Act V, Sc. V

Commendatory Verses and the Three Suns

Commendatory verses

Verses in praise of the late author appeared at the front of the First Folio compilation of Shakespeare's works. Ben Jonson's poem 'To the Memory of My Beloved, the Author' is so full of hints towards the identity of the true writer that we must place it at the head of the list to be analyzed. It was Jonson, of course, who also wrote a poem to Henry Neville, and who took overall charge of the publication of Shakespeare's collected works. The poem in its entirety is presented first, followed by notes on some of the lines. Then there follows a copy of Jonson's epigram to Sir Henry Neville. Finally, there are two more commendatory verses, by Leonard Digges and Hugh Holland, together with some suggestions of their cryptic meanings. In the actual Folio, Holland's was the 'cover sonnet'.

> ***To the Memory of My Beloved, the Author Mr. William Shakespeare:***
> ***And What He Hath Left Us***
> *To draw no envy (Shakespeare) on thy name,*
> *Am I thus ample to thy book, and fame.*
> *While I confess thy writings to be such,*
> *As neither man, nor muse, can praise too much*

'Tis true, and all men's suffrage. But these ways
Were not the paths I meant unto thy praise:
For seeliest ignorance on these may light,
Which, when it sounds at best, but echoes right;
Or blind affection, which doth ne'er advance
10 The truth, but gropes, and urgeth all by chance;
Or crafty malice, might pretend this praise,
And think to ruin, where it seemed to raise.
These are, as some infamous bawd, or whore,
Should praise a matron. What could hurt her more?
But thou art proof against them, and indeed
Above the ill fortune of them, or the need.
I therefore will begin. Soul of the age!
The applause, delight, the wonder of our stage!
My Shakespeare, rise; I will not lodge thee by
20 Chaucer, or Spenser, or bid Beaumont lie
A little further, to make thee a room:
Thou art a monument, without a tomb,
And art alive still, while thy book doth live,
And we have wits to read, and praise to give.
That I not mix thee so, my brain excuses;
I mean with great, but disproportioned muses:
For, if I thought my judgement were of years,
I should commit thee surely with thy peers,
And tell, how far thou didst our Lyly outshine,
30 Or sporting Kyd, or Marlowe's mighty line.
And though thou hadst small Latin, and less Greek,
From thence to honour thee, I would not seek
For names; but call forth thundering Aeschylus,
Euripides, and Sophocles to us,
Pacuvius, Accius, him of Cordova dead,
To life again, to hear thy buskin tread,
And shake a stage: or, when thy socks were on,
Leave thee alone, for the comparison
Of all that insolent Greece, or haughty Rome
40 Sent forth, or since did from their ashes come.
Triumph, my Britain, thou hast one to show,

To whom all scenes of Europe homage owe.
He was not of an age, but for all time!
And all the muses still were in their prime,
When like Apollo he came forth to warm
Our ears, or like a Mercury to charm!
Nature herself was proud of his designs,
And joyed to wear the dressing of his lines!
Which were so richly spun, and woven so fit,
50 As, since, she will vouchsafe no other wit.
The merry Greek, tart Aristophanes,
Neat Terence, witty Plautus, now not please;
But antiquated, and deserted lie
As they were not of nature's family.
Yet must I not give nature all: thy art,
My gentle Shakespeare, must enjoy a part.
For though the poet's matter, nature be,
His art doth give the fashion. And, that he,
Who casts to write a living line, must sweat,
60 (Such as thine are) and strike the second heat
Upon the muses' anvil: turn the same,
(And himself with it) that he thinks to frame;
Or for the laurel, he may gain a scorn,
For a good poet's made, as well as born.
And such wert thou. Look how the father's face
Lives in his issue, even so, the race
Of Shakespeare's mind, and manners brightly shines
In his well-turned, and true-filed lines:
In each of which, he seems to shake a lance,
70 As brandished at the eyes of ignorance.
Sweet swan of Avon, what a sight it were
To see thee in our waters yet appear,
And make those flights upon the banks of Thames,
That so did take Eliza, and our James
But stay, I see thee in the hemisphere
Advanced, and made a constellation there!
Shine forth, thou star of poets, and with rage,
Or influence, chide, or cheer the drooping stage;

Which, since thy flight from hence, hath mourned like night.
80 And despairs day, but for thy volume's light.

Ben Jonson

Commentary

To draw no envy (Shakespeare) on thy name,
Am I thus ample to thy book, and fame. (ll.1–2)

I do not wish to draw attention to your name, only to comment on your book, and your fame. Also, if the letters NV (envy) are 'drawn', this surely leads to Neville's name.

'Tis true, and all men's suffrage. (l.5)

It's true, and everybody agrees

Thou art a monument, without a tomb, (l.22)

If Neville does indeed lie in the family vault at Waltham St Lawrence, then his grave is unmarked. There is a family monument above ground, but no tomb.

And though thou hadst small Latin, and less Greek, (l.31)

'And if you had small Latin and less Greek' – the suggestion here is that the true writer was indeed learned so he, Jonson, can compare him with the great classical writers; whereas had the writer not been a classical scholar, then he would not have made those comparisons.

When like Apollo he came forth to warm
Our ears, or like a Mercury to charm! (ll.45–6)

Neville's family were always associated with the sign of the sun. (Note the appearance of the three exploding suns before the battle of Mortimer's Cross. Note also the sign of the sun in the top ring on his life-size portrait.) He was also an ambassador, therefore a 'message bearer', like Mercury.

Nature herself was proud of his designs,
And joyed to wear the dressing of his lines! (ll.47–8)

As a keeper of Windsor Forest, Neville 'dressed' Nature.

Yet must I not give nature all: thy art,
My gentle Shakespeare, must enjoy a part.
For though the poet's matter, nature be,
His art doth give the fashion. And, that he,
Who casts to write a living line, must sweat,
(Such as thine are) and strike the second heat
Upon the muses' anvil: turn the same,
(And himself with it) that he thinks to frame;
Or for the laurel, he may gain a scorn,
For a good poet's made, as well as born.
And such wert thou. (ll.55–65)

Jonson is anxious to make everyone realize that the true author was not an unlettered peasant, but a well-educated, hard-working man. Note the ironworking imagery of the anvil: this also acts as an anagram of a French version of his name, Navil.

Look how the father's face
Lives in his issue, even so, the race ... (ll.65–6)

... 'of the Neville's noble race' – in *2 Henry VI*, also at the head of their family tree. Shakespeare of Stratford had no surviving male issue: Neville had five sons.

manners brightly shines

Ironworking imagery again! His

In his well-turned, and true-filed lines:
In each of which, he seems to shake a lance,
As brandished at the eyes of ignorance. (ll. 67–70)

'lines' become synonymous with the imagery of his profession and his pseudonym.

Sweet swan of Avon, what a sight it were
To see thee in our waters yet appear,
And make those flights upon the banks of Thames,
That so did take Eliza, and our James (ll.71–4)

In the Celtic languages, Avon just means 'river'. The swan is a mute bird.

But stay, I see thee in the hemisphere
Advanced, and made a constellation there!
Shine forth, thou star of poets,
(ll.75–7)

This could easily be a reference to Neville's interest in astronomy.

and with rage,
Or influence, chide, or cheer the drooping stage; (ll.77–8)

As a politician, Neville had political influence.

To Sir Henry Nevil

Who now calls on thee, Nevil, is a muse,
  That serves nor fame, nor titles; but doth choose
Where virtue makes them both, and that's in thee:
  Where all is fair, beside thy pedigree.
Thou art not one, seek'st miseries with hope,
  Wrestlest with dignities, or feign'st a scope
Of service to the public, when the end
  Is private gain, which hath long guilt to friend.
Thou rather striv'st the matter to possess,
  And elements of honour, than the dress;
To make thy lent life, good against the Fates:

And first to know thine own state, then the State's.
To be the same in root, thou art in height;
*   And that thy soul should give thy flesh her weight.*
Go on, and doubt not, what posterity,
*   Now I have sung thee thus, shall judge of thee.*
Thy deeds, unto thy name, will prove new wombs
*   Whilst others toil for titles to their tombs.*

Ben Jonson

To the Memorie of the deceased Authour Maister W. Shakespeare

Shake-speare, at length thy pious fellowes give
The world thy Workes : thy Workes, by which, out-live
Thy Tombe, thy name must when that stone is rent,
And Time dissolves thy Stratford Moniment,
Here we alive shall view thee still. This Booke,
When Brasse and Marble fade, shall make thee looke
Fresh to all Ages : when Posteritie
Shall loath what's new, thinke all is prodegie
That is not Shake-speares; ev'ry Line, each Verse
Here shall revive, redeeme thee from thy Herse.
Nor Fire, nor cankring Age, as Naso said,
Of his, thy wit-fraught Booke shall once invade.
Nor shall I e're beleeve, or thinke thee dead.
(Though mist) untill our bankrout Stage be sped
(Imposible) with some new straine t'out-do
Passions of Juliet, and her Romeo ;
Or till I heare a Scene more nobly take,
Then when thy half-Sword parlying Romans spake.
Till these, till any of thy Volumes rest
Shall with more fire, more feeling be exprest,
Be sure, our Shake-speare, thou canst never dye,
But crown'd with Lawrell, live eternally.

Leonard Digges

Neville was a friend and relative of Leonard Digges, who was also an officer in the Virginia Company. Holland's verse (below) gives some possible hints to Shakespeare's true identity as Neville. Notice how Digges's last line could also be an anagram about Neville: 'But crown'd with all Law't reely neville'.

Upon the Lines and Life of the Famous Scenicke Poet, Master William
   Shakespeare
Those hands, which you so clapt, go now, and wring
You Britaines brave; for done are Shakespeares dayes :
His dayes are done, that made the dainty Playes,
Which made the Globe of heav'n and earth to ring.
Dry'de is that veine, dry'd is the Thespian Spring,
Turn'd all to teares, and Phoebus clouds his rayes :
That corp's, that coffin now besticke those bayes,
Which crown'd him Poet first, then Poets King.
If Tragedies might any Prologue have,
All those he made, would scarse make a one to this :
Where Fame, now that he gone is to the grave
(Deaths publique tyring-house) the Nuncius is,
For though his line of life went soone about,
The life yet of his lines shall never out.

Hugh Holland

Hugh Holland was a Welsh Catholic, but he was also a friend of Neville's, joining with him in both the Virginia Company and the Mitre Club. Notice how he lays stress on the word 'ring' and that this is associated with the rays of the sun. Again, such imagery is present in his portrait. Notice too the anagramatic nature of his last line, which could read: 'The life yet of his lines has Nevell rout'. It is also to be noted that the majority of the writers of the Commendatory Verses were not well-known poets but were members of the Virginia Company.

The three suns

Regarding the rays of the sun, one is reminded of Neville and the three suns before the Battle of Mortimer's Cross in the Wars of the Roses. As a result of this incident, the Nevilles took the three suns as their sign on the banner they carried into battle. The incident is recounted in *3 Henry VI*. Edward, Duke of York, the future King Edward IV, is moving east through Gloucestershire in 1461. He and his brothers (sons of Richard Plantagenet and Cecily Neville) are about to fight the Lancastrians at the Battle of Mortimer's Cross – a very important battle in the long Wars of the Roses, in which the victories of first the Yorkists then the Lancastrians protracted themselves across so many troubled years. It is early in the morning, and (historically speaking) the Duke of York's troops notice a strange phenomenon – three suns shining in the sky. However, in 'Shakespeare's' version, it is Edward Neville-Plantagenet himself who notices it:

EDWARD. *Dazzle mine eyes, or do I see three suns?*
RICHARD. *Three glorious suns, each one a perfect sun;*
    Not separated with the racking clouds,
    But sever'd in a pale clear-shining sky.
    See, see! they join, embrace, and seem to kiss,
    As if they vow'd some league inviolable.
    Now are they but one lamp, one light, one sun.
    In this the heaven figures some event.
EDWARD. *'Tis wondrous strange, the like yet never heard of.*
    I think it cites us, brother, to the field,
    That we, the sons of brave Plantagenet,
    Each one already blazing by our meeds,
    Should notwithstanding join our lights together
    And overshine the earth, as this the world.
    Whate'er it bodes, henceforward will I bear
    Upon my target three fair shining suns.
RICHARD. *Nay, bear three daughters – by your leave I speak it,*
    You love the breeder better than the male.

Act II, Sc. I

The connection between the three suns and the name of Shakespeare is an interesting one. To begin with, it is now known that a rare natural event caused this unusual phenomenon. It is called a parhelion, or mock sun, which happens when light is refracted through ice crystals.[1] However, it had hardly been witnessed at that time, and certainly never understood. The only mention of the three 'lights' an Elizabethan writer would have heard about were probably the three lights said to shine above the statue of the goddess Pallas Athena in Athens. Athena, bride of Apollo (the sun god) held a great shining spear, from which the light was reflected in such a way that three sections of sunlight were said to emanate from it. She is also known as the Tenth Muse, whose qualities encompass those of all the others. Her name in Greek actually means 'spear shaker'.

To know 'Shakespeare' is to know complexity; conundrum within conundrum. As John Milton later wrote about him 'Then thou our fancy of it self bereaving, / Dost make us Marble with too much conceaving;'[2] But Sir Henry Neville never leaves us without tantalizing clues: the jesting 'footnote' to this speech about the three suns talks of the Plantagenets' love of 'the breeder' – females – and daughters. It was from a *female Neville* that these Plantagenet brothers were descended. Who but a Neville would have bothered to add such a telling detail? And from here onwards the plays and poems are peppered with imagery of the sun – the emblem the Plantagenets chose to emblazon on their banner after their victory at Mortimer's Cross.

Mortimer's Cross was also the battle in which Owen Tudor, progenitor of the Tudor dynasty, was killed. Portraying his defeaters as such bold knights would have come naturally to a young Neville, but any other writer would surely have been more diplomatic when writing a play which a living Tudor monarch (Elizabeth I) would come to know. But 'Shakespeare' was obviously a safe cover for Neville, and the young Neville had not yet suffered 'the thousand natural shocks' that taught him to be more diplomatic.

Sir Henry Neville and the Essex Rebellion

W hy did Neville finally agree to listen to the Earl of Essex's plans? It has been said by some historians, and even by his own contemporaries, that it was pure ambition that made him do so. He knew that the Earl liked his work and ideas, and knew too that he would prefer him to be in Cecil's place. However, there may have been factors that were even more pressing than ambition itself.

Just at the time Essex began planning his rebellion, Neville had come back to England before his two-year term in France was up. He did not like France, was finding it expensive to stay there, and hated the Treaty of Bolougne negotiations, which had failed miserably. The Queen kept refusing him permission to return home from his ambassadorship, however, until Neville wrote in desperation to Robert Cecil that he would 'return and live hermit in the Forest of Windsor and contemplate my time as a bad ambassador',[1] if he were not given official permission to return. (Shades of Jacques in *As You Like It?*)

At last the Queen relented, but when Essex broke the idea of rebellion to Sir Henry, he was within only a few weeks of being sent back to France. Henry probably feared that, with his facility at languages and disguise,[2] he would be used there eventually as a double agent, instead of being recalled to England once his two-year contract was up. He had convinced himself that the Queen neither liked nor trusted him and suspected that she intended to send him to France and leave him there. Thus when Essex offered him the chance of political promotion in England Neville must have thought he had nothing to lose in joining with him. If he did not take the chance, then he would most assuredly be returned to France; whereas if he took the chance he might gain the most important political position in England. He would then be able to institute constitutional reforms, bring education and hygiene to the common people. Like Brutus, he would not have done anything 'in envy of great Caesar. He only, in general honest thought and common good to all' would make one of them. And if he could make his involvement in the projected uprising look accidental and marginal, then the worst that would happen to him would be imprisonment, if Essex's project failed. But his imprisonment would have to be in England and he would surely be allowed to write. Either way, therefore, whether Essex succeeded or failed, Neville's situation would be preferable to returning to France and ultimately being stranded there.

Many older aristocrats of the day saw Essex as a rash young man. However, he must have been charismatic and intelligent. It has not been stated often enough that he gave huge amounts of money for endowing libraries at Oxford and Cambridge. This fact alone would have caused Neville to respect him. Unlike most earls, he was also no snob. He even noticed talent in the pig man on his estate, promoting him to become a comic actor. Most earls would not even deign to speak to members of the House of Commons, let alone to lowly workers on their estates. To the people, therefore, he was a hero, his campaigns at Cadiz and in the Lowlands adding to his reputation. Even the King of Spain remarked how well Essex disciplined his soldiers and that he did not hurt the innocent women and children of the town.

It was clear Essex was also able to unite people from different sides of the religious divide; moderate Catholic and Protestant lords alike supported his stance against the Queen. The troops who had followed him in Ireland loved him, and it must have seemed to Elizabeth that they might be prepared to rise at his call, on their return to England. So now Essex threw his London house open to all his admirers. Puritans as well as many middle-of-the-road London citizens gathered around him, hanging on his every word.

No one could believe he would stay long out of the Queen's favour. True, he had failed to engage the enemy or triumph in any way in Ireland, but surely that was not enough reason for the Queen to remain angry for ever. Even his sudden, unannounced entry to her 'undressed' presence on his return would seem nothing more than a boyish prank, in time. The Earl of Southampton therefore advised him to go abroad until she cooled down, but it seems Essex did not wish to leave his admiring crowds. Eventually, the Earl of Southampton himself acceded to Essex's wish that he should return from the Lowlands, where he had been for some time. (One wonders if Neville visited him there during his 'incommunicado period', when he should have been in Boulogne.) In fact, Essex's followers now seemed to be travelling from every part of England too, in order to rally round him.

Among these, Sir Charles Danvers and Sir Christopher Blount were both secret Catholics who responded to Essex's summons. So was Lord Monteagle, the man who was later to expose the Gunpowder Plot. Nevertheless, the Protestant Earl of Rutland joined them, as did the Earl of Bedford and Lord Sandys. Even an ancestor of Oliver Cromwell counted himself among their number, having grown to respect Essex after serving him in Ireland. For such a diversity of men to have followed him, it is certain that they had cause for complaint against Elizabeth and the Cecils, though whether that complaint was simply that they were themselves less influential than they thought they should be, or whether they were mainly motivated by concern for what would happen to the country after the Queen's death, is debatable. It was probable that both reasons played their part to a greater or lesser extent in each individual follower of Essex.

The mixture of religious opinion following the Earl surely demonstrates the correctness of Neville's own opinion: that there were English Catholics who were just as afraid of the might of Spain as any Protestant in the kingdom. Indeed, fear of Spain and love of Essex seem the two common, uniting factors amongst all of them. But what were their aims? Did they wish to invite James VI of Scotland to take over the country with their blessing, so that there could be a smooth transition from one monarch to the next? This is the most usual opinion put forward by historians, but there is one overwhelming reason why it does not entirely match the facts of the situation. All of Essex's followers respected Sir Henry Neville's knowledge of international affairs, and he was unsure whether the King of Scots had been won over by the Spanish faction. Putting this together with other hints about Neville's opinions, it looks very much as if the conspirators may have been intending a (perhaps temporary) republic. Neville, Essex and

Southampton had all fallen foul of Queen Elizabeth, while Henri of Navarre, for whose monarchical succession they had fought, had subsequently proved a selfish, womanizing disappointment. If Neville did indeed write the works of Shakespeare, then they demonstrate mainly situations of kingship in crisis. Even the introduction to *Lucrece* blandly announces that where emperors have failed the people, then the only traditional answer has been for consuls to take over the country:

> *Brutus acquainted the people with the doer and manner of the vile deed, with a bitter invective against the tyranny of the king: wherewith the people were so moved, that with one consent and a general acclamation the Tarquins were all exiled, and the state government changed from kings to consuls.*

Added to this, there is the fact that Neville himself was known as the 'English Tacitus'. Apart from Tacitus having been a great orator, he was known to hold the opinion that the office of monarch was the most corrupting on earth. He argued that however 'good' and incorruptible a person might be, merely seating him on a throne and announcing that he had almost invincible power changed him into a monster. By choosing a man with such an epithet as 'Tacitus', therefore, for their head of state, the rebels must have been choosing someone who was happy to take on the reins of republican, parliamentary government.

However, even if these were their secret aims, they had insufficient time to discuss and plan their methods of achieving them. The idea that it could have been Neville's imminent return to France that forced them into hasty action has been overlooked by most, if not all, historians. It is always easier to research known 'big names' when one is reviewing the past, simply because so much more has already been written about them. Neville, through his complexity and no doubt also through his own desire for secrecy, has been less known and consequently more difficult to research. Thus it comes about that he has not previously been given his true status in the Essex equation. If all Essex's followers agreed that he should be named as head of state, then he must have been greatly loved and greatly respected by many of the greatest personages of the era. Twenty-one of the aldermen of London backed Essex's ideas, even if most of them were afraid to take direct action. So too did some of the most educated graduates of Oxford and Cambridge, together with a majority of the ablest aristocracy. In theory, then, these men also backed Neville.

Whereas, therefore, it has for centuries been the received wisdom to
label the Essex conspirators as madcap and hot-headed and to state
these unspecific qualities as the causes for their over-hasty action, it is
difficult to equate such a debased mentality with the quality of the
brains that backed that daring Earl. Only when Neville is added to the
equation is there a specific, assignable cause for their haste. Neville was
the man they all wanted, yet Neville was 'under sentence' to return to
France.

But these conspirators were also humanists. They seemed reluctant to
admit that their actions would probably lead to the shedding of the Queen's
and Cecil's blood, yet they were forced into a realization of this situation.
Neville immediately stated that he could have no part in harming Cecil, his
boyhood friend. The other conspirators readily understood his position and
devised a plan whereby Neville should go early on the morning of the rebellion to a certain chamber at Court, in which he should lock himself until all
the business was over, thus being ready to be called upon to take his place
of honour, at their success. Of course, on hearing of their *failure*, Neville
was not immediately found, and therefore not immediately implicated. But
the fact that he actually went to this chamber and waited showed he was
indeed playing his part.

However, not all these facts came out immediately. Returning to
Neville's original meeting with the conspirators at Drury House – the Earl
of Southampton's residence – the contemporary historian, Camden,
recounts what several witnesses later testified:

*Sir Henry Nevill ingenuously confessed (if my memory faile mee not, for I was
then present and heard his confession read) that Cuffe [Essex's agent] had
suggested unto him at his the said Nevils returne out of France, that it would
be imputed to* **him** *that the treaty at Boloigne failed of successe; that hee came
to him oftentimes afterward and perswaded him to come and see the Earle,
which once hee did; that after this, when hee was even ready to returne into
France, he intreated him to goe to Drury house and heare what should be consulted on, protesting that nothing was to be propounded there which was not
for the good of the kingdome and of the Earle, and which hee might heare
without breach of loyalty to the Queene; and lastly that hee prayed him to be
present with the Earle when hee should invade the Court, and laid open unto
him the whole plot; which when Nevill misse-liked as a matter full of danger,*

*difficulty, and wickednesse, and smiling at it, said it was in the number of those things **which are never praised till performed**.*[3]

There is a menacing drama about Neville's final words on the matter, and a kind of 'stage' metaphor, such as we shall again find him reported to have used in speech, but which he was so careful to keep out of his diplomatic dispatches. Neville must have been a very great orator indeed to be able to overcome this kind of evidence given against him at his trial – a feat that he must have performed, otherwise he would scarcely have escaped with his life.

On the eve of the revolution, the play *Richard II* was performed in 40 taverns and private houses up and down London. This was obviously because it contained the deposition of a monarch. Essex's representatives had offered substantial amounts of money to all actors who agreed to appear in it, and even the Globe company partook in the scheme. On investigating, the Queen was satisfied that neither Shakespeare nor his company knew anything of the purpose for which the work was intended, namely the incitement of the public towards a *coup d'état*. (If ever proof were needed that those in power knew that plays could be used as political propaganda, then here we have it.) It is indeed most surprising that Shakespeare, if he were truly the writer of the play, was exonerated from all blame. How could it have been performed everywhere without his permission? The only answer is that the Queen herself must have known that 'Shakespeare' was a mere pseudonym for the true writer. She is reputed to have gone from one courtier to another demanding the naming of the real author. Unsurprisingly, many truly had no idea, while those who knew would not have wished to be accused of complicity; so everyone probably kept his silence.

Of course, with Neville being the true author, the conspirators eventually had no problem obtaining authorial consent for the performance of the 'dissident' play. They wanted him for their ultimate political leader too. His approval was therefore a key factor in their enterprise. No wonder the Earl of Essex's men had tried so persistently to achieve Neville's consent, and only after gaining that consent struck the all-too-precipitate blow forced on them by Henry's imminent ejection from the country. But when the failed coup was over, no immediate suspicion attached to Neville. He had visited the conspirators only by night, had probably gone in disguise, and had not taken part in the direct action. Obviously, however, he could not be sure that none of them would give him away under torture or the threat of it. He still had his passport. He therefore made haste to take up his post in France.

As he had written to Winwood, he intended to leave his wife at home so that she could remind the Queen of her promise to allow him to return to England, once his two-year service was over. However, it was now possible that she and his children might never see him again, if any of the conspirators told his story. The whole family therefore set out to accompany Henry as far as Dover in order to bid him what might well be a last, sad farewell.

Henry's worst fears soon came to pass. Back in London, the young Earl of Southampton was telling all. His 'confession' was given to Cecil, so it is probable that not all of it came out in court, since it contained details of how Henry Neville was proposed to take over Cecil's own role. Obviously, Robert Cecil would not have liked this to have come out in court, since it would have meant certain death for Neville, his kinsman and favourite cousin's husband. Cecil had no need to kill Neville; he knew his secrets: he could control him. Also, if Neville had been shown openly to have been involved to such an extent, then some unwelcome questions would be asked. Why had Neville, of all people, turned against Cecil? Did Sir Henry know anything about the performances of *Richard II* on the eve of the revolution? Well, yes, but he also knew that Cecil himself had once gone to a relative's house to see a private performance of that play.[4] If one thing then led to another, it would eventually be assumed that those sonnets flying around 'among his private friends'[5] had probably been written by Neville to Southampton at Cecil's father's own behest. The Cecils would thus be revealed to Elizabeth as having known a secret which they plotted to keep from the Queen. And what of Sir Francis Bacon – the major prosecution lawyer at the Essex trials? He worked in Parliament with Sir Henry; indeed, Neville's stepmother was Francis' half-sister. How, then, could Sir Francis not know of Neville's authorship? The Queen would soon see them all as complicitous and so, in her present mood, might recommend a general culling and blood bath.

The 'Confession of Henry, Earl of Southampton' is to be found among the Salisbury papers, vol. xi, p.72. If it is all true, then it shows not only Neville's willing and open-eyed involvement in the plot, but also an attitude similar to that of his ancestor, the Kingmaker himself, in *Henry VI*:

> *There bee two thinges which I have forgotten to sett in their right places, your Lordship must bee therefore pleased to take them in this postscript. One is, that*

not longe before the day of our misfortune my Lord of Essex towld mee that Sir
Henry Nevill, that was to goe embassador into Fraunce, was a man wholy att
his devotion, and desiered to runn the same fortune with him, and therfore hee
towld mee that hee would appoint him to come to my lodginge in Drury House,
and I should make him acquainted with his porpose of goinge to the Courte,
which I did ackordingly, after this manner;

I towld him that I understood by Cuff . . . that hee had devoted him selfe to
my Lord of Essex, and that hee desiered to engadge him self in any thinge
wherby his fortune mought bee re-established. If it weare so, I had somewhat to
say to him from my Lord of Essex, and therfore wished him to lett mee know his
mind. Hee answered mee, that what Mr. Cuff had sayed hee would performe,
therefore desiered mee to say on. So I delivered unto him what my Lord of Essex
intended, which hee allowed of, and concluded that when hee should bee app-
pointed, hee would bee att the Courte before, to gyve him fartherance with
himself and his people . . . I once again bseech your Lordship to marke, that I
have never been mover nor instigator of any of these thinges, but drawen into
them by my best frendes.

Neville's promise to 'be at the court before' surely reminds one of his
ancestor Earl of Warwick's words in *2 Henry VI*, where, at the end of the
play, the Duke of York suggests that they follow the King to London, while
Richard Neville, Earl of Warwick, says – just like our Henry Neville – that
he will go before and prepare the way:

> *YORK. I know our safety is to follow them;*
> *   For, as I hear, the king is fled to London*
> *   To call a present court of Parliament.*
> *   Let us pursue him ere the writs go forth.*
> *   What says Lord Warwick? – shall we after them?*
> *WARWICK. After them? Nay, before them if we can . . .*
>
> *Act V, Sc. III*

So Neville was like the scheming Earl of Warwick, and Neville was a 'best
friend' of the Earl of Southampton. It will be well to bear these two facts in
mind when examining subsequent events in the story.

While all this was happening in London, then, Neville was 'escaping'.
But word of his involvement was now out; Cecil had signed an order for
Neville's arrest, so armed soldiers were now galloping along his escape

route. They caught up with him at Dover. Neville saw them coming and jumped on a horse, galloping away with his children crying after him. Henry was a heavy man, so it was inevitable that the soldiers would soon catch up with him, and when they did, Neville put up no resistance, agreeing to go with them to London. However, Anne and her large family now had to make their own way home.

When they all finally arrived back at Lothbury, Anne's father refused to let them in. This may seem a heartless gesture, but viewed from his perspective at the time, it was a necessary act. Killigrew and the rest of his family must not be implicated in the plot, and the only way he had of demonstrating his complete non-involvement was to take the drastic step of cutting off his own daughter and grandchildren. To his credit, Robert Cecil understood this too, and so made an Order in Council forcing Anne's father to allow them all to live at Lothbury as before. Soon afterwards, soldiers marched into Henry's study at his father-in-law's house, searching it for possible evidence. It is of course highly probable that any incriminating papers had been cleared by this time. Unfortunately, papers involved with Henry's secret writing must have been similarly cleared away. Anne and her father were nothing if not resourceful: generations of the fighting Killigrews had gone into training them. Whether papers were destroyed or hidden by the Killigrews still remains to be investigated, though it is unfortunately the case that the Great Fire of London did away with much important documentary evidence in that area of the City. Anne's own records, together with those of her second husband, the Bishop of Chichester, are said by the curator at Chichester Cathedral to have disappeared during the Civil War. We do not even know her burial place.

So Neville was now thrown into the position of preparing his defence against a charge of treason. His first attempt has a desperation about it, in effect claiming that he had nothing to do with the errant earls. This was the substance of his first hearing in the Privy Council. It ran thus: he had not seen Essex immediately before the uprising but had seen Cuffe, his man. He desired him to meet with the Earl of Southampton and Sir Charles Danvers at Drury House. On Monday, 'Candlemass Day, at four of the clock', he had been coming out of Sergeant's Inn when he saw a carriage pass by. In that coach were the Earl of Essex, the Earl of Southampton, Sir Christopher Blount and Sir Charles Danvers. 'There, after some ordinary salutations, because I had never spoken with my Lord of Southampton since he was a child in my old Lord Treasurer's House, my Lord began to break to me their plans.'

Even thus far, Henry's testimony seems so full of holes as to have been drawn up in some panic. Neville at first says that the coach was 'passing by', then says that he paid Southampton some 'ordinary salutations'. He never mentions that the coach even stopped. And why is he at such pains to make a statement about his lack of contact with Southampton, when it is his contact with the Earl of Essex which is primarily under investigation? The answer must be that he wished above all not to be traced as the author of the published *Lucrece,* which all the world knew had been dedicated to Southampton, for this would then betray him as the author of the plays, including *Richard II* – the play that Essex had paid both the Globe and other actors to perform all around London on the eve of his uprising. It would not have been difficult for someone at his hearing to put two and two together if the longstanding friendship between Neville and Southampton had been admitted by the older, wiser man.

However, if we look for a deeper layer within Neville's testimony so far, we can see that some of the illogicalities also serve as inferences. By concentrating on the Earl of Southampton, he does not have to say openly whether or not he also spoke personally with Essex. He is therefore avoiding questioning on the words he and Essex may have exchanged at that time. Neville also casually remarks that he was just leaving Sergeant's Inn. Only those highly trusted by the judiciary were allowed to enter this place, so Neville, without saying it in so many words, is reminding the Privy Counsellors just what a trusted servant of the Queen he has been. Like a clever writer, Henry is able to make subtle suggestions which the hearers or readers can piece together in their own minds, padding them out with their own images.

Yet it is still strange that neither Francis Bacon nor Robert Cecil openly questioned the glaring discrepancy that now appeared between Southampton's and Neville's testimonies. Southampton had declared that Essex, Cuffe and Neville were his best friends, while Neville had claimed no meetings with Southampton since he was a child. Francis Bacon was the barrister who gathered together evidence against Essex and whose arguments, above all others', finally saw him sentenced to death. Bacon did this in spite of the fact that Essex was once his good patron, which argues against his having scruples that would have prevented him from also indicting Neville.

Cecil too never showed much sensitivity when providing evidence against anyone when it would advance his own standing to do so. Their restraint when it came to Neville, therefore, must have stemmed from a secret cause. We maintain that the main cause was that both these men knew that Neville was truly Shakespeare, and that any public suggestion of an association between him and Southampton would immediately tie up with Shakespeare's dedication of his works to this earl. With Bacon and Cecil both being Neville's cousins, the whole matter would then surely have grown large enough to have encompassed the two of them.

Cecil has often been portrayed as a Court rival to Essex, yet appearances could be meant to be deceptive during the latter days of Queen Elizabeth I. The Tudor dynasty was coming to an end. In theory, anarchy could take advantage of the lack of clear successor. In practice, then, both Cecil and Essex were working secretly towards the smooth transition from Tudors to another dynasty. Yet while her court appeared to be divided, Elizabeth was going to be far more likely to impart some of her thoughts and schemes to one side, feeling sure that any secrets would be safe from the opposition. Without such a perceived division among her courtiers, the Queen was far more likely to fly kites of her own and so bring all their plans to confusion.

However, towards the end there was doubtless a power struggle going on. The side which successfully brought about the reign of the new monarch would be the side favoured by that new King or Queen. There was therefore some vying as to who was going to be first to furnish the monarch's route to the throne. We see from Henry's later 'Letter to a noble Lord' that there was even rivalry within the group in this respect:

> *Trew it is that I have been told that some proceedings of Sir Edwin Sandes, when he went downe first to his majesty into Scotland (at which both your Lordship and other greate persons tooke offence) have bin imputed to me.*[6]

But Neville crossed this through in his own draft. He obviously did not wish to leave any trace behind of his secret early connections with Scotland, and therefore also with the Earl of Essex.

From the available evidence, therefore, it seems as if the Essex conspirators might well have been hoping to set up a temporary republic, keeping in reserve the eventual probablility of inviting the King of Scotland to become their head, should he prove to be as fixedly against Spain as were the English, or should the people demand a monarch rather than a president.

That the Earl of Essex personally foresaw the possibility of proclaiming himself King, however, could be inferred from his first astonishing reaction at his trial. He begins by naming and blaming anyone and everyone who followed him, ending with an incredible attack on his sister who, he said 'did continually urge me on with telling me how all my friends and followers thought me a coward, and that I had lost all my valour ... She must be looked to, for she has a proud spirit.'[7] It is unlikely that his sister would have urged him to become the leader of a republic. That aristocratic lady doubtless had him in mind for the next monarch. It shocked everyone that Essex blamed her in this manner and, after all, her arguments must have fallen on willing ears.

By the time his next, more open hearing arrived, Neville had realized that he could no longer claim to have been as ignorant of Essex's designs as he had previously set out to convince everyone. He therefore decided that his best tactic would be to say that yes, he was aware of their 'fantasies', but that he neither took them seriously nor took part in them. 'It was not a matter that originally entered into my Thoughts, but that I was enticed, and in a manner enforced to hear it.' He emphasized how many assurances of 'no harm' to the Queen he had insisted upon from Cuffe, the Earl's representative, before he would even agree to give them half an ear. 'With these Protestations and Assurances how could I well have refused, and who might not have been abused as well as I?'[8] And, he said, even then he had only listened, nothing more.

So Neville himself had now been forced to label the rebels as basing their ideas on an unsound foundation – on a 'fantasy' that would 'vanish of itself' – but this assessment was a construction given by Neville only when he was desperate, and desperately scratching round for an explanation as to why he did not inform the Queen that he had heard their plans. It is ironic that this, Neville's 'construction' of the conspirators' inadequacies, has been believed ever since – ironic, but not surprising. If Neville was Shakespeare, then he was expert at 'constructing' events in such a way that everyone who heard or read them was drawn into believing. He was very persuasive. Of course, Neville would be the last person to admit in Court that it was he himself, and his own situation vis-à-vis his return to France, that had caused the rebels' 'madcap haste'. Of course he had to play down his fellow-conspirators' strategic abilities too. In English law, 'malice aforethought' adds an extra dimension of guilt to any criminal's deeds. Yet when facts are allowed to speak more loudly than words, the truth of the situation shines clearly. Neville was indeed a key man in the Essex affair, just as so many witnesses of the time attested.

Despite the testimony of these witnesses, however, Neville steadfastly denied he played any role in the uprising. 'Secondly', he continued,

> *I desire that it may be remembred, that this Meeting at Drewry-House was not till Candlemas; whereas her Majesty had signed my Privy Seal and all my Dispatches, at the least four days before; and in Truth if I could have got my Money (which I laboured with all earnestness both my Lord Treasurer and Mr. Skinner, and was at length forced to signify to Mr. Secretary that I could not get it, albeit my Journey staid for nothing else,) I fully purposed to have set forward upon the Thursday after Candlemas day at the farthest; and if that had been so, undoubtedly I had never met with them ... What likelyhood is there that the Earle should build upon any thing from me, in that I was not likely to see the Issue of it?* [9]

Neville was clever and tricky. He turned what was probably the conspirators' reason for their hasty action – namely that they wanted to finish the business before Neville was forced to return to France – into a reason against the probability of his ever being so deeply involved with it. The truth, however, is that Neville was doing all he could to delay his return to France, as we have seen. He wrote as much in a letter to Winwood on 28 January 1600:

> *I may perhaps put off my Journey, some three or four Days longer than I wrote in my last; and if I could, I would be glad to deferr it till the end of the Term, which is the 12th of February; for I have much busyness to dispatch about my own private Estate.* [10]

No one at the hearing knew of this letter at the time, but Elizabeth sensed she was being bamboozled, and gave Neville a heavy sentence. She did not accept his plea that his only crime had been one of omission, in not informing her of the conspirators' plans, which he blamed partly on the fact that he thought their ideas so ill thought out that the project would 'vanish of it self whensoever they should have laid aside the Passion of Discontentment and examined it with reason';[11] and partly upon *an Imbecillitie and weakness of my own Nature, (if so it be to be termed) which could not resolve to become an Accuser; which how odious a thing it is, all the World knoweth; especially in respect of the Person whom I must have accused [i.e. Essex]; who I desire may be so considered, not as he hath been found since, but as he was reputed.*[12]

David Hume, the eighteenth-century philosopher, rightly praised Neville for his eloquence, finding his balanced, expressive phrases a joy to read, in contrast with the staccato, often opaque style of his diplomatic peers. Yet all the eloquence in the world could not save him now. Sir Henry was sentenced to house arrest, for a little while with his own father-in-law, and then with the Lord Admiral in Chelsea, before ultimately being sent to the Tower.

From a 'Report on the Manuscripts of the Duke of Buccleuch and Queensberry, preserved at Montagu House' it would appear that he did not altogether dislike his home with the Lord Admiral:

... where I am in a very honorable prison.' – Supposes Winwood will have heard of his misfortune. Will be 'unable to requite my pains, faith and love, but wish I may find other friends ... Your letter by Simons I received upon my way at Rochester. Since that I have been in trouble, and heard nothing. But I am commanded by Mr. Secretary [Cecil] to write unto you to continue your charge, till her Majesty take some other order for the supplying of the place I held there.'

Is licenseed to dissolve his family there. Desires that an account be taken both of his steward and Richard Hauthorne, and that the butcher and rotisseur be paid. Stallin to be paid 100 crowns for wages. Some of his stuff is to be sold; part had been sent to England with Hammon; the rest Winwood may have. The provisions of spice, sugar, grocery ware, wine lights, and such like may be sold, 'and so the house discharged and my people with the stuff sent by water to Rouen and from thence the directest way for England.' From Rouen it may be converyed overland to Deepe, and there shipped for Dover in some safe passage, 'because there is matter of charge of the Queen's plate and mine own, among it.'

Various other directions in which Mr. Willaston, young H. Savile, Mr. Bashe, and mine host of Orleans are mentioned.[13]

It is significant that Neville's only concerns are that he is unable 'to requite my pains, faith and love'. Clearly he was missing his wife, and by his 'faith' he obviously meant his religion, since the Lord Admiral was one of the Howard family of Catholics. His 'pains' probably refer to the gout that was troubling him increasingly. At home, he knew of herbal medicine and its preparation, but he obviously had no access to it there.

According to Cecil, however, Neville was also very angry. He had been fined first £10,000 by Elizabeth. Although this was now under consideration to be reduced and to be paid by instalments, he still felt the injustice of it. He had already spent £4,000 of his own fortune in France, thus making the Queen's debt to him another cause of his joining the conspirators. To Neville, she must have seemed a hypocritical thief. She had sent him to France to recover a loan, while at the same time refusing to pay him his due allowances. She now insisted on Neville drawing up a list of all his real estate, so that she might choose which rents she could 'dip into'. His original list is still available in the Berkshire Record Office. He begins by writing it in a 'Court hand', but this gradually deteriorates into a scrawled Elizabethan script, probably signifying his growing disgust at having to provide her with such a personal document.

It was not long before he was sent to the Tower of London along with his 'champion', the Earl of Southampton. Everyone was surprised and relieved that Southampton had escaped the death sentence, but it is significant that he and Neville remained in the Tower longer than any of the other conspirators. In fact, they were only released when King James succeeded to the throne.

On 25 February 1601 Essex was led to his death. The Queen had granted him the final boon of being executed in a private courtyard rather than in the open, public green. Even so, about a hundred onlookers were present. He dressed elegantly as always. Adding a touch of theatre right to the end, he took off his cloak to reveal a scarlet velvet tunic. Essex, on forgiving the executioner, said that, after all, he had deserved his fate and was sorry for what he had attempted.

Danvers, Sir Gelly Meyrick and Cuffe all received the death sentence too. Henry Cuffe was an extremely educated man, being a noted classical scholar. He made a speech at the scaffold, speaking of Neville with his dying breath:

I confesse (saith he) *that it were a high offence, yea Treason, if a subject cast out of favour and degree of honour should by force and armes make his way to the Queenes Majesty. But I never incited any man to arms against the Queene. But whereas I have brought that Noble Knight Sir Henry Nevill into danger, I am hartily sory for it, and I earnestly intreat him to forgive mee. And whereas I said that of the 24 Aldermen of London 21 were at the Earles devotion, this I meant of their most favourable affection unto him, and not that they would take armes for him.*[14]

Finally, with Neville's involvement with the Essex rebellion, the real reason behind the continuing concealment of the true writer is revealed. If Neville himself had at any time past been half wondering whether he might eventually decide to uncover his identity as Shakespeare's shadow, then the Essex trouble surely must have put a stop to any such thoughts. His friends too would have persuaded him not to besmirch their own immortal reputations by telling the true story.

Did a conspiracy of silence therefore ultimately transmute itself into a sea of forgetfulness, when it came to the Shakespeare cover-up? This might indeed have been the case, especially after the splitting of the Neville family during the Civil War and subsequent Commonwealth (1640–60). At this time, Neville's eldest grandson (also Henry) became a political writer and satirist, first supporting Cromwell and then being imprisoned by him for criticizing his dictatorial conduct. His brother Richard, however, was one of the main leaders of the Royalist forces. The Killigrews were originally Parliamentarian – so much so that their home in Cornwall was the first 'grand house' to be destroyed by the Royalists. However, at the end of the Civil War, some of the Killigrews' descendants became Royalist playwrights. One of them opened a theatre and was even given a sole licence to perform Shakespeare's plays in London, his partner being none other than William Davenant, reputed illegitimate son of Shakespeare (the actor) himself.[15]

Richard Neville indeed seemed to gain the love of a king, which was always something that eluded his grandfather. Charles II held his Restoration Party at Billingbear House, and this was a popular choice. King Charles was probably the kind of 'constitutional monarch' Henry Neville always had in mind, though his womanizing would not have pleased him. However, one of the Killigrew girls had a child by Charles, so the old political divisions must have been virtually healed. The Nevilles and Killigrews were attractive and obviously continued to inspire admiration, just as they had always done.

Neville's neighbours and relatives, the Hobys, were convinced that, had he possessed the patience to wait long enough, he would have been eventually invited by the status quo to take on a senior political role. (And it should be noted that they must therefore have been sure he always intended to take part in the Essex rebellion and become head of state.) Neville may have had to wait for a new monarch in order for this to happen, they thought, but it would nevertheless come to pass. But they and others may all have been forgetting just how much Neville's old dynasty was still feared by the Tudors. Could such a family ever be content to take on the role of state servant rather than state leader? In later years, the Nevilles' relatives, the Spencers, whose coat-of-arms was quartered with their own, were to suffer the same suspicions from those on high.

Appendix 3

Sir Henry Neville's Voyage to France, and its Double

‹❦›

Neville and the Savile group must have spent a few weeks in France while visiting Anthony Bacon, as Sir Henry was known to be skilled in French, even as a young man. On arriving at the French Court in May 1599, Sir Henry proudly wrote to Cecil that Henri IV embraced him like an old friend when he first greeted him. This probably meant that he had met that King when he was Henri of Navarre, in those early days with Anthony Bacon, or at least that the King knew of Neville's reputation as a great intellectual. Henri himself was interested in literature and philosophy, so would probably have been careful to be well-informed of all the like-minded men of Europe.

It may be recalled too that the Earl of Essex knew and worked with Henri, that the young Earl of Southampton had run away in order to assist Henri of Navarre (as he then was) in his efforts to become King of France, and also that Neville hunted with the Queen and Biron (friend of Henri and the then French Ambassador) when he stayed in England. Henry Neville and his wife now lodged at his father-in-law Killigrew's house in Lothbury. As Killigrew had a young French wife by 1592, it could be surmised that Henry had a great opportunity to keep in practice with the language.

One can begin to understand why Queen Elizabeth saw Neville as the perfect man for the ambassadorship, and why she was so insistent he should go, despite all his pleadings to the contrary. Perhaps too she had a nagging feeling that such a highly intelligent man from a rival dynasty who also knew how to make weapons, but whom she had just forced to sell his business, and whose friend's sufferings she had ignored,[1] was better kept as far from her Court as possible. However, she must have been at least a little troubled by the vehemence of his reluctance to accept the office, and even more concerned when she discovered that the Earl of Essex had been able to persuade him where she herself had failed. She favoured men who flattered her and were persuaded by her. With Sir Henry Neville she got no satisfaction in either regard. It seems likely that Henry was at this time (1599) involved in writing *Henry V*, and that Essex, who had his own troupe of actors, was partly supporting his playwriting. Also, both men were excitedly awaiting the completion of the Globe Theatre, and Neville must surely have been anxious to attend the first performance of *Julius Caesar*, even if in disguise. No wonder Henry did not wish to accept the post that would take him abroad.

However, France was the country in which much of his ongoing play was set. It is probable that he had completed most of *Henry V* by the time he undertook the journey there, but a little additional verisimilitude of place and action certainly did not harm the play. Henry obviously continued to write it in France, where he was surrounded by the French language and ambience. And there is indeed textual confirmation for these suppositions: to begin with, the 'Chorus' in the play follows closely Neville's own experiences of travelling to France. Then there is a scene written wholly in French, plus a mention of the Earl of Essex in its text. Added to all this, there is a reference to an allowance of money given to Henry V for his wars. This is described as the largest amount ever given for such a purpose, which was precisely the case with the 'war loan' Elizabeth had granted Henri IV. (She had been unable to send him men to assist in his fight against the Spanish, but had sent him gold to support his own troops; now she wanted Sir Henry to go and persuade him to pay back this money.)

The evidence for the parallels between Neville's personal situation and the play of *Henry V* consists of Neville's letters, which were preserved by his friend and secretary, Ralph Winwood, intertwined with extracts from the play itself. There will be seen to be much overlapping between the two sets of texts.

Neville began his journey from London to Paris in April, 1599. On reaching Dover, he had to stay at an inn and wait several days for the wind to change:

Dover, 26th April 1599

Right Honourable [Robert Cecil, Secretary of State]

I receaved at my coming to Dover, a Letter from my Steward, who is attending me at Deipe [Dieppe], dated two days since; wherein he writes, that Monsieur de Cuchon, Lieutenant Governor of Deipe, hath receaved advertissement that all French Ships are staied in Spain, . . . I am heere attending the Wind, which is yet directly contrarie; as soone as it turnes I will loose no opportunity . . .

Your Honor's very humbly to be commanded

HENRY NEVILLE[2]

At the same time as Henry wrote this, Cecil was writing a private letter to him, ending 'Your loving Kinsman and Friend'. (Cecil was always very careful to tell Neville that he should write in a very different manner when he wrote actual dispatches, as the Queen was obliged to see them, but when writing a personal letter, he should use different channels for its delivery. Only in their personal correspondence would they divulge their true feelings and boyhood friendship – a friendship that was to be sorely tested during Neville's stay in France.)

The wind did not change for another three days, so Henry was forced to remain at the inn in Dover, always concerned about his anxious family: 'I would gladly settle myselfe and my familie, before I undertake so long a Voiage',[3] he wrote on hearing that the French King was leaving Paris and travelling south. He wanted to settle his wife and family in Paris, not to leave them there alone in a foreign city, as soon as they arrived. He desperately hoped that the Queen would not wish him to follow the King immediately so far down country, but would be content for him to wait for Henri's return. But Elizabeth valued Neville's skills too highly to consider their being wasted: if the King were gone away when Henry reached Paris, then he must follow.

How heartless this Queen was turning out to be! Neville might have added that his wife was several months' pregnant, hoping that this would then soften Elizabeth's attitude. However, such a protestation would have caused even more problems: any child born abroad of a father employed abroad was refused English citizenship, so Neville probably hoped that the baby would be born soon, so that he might keep its birthplace secret and pretend it had arrived just before they embarked from Dover.

The delayed journey, sojourn at an English inn, and desperate worry about the effect of protracted travel on the stomach are all echoed in *Henry V*. King Henry V is similarly delayed by a 'contrarie' wind, and is forced to wait at Southampton. In fact, scholars have often discussed why the writer made this 'mistake'. Henry V did in fact also embark from Dover; but perhaps Neville thought the parallels between himself and the play might become too noticeable if he included this fact:

> CHORUS. . . . *The King is set from London, and the scene*
> *Is now transported, gentles, to Southampton;*
> *There is the play-house now, there must you sit,*
> *And thence to France shall we convey you safe*
> *And bring you back, charming the narrow seas*
> *To give you gentle pass; for, if we may,*
> *We'll not offend one stomach with our play.*
> *But, till the King come forth, and not till then,*
> *Unto Southampton do we shift our scene.*
>
> *Act II, Prologue*

And while the King is involved in this journey, Falstaff is dying at the inn in Eastcheap. It is as if Neville is saying farewell to his old life, and perhaps also to his father, as he had become a very Falstaffian figure in some ways – jesting, overweight, fond of his food, and somewhat disabled from gout, which was eventually to be Henry's own destiny. Then, for King Henry V as well as for Neville, the wind changes:

> KING HENRY. *Now sits the wind fair, and we will aboard.*
>
> *Act II, Sc. II*

And next we are surely treated to a picture of Neville's own start of journey, together with the feeling of adventure welling up inside him, counterbalancing his worry for his wife and children, and accompanied with memories of the great 'ordnance' (once his daily concern), and of the fleet he once sailed with to Cadiz:

> CHORUS. *Thus with imagin'd wing our swift scene flies,*
> *In motion of no less celerity*
> *Than that of thought. Suppose that you have seen*
> *The well-appointed King at Hampton pier*

Embark his royalty; and his brave fleet
With silken streamers the young Phoebus fanning.
Play with your fancies; and in them behold
Upon the hempen tackle ship-boys climbing;
Hear the shrill whistle which doth order give
To sounds confus'd; behold the threaden sails,
Borne with th' invisible and creeping wind,
Draw the huge bottoms through the furrowed sea,
Breasting the lofty surge. O, do but think
You stand upon the rivage and behold
A city on th' inconstant billows dancing;
For so appears this fleet majestical,
Holding due course to Harfleur. Follow, follow!
Grapple your minds to sternage of this navy
And leave your England as dead midnight still,
Guarded with grandsires, babies, and old women,
Either past or not arriv'd to pith and puissance;
For who is he whose chin is but enrich'd
With one appearing hair that will not follow
These cull'd and choice-drawn cavaliers to France?
Work, work your thoughts, and therein see a siege;
Behold the ordnance on their carriages,
With fatal mouths gaping on girded Harfleur.
Suppose th' ambassador from the French comes back ...

Act III, Prologue

(As far as we are aware, Shakespeare of Stratford never left the shores of England.)

Perhaps too, Neville was imagining the fleet of French ships now captured by the Spanish, as he wrote in his letter of 26 April (quoted above.) He now describes to Cecil the extent of that captured French fleet:

Deipe, 3rd May, 1599 O.S.
Yt may please your Honor to understand, that I arryved in this Towne the second of May, having continued almost 3 Dayes upon the Sea. I found the Gouvernor, and his Leiutenant, both absent; but have receaved great Curtesies of the Sergent Major of the Towne, called Monsieur Favet ... Touching the

Arrest of the Frenche Shipps, whereof I wrote unto your Honor from Dover, I learne heere that yt is of all Ships (above a hundred) and that he offers them very good Entertainement. Among the rest, there is one Shipp staied, belonging to the Gouvernor of this Towne, the Captaine whereof hath written hither that the Fleet which that King prepares consisteth of some 38 great Shipps, and 50 Gallies.

... This place affords no other News at this tyme, that I dare wryte to your Honor; yet some bruits I heare, that the Duke of Savoy fortifieth his Frontiers towards France; which should argue no great intention to satisfie the King for the Marquisat; but of that I shall certifie your Honor more from Paris. I purpose to go hence to morrow to Rouen, where I expect answere, by a Messenger I sent Post of purpose to Mr. Edmonds,[4] of the certaintie and speede of the King's remoove. That little tyme I remaine there, I meane to imploy, in learning as much as I canne by our English Merchants, of the Nature and Valew of those Customes, which are by the Contract to be assigned to her Majestie, for her remboursement. I hope e're I arryve at Paris, I shall receave answere from your Honor of both the Letters I wrote from Dover.

Perhaps the news he dare not write concerns the state of poor Anne's pregnancy – Robert Cecil was genuinely fond of Anne Killigrew Neville, his first cousin.

Once in France, Neville is relieved to find King Henri still resident in Paris, though secretly staying at a friend's house. But as far as his writing of *Henry V* is concerned, Neville becomes more French and more ambassadorial in style, for a while. One word that keeps appearing in his dispatches is 'touching', meaning 'regarding'. We have 'Towching the States Navie...'[5] 'Towching the 20000 Crowns...'[6] etc. Indeed, the word is used a great deal by members of the diplomatic service at that time. Now, the first half of *Henry V* also contains frequent use of the word. And then it stops, as if Neville suddenly realizes he might be giving himself away:

CANTERBURY. *... And in regard of causes now in hand,*
    Which I have open'd to his Grace at large,
    *As **touching** France – to give a greater sum*
    Than ever at one time the clergy yet
    Did to his predecessors part withal.

Act I, Sc. I

KING HENRY. *... **Touching** our person seek we no revenge ...*

Act II, Sc. II

> *FLUELLEN. . . . as partly **touching** or*
> *concerning the disciplines of the war, . . . as **touching** the direction of the*
> *military discipline, that is the point.*
>
> Act III, Sc. II

Notice how Fluellen feels he has to add the substantive 'concerning' when he uses 'touching'. It is as if the writer is beginning to feel that perhaps the general audience may not have heard the diplomatic terminology before. And besides the actual vocabulary used, it will be noticed that Canterbury is referring to a grant of money offered to King Henry V by the Church for his French escapade, just as Henri IV of France had received money from Elizabeth to help his fight against the Spanish. It was precisely this loan of 20,000 Crowns that Neville had been sent to retrieve, so money for wars was most definitely in his mind at the time. There is indeed much talk of Crowns in *Henry V.* And the words 'French Crown' carried at least three meanings at the time: 1) the imperial crown of state; 2) coinage; 3) venereal disease. Knowing the true authorship and circumstances of the play, one wonders whether the reference to 'twenty crowns' made by Henry V himself is entirely arbitrary:

> *KING HENRY. Indeed, the French may lay twenty French crowns to one*
> *they will beat us, for they bear them on their shoulders; but it*
> *is no English treason to cut French crowns, and to-morrow the*
> *King himself will be a clipper.*
>
> Act IV, Sc. I

It was, after all, 20,000 Crowns that were now owed to Queen Elizabeth. And as for the third meaning, Henri IV was known as a womanizer. Indeed Neville was to become disgusted with his treatment of his wife, and his flaunting of mistresses at the French Court.

The French Ambassador plays his role in the drama too. And Henry V displays a wish to carry out background research before meeting with ambassadors – just the same wish Neville displays in his letter to Cecil, quoted above: 'That little tyme I remaine there, I meane to imploy, in learning as much as I canne by our English Merchants, of the Nature and Valew of those Customes, which are by the Contract to be assigned to her Majestie, for her remboursement'.

WESTMORELAND. Shall we call in th' ambassador, my liege?
KING HENRY. Not yet, my cousin; we would be resolv'd,
  Before we hear him, of some things of weight
  That task our thoughts, concerning us and France.

Act I, Sc. II

Neville too always wished to be well prepared, constantly insisting with Cecil that the Queen should communicate her thoughts to him before he committed himself to an audience with the King of France or his representatives. Indeed, King Henry V shows yet another striking similarity to Neville's own way of thinking. When the King of Spain dies in June 1599, Neville is invited to the funeral, but writes to tell Cecil that he will not go; because...? Well, because of all sorts of complicated reasons. Yet he finally confesses that he went after all, but in disguise:

> *This Day were the Obsequies of the King of Spaine performed, and whereunto I was invited, but excused my selfe, That I was very willing to do the King any Honor, but this Action being desseigned wholly to the Honor of the King of Spaine, who dyed not in Amitie, but rather in Hostillitie with her Majestie, and his Son continuing the same Termes, yt would very evill beseeme me to be Partaker of yt, and besydes my Presence would but trouble the Feast; for I thought the Spanishe Ambassador would insist upon his Master's Place and Honor, and so would I upon the Queen's my Mistresses; which might easily produce Effects that would not be pleasing to this King, especially at suche a tyme.*
>
> *My excuses were well taken, and I was offered a private Place to see the Solemnity yf I would; I accepted yt for the Gentlemen of my Company, but indeed I went also disguised my selfe, and repented me of my paines, having never seene a poorer thing.[7]*

The somewhat black humour of the situation and of Neville's writing cannot be missed: he had experienced many a crossed sword with the Spanish Ambassador's representative by this time, and was destined to cross him more. Neville's father had gone on a mission to France in disguise too. His uncle had disguised as King Henry VIII at a party – there was definitely always a touch of the dramatic about the Nevilles.

It is impossible not to equate Neville's disguising with that of Henry V before the battle of Agincourt, when he wanders cloaked among his men in order to hear the truth of their sentiments, and perhaps also to avoid the wrath of any who are angry that they ever followed him to the benighted battlefield:

> HENRY ... *Lend me thy cloak, Sir Thomas ...*
> PISTOL. *Qui va là?*
> KING HENRY. *A friend.*
> PISTOL. *Discuss unto me: art thou officer,*
>   *Or art thou base, common, and popular?*
> KING HENRY. *I am a gentleman of a company.*
> PISTOL. *Trail'st thou the puissant pike?*
> KING HENRY. *Even so. What are you?*
> PISTOL. *As good a gentleman as the Emperor.*
> KING HENRY. *Then you are a better than the King.*
> PISTOL. *The King's a bawcock and a heart of gold,*
>   *A lad of life, an imp of fame;*
>   *Of parents good, of fist most valiant.*
>   *I kiss his dirty shoe, and from heart-string*
>   *I love the lovely bully. What is thy name?*
> KING HENRY. *Harry le Roy.*
> PISTOL. *Le Roy! a Cornish name; art thou of Cornish crew?*
> KING HENRY. *No, I am a Welshman.*
>
> *Act IV, Sc. I*

Finally, we are now able to understand why the writer of *Henry V* was concerned enough about Essex's campaign in Ireland to use it as an image in the play. The reference to the Earl of Essex being in Ireland at the time it was written actually dates its composition as between 27 March 1599 and his return on 28 September of that same year:

> CHORUS. ... *How London doth pour out her citizens –*
>   *The mayor and all his brethren in best sort,*
>   *Like to the senators of th' antique Rome*
>   *With the plebeians swarming at their heels,*
>   *Go forth and fetch their conqu'ring Caesar in –*
>   *As, by a lower but loving likelihood,*
>   *Were now the **general of our gracious empress**,*
>   *As in good time he may, from Ireland coming,*

Bringing rebellion broached on his sword,
How many would the peaceful city quit
To welcome him! Much more, and much more cause,
Did they this Harry.

This places the writing firmly within Neville's ambassadorship in Paris. The 'general of our gracious empress' was none other than Essex himself. Henry's friend Essex knew of his predicament. He had indeed persuaded him to go over there partly as his own representative. We do not appear to have any letters that passed between them at this time, but this is hardly surprising, since Essex found it difficult to receive and write letters while involved in his Irish campaign. After this, Essex was in disgrace, so it may well be that both men thought it safer not to correspond. Then Neville returned to England for a break (ostensibly on the grounds of increasing deafness) in July 1600, so the two communicated in person after that date.

And throughout his embassy in France, Neville writes to Cecil asking news of Essex and his Irish campaign, to which Cecil does his best to reply optimistically. Even while still at Dover, Cecil writes to Neville about Essex, thus proving that he knows of his concern:

26th Aprill 1599

We have receaved Newes that the Earl of Essex is well arrived; and here all things are as they were . . . I find the Queene will lyke yt well, yf you do procure the King accidentally, to send hyther to be installed . . . [as a Knight of the Garter].[8]

Then in a private letter to Cecil, Neville tells him of a conversation he had with King Henri IV concerning Essex:

. . . he asked me yf my Lord of Essex and my Lord Admirall were made Freends before his Jorney [into Ireland]. I answered, I knew of no other but frendly Disposition betwene them, and yf there had bin any other at any tyme, yet at the tyme of his Departure I knew they were in very kynd Termes. Then he asked me, whether your Honor and my Lord of Essex did agree any better than you did. These Questions were strange to me, and I answered, that I knew of muche Kindnes that had passed betwene your Honor and him, but never of any Unkindnes. He sayd, Yes, yes; and that he had hard much of yt. I told him, that in matters of Advice and Counsail, you might perhaps have differed some-

> *tyme in Opinion, which was ordinary in Princes Counsails, and I thought his*
> *Court was not free from yt; No, no, said he, I have had the greatest paine in*
> *the World to containe them, but I have made them know my Mind, that I will*
> *have them agree, and I thinck that the best course for the Queene your Mistres*
> *also. . . .*

Neville here plays his cards very close to his chest. King Henri seems to know quite a lot about factions at the English Court. The Lord Admiral was a Catholic and a member of the Howard clan, and thus not on particularly good terms with the Earl of Essex or the Nevilles. But Henry is not going to give him any chance to dig more deeply into that hole. He knows the Queen wishes all foreign potentates to see her as head of a united crew. Of course, the King knows the truth of the matter and understands Henry's posturing. Neville has no need to explain all this to Cecil, as he too understands. So he next proceeds to display a little bawdiness in his sense of humour – an aspect of Neville's personality we are generally only permitted to see in the plays:

> *Then he [King Henri] told me a Merriment, that he understood that the*
> *Archduke that Night he was married, was not able to consummat Matrimony*
> *with the Infanta, which he had likewise related to the Generall of the*
> *Cordeliers, who had answered that yt might well be, for he had hard the*
> *Archduke's Confessor affirme, that he knew, when he was 37 Years old he had*
> *never towched Woman. Thus praying Pardon of your Honor, yf whiles I thought*
> *to relate you all that passed, I have troubled you with more than needed, I*
> *humbly take my leave.*[9]

The somewhat over-officious Cecil had written to Neville to tell him to be sure to relate *everything* in his personal letters. Clearly, Neville wanted to teach him the lesson that it was perhaps best if he edited out some things that were said at the French Court!

Next come letters from Neville telling of 'bruits' he has heard concerning the Earl of Essex, and he wonders whether Cecil can confirm them. ('Bruits' was the diplomatic term for partially substantiated rumours – a word that is often used in 'Shakespeare', though it is not ordinarily found outside diplomatic circles at the time.) By 15 May 1599, Neville has heard that Essex has already put down the Earl of Connaught. But Cecil replies to Neville telling him he must be very selective with the information he receives. Cecil urges him to trust *his* reports only, and assures him he will tell him as soon as any such positive news of Essex reaches him. In the meantime, Neville must not in any way give the impression in the French Court that the Queen is criticizing Essex's failure to engage the enemy. Cecil writes:

> *many things fly over by common bruits, whereof you have not hard by me: . . . In this Point I confesse I mean to deal curiously, in a common respect to us bothe, . . . knowe this from me, that yf any one of the Great of Ulster or Connaght be reduced, yt is more than the Queene of England to my Knowledge understandeth; only this is true, that in the Countries of Lempster and the Pale . . . offer submission.*
>
> *Thus much doe I particularise unto you, nether to the intent should you make them there thinck us less happy, or yet to diminishe the Reputaion of my Lord's [Essex's] Proceedings; for he, arriving not in Ireland before the 17th April, must have wrought Miracles, to have settled and distributed an Army of 16000 Foote and 1300 Horse, and to have accomodated them with all Necessaries in a Countrey full of Misery and Disorder, in a shorter Tyme than he did . . .*[10]

Neville is sensitive enough to assure Cecil that he did not mean to imply that he (Cecil) had not related the news quickly enough to him:

> *I beseech you, Sir, to be assured, that I had no purpose any way to challenge you of any omission, in that I was not advertised of the Newes of Ireland, which the King told me; for I had even the same conceyte of yt, which I find now to be trew, that the Ambassador, had taken up the Newes there at the Exchange: but de bene esse, I made that Answere I wrote of. I beseeche you thincke that I shall take all you wryte me to be of favor, and what you write not, to be forborne on good respects.*[11]

Stylistically speaking, it can be noted how much more fluent Neville is than Cecil. David Hume, the Scottish philosopher, was later to note that Neville's was the best and liveliest diplomatic style he had ever read. It may also be seen just how frequently Neville changes his spelling – he will happily spell the same word differently on the same page. And these transcriptions are true to Neville's originals, many of which can be found in the Public Record Office. Shakespeare scholars have for centuries debated whether the original printers were eccentric in their varied spellings rather than the writer; the matter is now solved – the true writer cared more for style and fluency than he did for formal spelling. One gets the impression he is writing so quickly that he spells in whichever way comes first to mind.

And thus the correspondence over Essex continues, until Neville hears that he has returned from Ireland, displeased the Queen and so had his right to the tax on the importation of sweet wines taken from him. Neville interprets this, correctly, as a bad sign. Many scholars have thought Sonnet 125 to be a reference to it:

> *Have I not seen dwellers on form and favour*
> *Lose all, and more by paying too much rent*
> *For compound sweet; forgoing simple savour,*
> *Pitiful thrivers in their gazing spent? ...*

It was said that Essex, on his return, burst all muddy and unannounced into Elizabeth's private chamber, arriving just as she was dressing. Instead of leaving, he stood and gazed. The 'compound sweet' is thought to refer directly to the tax on sweet wines. Neville was definitely concerned with the same things as Shakespeare, as seen in a letter from Neville to his secretary Winwood, dated from London, 2 November 1600 (Neville had by this time been allowed to return to England for a break):

> *The Earle of Essex continueth yet without Access to the Court. At Michaelmas last his Lease of the Sweet Wines expired; and after a Moneths Suspence, whether it should be graunted him or nay, it is at length put into Sir Henry Billingsley's Hands and others to husband it for the Queen, which is no Argument of any such relenting Disposition towards him as was supposed. Yet notwithstanding there is an Expectation of his running at the Coronation-Day, and that it shall be the first step of his Grace and Access to the Court: But I am not very prone to beleeve it.*[12]

(Each anniversary of Elizabeth's coronation was a public holiday and time of celebration.) But Neville was still playing his cards close to his chest, not mentioning even to Winwood (his friend as well as his secretary) that he had had contact with the Earl of Essex's companions.

Appendix 4

A Review of *Shakespeare and the Founders of Liberty in America*

In 1917 Charles Mills Gayley published *Shakespeare and the Founders of Liberty in America* (New York, 1917). At the beginning of the book he describes how:

> *The adventurers and planters of Virginia, in later years when Shakespeare was writing* Troilus and Cressida, Coriolanus *and* The Tempest, *were of his blood and temper, the blood and temper of the forefathers of many of us today. Their ventures and failures, their faults and virtues, are our history, Anglo-Saxon and American, as well as theirs. It was a group of patriots clustered about Shakespeare's patron, the Earl of Southampton, and Sir Edwin Sandys, Southampton's ally – a group of patriots, some of them friends of Shakespeare, some of them acquaintances, – that laid the foundations of constitutional government in the New World. (pp.1 and 2)*

Sir Henry Neville was prominent among the 'adventurers' and political thinkers cited above, and is celebrated as such in Gayley's book. In fact, he even provided wood from his estate to build the ships that took the 'planters' to the new colony. Gayley establishes a definite connection between the works of 'Shakespeare' and the men who initiated the Virginia Company. He thinks of Neville as being separate from 'Shakespeare' and yet shows how they shared the same friends, were influenced by the same writers and thinkers, even appeared in the same clubs, but were never together at the same time in the same venue. There is an unbridgeable gap in his reasoning, however: Shakespeare was never a member of the Virginia Company. But Gayley never knew that Shakespeare, the writer, and Henry Neville, the politician, were one and the same person.

Gayley was later to be a fellow researcher with Dr Leslie Hotson, the famed literary sleuth, but both were seeking Shakespeare's connections – a quest which they never extended into a search for his identity. There is thus one major flaw in Gayley's chain of thought: yes, 'Shakespeare' must have shared ideas, political ideals and friends among the members of the Virginia Company, yet an explanation of how the lowly actor managed to contact all these elevated men and become privy to their philosophy, learning and private information is never attempted. So even though Gayley's research strongly implies that 'Shakespeare' and his ideology were to be found among the members of the Virginia Company, we know that the name 'Shakespeare' did not appear in its meticulously kept lists. Yet no one outside that company would have been allowed to read their private letters, as the author of *The Tempest* so obviously did. The conclusion is surely that Gayley would have done well to look through the lists for another name and another identity.

However, even though he does not actively seek a different authorial identity, the writer painstakingly puts together evidence which demonstrates how the ideals associated with the leaders of the Virginia Company are presented in the works of William Shakespeare. In doing this, he has provided yet more intertextual arguments for the true author being listed among these 'Patriots', as they called themselves.

Gayley explains how the group of friends and associates who began the Virginia Company constructed *ab initio* an association dedicated to political reform. They had been disappointed at James I's failure to reform areas of state abuse left over from Elizabeth's reign. They wanted to bring an end to favouritism, monopoly and monarchical interference in control of taxation; they wished also for freedom of election, person and speech, and so inaugurated a 'company' in which these ideals could serve as a model for the state. This means that their ideals became the basis for the American

Constitution. By extension, therefore, we can now say with confidence that the ideas and ideals encapsulated in Shakespeare's (Neville's) works are those still perpetuated in the Constitution of the United States.

A mainstay of Gayley's argument is his drawing of parallels between the sermons and writings of a certain Richard Hooker and those ideas expressed by 'Shakespeare'. As we shall see, Neville was in contact with Hooker and knew his philosophy, whereas there is no known connection between Hooker and the Stratford actor.

Richard Hooker (*c.*1554–1600) was born in Exeter and attended Corpus Christi College, Oxford. He became a fellow of that College in 1577, which was the year Neville graduated from that same university. He was ordained in 1581 and moved to London in 1584 – the year Neville became an MP. Hooker married the daughter of a prominent member of the Merchant Taylors' Company, and from Neville's concern for workers in the cloth trade there is a suspicion that he too was allied with this company and with the Dyers' Company. In 1585 Hooker became Master of the Temple, in which position he was concerned with refuting Puritanism. He soon produced political–religious books, including *The Laws of Ecclesiastical Polity* (published in 1593.)

Above all, Hooker was concerned with examining and rebuking the basis of many accepted beliefs, including both Presbyterianism and Roman Catholicism, and, most significantly, denying the Royalist doctrine of the Divine Right of Kings. In this way, therefore, Hooker can be seen as being very much in line with the rather Templar beliefs expressed throughout the works of Shakespeare – that the position of monarch bears responsibility to the people and a duty of care to the state, not a Divine Right to rule as he pleases.

Gayley maintains, correctly, that these latter ideas are those expressed in *Richard II* (1595–97) 'and of the later plays in so far a reference is made to the relation of ruler and subject' (p.84). He also stresses that Sir Edwin Sandys was a Virginia Company member who was a particular follower of these ideals, along with his friend and political associate, Sir Henry Neville. Indeed, it was Sandys who was later to declare Virginia a Republic, but who was placed in the Tower by King James for doing so. As a result, James dissolved the Virginia Company and declared the state a Crown Colony.

The papers of the Virginia Company are now to be found among those left by Thomas Jefferson, and there is no doubt that its constitution greatly influenced the ideas on which the (eventually) independent United States of America was based. Gayley also notes that Francis Bacon, despite being more reactionary in his politics than Neville and Sandys, did help to prepare letters patent for Virginia. (Having traced Neville's connection with the Bacons, we can all guess at whose instigation Sir Francis agreed to do this.)

Regarding Sir Henry himself, Gayley notes how he was friends with Sir Robert Sidney and 'As Baron Penshurst in 1603, and afterward as Lord Lisle, Sidney threw open his home at Penshurst to the poets – Ben Jonson and many another friend of Shakespeare. That the Sidney and Shakespeare of this circle of common acquaintance did not know each other is, to say the least, unlikely' (p.16). However, there is no record of Shakespeare ever having known Sir Robert, whereas there is direct evidence of a friendship existing since teenage years between Sidney and Neville, and also documentary proof of Jonson's visits to Penshurst Place.

We may well smile at Gayley's very next comment:

The interests and intimacies of Shakespeare and Henry Neville, of Billingbear in Berkshire, coincided in half a dozen different ways. Another of Essex's knights of Cadiz, Sir Henry had participated in the Earl's conspiracy of 1601, had been convicted of treason, thrown into the Tower with Southampton, and held there till the accession of James I. He was for years a close companion of Shakespeare's devoted panegyrist, Hugh Holland, and of Holland's friend Christopher Brooke, another of Shakespeare's personal admirers. He was an excellent patron of poets, this Sir Henry – of Davies of Hereford, Ben Jonson, Beaumont and Fletcher, all well known to Shakespeare. His name is to be seen scribbled over the fly-leaf of a manuscript of 'Mr. Frauncis Bacon's' essays and speeches (about 1597) together with those of Bacon (a relative) and Shakespeare [i.e. The Northumberland Manuscript] ... Neville was early interested in the Virginia enterprise, a member of the council from 1607 until his death in 1615, and one of its Patriots and a leader of the Independent Party in Parliament. His independence, indeed, prevented him, in 1612, from becoming Secretary of State. His son and successor, of the same name, was a subscriber to the Plantation in 1611; and one of his daughters, Elizabeth, married a brother of Sir William Berkeley, afterwards Governor of Virginia. Though we have no testimony concerning his (Sir Thomas Gates') immediate acquaintance with Shakespeare we know that they had associations and infor-

mation in common. Gates, like Pembroke and Neville, was a knight of the Essex creation and supporter of the liberal faction in the Virginia Company. With his adventures in the New World in 1609–10 Shakespeare was extraordinarily familiar. In The Tempest, *written soon afterward, he makes use of minute details of Gates's shipwreck off Bermuda in 1609, of his life on the island, and of his experiences as Lieutenant-General and Administrator of Virginia. Of these details some, as we shall presently see, were derived from a confidential account set down in the colony, brought over to England by Gates, and not made public for years after Shakespeare's death.*

Gayley later goes on to say how Neville was a member of the Mitre Club, known to be a merry literary company, of which John Donne was also a member. Then he relates how Richard Martin (whose connection with Neville we have discussed elsewhere) was also a friend of the poet Chapman who, says Gayley, 'was variously connected in literature and life with Shakespeare and closely with Ben Jonson'. He also describes John Donne as 'An adherent of Essex in 1596–7, his political, literary, and social affiliations were in half a dozen ways interwoven with those of Shakespeare'. It is surely by now becoming obvious that Shakespeare is the ghostly, unspecific, unrecorded, missing factor. Everyone else's presence is reliably witnessed, but 'Shakespeare' is never there.

Now what of those specific instances of Hooker's ideas included within the works of William Shakespeare? Gayley reckons it does not stop with 'ideas' alone: there are even specific parallels between the language used by Shakespeare and Hooker. As an example of this he quotes from Ulysses' speech on 'degree' from *Troilus and Cressida*. It is clear that neither 'Shakespeare' nor Hooker thought that liberty and equality before the law should extend its meaning to include an idea that everyone in society is equal in every way. Respect for the rule of law and respect for learning and position must still be maintained, in any civilized society. For ease of linguistic and semantic comparison, we can set Shakespeare and Hooker side by side:

Troilus and Cressida

The specialty of rule hath been neglected;
And look how many Grecian tents do
stand

Hollow upon this plain, so many hollow
factions.

When that the general is not like the
hive
To whom the foragers shall all repair,
What honey is expected? Degree being
vizarded,
Th' unworthiest shows as fairly in the
mask.

The heavens themselves, the planets,
and this centre,

Observe degree, *priority, and place,*
Insisture, course, *proportion,*
season, *form,*
Office, and custom, in all line of
order;
And therefore is the **glorious planet**
Sol
In noble eminence enthroned and
sphered
Amidst the other, whose med'cinable eye
Corrects the ill aspects of planets evil,
And *posts* **like the commandment**
of a king,
Sans check, to good and bad. **But**
when the planets
In evil mixture to disorder wander,
What plagues and what portents,
what mutiny,

Hooker's Ecclesiastical Polity, Bk.1

God's commanding those things to be
which are, and to be in such sort as they
are, to keep that tenure and course
which they do, importeth the establishment of nature's law … And as it
cometh to pass in a kingdom rightly
ordered, that after a law is once published, it presently takes effect far and
wide, all states framing themselves
thereunto, even so let us think it fareth
in the natural course of the world, since
the time that God did first proclaim the
edicts of his law upon it, heaven and
earth have hearkened unto his voice,
and their labour hath been to do his
will: He made a law for the rain; he
gave his decree unto the sea that the
waters should not pass his commandment. Now if nature should intermit
her course, and leave altogether though
it were but for a while the observation
of her own law; if those principal and
mother elements of the world, whereof
all things in this lower world are made,
should lose the qualities which now they
have; if the frame of that heavenly arch
erected over our heads should loosen
and dissolve itself; if celestial spheres
should forget their wonted motions,
and by irregular volubility turn themselves any way as it might happen; if
the prince of lights of heaven, which
now as a giant doth run his unwearied
course, should as it were through a lan-
guishing faintness begin to stand and

What raging of the sea, **shaking of earth,**
Commotion in the winds, *frights, changes, horrors,*
Divert and crack, rend and deracinate,
The unity and married calm of states
Quite from their fixture! O, when degree is shaked,
– Which is the ladder to all high designs –
The enterprise is sick ...

Act I, Sc. III

to rest himself; if the moon should wander from her beaten way, the times and seasons of the year blend themselves by disordered and confused mixture, the winds breathe out their last gasp, the earth be defeated by heavenly influence, the fruits of the earth pine away as children at the withered breasts of their mother no longer able to yield them relief: what would become of man himself, whom these things do all serve? See we not plainly that obedience of creatures unto the law of nature is the stay of the whole world?

The emboldened words in the passage from *Troilus and Cressida* represent the vocabulary Gayley saw as overlapping with that of Hooker. However, when we know that Neville is the true author, I think we can add yet a further observation. Neville was especially keen on astronomy and the natural sciences: it is this very vocabulary and these very images that he has chosen to overlap with Hooker's imagery.

Of course, the above passages represent only a tiny proportion of Gayley's total evidence linking 'Shakespeare' with Hooker. By the time he has finished the comparisons, he has indeed made his point: the writings of the writer he knew as Shakespeare definitely encapsulate the ideas and spirit of Hooker and, in turn, it is Hooker's philosophy and wisdom that is seen as one of the paradigmatic influences towards the American Constitution. Gayley has indeed established the links; just one small step further and he might have established the author. As he says in his extension of Jefferson's words, 'the ball of the Revolution received its first impulse, not from the actors in the event, but from the first colonists'. He might well have added: 'and from the Jacobean protagonists of colonial rights, their brothers in England; from the word oft reiterated in Parliament by Sandys and Selden and Brooke, Fulke Greville, by Phillips, Neville, Sackville, and Digges; from the motive and deed of Southampton and Cavendish and the other Patriots of the Virginia Company; and from their instructor in the principles of equal opportunity, self-government, justice and liberty – ... the most judicious political philosopher of the Shakespearian age, the friend of Shakespeare's friends – Richard Hooker'.

Altogether, reading this book brings one aspect of Neville's predicament home very strongly. The circle in which he belonged was a progressive but still elevated one in which anyone who was involved in writing wrote poetry, not plays for the public theatre. Ben Jonson was welcomed in from time to time, but on the basis that he was still something of an outsider – he was not born into their social class, even though he had gained his education and patronage through their class and, more specifically, through their progressive circle. Neville, however, was born into their class, and so had to be seen to abide by the class rules. If he had chosen merely to write adulatory verses to his friends, and philosophical poems concerning the nature of Man, religion or the universe, he could have written under his own name. However, the public theatre was not generally recognized as even a respectable institution at that time, and was certainly not considered a venue for works of art. It was indeed Ben Jonson who gradually changed English upper-class opinion in this respect, and he and his patrons (who were also Neville's friends in the Virginia Company and at Court) finally used 'Shakespeare's' plays as their most convincing argument.

All this means that if Neville wished to retain respect amongst the upper classes as a whole, he had to play out an elaborate charade of being just a politician and gentleman – either that, or he had to cease writing for the public theatre and write only poetry. His missions in life to educate the lower classes and to bring the theatre respect as an art form were obviously so great that he refused to concentrate on poetry alone. In refusing to do this he therefore did not fit into the mould, and so would have wished to write anonymously in order not to bring controversy onto either his close friends (who knew his secret) or the upper class as a whole. Ulysses' speech in *Troilus and Cressida* demonstrates how much he dreaded untuning even a single string of society's harmony by undermining the concept of 'degree':

> *Take but degree away, untune that string,*
> *And hark what discord follows: each thing meets*
> *In mere oppugnancy. The bounded waters*
> *Should lift their bosoms higher than the shores,*
> *And make a sop of all this solid globe;*
> *Strength should be lord of imbecility,*
> *And the rude son should strike his father dead;*
> *Force should be right, or, rather, right and wrong*
> *– Between whose endless jar justice resides –*
> *Should lose their names, and so should justice too.*
> *Then everything includes itself in power,*
> *Power into will, will into appetite,*
> *And appetite, an universal wolf,*
> *So doubly seconded with will and power,*
> *Must make perforce an universal prey,*
> *And last eat up himself.*

Act I, Sc. III

From occasional hints in the Tower Notebook, it seems Neville may have been concerned about the strict laws regulating plays produced on the public stage. He felt so strongly about degree and the rule of law that he declares the only solution was therefore to 'lye in all' regarding his identity. He regretted this, but only by doing it could he protect both himself and society's harmony. His immediate circle of upper-class friends knew of his writing but understood both his feelings and the social dilemma in which he was placed. Add to this the dangers in which he and his family were placed because of his involvement with the Earl of Essex, and there can no longer be any wonder that he chose to keep his secret, protected by a powerful and loyal circle, which probably eventually included the collusion of even the King himself. All would have agreed – if any string of society was to be either untuned or retuned, it had to be done carefully and gradually, not by a sudden force that would break it, and thus throw society and nature itself to the mercy of the four winds.

Neville's secret agenda, however, was still there at the back of his mind: if all the careful retuning of society was to no avail, if those with 'power' refused to submit to the forces of justice and enlightenment, then the short, sharp strike must come. We are not therefore to confuse intelligence-gathering and 'preparation of the way' with ultimate passiveness or cowardice –

> *They tax our policy and call it cowardice,*
> *Count wisdom as no member of the war,*
> *Forestall prescience, and esteem no act*
> *But that of hand. The still and mental parts*
> *That do contrive how many hands shall strike*
> *When fitness calls them on, and know by measure*
> *Of their observant toil the enemy's weight –*
> *Why, this hath not a finger's dignity:*
> *They call this bed-work, mapp'ry, closet-war;*
> *So that the ram that batters down the wall,*
> *For the great swing and rudeness of his poise*
> *They place before his hand that made the engine,*
> *Or those that with the fineness of their souls*
> *By reason guide his execution.*

Act I, Sc. III

Would Shakespeare/Neville therefore have agreed that 'fitness' had called the American population to use its 'many hands' to 'strike' for independence after all the 'prescience' and 'wisdom' had done its best to delay and prepare the moment? Perhaps he would.

Appendix 5

Genealogical Notes

Notes from the Neville family tree, 1729 (Essex Record Office)

Margaret Neville m. Henry Lord Piercy, first Earle of Northumberland.

Raufe, Lord Neville of Raby and Mydelham d. 5 August 1368. He married Alice, daughter of Sir Hugh Awdeley, Lord Audley of Heleigh Castle [who was also a Spencer descendant. The full Neville Coat of Arms includes the Spencer Device.]

Notes from R.A. Neville's eighteenth-century notebook

[The notes are R.A.'s own, with my observations added within square brackets.]

Elenor Neville m. Thomas, Lord Stanley, Earl of Derby.

Margaret Neville m. Sir Robert Southwell.

The rose on the cross of the Billingbear Nevilles is the Rose of Lancaster, from the Lady Joanne Beaufort.

Bulmer, Lord of Branspeth and Sherryhutton is also part of the family, as was Sir Ralph Glanvile, Lord Chief Justice of England.

The pedigree makes the point that the Earls of Westmoreland were the progenitors of the Earls of Northumberland during Saxon times, 'before the Norman Conquest'.

A Neville was admiral to William the Conqueror.

The Nevilles are also descended from the Kings of Scotland, Spain, Portugal and Navarre, and from Edmund of Langley, Duke of York. [He was obviously also related to the Spencers through Constantia Langley – see the family tree on page xxiv.]

The Nevilles are also related to the Blunts.

Henry Neville [senior] was knighted on 11 October 1551. He was Sheriff of Berkshire in 1570, and then Sheriff of Reading and Wokingham in 1587, and was also still Sheriff of Berkshire.

Henley on Thames church contains the monument to Elizabeth, Lady Peryam [formerly Elizabeth Bacon-Neville.]

Statement at the front of the full Neville family tree, 1729

The noble family of the NEVILLES descended from the ancient Earles of Northumberland before the Norman Conquest and spread into many branches whence not only the late Earles of Westmoreland, Warwick and Salisbury but sundry other honourable personages are known (sic) to have their derivation whereof in this project the lords and Barons of Abergavenny together with the several inheritable houses wherewith they have matched as also to shewe how they do participate in blood with all ye noble lines here described.

The Coat armour, and some of the quarterings of the noble NEVILLES of Billingbere in Berkshire who are a branch of the right honourable the NEVILLES, Lord Abergavenny, and the offspring of the most illustrious Ralph, Lord Neville of Raby Castle, the first Earl of Westmoreland, and of his wife Lady Joane Beaufort, the sister of King Henry the fourth the names as they are here in order marshalled as these:

Westmoreland Midelsham Chester Arundell Warwick Spencer Gloucester

Sir Edward Neville, knight, fourth son of Ralph Neville of Westmoreland by his second lady, Joanne Beaufort, Daughter of John of Gaunt, Duke of Lancaster, King of Castile and Leons and fourth son to Edward III of England, was first Lord of Abergavenny.

[The Spencer Device is similar to the Nevilles' but with no rose, and it includes a square (or, rather, lozenge) intertwined with the cross.]

Appendix 6

The Chronology of Shakespeare's Works

Since the late eighteenth century, scholars have attempted to compile a chronology of Shakespeare's works. The consensual view of the dating of his works is given here. In many cases, dates are approximate; in other cases, we are certain or fairly certain of the first performance of a play or the publication of a poem. Occasionally, when there is a difference of opinion among scholars, alternative dates are given in brackets. Some minor poetry and plays whose authorship is disputed have been omitted. As noted in the text, we have always accepted the accepted chronology of the plays in setting out the life of Sir Henry Neville.

1589–90	*1 Henry VI*	May 1594	*The Rape of Lucrece*
1590–91	*2 Henry VI*	1594–95	*The Two Gentlemen of Verona*
	3 Henry VI (1587–92) for the Trilogy)		*Love's Labour's Lost*
1592–93	*Richard III* (1591)	1595–96	*Romeo and Juliet*
	Titus Andronicus		*Richard II*
April 1593	*Venus and Adonis*		*A Midsummer Night's Dream*
1593–94	*The Taming of the Shrew*		
	The Comedy of Errors	1596–97	*King John*

	The Merchant of Venice	1605–06	King Lear (1607)
			Macbeth (1607)
1597–98	1 Henry IV		
	2 Henry IV	1606–07	Anthony and Cleopatra
	The Merry Wives of		(1608)
	Windsor (1602)		
		1607–08	Coriolanus
1598–99	Much Ado About		
	Nothing	1608–09	Pericles, Prince of Tyre
	Henry V		
		1609–10	Cymbeline
1599–1600	Julius Caesar		Shake-speares Sonnets
	As You Like It		(published June
	Twelfth Night		1609)
1601–02	Hamlet	1610–11	The Winter's Tale
	Troilus and Cressida	1611–12	The Tempest
	(published 1609)		
	Othello	1613–14	Henry VIII
	All's Well that Ends		The Two Noble Kinsmen
	Well		
		1623	The First Folio
1603–04	Measure for Measure		published
1604–05	Timon of Athens		

Notes

Chapter 1 The Shakespeare Authorship Question

1 Cited in, e.g. Anthony Holden, *William Shakespeare: His Life and Work* (London, 1999), p.40.

2 Cited in 'XIII. John Aubrey (1681)' in E.K. Chambers, *William Shakespeare: A Study of Facts and Problems*, vol. 2 (Oxford, 1930), p.252.

3 Park Honan, *Shakespeare: A Life* (Oxford, 1999), pp.44–5.

4 Ibid., p.52.

5 Similarly, F.E. Halliday's valuable and reliable, *A Shakespeare Companion 1564–1964* (London, 1964), states (p.253) that 'Jenkins was a Welshman and may be the original of Sir Hugh Evans in *The Merry Wives*'. According to Park Honan (p.51), however, Jenkins was 'a Londoner . . . the son of an "old servant" of Sir Thomas White, founder of St. John's College, Oxford'.

6 Indeed had a schoolmaster truly taken a special interest in Shakespeare, then he would have been put forward for a scholarship to unversity, as was young Christopher Marlowe (the son of a cobbler from Canterbury). Shakespeare, however, was never mentioned in this connection and did not attend university.

7 Honan, *Shakespeare*, op. cit., pp.14–15.

8 See Donna B. Hamilton, *Shakespeare and the Politics of Protestant England* (Hemel Hempstead, 1992).

9 Diana Price, *Shakespeare's Unorthodox Biography: New Evidence of an Authorship Problem* (Westport, CT, 2001), p.248, citing Samuel Schoenbaum, *Shakespeare's Lives* (Oxford, 1991), p.103. Price's excellent book is the best, most learned and rational, and most devastating account of the insuperable difficulties involved in accepting the view that Shakespeare of Stratford wrote the works attributed to him. See also John Michell, *Who Wrote Shakespeare?* (London, 1996), pp.23–6, and virtually any other work by an anti-Stratfordian, e.g. Charlton Ogburn, *The Mystery of William Shakespeare* (London, 1988), pp.239–42, probably the leading recent Oxfordian text.

10 Price, *Shakespeare's Unorthodox Biography*, op. cit., p.248, citing Selma Guttman, *The Foreign Sources of Shakespeare's Works* (New York, 1947), pp.121–2.

11 R.C. Churchill, *Shakespeare and His Betters: A History and a Criticism of the Authorship Question* (London, 1958), p.176.

12 Ibid., p.178.

13 Katherine Duncan-Jones, *Ungentle Shakespeare: Scenes from His Life* (London, 2001), p.115.

14 N.B. Cockburn, *The Bacon Shakespeare Question: The Baconian Theory Made Sane* (Wimbledon, 1998), p.85.

15 Churchill, *Shakespeare and His Betters*, op. cit., p.175. Yet another theory (cited in Cockburn, *The Bacon Shakespeare Question*, op. cit., pp.85–6) is that he used John Stow's library, although there is no evidence for this.

16 Churchill, *Shakespeare and His Betters*, op. cit., p.175.

17 These include, in particular, Ernesto Grillo, *Shakespeare and Italy* (Glasgow, 1949); Karl Elze, *Essays on Shakespeare* (London, 1874); George Lambin, *Voyages de Shakespeare en France et en Italie* (Geneva, 1962); and Cecil Roth, 'The background of Shylock', *Review of English Studies* IX (1933), pp.148–56. There is a lengthy list of such works in Dr Noemi Magri, 'Places in Shakespeare: Belmont and thereabouts', in the *De Vere Society Newsletter*, June 2003. See also Eddi Jolly, 'Voyages de Shakespeare en France et en Italie: an overlooked masterpiece', in the *De Vere Society Newsletter*, June 2003.

18 Grillo, *Shakespeare and Italy*, op. cit., p.133. Grillo believes that 'we can fix with some certainty the date of his journey between the autumn of 1592 and the summer of 1593', when the plague raged in London.

19 Cited in Cockburn, *The Bacon Shakespeare Question*, op. cit., pp.705–6.

20 Ibid., p.710. See also Michell, *Who Wrote Shakespeare?*, op. cit., p.223.

21 Chambers, *William Shakespeare: A Study of Facts and Problems*, op. cit., vol. 1 p.61. For further evidence that Shakespeare must have visited Italy to have acquired the detailed knowledge demonstrated in his plays, see also the essays by Noemi Magri, a scholar resident in Venice, in Richard Malim, ed., *Great Oxford: Essays on the Life and Work of Edward De Vere, 17th Earl of Oxford, 1550–1604* (Tunbridge Wells, 2004), pp.45–106.

22 It should be noted that Shakespeare's evident knowledge of Italy contrasts with his apparent lack of detailed knowledge of Elsinore and Denmark. In the first edition (Q1) of *Hamlet*, published in 1603, Shakespeare made all sorts of mistakes about Danish matters: not surprisingly, given the true author's inability to advance his knowledge in 1601–02, when the play was apparently written. The second edition (Q2) of *Hamlet*, published in 1604, greatly revised and rendered more accurate the play's details. It is possible that the author visited Denmark in this period, or that he learned of them from Anne of Denmark, James I's Queen, or one of her entourage. Roger Manners, fifth earl of Rutland (1576–1612), sometimes mentioned as a possible Shakespeare author (despite the fact that he would have been only 14 or so when the first of Shakespeare's plays appeared) visited Elsinore in mid-1603 as temporary Ambassador for the christening of the royal heir; he is another possible source of information. (Michell, *Who Wrote*

Shakespeare?, op. cit., pp.212–13, 220–2). Grillo (*Shakespeare and Italy*, p.146) also contrasts Shakespeare's profound knowledge of the geography of Italy with 'his ignorance' of the geography of many French towns.

23 See Price, *Shakespeare's Unorthodox Biography*, op. cit., p.270, and the explanation by Brenda James in this work.

24 See, for example, the commentary by Stephen Booth, ed., *Shakespeare's Sonnets* (New Haven, CT, 1977), pp.429–30, where 'various commentators have explained' that a religious procession such as the Holy Communion is meant.

25 This is the standard and oft-repeated view, which seems compelling, but it has been denied by some commentators such as Sir Israel Gollancz, who believed, implausibly, that Polonius was supposed to be Polish bishop and statesman Warwrzyniec Goslicki. (Harold Jenkins, ed., *The Arden Shakespeare: Hamlet* (London, 1982), pp.421–2.)

26 Cited in Cockburn, *The Bacon Shakespeare Question*, op. cit., p.338.

27 Edgar I. Fripp, *Minutes and Accounts of the Corporation of Stratford-upon-Avon* (Oxford, 1921), p.lviii.

28 Cited in O. Hood Wilson's excellent study *Shakespeare and the Lawyers* (London, 1972), p.182.

29 Ibid., p.186.

30 Ibid., pp.186, 188–9.

31 Ibid., pp.64–7.

32 In Elizabethan England, Justice of the Peace (JP) was a legal officer, appointed by the Lord-Lieutenant of each English county or by the Lord Chancellor, who tried minor cases of law-breaking at Quarter Sessions and who collectively functioned in each county as the primary administrators of local government. There were several dozen (or more) JPs in each county, most of whom were well-regarded local landowners, men of property, or clergymen; many (like Justice Shallow) had no formal legal training.

33 Peter Usher, 'Shakespeare's support for the new astronomy', *The Oxfordian*, 5 (October 2002), pp.132–46. Usher is Professor Emeritus of Astronomy and Astrophysics at Pennsylvania State University.

34 Ibid., p.143.

35 One suggestion is that Shakespeare learned about astronomy from Thomas Digges (1545–95), a prominent mathematician who was in contact with Tycho Brahe (Usher, 'Shakespeare's support'). He was the father of Leonard Digges (1588–1635), who wrote a commendatory verse for Shakespeare in the First Folio. Digges's only previous known connection with Shakespeare is that in 1603 his widowed mother married Thomas Russell of Stratford (1570–1634), whom Shakespeare appointed overseer of his will. While this is possible, it should be noted that Digges's widow remarried eight years after Thomas Digges's death. There is no direct evidence that Shakespeare of Stratford had even met Thomas Digges or, for that matter, his son. Another suggestion is that Shakespeare might have learned about the latest scientific advances at Gresham

College in London, but Gresham College simply did not disseminate scientific advances in this way. See the discussion of 'Gresham College and its role in the genesis of London science' in Mordechai Feingold, *The Mathematicians' Apprenticeship: Science, Universities and Society in England, 1560–1640* (Cambridge, 1984), pp.166–89.

36 Price, *Shakespeare's Unorthodox Biography*, op. cit., p.256.

37 Schoenbaum, *Shakespeare's Lives*, op. cit., pp.92–3.

38 'The Wallaces', in Schoenbaum, *Shakespeare's Lives*, op. cit., pp.464–72.

39 Anthony Holden claims that Shakespeare 'had probably known them [the Mountjoys] some years, as he had given their Huguenot name to the French herald in *Henry V*, written ... in 1599' (Holden, *William Shakespeare*, op. cit., p.214). There is no evidence for this claim, nor for Holden's claim that 'Probably he met them through his friend Richard Field ... whose French wife Jacqueline would have worshipped alongside Mary Mountjoy at London's French church' (ibid.). Shakespeare clearly stated in his evidence that he had known them since about 1602, not earlier.

40 Honan, *Shakespeare*, ibid., p.327. *All's Well* is usually dated as written about 1602–03, but may well be a revision of a play composed five or six years earlier (Halliday, *Shakespeare Companion*, op. cit., p.29).

41 Shakespeare did state that, at the behest of Marie Mountjoy, the daughter, he 'did solicitt and entreat [him] ... to move and perswade' Bellot to marry, which he did (Honan, *Shakespeare*, op. cit., p.327). This, however, seems very far from the situation of Helena (in *All's Well*) and Duke Vincentio (in *Measure*) which Professor Honan argues may be based upon Shakespeare's role in the Bellot–Mountjoy alliance (Honan, *Shakespeare*, p.327). The plots of both plays have in any case been traced to much earlier published works.

42 Strictly speaking, while Sir Thomas Hesketh of Rufford, the second of these gentry households, was a Catholic, Alexander Houghton of Lea Hall was a Protestant, although his wife and a brother were Catholics. Alan Keen and Roger Lubbock, *The Annotator: The Pursuit of an Elizabethan Reader of Halle's Chronicles, Involving Some Surmises About the Early Life of William Shakespeare* (London, 1954), pp.77–80.

43 Cited in Schoenbaum, *Shakespeare's Lives*, op. cit., p.535.

44 *The Annotator* is an account of a copy of *Halle's Chronicles* of 1550, which the authors claim was annotated in its margins by Shakespeare.

45 Schoenbaum, *Shakespeare's Lives*, op. cit., pp.536, footnote.

46 E.A.J. Honigmann, *Shakespeare, The 'Lost Years'* (Manchester, 1998), p.34.

47 Ibid.

48 For an exposition of this theory see, for instance, Ian Wilson, *Shakespeare: The Evidence: Unlocking the Mysteries of the Man and His Work* (London, 1993), esp. pp.44–58 and 92–112. See also the useful discussion in Eric Sams, *The Real Shakespeare: Retrieving the Early Years, 1564–1594* (New Haven, CT, 1995), pp.36–8.

49 R. Philips, in *The Monthly Magazine*, 45(1) (1818), p.152. Cited in Sams, *The Real Shakespeare*, op. cit., p.210.

50 Aubrey's claim was made, according to him, on the authority of the actor William Beeston (d. 1682), whose father Christopher belonged to the Chamberlain's Men Acting Company, to which Shakespeare belonged, apparently from about 1598 to 1602. Christopher was still alive in 1637, although his date of death is unknown. It is not known when Aubrey collected his material on Shakespeare, but the senior Beeston must probably have known Shakespeare no more recently than 60 or 70 years earlier. Aubrey also states that 'this Wm. being inclined naturally to Poetry and acting, came to London I guess about 18', making no mention of Lancashire.

51 Cited in Wilson, *Shakespeare: The Evidence*, op. cit., p.410.

52 Shakespeare's Protestantism is apparent to many historians who believe in the 'Shakeshafte' theory. Honigmann, *The 'Lost Years'*, op. cit., p.122, notes that the apparent anti-Catholic bias of plays like *King John* 'is disconcerting, I admit', but regards its author as a 'lapsed Catholic' who might have returned to Catholicism on his deathbed. This is, however, to overlook the consistent pro-Puritanism in Shakespeare's later plays. For a compelling and valuable account of Shakespeare's obvious Protestantism and the close connection of his plays, especially the later ones, with the pro-Protestant politics of the 1600s, see Hamilton, *Shakespeare and the Politics of Protestant England*.

53 Schoenbaum, *Shakespeare's Lives*, op. cit., p.536.

54 Duncan-Jones, *Ungentle Shakespeare*, op. cit., p.xii.

55 Cited (among other places) in Michell, *Who Wrote Shakespeare?*, op. cit., p.249; see also Wilson, *Shakespeare: The Evidence*, op. cit., pp.216–17.

56 Michell, *Who Wrote Shakespeare?*, op. cit., p.250.

57 Wilson, *Shakespeare: The Evidence*, op. cit., p.216.

58 Duncan-Jones, *Ungentle Shakespeare*, op. cit., pp.205–7; Honan, *Shakespeare*, op. cit., pp.328–9. Both writers cite the research of Roger Prior on Wilkins: Roger Prior, 'The Life of George Wilkins', *Shakespeare Survey* 25 (1972), op. cit., pp.137–52.

59 Honan, *Shakespeare*, op. cit., p.329.

60 Some historians believe that the so-called 'Hand D' in the manuscript of part of the play *Sir Thomas More* is in Shakespeare's handwriting. No authors' names are attached, and the possibility that 'Hand D' (one of six separate scribes) is Shakespeare was proposed first in 1871–72 (based upon its style) and again in 1916 (based on palaeographic evidence). This is possible, but there are serious objections: we can have no real palaeographic evidence since, as noted, the six signatures on legal documents comprise the only basis of comparison. Also, most of the other supposed writers (Munday, Chettle, Dekker) worked for the Admirals' Company, the rival group to Shakespeare's Chamberlain's Company.

61 Michael Wood, *In Search of Shakespeare* (London, 2003), pp.38–42. This volume accompanied the series.

62 Ibid., p.39.

63 This discovery does, however, have a certain value in showing that John Shakespeare sailed close to the legal wind in his business dealings; his son might conceivably have learned traits at his father's knee.

64 Price, *Shakespeare's Unorthodox Biography*, op. cit., p.150.

65 'Shakspere' is her name for the man from Stratford, as opposed to the author of the works, ibid., p.299.

66 See the discussion in Schoenbaum, *Shakespeare's Lives*, op. cit., pp.526–8.

67 Holden, *William Shakespeare*, op. cit., p.153.

68 R.W. Chambers, *The Jacobean Shakespeare and Measure for Measure* (London, 1937), p.56, cited in Schoenbaum, *Shakespeare's Lives*, op. cit., p.528.

69 Duncan-Jones, *Ungentle Shakespeare*, op. cit., p.134.

70 Price, *Shakespeare's Unorthodox Biography*, op. cit., pp.141–4.

71 'Hunsdon, George Carey, 2nd Lord (1547–1605)' in Halliday, *Shakespeare Companion,* op. cit., p.238.

72 Despite the paucity of information which exists on the life of Shakespeare of Stratford, however, commentators have drawn attention to a number of inconsistencies which apparently exist between his life and the chronology of the plays. Most strikingly, what was probably the earliest performance of *The Comedy of Errors* took place at Gray's Inn on the night of 28 December 1594, at a performance so memorable for its confusion that it became known as the 'night of errors'. On the same night, however, Shakespeare's company, the Lord Chamberlain's Men, was performing for the Court at Greenwich, eight or nine miles away, for which they received payment from the Treasurer of the Chamber Accounts. Given the difficulty of explaining how either Shakespeare or his company could be in two places at once, orthodox scholars have decided that the entry relating to the Greenwich performance has 'possibly [been] . . . misdated'. As R.A. Foakes points out, 'there seems to be no other way out of the difficulty' ('Appendix II: The Gray's Inn Performance of 1594', in R.A. Foakes, ed., *The Arden Shakespeare: A Comedy of Errors* (Cambridge, MA, 1962), p.116). See also N.B. Cockburn, *The Bacon Shakespeare Question*, op. cit., pp.121–5. Shakespeare is actually listed in the Chamber Accounts as (with William Kempe and Richard Burbage) receiving £20 payment for the Court performance.

73 This is discussed at great length by Price, *Shakespeare's Unorthodox Biography*, op. cit., esp. pp.45–152.

74 The best-known recent general account of the authorship candidates is Michell, *Who Wrote Shakespeare?* The two other well-known post-war general accounts of the rival authors are H.N. Gibson, *The Shakespeare Claimants* (London, 1962). and Churchill, *Shakespeare and His Betters*, op. cit., which includes a very comprehensive bibliography. Schoenbaum, *Shakespeare's Lives*, op. cit., pp.385–454, contains a comprehensive account of the rival authors from an uncompromisingly pro-Stratfordian viewpoint. Each of the major alternative Shakespeares has had a very considerable literature advancing their candidacy, only a small part of

which can be cited here. The Baconians have not done especially well in recent years, with the notable exception of the outstanding work by Cockburn, *The Bacon Shakespeare Question*, op. cit., and the works of Peter Dawkins, such as *Francis Bacon – Herald of a New Age* (London, 1997). The Oxfordians, who are clearly now the dominant anti-Stratfordian group, have been far luckier, with a range of well-known publications by mainstream publishers such as Ogburn, *The Mystery of William Shakespeare*; Joseph Sobran, *Alias Shakespeare: Solving the Greatest Literary Mystery of All Time* (New York, 1997); and Richard F. Whalen, *Shakespeare: Who Was He? – The Oxford Challenge to the Bard of Avon* (Westport, CT, 1994). All the rival candidates have well-organized societies and websites. The Shakespeare Oxford Society in Washington, DC, publishes a genuinely impressive annual journal, *The Oxfordian*, and several of the newsletters produced by these societies are also very valuable. Professor Daniel Wright of Concordia University, Portland, Oregon, a leading pro-Oxfordian, has organized, on an annual basis, a very interesting and well-attended pro-Oxfordian and anti-Stratfordian conference at his university since the mid-1990s.

75 Professor Daniel Wright, working with Dr John Rollett of Ipswich, has found that no 'Ipswich Philosophical Society' ever existed, and no trace could be found in any source of a John Corton Cowell. Professor Wright has suggested that a pro-Baconian enthusiast may have forged this paper in the 1920s to meet the threat posed by the theory that the seventeenth Earl of Oxford wrote the plays, first proposed in 1920, although much about this affair remains mysterious. There certainly was a Rev. James Wilmot, a Cambridge graduate whose notice appears in the *Dictionary of National Biography*. Interestingly, Wilmot was proposed in 1813 as the possible author of *The Letters of Junius*, whose authorship remains unknown.

76 On Delia Bacon see Schoenbaum, *Shakespeare's Lives*, op. cit., pp.385–94.

77 See Michell, *Who Wrote Shakespeare?*, op. cit., pp.113–60.

78 Ibid., pp.131–4.

79 Spelled out very fully in Cockburn, *The Bacon Shakespeare Question*, op. cit.

80 See 'Appendix I – Some Bacon Poems', in ibid.

81 Ibid., pp.89–90.

82 Shakespeare is mentioned only once in this 637-page book, while the theory that Bacon was Shakespeare is not mentioned at all.

83 On Looney see Schoenbaum, *Shakespeare's Lives*, op. cit., pp.430–40 and Michell, *Who Wrote Shakespeare?*, op. cit., pp.161–89. Looney is a Manx name, pronounced 'Loney'.

84 In 1596, a play about Hamlet was certainly being performed, because one contemporary referred to '. . . the Vizard of ye ghost which cried so miserably at ye theator like an oister wife, Hamlet, revenge'.

85 On Marlowe see Michell, *Who Wrote Shakespeare?*, op. cit., pp.227–40.

86 Ibid., pp.190–226, contains details and a bibliography.

87 She was proposed as a candidate (as one of a group) by George and Bernard

Winchcombe, in *Shakespeare's Ghost Writers* (Esher, Surrey, 1968); the case for the Countess of Pembroke has recently been revived by the American writer Robin Williams.
88 See the bibliography (pp.225–46) in Churchill, *Shakespeare and His Betters*, op. cit., which lists works on over 20 possible authors.

Chapter 2 The real Shakespeare

1 Further evidence in favour of the attribution of the Tower Notebook to Sir Henry Neville is also to be found in Chapter 11 of this book.
2 See the section on King Henry VIII in *Hall's Chronicle; Containing the History of England during the Reign of Henry the Fourth, and the Succeeding Monarchs, to the end of the Reign of Henry the Eighth in which are Particularly Described the Manners and Customs of those Periods*. Halle, Edward [d. 1547] (and Richard Grafton, Printer). Reprinted, London, 1809.
3 Calendar of State Papers, Domestic, 'James I: Volume 2: June–July, 1603' 17.59. : 'Answers and assertions of Geo. Brooke. Part taken by Lord Grey in the conspiracy'.
4 See Zachary Lesser, 'Mixed government and mixed marriage in *A King and No King*: Sir Henry Neville reads Beaumont and Fletcher', *ELH*, vol. 67 (2002), pp.947–78.
5 For the impact of Halle's *Chronicles* on Shakespeare's history plays, see Lily B. Campbell's book, *Shakespeare's History Plays* (London, 1968).
6 See Keen and Lubbock, *The Annotator*, op. cit., p.92.
7 E.g. by typing in http://drk.sd23.bc.ca/DeVere/Annotator_5_of_5-56.pdf
8 'The Commonplace Book of Richard Alldworth Neville (1717–93)', Essex Record Office, ref. D/DBY. F60.

Chapter 3 The Neville heritage

1 Charles R. Young, *The Making of the Neville Family in England, 1166–1400* (Woodbridge, Suffolk, 1996), p.1.
2 *Richard II,* Act I, Sc. I.
3 Owen Lowe Duncan, 'The political career of Sir Henry Neville: an Elizabethan gentleman at the Court of James I', unpublished doctoral dissertation, Ohio State University, U.S.A. (1974), p.1 (hereafter 'Duncan').
4 Cited (without a complete reference) in Henry J. Swallow, *De Nova Villa: or, the House of Neville in Sunshine and Shade* (Newcastle upon Tyne and London, 1885), pp.248–51.
5 Duncan, op. cit., pp.3–7. The genealogy of the Neville family is bewilderingly complex and confusing even to experts.

6 'Sir Henry Neville (d. 1593)' in P.W. Hasler, *The House of Commons, 1558–1603, Volume III: Members M–Z* (London, 1981), p.124 (hereafter 'Hasler').

7 Duncan, op. cit., pp.5–6.

8 'Sir Edward Neville (d. 1538)', *Dictionary of National Biography* (hereafter *'DNB'*).

9 *Notes and Queries* (1st series), vol. 2 (1851), p.307, cited in Duncan, op. cit., p.17.

10 Tacitus was a classical writer who thought that the office of monarchy automatically corrupted its owner, whoever he or she might be. Duncan, op.cit, p.5, n.11.

11 Hasler, op. cit., p.124.

12 Hasler, op. cit.

13 Ibid.

14 Ibid.

15 Duncan, op. cit., p.19.

16 Irwin Smith, *Shakespeare's Blackfriars Playhouse: Its History and Design* (New York, 1964), pp.101–2, 134–5, 453–6.

17 'Sir Henry Neville (*c.*1520–93)', in *Oxford Dictionary of National Biography* (hereafter *ODNB*).

18 See the portrait of Sir Henry Neville in ibid.

19 Ibid.

20 Ibid.

21 See Jardine and Stewart, *Hostage to Fortune*, op.cit., pp.25–6.

22 Although Sir Henry I is believed to have married Elizabeth Gresham by 1567, some evidence exists that they might not have been married until a year after our Sir Henry was born. If so, this might help to explain Shakespeare's apparent obsession with bastards, illegitimacy, secret relatives who mysteriously turn up, and the like.

23 'Sir Richard Gresham (*c.*1485–1549)', in *ODNB*. (Sir Richard was Sir John Gresham's elder brother).

24 William D. Rubinstein and Philip Beresford, 'Richest of the Rich', *Sunday Times* Supplement, April 2000, pp.18–19.

25 'Gresham College', in Ben Weinreb and Christopher Hibbert, *The London Encyclopedia* (London, 1983), p.338; Francis Ames-Lewis, ed., *Sir Thomas Gresham and Gresham College: Studies in the Intellectual History of London in the Sixteenth Century* (Aldershot, 1999); Richard Chartres and David Vermont, *A Brief History of Gresham College, 1597–1997 (London, 1998)*.

26 David Honeyman, *Closer to Shakespeare* (Tiverton, Devon, 1990), p.172.

27 Ibid.

28 See Alan Macfarlane, *The Origins of English Individualism: The Family, Property, and Social Transition* (Oxford, 1978).

29 When Neville's mother died on 7 November 1573, he was described in her funeral certificate as '10 1/2 years old', suggesting that he was born between November 1562 and June 1563. (John Harley, '"My Ladye Nevell" Revealed',

Music and Letters, 86, no.1 (February, 2005), p.5, n.32.) The balance of evidence is that Neville was probably born in late 1562.

30 See Professor John Bossy, *Giordano Bruno and the Embassy Affair* (New Haven, CT, 1991). See also Thomas Vautroullier, *A Booke Containing Divers Sortes of Hands* (London, 1570).

31 Vautroullier, ibid.

32 C.C. Stopes, *The Life of Henry, Third Earl of Southampton* (Cambridge, 1922).

33 Among the victims of this outbreak of the plague was Sir Robert Doyly, High Sheriff of Oxfordshire, whose widow remarried Sir Henry's father (as his third wife) in 1579. (Duncan, op. cit., p.45).

34 Duncan, op. cit., citing Francis Gribble, *The Romance of the Oxford Colleges* (London, 1910), p.60. Recently, Clare Asquith has argued that *Love's Labour's Lost*, probably written around 1594–95, shows clear indications that its author was familiar with Oxford University, including several of its academics, and with the town of Oxford. (Clare Asquith, 'Oxford University and *Love's Labour's Lost*', in Dennis Tayllor and David Beauregard, eds., *Shakespeare and the Culture of Christianity in Early Modern England* (New York, 2003), pp.80–102.) There is, of course, no reason to suppose that Shakespeare of Stratford would have had any familiarity with Oxford University. Although the Chamberlain's Men (Shakespeare's acting company) performed at Cambridge in 1594–95, it never performed in Oxford. (Andrew Gurr, *The Shakeapearean Playing Companies* (Oxford, 1996), p.303.)

35 Duncan, op. cit., pp.54–5.

36 See Adam Nicolson, *Power and Glory: Jacobean England and the Making of the King James Bible* (London, 2003). Regrettably, there is no biography of Savile, but see the lengthy entries on his life in the *Dictionary of National Biography* and the *Oxford Dictionary of National Biography*. Savile was an obvious possible model for Holofernes, the pedantic schoolmaster, in *Love's Labour's Lost*.

37 John Aubrey, *Lives of Eminent Men*, vol. 2, p.215, cited in 'Sir Henry Savile' in *DNB*, op. cit.

38 Duncan, op. cit., p.55.

39 Because of its importance in bringing recent European scientific knowledge to Elizabethan England, this tour has been studied by a number of recent historians. Writings about the tour include Mordechai Feingold, *The Mathematicians' Apprenticeship: Sciences, Universities, and Knowledge in England, 1560–1640* (Cambridge, 1984), p.126; Robert B. Todd, 'Henry and Thomas Savile in Italy', *Bibliothèque d'Humaisme et Renaissance*, LVIII (1996), pp.439–44; Jardine and Stewart, op. cit., pp.57–63; and Nicolson, op. cit., p.165, where Neville is inaccurately described as 'later a Jacobean diplomat'.

40 Todd, op. cit, p.440.

41 Ibid.; 'Sir Henry Savile', *DNB*, op. cit.

42 This diary is reviewed by A.L. Rowse in *Ralegh and the Throckmortons* (London, 1962).

43 Todd, op. cit.; Nicolson, op. cit.

44 Tycho Brahe sent an engraving of himself to Henry Savile's brother, Thomas, which has a direct bearing on the Danish play. The presentation was accompanied by a request, begging Thomas Savile to be so kind as to print copies of it and distribute them among 'the friends' in England. Neville was assuredly in this category, and so would have received a print of this engraving, which included the names and arms of Rosenkrantz and Guildenstern (Tycho's ancestors) on its border. (Mordecai Feingold, *The Mathematician's Apprenticeship*, Cambridge, 1984.)

45 'Dudith (Duditius), Andreas', in Charles Coulston Gillespie, ed., *Dictionary of Scientific Biography,* vol. 4 (New York, 1971), p.212. Dudith was also the subject of a biography in French by Peter Costil, *André Dudith: Humaniste Hungrois, 1533–1589* (Paris, 1935).

46 Costil, ibid., p.135.

47 Gillespie, op. cit., p. 213 describes the comet controversy, which may have found an echo in the famous lines in *Julius Caesar*, 'The fault, dear Brutus, is not in our stars but in ourselves.' (Act I, Sc. II, ll. 140–1)

48 Peter Usher, 'Shakespeare's support for the New Astronomy', *The Oxfordian*, vol. 5 (2002), pp.132–46.

49 Steven Sohmer, *Shakespeare's Mystery Play: The Opening of the Globe Theatre 1599* (Manchester, 1999).

50 Feingold, op. cit., p.129.

51 Cited in N.B. Cockburn, op. cit., p.705

52 Ernesto Grillo, *Shakespeare and Italy* (Glasgow, 1949), p.163. Significantly, Grillo does *not* question that Shakespeare of Stratford wrote the works attributed to him, and is *not* making a case for another author. Other works (of many) making the point that Shakepeare *must* have visited Italy include Karle Elze, *Essays on Shakespeare* (London, 1874); George Lambin, *Voyages de Shakespeare en France et en Italie* (Geneva, 1962); and Cecil Roth, 'The Background of Shylock', *Review of English Studies,* vol.9, no.35 (July 1933), pp.148–56. See also the essays on this subject by Dr Noemi Magri in Richard Malim, ed., *Great Oxford: Essays on the Life and Work of Edward De Vere, 17th Earl of Oxford* (Tunbridge Wells, 2004), pp.45–106, which includes a lengthy biography (pp.105–6).

53 Ibid., p.710.

54 Ibid.

55 Ibid., p.712.

56 From his surviving letters and papers, it is clear that Neville was fluent in French and Spanish, and was able to read Italian, German, and Dutch; of course he could read Latin and Greek.

57 Cockburn, op. cit., pp.71–2; F.E. Halliday, *A Shakespeare Companion, 1564–1964* (Harmondsworth, 1964), pp.316, 506. A very detailed recent study of Shakespeare's sources is Stuart Gillespie, *Shakespeare's Books: A Dictionary of Shakespeare's Sources* (London, 2004).

58 Letter from Carleton to Chamberlain, Eton, 20 Sept. 1608, in Maurice Lee, Jr, ed., *Dudley Carleton to John Chamberlain, Jacobean Letters 1603–1624* (Rutgers University, NJ, 1972), p.105.

59 Letter from Carleton to Chamberlain, London, 20 August 1606, transcribed in ibid., p.88.

60 See O. Hood Wilson, *Shakespeare and the Lawyers* (London, 1972), p.186, and B.J. Sokol and Mary Sokol, *Shakespeare's Legal Language: A Dictionary* (London, 2000), pp.1–2.

61 Wilson, ibid., pp.64–7.

62 'Sir Henry Neville II (*c.*1562–1615)' in Hasler, op. cit., p.123.

63 Ibid., and Duncan, op. cit., pp.66–72. Shakespeare also demonstrated a reasonably good knowledge of ships and maritime language, something rather curious in a man born literally in the middle of England, whose only experience on a water-borne vessel might well have been as a passenger on the ferries linking the two banks of the Thames. (See Alexander Frederick Falconer, *Shakespeare and the Sea* (London, 1964)). Apart from his cross-channel travels, it is difficult to believe that as a young man Neville did not take an interest in the trading vessels of the great Gresham mercantile enterprise which must have been very prominent in the port of London.

Chapter 4 Becoming William Shakespeare, 1582–94

1 Hasler, op. cit., pp.122–3.

2 Duncan, op. cit., p.65.

3 Ibid., pp.64–5.

4 Ibid., citing *Victoria County History: Sussex*, vol. 2, pp.68–70.

5 Duncan, op. cit., pp.68–70.

6 'Sir Henry Killigrew (*c.*1525–1603), diplomat', in *ODNB*; 'Henry Killigrew (*c.*1528–1603)', in Hasler, op. cit., vol. 2, pp. 394–5. On Neville's marriage dates, see Duncan, op. cit., p.74, although there is some doubt about the precise date. Killigrew, who may have attended Cambridge without taking a degree, was the subject of a biography by Amos C. Miller, *Sir Henry Killigrew: Elizabethan Soldier and Diplomat* (Leicester, 1963).

7 Duncan, op. cit., p.74.

8 Hasler, vol. 2, op. cit., p.394.

9 Miller, op. cit., p.97.

10 'Sir Henry Killigrew', *ODNB*, op. cit. In his will, Killigrew left no legacies to Neville or Neville's wife (ibid.), presumably because of his anger at his son-in-law's role in the Essex rebellion. By his second wife, whom he married in 1590, he had three sons and a daughter. (Ibid.)

11 Duncan, op. cit., pp. 74–5.

12 E.A.J. Honigmann, *Shakespeare: The 'Lost Years'* (Manchester, 1998), pp.90–113.

13 Duncan, op. cit., p.74.

14 Ibid.

15 'Sir Henry Neville II (c.1575–1641) in Hasler, vol. 3, op. cit., p.125.

16 'Edward Neville I (c.1575–1622) in ibid., p.122.

17 Several alleged earlier references cited, for instance, in E.K. Chambers, *William Shakspeare: A Study of Facts and Problems*, vol.2 (Oxford, 1930), pp.186–90 do not necessarily refer to Shakespeare of Stratford. The meaning of the famous passage in Greene's *Groatsworth* remains extremely obscure and ambiguous. The author (Greene on his deathbed, but more likely Henry Chettle) appears to be warning three well-established playwrights (usually taken to be Marlowe, Nash, and Peele) about an 'upstart crow', a new playwright, namely 'Shake-scene'. But why would Greene/Chettle do this, and for what possible reason? New writers were appearing all the time; some were former actors. They did not threaten well-established playwrights. Greene/Chettle *seems* to be making the point that 'Shake-scene' was a detestable fellow of some kind, possibly because he was a rapacious money-lender or a thief of others' work. (See Price, op. cit., pp.45–57.) Nor is there any evidence that Greene/Chettle knew the identity of the author of *Henry VI*, apparently referred to in the famous passage, only that Shakespeare, its supposed author, was detestable. For an orthodox view of Shakespeare as probably being an unpleasant individual (one of several such recent works), not 'gentle Will', see E.A.J. Honigmann, op. cit. (London, 1982).

18 Halliday, op. cit., pp.90, 133–4.

19 Chambers, op. cit., p.30.

20 Ibid., pp.30–2.

21 'Nicholas Rowe (1709)', in ibid., pp.266–7, which reprints most of Rowe's Life of Shakespeare.

22 This might have been a major reason why *As You Like It*, *Henry V*, and *Much Ado About Nothing* were not recorded in Stationers' Register until a few days before Neville returned from Paris, where he had served as Ambassador, to London. This is discussed below.

23 On aspects of this topic, see Halliday, op. cit., pp.216–18; Andrew S. Caincross, ed., 'Introduction' to *The First Part of King Henry VI* (Arden Edition, London, 1969), pp. xxviii–xxxviii; idem., *The Second Part of King Henry VI* (Arden Edition, London, 1962), pp. xxi–xlix; Randall Martin, ed., 'Introduction' to *William Shakespeare: Henry VI, Part Three* (Oxford Edition, London, 2001), pp.96–132; and Chambers, op. cit., vol. 1, pp.277–93.

24 On the dating of *Richard III* see Antony Hammond, ed., 'Introduction' to *King Richard III* (Arden Edition, London, 1981), pp.54–61. Hammond concludes (p. 61) that 'Shakespeare's first tetralogy was begun by 1590 and concluded with *Richard III*, probably late in 1591'. It is possible that *Edward III,* now attributed to Shakespeare by some scholars, was also written at this time or slightly later.

25 Hasler, vol. 3, op.cit., p.124; 'Sir Henry Neville (*c.*1520–1593)', in *ODNB*, op. cit. In July 1850 a correspondent named S.W. Singer sent the following extraordinary letter to the recently-founded *Notes and Queries* magazine; it was printed in issue no. 42 (August 17, 1850), p.182:

QUERIES

ESSAYES OF CERTAIN PARADOXES: POEM ON NOTHING.

Who was the author of a thin 4to. volume with the above title, printed for Tho. Thorpe, 1616? The contents are, 'The Praise of K. Richard the Third- The French Poetes- Nothing- That it is good to be in Debt.'

The late Mr. Yarnold has a MS. copy of the 'Praise of K. Richard', which is prefixed the following dedication–

'TO THE HONOURABLE SIR HENRY NEVILL, KNIGHTE.'

'I am bold to adventure to your hoonors viewe that this small portion of my privatt labors, as an earnest peny of my love, being a mere Paradoxe in prayse of a most blame-worthie and condemned Prince, Kinge Richard the Third; who albeit I shold guilde with farre better termes of eloquence then I have don, and freate myself to deathe in pursuite of his commendations, yet his disgrace beinge so publicke, and the worlde so opninionate of his misdoings, as I shold not be able so farre to justifie him as they to condemne him. Yet that they may see what may be saide, and to shew how farre they haue mispraysed his vertues, this following Treatise shall make manyfest. Your honour may peruse and censure yt at your best leisure, and though yt be not trickt up with elegance of phrase, yet may it satisfye a right curious judgement, yf the reasons be considered as they ought. But, howsoever, yf you please to accepte it, I shall thinke my labors well bestowed; who, both in this and what ells may, devote myself to your honour, and rest,

Your honours most affecionat servant,

HEN. W.

The praise of Nothing is very well versified from the Latin of Passerat, whose verses Dr Johnson thought worthy of a place in his *Life of Lord Rochester.* Besides Rochester's seventeen stanzas 'Upon Nothing', there appears to have been another copy of verses on this fertile subject; for Flecknoe, in his *Epigrams of All Sorts*, 1671, has 'Somewhat to Mr. J.A. on his excellent poem of Nothing.' Is *anything* known of *Nothing*?

S.W. SINGER, Mickleham, July 29, 1850.

If 'HEN. W.' is indeed Henry Wriothesley, Earl of Southampton, this Dedication raises very many questions. Most obviously, when was it written, and why? Southampton, it should be noted, was baptized a Roman Catholic, and might have been attracted to the last King of an exclusively Catholic dynasty. Was it written in the early 1590s, just before or after Shakespeare's drama appeared? Neville was not knighted until the mid-late 1590s, but was a Knight of the Shire of Sussex from 1589–93, at the time *Richard III* was written, and was entitled to be formally addressed as 'Sir Henry'. The tone of the letter could certainly be that of a younger, hesitant man to a respected elder. (Southampton was eighteen in 1591.) And why was it written at all? Sir Henry Neville had no ostensible interest in King Richard III. The final sentence, in which the author promised to 'devote myself to your honour', although it may simply be the standard formula of flattery, seems to have echoes in the Dedication of *Venus and Adonis* of 1593. It is of course quite possible that Sir Henry Neville and Lord Henry Wriothesley wished to confuse the issue regarding their identification.

26 Hasler, op. cit.

27 Duncan, op. cit., pp.75–7. Remarkably enough, however, one room of Billingbear survives today at Pace College in Manhattan, near New York's City Hall, where it was rebuilt in the early twentieth century. It is said to be haunted.

28 Duncan, op. cit., p.75. Henry Neville's younger brother Edward (d. 1567), of whom little is known, was elected at the same time as the other MP for New Windsor, which returned two members.

29 On Field's career, see 'Richard Field (bap. 1561, d. 1624), printer', *ODNB*, and Colin Burrow, 'Introduction' to *William Shakespeare: The Complete Sonnets and Poems* (Oxford, 2002), pp.6–10.

30 Among Neville's accounts at the Berkshire Record Office, however, there is a bill paid to Newbury for £105 – a tremendous sum in those days. Also, Ralph Newbury was an executor and beneficiary under Neville's will, so it is quite possible that he was involved in some way with Neville's work.

31 Irwin Smith, *Shakespeare's Blackfriar's Playhouse*, op. cit., p. 172.

32 On the dating and authorship of *Titus* see, for instance, Alan Hughes, 'Introduction' to *Titus Andronicus* (New Cambridge Shakespeare, Cambridge, 1994), pp.1–22.

33 Clifford Leech, 'Introduction' to *The Two Gentlemen of Verona* (Arden Edition, London, 1969), pp.xxi–lxxv.

34 T.S. Dorch, 'Introduction' to *The Comedy of Errors* (New Cambridge Shakespeare, Cambridge, 1988), pp.1–16.

35 Cockburn, op. cit., p.106.

36 Ibid., p. 14. This was first pointed out by Charlotte Stopes in 1916. Recent orthodox biographers of Shakespeare have suggested that the performance at Greenwich was held in the daytime, with the entire company then travelling to Gray's Inn for a night-time performance, presumably without rehearsing. But Chambers pointed out in 1907 that 'the Court performances were always held at night, beginning about 10 p.m. and ending about 1 a.m.' (Cockburn, ibid., p.123).

37 Ibid., pp.120–2, citing E.K. Chambers, *The Elizabethan Stage* (London, 1923), vol. 4, pp.164–5.

38 Michael Dobson and Stanley Wells, eds., *The Oxford Companion to Shakespeare* (Oxford, 2001), p. 86.

39 H.R. Woudhuysen, ed., *Love's Labour's Lost* (Arden Edition, London, 1998), pp.59–61.
40 Harold F. Brooks, ed., 'Introduction' to *A Midsummer Night's Dream* (Arden Edition, London, 1979), pp.xxxiv–lxviii.
41 Duncan, op. cit., p.79.

Chapter 5 The road to the top, 1595–99

1 Hasler, op. cit., p. 123. The MPs elected for New Windsor in 1597 were Sir Julius Caesar – that was his name – a Privy Counsellor who was at Oxford at the same time as Neville, and John Norreys. (Duncan, op. cit., p.81.)
2 Duncan, ibid., p.82.
3 Ibid., p.81.
4 Ibid., p. 85; Hasler, op. cit., p.123.
5 Dobson and Wells, *Oxford Companion*, p.292; Halliday, op. cit., p.314.
6 'Venice', in the *The Encyclopedia Judaica* (Jerusalem, 1971), vol. 16, p.98.
7 '3,000 ducats is precisely the sum involved in a trial that took place in 1567 between a Jew and a Christian [in Venice] … The Ribeiras were discovered to be crypto-Jews … The Ribeiras did not reside in the Ghetto … showing how Jewish geography was more complicated', Shaul Bassi, 'The Venetian ghetto and modern Jewish identity: from all their habitations', *Judaism, Quarterly Journal of Jewish Life and Thought* (Autumn, 2002). According to *The Encyclopedia Judaica* (ibid.), 'a considerable number' of Venetian Jews 'had established partnerships with Christian merchants'.
8 Neville's step mother-in-law, Jael de Peigne, was a Huguenot. It may of course have been through her that the Mountjoy lodgings were found for Shakespeare, the actor. In this case, it is quite possible that all concerned would be very careful to keep quiet about the Huguenot connection, as this might then lead straight back to Neville.
9 Holden, *William Shakespeare*, p.214
10 Honan, *Shakespeare,* p.327
11 See, for instance, Richard Whalen, *Shakespeare: Who Was He? The Oxford Challenge to the Bard of Avon* (Westport, Conn., 1994), pp.106–7.
12 Alan H. Nelson, *Monstrous Adversary: The Life of Edward De Vere, 17th Earl of Oxford* (Liverpool, 2003), p.187.
13 Ibid., pp.188–9.
14 Ibid., pp.397–8.
15 Accounts of this wretched affair may be found in Robert Lacey, *Robert, Earl of Essex: An Elizabethan Icarus* (London, 1971), pp.115–20, and Noel Green, *The Double Life of Sr. Lopez* (London, 2002).
16 Machiavelli was not translated into English until the seventeenth century; only Italian (and translated Latin and French) versions were available in London at

this time. Although manuscript English translations also existed from *c.* 1585, Shakespeare appears to have been very familiar with Machiavelli's writings and his influence. On this question see Gillespie, *Shakeapeare's Book*, op. cit., pp.311–16.

17 See 'XVIII. Elizabeth Wriothesley, Countess of Southampton (1599)', in Chambers, *William Shakespeare,* vol. 2, op. cit., p.198; Halliday, op. cit., p.107.

18 *Memorials of Affairs of State in the Reigns of Q. Elizabeth and K. James I, Collected (chiefly) from the Original Papers of the Right Honourable Sir Ralph Winwood, Kt.*, published in three volumes by Edmund Sawyer of Lincoln's Inn, London 1725, vol. 1, p. 115. (Hereafter *Winwood's Memorials.*)

19 Miller, *Killigrew*, op. cit., p.198.

20 Chambers, op. cit., p.198.

21 Leslie Hotson, *Shakespeare's Sonnets Dated*, (London, 1949), p.156.

22 Charles R. Forker, 'Introduction' to *King Richard II* (Arden Edition, London, 2002), p.112.

23 Andrew Gurr, 'Introduction' to *King Richard II* (New Cambridge Shakespeare, Cambridge, 1990), p.1.

24 Halliday, op. cit., p.412; Anne and Veronica Palmer, *Who's Who In Shakespeare's England* (London, 2000), pp.37–8, 119.

25 Chambers, op. cit., vol. 1, pp.352–4 makes the case that this linkage was widely seen at the time.

26 A.R. Braunmuller, 'Introduction' to *The Life and Death of King John* (Oxford Edition, Oxford, 1989), p.26. The anti-Catholic tenor of this play has been widely noted.

27 On its dating, see Chambers, op. cit., vol. 1, p.375. It is possible that fragments of this play, now in the Folger Library, were written earlier.

28 Dobson and Wells, *Oxford Companion*, p.188.

29 H.J. Oliver, 'Introduction' to *The Merry Wives of Windsor* (Arden Edition, London, 1971), p.xliv.

30 Chambers, op. cit., vol. 1, p.426; Halliday, op. cit., p.314.

31 See, for instance, Oliver, 'Introduction', op. cit., pp.xliv–liii; Dobson and Wells, *Oxford Companion*, op. cit., p.292.

32 A.R. Humphreys, ed., 'Introduction' to *The Second part of King Henry IV* (Arden edition, London, 1966), p.xiv.

33 Gary Taylor, ed., *Henry V* (Oxford, 1984), pp.4–5. It is possible that Neville began *Henry V* in England and completed it in France.

34 Duncan, op. cit., p.99; Alan Haynes, *Robert Cecil, Earl of Salisbury, 1563–1612: Servant of Two Sovereigns* (London, 1989), p.86

Chapter 6 Ambassador to France, 1599–1600

1 Duncan, op. cit., p.150.

2 Ibid., p.95.

3 Ibid., p.101.

4 See V. Wheeler Holohan, *The History of the King's Messengers* (London, 1935). One of the Queen's Messengers who delivered correspondence for Neville was the poet Aurelian Townshend (before 1583–*c*.1649). Especially recommended by Robert Cecil, he served in this post for a year from 1600. ('Aurelian Townshend [Townsend]' (fl. 1583–1649?), *ODNB.*) At least three other Queen's Messengers served Neville when he was an Ambassador.

5 Duncan, op. cit., p.99.

6 Ibid.

7 Ibid., p.115.

8 Ibid., pp.125–9.

9 Ibid., p.148.

10 *Satire Menipe* (1594) cited in Patrice Higonnet, *Paris: Capital of the World* (Cambridge, MA, 2002) p.23

11 'Montaigne, Michel de (1533–92)', in Halliday, op. cit., p.321.

12 Orthodox historians also suggest that 'it is probable that Shakespeare knew Florio through their common patron, Southampton'. (Halliday, ibid., p.168.) But as has been repeatedly noted, there is no evidence that Southampton was actually Shakespeare's patron.

13 Price, op. cit., p.16; Honan, op. cit., pp.240–51; Chambers, op. cit., vol. 2, pp.52–106.

14 Halliday, op. cit., pp.372–3.

15 Cited in T.S. Dorsch, 'Introduction' to *Julius Caesar* (Arden Edition, London, 1965), p.vii.

16 On the connections between the Neville household and Morley, see Harley, 'My Ladye Nevell', op. cit.

17 Honan, op. cit., p. 246.

18 Duncan, op. cit., p.134, citing *Calendar of State Papers (Domestic) (1598–1601)*, p. 379; 'Neville (1562–1615)', in Hasler, op. cit., p.123. Ashridge is in Sussex, near Neville's former estate in Mayfield. On the dating of *As You Like It*, see Chambers, op. cit., vol. 1, pp. 401–4, and Alan Brissenden, 'Introduction' to *As You Like It* (Oxford Edition, Oxford, 1993), pp.1–5.

19 From the Neville papers, Berkshire Record Office, ref. D/EN F6 5/7.

20 See Chambers, op. cit., vol. 1, pp.405–7.

21 *Winwood's Memorials*, vol. 1, p.275, letter from Sir Ralph Winwood to Sir Henry Neville, 20 November 1600.

22 *Winwood's Memorials*, vol. 1, p. 302; Halliday, op. cit., p.505. Hotson's suggestion that it was meant to be performed at Candlemas has been disputed by some. Neville also possibly wrote *Much Ado About Nothing* at this time, although it is sometimes linked to events in 1598. Nevertheless, it was included among the three Shaespearean plays 'staied' in August 1600.

23 Under a 1586 decree of the Star Chamber, all books had to be licensed for printing by the Archbishop of Canterbury, the Bishop of London, or their

deputies. Once this was done, the book would be entered by its publisher in the Register of the Stationers' Company or its Wardens. As none of these four plays had been published, it *seems* that their being 'staied' marked an intention eventually to publish them, a kind of proto-copyright which allowed their owners, in this case the Chamberlain's Company, to perform them without their being memorized and used by another acting company. (see Chambers, op. cit., vol. 1, p.145.) But the whole procedure remains rather obscure.

24 Brissenden, *As You Like It*, op. cit., p.2.

25 Chambers, op. cit., vol. 1, p.389.

Chapter 7 The Catastrophe, 1601–03

1 On Essex see G.B. Harrison, *Life and Death of Robert Devereux* (London, 1937); Robert Lacy, *Robert, Earl of Essex* (New York, 1971); and other standard sources.

2 Cited in 'Henry Neville (1562–1615)', in Haslar, op. cit., p.124.

3 Robert Boies Sharpe, *The Real War of the Theatres: Shakespeare's Fellows in Rivalry with the Admiral's Men*, 1594–1603 (Boston, MA, 1935).

4 The Admiral's Men were under the patronage of Charles Howard, Lord Howard of Effingham and first Earl of Nottingham (1536–1624), who commanded the Armada fleet as Lord High Admiral of England. He was an extremely popular figure, certainly more popular and better-known than the patron of the Chamberlain's Men, Lord Hunsdon. The Admiral's Men, normally working out of the Rose and later the Fortune Theatres, included among others Edward Alleyn (the founder of Dulwich College) and Philip Henslowe, whose *Diary* is one of the great sources of information about the Elizabethan theatre. Ben Jonson wrote many (not all) of his plays for the Admiral's Men, as did, among others, Michael Drayton and Thomas Dekker.

5 Duncan, op. cit., p.151; 'Henry Cuffe (1562/3–1601)', in *ODNB*; A. and V. Palmer, op. cit., p.58.

6 Duncan, op. cit., p.152.

7 Ibid., p.154.

8 Ibid., p.155; Chambers, op. cit., vol. 1, p.389.

9 Duncan, op. cit., p.156.

10 Ibid., pp.157–60.

11 Ibid., p.163.

12 Ibid., p.162.

13 Ibid., p.163.

14 Ibid., p.165; Charlotte Stopes, *The Life of Henry Third Earl of Southampton* (London, 1922), p.203; 'Sir Henry Neville', *DNB*.

15 Haslar, op. cit.; Duncan, op. cit., pp.166–7.

16 Duncan, ibid., pp.167–9.

17 Chambers, op. cit., vol. 1, pp.354–5; Halliday, op. cit., pp.366–7.

18 Chambers, ibid., p.354.

19 Duncan, op. cit., pp.170–1

20 Ibid., p.173.

21 Ibid., pp.173–4.

22 Ibid., p.173.

23 Ibid.

24 Halliday, op. cit,.p.334; Mitchell, op. cit., pp. 48–9.

25 Nelson, op. cit., pp.323, 397.

26 Ibid., 386–7.

27 They are also extremely misogynistic, while Shakespeare was one of the earliest writers to create three-dimensional female characters (ibid., pp.388–9).

28 Halliday, op. cit., p. 429; A. and V. Palmer, op. cit., p. 213. Sadler was also a witness to Shakespeare's will.

29 Harold Jenkins, 'Introduction' to *Hamlet* (Arden Edition, London, 1982), p.13.

30 Ibid., p.6.

31 Ibid., pp.3–7.

32 Halliday, op. cit., p.429; A. and V. Palmer, op. cit., p.213.

33 Kenneth Palmer, 'Introduction' to *Troilus and Cressida* (Arden Edition, London, 1982), pp.1, 17.

34 *Troilus and Cressida* in Dobson and Wells, *Oxford Companion*, op. cit., pp. 63–5, 487.

35 It is not discussed, for example, in Chambers' two-volume work, although the Epistle is reprinted in full in Chambers, op. cit., vol. 2, pp.216–17.

36 On the festivities of the Inns of Court and their 'Princes', see *Mr W.H.*, by Leslie Hotson (Rupert Hart-Davis, London, 1964), p.51.

37 It is possible that Neville was in a more expansive and optimistic mood in early–mid-1609 than he had been in some time. His elder son had just married an heiress, and he was apparently hopeful of emerging from his financial straits with the official start of the second London Virginia Company in May 1609. The Sonnets were certainly published in May 1609 in connection with the launch of the second London Virginia Company, of which Neville was director.

38 G.K. Hunter, 'Introduction' to *All's Well that Ends Well* (Arden Edition, London, 1962), pp.xviii–xix.

39 Ibid., p.xx. Hunter states that 'with this view no one presumably would quarrel'. This quotation he cites from an edition of the play, edited by Eversley, published in 1899.

40 Chambers, op. cit., vol. 1, p.426.

41 One person whom Neville would probably have met when imprisoned in the Tower was Sir Anthony Dering (*c.* 1557–1636) who was then deputizing for his mother's step-father as Lieutenant of the Tower of London. Either Dering or his son Sir Edward Dering (1598–1644; he was born in the Tower) owned the earliest extant manuscript copy of a Shakespeare play, a version of the two parts of *Henry IV* known as the 'Dering Manuscript'. Formerly dated to 1613, the Manuscript is now generally dated to about 1622–23. It is reasonable to assume

that Sir Anthony Dering might have known about Neville's secret identity and that they became friends when he was a prisoner. *If* the Manuscript dates from 1613, it was presumably written with Neville's approval, in his lifetime.

Chapter 8 Freedom and disappointment, 1603–08

1 From *Englandes Mourning Garment*, registered in the Stationers' Register on 25 April 1603; cited in Chambers, op. cit., vol.2, 189. That Chettle, even in 1603, evidently did not know Shakespeare's true identity should be noted in considering *Greene's Groatsworth of Wit* of 1592.

2 Nicholas Rowe, Shakespeare's first biographer, claimed in 1709 that 'Queen Elizabeth had several of his plays acted before her, and without doubt gave him many gracious marks of her favour'. Rowe provides no source for this information, nor for his further well-known claim that Shakespeare wrote *The Merry Wives of Windsor* at the Queen's command.

3 On interpretation of this Sonnet, see Stephen Booth, ed., *Shakespeare's Sonnets* (New Haven, CT, 1997), pp.342–8. Booth cites several previous authorities who have commented on the difficulty of knowing what the Sonnet is supposed to be about, with, for instance, H.C. Beeching noting (p.346) in 1904 that 'though it seems at first sight a simple and natural allusion to a well-known historical event', it is, nevertheless, 'the most difficult of the sonnets'. Most commentators, however, have certainly identified the 'eclipse' of the 'mortal moon' with Queen Elizabeth's death, which is an accurate reading.

4 Duncan, op. cit., p.189.

5 Ibid., p.170. Neville had acquired this reputation in part while abroad in France, but the man who wrote it appears to have been a disgruntled Englishman abroad whom Neville had put off seeing. This anonymous Englishman therefore wrote that he thought Neville must be some sort of Puritan and 'wholly Scottish', both of which remarks were brought on by the fact that Neville seemed to surround himself with more Scottish than English friends at the time. This was probably because he was quietly planning the succession of James VI of Scotland to the English throne, as he (James) was then just about the only possible Protestant successor to Queen Elizabeth.

6 James's mother, Mary Queen of Scots, in her will, 'bequeathed' the throne of England to her son after Elizabeth's death, provided that he (James) remained true to the Catholic faith. If he did not, then she decreed that the King of Spain ought to become the monarch of England. As can be seen in the early pages of Volume 1 of *Winwood's Memorials*, it was then essential that James should appear to the Spanish to be at least a crypto-Catholic, while to the English he had to appear wholly Protestant. This must have been a difficult line to tread, and he was no doubt aided in its treading by Neville's careful treatment of the Scottish Catholic faction, then in France.

7 Duncan, op. cit., p.191. An account of this incident may be found in G.P.V.

Akrigg, *Shakespeare and the Earl of Southampton* (London, 1968), pp.140–1. Proponents of the Earl of Oxford as the true Shakespeare often point out that this occurred shortly after Oxford's death, but it is difficult to see any connection whatever between the two events. (The only apparent connection is De Vere's purported relations with Southampton, but, to reiterate, there is no evidence of any linkage between the two.) Lord Danvers had been a prominent associate of Essex and Southampton, although in Ireland at the time of the rebellion. Berkeley was Neville's brother-in-law, married to his wife's sister.

8 Duncan, op. cit., p.142.

9 Ibid., p.189.

10 Ibid., p.190.

11 *Winwood's Memorials,* vol.2, p.17.

12 Brian Gibbons, 'Introduction' to *Measure for Measure* (New Cambridge Shakespeare, Cambridge, 1991), p.1; Dobson and Wells, eds, *Oxford Companion*, p.184.

13 Dobson and Wells, eds, *Oxford Companion*.

14 HMC 'Salisbury' MSS, XI, 259 – letter from Anne Neville to Queen Elizabeth: '[it] pleased Her Majesty . . . to take a gracious course towards the offenders of all degrees and sorts, even in open action. If Mr. Neville may but taste of the same favor, and be restored to me and his poor children, though we live poorly together, I shall think myself happy and have cause to pray for you.'

15 Duncan, op. cit., p.193; Haslar, op. cit., vol. 3, p.123.

16 Duncan, op. cit, p.193.

17 Haslar, op. cit., vol. 3, p.124.

18 Halliday, op. cit., p.93.

19 Dobson and Wells, eds, *Oxford Companion*, p.72.

20 It may be significant, however, that King James I went to Billingbear to consult with Neville about something he (James) was writing. Dudley Carleton – diplomat, letter-writer, friend of Neville and cousin of the man who eventually married Neville's widow – wrote in September 1608: 'The king was there [Billingbear] lately and solemnly entertained, but was not so busy with the young wenches as the time before, having his head much troubled about an answer of his book, which is lately come over and done, as is thought, the most part by Parsons, though some of it by others, as may be seen by the difference of the style' (Lee, ed., *Jacobean Letters*, op. cit., p.105). King James also accompanied Neville at Oxford University when he received his MA (and the reason for Neville obtaining this degree at this time is unknown.)

21 Rosalind Miles, *The Problem of 'Measure for Measure': A Historical Investigation* (London, 1976), pp.13–14.

22 Ibid., pp.31–48.

23 Duncan, op. cit., p.195.

24 Haslar, op. cit., vol. 3, p. 124.

25 See a letter to him from 'the poor' on his estate, Berkshire Record Office, ref. D/EN F6 2/6.

26 Duncan, op. cit., pp.196–7.

27 Ibid., p.197.

28 Ibid., p.199. There might perhaps be a curious and otherwise inexplicable echo of this rumour. Between 1 November 1604 and 12 February 1605 a series of 12 plays were presented to the Court at Whitehall by the King's Men. Eleven of these were plays by Shakespeare. On 11 February 1605 the penultimate play in the series was presented, entitled *The Spanish Maze*. No one has ever satisfactorily explained what this play might have been: no play by this name survives, although the other 11 plays by Shakespeare (*Measure for Measure*, *The Comedy of Errors*, etc.) certainly do survive. In view of the rumours which were known to have existed at the time about Neville's supposed appointment as Ambassador to Spain, it is just possible that this was, indeed, a play by Neville about Spain which was written by him in effect to lobby for (or perhaps against) his appointment. Once his appointment fell through, it is possible that Neville suppressed the play, conceivably because its message was too overtly political. Obviously this is pure speculation, but, again, the coincidence of dates is very suggestive.

29 Duncan, op. cit., pp.200–2.

30 Ibid., p.203. These proposals had widespread support in Parliament.

31 *Winwood's Memorials*, op. cit., vol.2 p.216: Letter from Sir Henry Neville to Mr Winwood: '... Our Laws against Recusants have been very sharp, insomuch as we are devising already how we may quallify them in the execution'. Neville then goes on to point out a great disadvantage in one of them, viz. that the country will find it hard to get any Catholics to fight for England in future concerns abroad, because of the strictness of one proposed law saying that anyone now serving abroad will be deemed to be a felon under English law if he did not previously take oaths to the effect that, although a Catholic, he would fight exclusively in the interests of of the English Crown. Neville's point is that this will of course drive any English Catholic 'Voluntaries' serving abroad straight to the other side, for fear of coming back and being branded a felon, as they would find it difficult to prove that they ever took such an oath. It will also, says Neville, prevent many a moderate Catholic from ever considering to fight for England again, which would mean a serious diminution in our forces. 'Thus is my good intention clean perverted', as Neville says. There is also a hint that Neville was by this time very much involved in the making and judging of laws, for on 1 November 1604 there was a letter from him to Winwood, ending 'From my bed at the Star-Chamber' (*Winwood's Memorials*, vol.2, p.35).

32 Recent works arguing that Shakespeare was a secret Catholic include Ian Wilson, *Shakespeare: the Evidence* (London, 1993); Wood, *In Search of Shakespeare*; Richard Wilson, *Secret Shakespeare: Studies in Theatre, Religion, and Resistance* (Manchester, 2004), and Clare Asquith's *Shadowplay* (New York, 2005). Against the positive evidence in favour of this proposition – John Shakespeare's 'Spiritual Will', the supposed two years spent in Lancashire Catholic households, and so on – many points can also be raised, for instance, that Shakespeare of Stratford made no attempt to marry his two

daughters to Catholics; indeed his son-in-law Dr John Hall was an extreme Puritan. Of course, if one accepts that Shakespeare did not write the works attributed to him, his religion is of no real importance, and of no importance whatever in understanding these works, unless – which seems implausible – it somehow affected Neville's texts.

33 See the 'Introduction' to the Oxford University Press edition of the play, published in 1992, edited by R.B. Parker, with Stanley Welles, p.2: 'There is no entry for *Coriolanus* in the Stationers' Register before 1623 and no record of any contemporary performance, but consensus is that it was probably written and first produced in the period between mid 1608 and late 1609 ... Evidence is scanty, however, and mostly inferential ...'.

34 See, for example, Wilson, *Shakespeare: the Evidence*, p.314.

35 'Robert Armin', in A. and V. Palmer, op. cit.

36 Duncan, op. cit., p.208.

37 Ibid., pp.209–10.

38 Hamilton, *Shakespeare and the Politics of Protestant England*, p.xii.

39 Constance Jordan, *Shakespeare's Monarchies: Rules and Subject in the Romances* (Ithaca, NY, 1997), p.30. Jordan's work is concerned with the last plays, although she is here addressing the whole post-1603 era.

40 Kenneth Muir, 'Introduction' to *Macbeth* (Arden Edition, London, 1984), pp.xvii–xviii.

41 Chambers, op. cit., vol.1, p.475.

42 Dobson and Wells, eds, *Oxford Companion*, p.271.

43 'Abergavenny, Marquesses of', *Burke's Peerage*, 106th (1999) edition. The 'mormaers' were powerful territorial magnates, the equivalent of earls in England. See also Nick Aitchison, *Macbeth: Man and Myth* (Stroud, 1999), pp.17–19.

44 '...the Earls of Mar and Angus, and the Master of Glamis, the leaders of the English faction ...', Leo Hicks, *An Elizabethan Problem* (London, 1964), p.60.

45 Chambers, op. cit., vol.1, p.463.

46 Neville was always concerned about the welfare of his daughters and clearly loved them. When his oldest, Katherine, married a northern gentleman and went to live in Cheshire, her unhappiness in that area of the country moved her father to attempt to exchange some of his Berkshire lands for some of those of her father-in-law, so that she and her husband might come and live near him again. In his 'letter to a Noble Lord' (probably Southampton), Neville wrote and asked that Lord for help in obtaining a favour (such as a fee-farm) from the King, saying, 'I would be glad of some small amenities to my younger sons, whereby I might be able to give them good education at the least, being eased of that charge, to do the more for my daughters'. Berkshire Record Office, ref. D/EN F6 2/3. It was also the talk of the Court when Neville allowed one of his daughters to marry his manservant, even though he had originally intended her for a much richer husband.

47 Duncan, op. cit., p.214.

48 Dobson and Wells, eds, *Oxford Companion*, p.475.

49 Ibid.; H.J. Oliver, 'Introduction' to *Timon of Athens* (Arden Edition, London, 1963), pp.xxii–xxviii, xl–xliii.

50 Duncan, op. cit., p.199.

51 Michael Neill, 'Introduction' to *Anthony and Cleopatra* (Oxford Edition, Oxford, 1994). pp.20–2, who suggests a date of 'late 1606 or early 1607' for the play's 'first performance'. Dobson and Wells, eds, *Oxford Companion*, p.15.

52 Philip Brockbank, 'Introduction' to *Coriolanus* (Arden Edition, London, 1976), p.25; Chambers, op. cit., vol.1, pp.497–8.

53 Dobson and Wells, eds, *Oxford Companion*, p.90. Owing to its sources, the play must have been written between 1605 and 1609.

54 *Winwood's Memorials*, op. cit., vol.2, p.399, cited in Duncan, op. cit., p.214.

55 R.B. Parker, 'Introduction' to *Coriolanus* (Oxford Edition, Oxford, 1994).

56 Dobson and Wells, eds, *Oxford Companion*, p.342; F.D. Hoeniger, 'Introduction' to *Pericles* (Arden Edition, London, 1963), p.lxiv.

57 Hoeniger, 'Introduction' to *Pericles*, p.lxiv.

58 Dobson and Wells, eds, *Oxford Companion*, p.342; Hoeniger, 'Introduction' to *Pericles*, pp.liii–lxiii. George Wilkins, a rather shady contemporary writer, is generally seen as Shakespeare's collaborator.

Chapter 9 Towards closure: the last plays, the Sonnets and the parliamentary 'undertaker', 1609–15

1 'Letter to a Noble Lord', Berkshire Record Office, ref. D/EN F6 2/3.

2 See the draft of Sir Henry Neville's Will, Berkshire Record Office, ref. D/EN F6 1/8.

3 There may indeed be a hint that this secret was perhaps kept in the Stuart family for some time. Not only did Charles II hold his Restoration Party at Billingbear, he also gave an exclusive licence to Thomas Killigrew (nephew of Anne Killigrew, Neville's wife) and William Davenant (reputed to be Shakespeare's illegitimate son) to produce Shakespeare's plays in London.

4 One of the documents found in the Worsley collection in Lincolnshire Record Office (alongside the Tower Notebook) is a research paper on how much various monarchs in England and on the Continent have been allowed for their personal use down the ages. Judging by the accurate figures Neville later quoted the King when arguing against increasing his allowance, this document was almost certainly his, though whether it is the original or a copy of Neville's original has yet to be ascertained.

5 In 1611, two well-informed public servants, John More and Levinus Munck, discussed Neville's chances of becoming a Secretary of State or a Privy Councillor, with More noting that Neville's reputation had made any such appointment out of the question, 'which I think he would not have done if he

had aspired to any Court employment'. (Clayton Roberts, *Schemes and Undertakings: A Study of English Politics in the Seventeenth Century* (Columbus, OH, 1985), p.3.)

6 Richard L. Greaves and Robert Zoller, eds, *Biographical Dictionary of British Radicals in the Seventeenth Century* (3 volumes, Brighton, 1983), vol.2, pp.260–1.

7 Dobson and Wells, eds, *Oxford Companion*, p.101.

8 J.M. Nosworthy, 'Introduction' to *Cymbeline* (Arden Edition, London, 1969), p.xv. Chambers, op. cit., vol.1, p.485.

9 Chambers, ibid.

10 J.H.P. Pafford, ed., *The Winter's Tale* (Arden Edition, London, 1966), 'Appendix I', p.163, and 'Introduction', p.xxi.

11 Ibid., p.xxiii.

12 Chambers, op. cit., vol.1, p.489.

13 Pafford, ed., 'Introduction' to *The Winter's Tale*, p.liii.

14 Most unfortunately, the water has been muddied concerning a modern understanding of Sir Henry Neville senior's ownership of the Blackfriars property. The confusion has occurred because of the differences between English and American Law of Property (i.e. real estate). American researchers have seen that Sir Henry was a 'leaseholder' or 'lessee' and assumed this means that he was only *renting* Blackfriars. However, most property in Britain was leasehold, not freehold, until the 1960s, when an Act of Parliament gave leaseholders the right to buy the freehold for the first time. As a leaseholder, one effectively *owns* the property, having usually only to pay a few pounds in 'ground rent' per year to the person who owns the ground on which it stands (i.e. the freeholder). Under leaseholds, original buyers of the 'lease' own the property itself for any time specified by the owner of the ground. The freeholder then has no actual rights over that *property* until the lease is up. Usually, the lease is granted for between 99 and 999 years, during which time the leaseholder can sell or let that property, passing the remaining years onto the new owner. This therefore makes some of Irwin Smith's assumptions invalid. In his book *Shakespeare's Blackfriar's Playhouse* (New York, 1964), he states for instance that Sir Henry senior was unlikely to be the one altering the Blackfriars property as he only leased it. He even states that, therefore, some of the records are bound to be incorrect, whereas I am afraid that some of Smith's assumptions seem to be based on this confusion over what are, admittedly, very complex English property laws.

15 The description is in Richard Eede's poem, *Iter Boreale*.

16 Thomas Lodge, who wrote *Euphues Golden Legacy*, mentions this Luce in one of his poems 'A Fig for Monus', and it is very likely that Shakespeare's Sonnet 21 parodies Lodge's poem to Rosalind in the Euphues sequence.

17 Thorpe himself actually wrote dedications to two books he published by *dead* authors: a translation by Marlowe of Lucan and a 1616 edition of a translation by John Healey of Epictetus. (Colin Burrow, 'Introduction' to William

Shakespeare, *The Complete Sonnets and Poems* (Oxford, 2002), p.99.) In contrast, however, the author of the Sonnets was of course alive and active in 1609. Additionally, Thorpe's two other dedications, both to dead authors, look nothing like the dedication of *Shake-speare's Sonnets*, and are signed, respectively, 'Thom. Thorpe' and 'Th. Th.' (John M. Rollett, 'Secrets of the dedication of Shakespeare's Sonnets', in Malim, ed., *Great Oxford*, op. cit., pp.253–66.

18 Thomas Thorpe might well have been reluctant to go along openly with an overt deception of this kind; hence the use of his initials rather than his name in full.

19 A.L. Rowse, *Shakespeare's Southampton, Patron of Virginia* (London 1965), p.239.

20 Robert Giroux, *The Book Known As Q: A Consideration of Shakespeare's Sonnets* (New York, 1983), p.4.

21 Katherine Duncan-Jones, in her 'Introduction' to the Arden Edition of *Shakespeare's Sonnets* which she edited (London, 1997), states that the division of copies between two booksellers (named in different editions of the Sonnets) 'may suggest that a larger than normal print-run had been produced' (p.37). But no direct evidence for this is offered, and she bases her conclusion in part on the reference to the 'adventurer' setting forth, which, as we have seen, simply does not refer to the Sonnets' publication. Everything we know about the Sonnets suggests that the opposite was true: its print-run was small, and its publication made no impact.

22 Ibid., pp.4–5.

23 For instance, Neville supplied timber to the East India Company, as this letter from Sir Thomas Smythe makes clear. Berkshire Record Office Letter from Thos. Smythe to Sir Henry Neville, 10 Aug. 1609
The East India Company cannot 'finde the writing wherein you contracted the to deliver 100 lode of Timber ...' But it had nevertheless been delivered – they are now going to use it '... towards the finishing of the Shippes' and will '... paye as they did for the former ...' 'most hartie thankes to you and my Lady for my kind entertainment ...'

24 Alexander Brown, *The Genesis of the United States* (2 volumes, first published 1890; republished New York, 1964), vol.1, p.206.

25 Ibid., pp.228–9.

26 Ibid.

27 Duncan, op. cit., p.215.

28 Charles Mills Gayley, *Shakespeare and the Founders of Liberty in America* (New York, 1917), p.17.

29 See, for instance, Stephen Booth, ed., *Shakespeare's Sonnets* (New Haven, CT, 1977), pp.135ff; Burrow, 'Introduction' to *The Complete Sonnets*, p.100.

30 'Sir Thomas Smythe (*c*.1558–1625)', *ODNB*.

31 Ibid.

32 If Neville was, indeed, in an unwontedly euphoric mood in mid-1609, this may account for the decision to allow the publication of *Troilus and Cressida* at about

this time. The first Shakespeare play to be published in some time, it was registered in the Stationers' Register in January 1609, but then appeared, later in 1609, in two Quarto editions. The second Quarto edition contains the famous Epistle, written in facetious style, that the play 'never clapper-clawd' before, and was released 'by the grand possessors will' (Halliday, *Shakespeare Companion* p.502; Chambers, op. cit., vol.1, pp.438–9.) Presumably, then, the author of the Epistle knew about Neville, who could plainly have been described as a 'grand possessor'. It is thus conceivable that the author of the Epistle might have been Neville's friend Richard Martin, who was Ben Jonson's patron, a fellow-member of the Mitre Club, and a lawyer in the Virginia Company. This theory was put forward by Leslie Hotson, who finds traces in the play to suggest that it was meant for performance at the Inns of Court. Richard Martin had once been a Prince d'Amour at the Middle Temple. A treatise by Martin is also present in the Worsley documents in the Lincoln Record Office, alongside the Tower Notebook, and Martin had used Neville's scribe to pen it. Added to all this, Martin was the deviser of the 'Virginian Maske'(according to Gayley, *Shakespeare and the Founders of Liberty*) which was performed around the marriage celebrations of King James' daughter, alongside what Frank Kermode claims may also have been a performance of *The Tempest*, in which the nuptial masque was then inserted.

33 A typical dating of the Sonnets to the 1590s may be found in Burrow, ed., 'Introduction' to *The Complete Sonnets*, pp.144–50. Of course, 'Shakespeare' had written sonnets before 1598, *per* Meres.

34 Ibid., p.138.

35 Ibid., p.139.

36 Ibid., pp.139–40.

37 The Dedication to the Sonnets also, in our view, has another concealed meaning. It was written in the strange way it was in part so that it might contain precisely 144 letters, and could thus be arranged into a 12 × 12 square. Once arranged in this way, the Sonnets can be seen to be a code which can be decoded by applying a wordsquare and keyword decoding system, yielding a number of statements about its authorship, including, especially, 'The wise Thorp hid thy poet', 'Henry Poet' and 'He only be of the Sein[e]' encoded within its transformations. Since this will immediately strike many readers as redolent of the very worst of nineteenth-century Baconian charlatanism about secret codes in Shakespeare's works, it cannot be emphasized too strongly that the code derives from an authentic cryptographical device, and has not been artificially imposed. As a talented mathematician and a former Ambassador, Neville would have been familiar with this encoding method. There must be *some* explanation for the strange, even bizarre, pattern of the Sonnet Dedication. It was through the application of the keyword transformational system to the Dedication that Brenda James made the seminal breakthrough to solving the authorship question. She had never previously heard of Sir Henry Neville, and had no reason to connect him with the Seine, or with Shakespeare.

38 Chambers, op. cit., vol.1, pp.491–2. According to Dobson and Wells, eds, *Oxford Companion*, p.420, it was 'completed in 1611'.

39 Chambers, ibid., gives an excellent account.

40 Ibid., p.492.

41 Ibid.

42 Ibid. An excellent pro-Stratfordian website, compiled by David Kathman, 'Dating *The Tempest*' (www.Shakespeareauthorship.com), provides an excellent introduction to this question. Kathman, a leading defender of the Stratford man as author, is here writing to refute the claims of the Oxfordians, which he does very cogently. See also Frank Kermode, ed., 'Introduction' to *The Tempest* (Arden Edition, London, 1964), pp.xi–xxxiv.

43 Kathman, 'Dating *The Tempest*'. For an exposition of the Oxfordian case, see, for example, Ogburn, *The Mystery*, pp.340–2.

44 The case made on Kathman's website (www.shakespeareauthorship.com) seems totally persuasive.

45 Discussed by Kermode, 'Introduction' to *The Tempest*, pp.xv–xvii, who says (p.xvii) that this theory has 'very little to support it'. Chambers (op. cit., pp.493–4) is also dubious.

46 Halliday, op. cit., p.427.

47 Cited in Kathman, 'Dating *The Tempest*', p.11 of his website.

48 One possible 'linkage' posited by Gayley (*Shakespeare and the Founders of Liberty*, p.18) in 1917 and by others was – believe it or not – via Sir Henry Neville himself! (Gayley of course knew nothing of Neville as possible author). But the *only* ostensible linkage of Neville to Shakespeare before the publication of this book is that he was a friend of Southampton, Shakespeare's alleged patron 16 years earlier.

49 Kathman, 'Dating *The Tempest*'.

50 Chambers, op. cit., vol.1, pp.496–8; Dobson and Wells, eds *Oxford Companion*, p.6.

51 Dobson and Wells, eds *Oxford Companion*, p.500.

52 Halliday, op. cit., p.507.

53 Dobson and Wells, eds, *Oxford Companion*, p.66.

54 Duncan, op. cit., pp.222–5.

55 Ibid., p.67.

56 Ibid., pp.220–75; Roberts, *Schemes and Undertakings*; Wallace Notestein, *The House of Commons, 1604–1610* (New Haven, CT, 1971), pp.420–34.

57 R.C. Bald, *John Donne: A Life* (Oxford, 1970), p.191. Bald confuses our Sir Henry Neville with his namesake, Henry Neville, Lord Bergavenny.

58 On the Gatehouse purchase, see, for instance, Wilson, *Shakespeare: The Evidence* op. cit. pp.360–81.

59 Duncan, op. cit., p.269.

60 Ibid., p.270.

61 Ibid., p.273.

62 Ibid. Neville's symptoms are probably consistent with cirrhosis of the liver, a form of jaundice marked by bloating. It is thus possible that alcoholism killed 'Shakespeare'.

Chapter 10 Life After death: the First Folio and the apotheosis of Shakespeare

1 'George Carleton (1557/8–1628)', *ODNB*.
2 According to Neville's note on the lands in his possession in 1601 – just before going into the Tower – he still owned lands in Mayfield, even though he had sold his ironworks. (See ref. D/EN F6 1/8 in the Berkshire Record Office.) This means that he might, in theory, have lived in Mayfield from time to time and indeed there is a note in the Chichester Record Office that he was the sponsor for Carleton's appointment as the Vicar of Mayfield.
3 'George Carleton', *ODNB*, op. cit.
4 As noted, Neville's eldest son, Henry, married Elizabeth Smythe (or Smith). His second eldest daughter, Frances (1592–1659), married, first, Sir Richard Worsley and, after his death, Jerome Brett. Neville's other children were Catherine (*c.*1589–1650) who married Sir Richard Brooke; Anne, who was apparently unmarried; Elizabeth (1588–1656) who was married three times, to William Glover, Sir Henry Berkeley and Thomas Dyke; Dorothy (1596–1640) who married Richard Billingsley; William (1596–1640), married to Catherine Billingsley; Richard (1608–44); Edward (1602–32), a Fellow of King's College, Cambridge, married to Alice Pryor; Charles (1607–26); and Mary (1590–1642), married to Edward Lewknor. Edward was evidently conceived when Neville was imprisoned.
5 Nicholas von Maltzalin, 'Sir Henry Neville (1620–1694)', *ODNB*. In the eighteenth century one of Neville's female descendants married Field-Marshall John Grillin, ninth baron Howard de Walden (1719–97), who was also created first Baron Braybrooke in 1788. The peerage still survives, and its successive holders owned Billingbear until it was destroyed in a fire in the 1920s. Another descendant, from Neville's daughter Elizabeth, was Sidney Godolphin, first Earl of Godolphin (1645–1712), a leading politician of Queen Anne's time.
6 Halliday, op. cit., p.446.
7 'Descendants of Shakespeare's Nephew Thomas Hart ...', in Honan, *Shakespeare: A Life*, op. cit., p.413.
8 Chambers, op. cit., vol.2, p.214. It is sometimes said that its references to 'Kings' indicates the King's Company, although it seems hard to read this into the wording.
9 Price, op. cit., p.63, citing Roger Ascham's *The Schoolmaster* of 1750. Montaigne also mentioned Terence's reputation, in a work translated into English in 1603, (Price, ibid.).

10 Another contemporary poem often thought to refer to Shakespeare was 'Cephalus and Procris. Narcissus' by Thomas Edwards (or Edwardes), which appeared in 1595. Describing one 'Adon', often taken as a reference to Shakespeare's *Venus and Adonis*, published two years earlier, its second verse reads:

> *Eke in purple robes disdained,*
> *Amidst the Centre of this clime,*
> *I have heard say doth remain,*
> *One whose power floweth far,*
> *That should have been of our rhyme,*
> *The only object and the star.*

These lines could manifestly never refer to Shakespeare the actor, but only to a well-placed courtier and politician such as Neville. These lines *could* refer to De Vere or Bacon, although in 1595 Oxford was out of favour and engaged in tin-mining schemes to escape from poverty, while Bacon, although an MP, was only made a Queen's Counsel in 1596. Neville, in contrast, was a rising MP and the favoured kinsman of Burghley, as well as the scion of an illustrious family.

11 Price, op. cit., pp.111ff., makes this abundantly clear. She contrasts the complete lack of what she terms 'literary paper trails' for Shakespeare with his famous contemporaries. For instance – to cite some of countless examples – Henslowe's *Diary* recorded ten payments to Ben Jonson expressly for writing, while Court records note payments to Jonson 'the Poet' for writing masques and plays (ibid.). In contrast, there are no such records about Shakespeare – literally none – and all contemporary references to him are as a 'player' or a businessman.

12 Schoenbaum, *Shakespeare's Lives*, pp.104–10.

13 Ibid., p.86.

14 Ibid., p.93.

15 Halliday, op. cit., p.299.

16 William Camden (1551–1623) was an antiquarian and historian. He served as Headmaster at Westminster School from 1593 to 1598. Ben Jonson was one of his pupils, and Jonson always praised the special attention he had given him. Like Neville, Camden was in touch with the European humanists. Earlier in his life, Camden travelled throughout England for nearly ten years and charted his observations in *Britannia*, which was published in Latin in 1586. A translation of this into English was published in 1610. He was the principal founder of the original Society of Antiquaries. Through his friendship with the Cecils, Camden had access to recent state papers, which enabled him to publish his *Annals of the Reign of Elizabeth to the year 1589*. The second part of this work was published in 1615 and 1625, and this contained information on the Essex Rebellion, including the part played by Neville in it. William Camden is buried in Westminster Abbey.

17 Duncan, op. cit., p.275. Jonson's line 'thy soule should give thy flesh her weight' may refer to Neville's overweight by the end of his life.

18 W.W. Greg, *The Shakespeare First Folio: Its Bibliographical and Textual History* (Oxford, 1955), pp.9–11.

19 Ibid., p.461.

20 See Appendix 1 for an analysis of the commendatory verses.

21 Greg, op. cit., p.1; Price, op. cit., pp.170–4.

22 Greg, op. cit., p.461.

23 Charlton Hinman, *The Printing and Proof-Reading of the First Folio of Shakespeare* (2 volumes, Oxford, 1963), vol.2, p.328; vol.1, p.362.

24 Rosalind Miles, *Ben Jonson: His Life and Works* (London, 1986), p.216.

25 Ibid.

26 Ibid., p.222.

27 Richard Chartres and David Vermont, *A Brief History of Gresham College, 1597–1997* (London, 1981), p.13; Miles, *Ben Jonson*, p.222.

28 Miles, ibid.

29 Ibid., p.206.

30 Jonson was friendly with two Gresham professors, Gunter and Osbaldson, but they were professors of geometry and divinity. Miles, ibid., p.224.

31 On Jonson's stay at Gresham College, see also ibid., p.223; 'Ben Jonson' in *ODNB*; C.J. Sisson, 'Ben Jonson of Gresham College', *Times Literary Supplement*, 21 September 1951; and the letter by George Burke Johnston, 'Ben Jonson of Gresham College, *Times Literary Supplement*, 28 December 1951.

32 Vanessa Harding, 'Citizen and mercer: Sir Thomas Gresham and the social and political world of the City of London', in Francis Ames-Lewis, ed., *Sir Thomas Gresham and Gresham College* (Aldershot, 1999), p.34.

33 Ibid.

34 Ibid., pp.35, 59.

35 Greg, op. cit., p.6; David Honeyman, op. cit., Map IV, p.196.

36 Cited in Chambers, op. cit., vol.2, p.224; spelling and punctuation modernized.

37 Ibid.

38 Ibid., p. 223. Chambers believed that the reference here was either to the installation of a Garter Knight at Windsor, or to Lord James Hay, who 'had a tawny livery on an embassy to France in 1616'. (Ibid.) The reference could thus be to Neville's livery as Ambassador to France. Chambers (ibid., pp. 223–4) dates the poem to 1615. Neville died in July 1615, Beaumont in March 1616, a month before Shakespeare.

39 Cited in ibid., pp.206–7, spelling modernized.

40 Greg, op. cit., p.455.

41 Ibid., pp.45–57.

42 Ibid., p.456.

43 Halliday, op. cit., p.170. See also Anthony James West, *The Shakespeare First Folio: The History of the Book*, vol.1 (Oxford, 2001). In his outstanding study,

West concludes that about 750 copies of the First Folio were printed, with the price of an unbound copy about 15 shillings, and 16 shillings – one pound for a bound copy. (Ibid., p.4.) The cost of producing a copy was about 6 shillings 8 pence, or 33.3 p. The cost of publishing 750 copies was thus about £250, or £250,000 in today's money. This sum had to be set out in advance, with at least 250–300 copies sold before the venture could break even.

44 Duncan-Jones, *Ungentle Shakespeare*, p.282.

45 Dobson and Wells, eds, *Oxford Companion*, p.147.

46 Halliday, op. cit., p.171.

47 Publication of the First Folio was announced in the catalogue of the Frankfurt Book Fair as being printed between April and October 1622, and printing of the Folio apparently began in early 1622. (Dobson and Wells, eds, *Oxford Companion*, p.145.) Thus, the publication could not have been initiated because of the political situation surrounding the Spanish marriage. But Jonson might have been keen to have been brought into the First Folio project, with its Protestant orientation. It is known that Jonson 'found the proposed match abhorrent' (Miles, op. cit., p.221).

48 Price, op. cit., p.164. 'Thy name from hence immortal life shall have/ Though I, once gone, to all the world must die' (Sonnet 81). This is clearly the statement of someone who had never published any work *under his own name* which might survive him.

Chapter 11 Documentary evidence: analyses and Shakespearean parallels

1 Several books on this subject were produced in previous centuries, though recent works on the topic are rare. Those past books included L. G. Wickham Legg, *English Coronation Records*; Roxburgh Club: *Liber Regalis* (London, 1870); Anon., *A Complete Account of the Ceremonies observed in the Coronations of the Kings and Queens of England* (London, 1727); F. Sandford, *Description of the Coronation of James II.* (1687).

2 Dr Geoffrey Parnell, personal communication.

3 ARCHON ref. C 57 Chancery and Lord Chancellor's Office: Crown Office: Coronation Rolls

4 See, for example, Society of Antiquaries of London, ref. SAL/MS/231 Liber Regalis. A translation into English of the *Liber Regalis*: *The Westminster Abbey MS of the Liber Regalis or order for the coronation of a king and a queen*, was reproduced by Lord Beauchamp for the Roxburghe Club, Vol. 93 (1870).

5 Calendar of State Papers, Domestic, 'James I: Volume 2: June–July, 1603'.

6 See the section on King Henry VIII in *Halle's Chronicle; Containing the History of England during the Reign of Henry the Fourth, and the Succeeding Monarchs, to the end of the Reign of Henry the Eighth in which are particularly described the*

manners and customs of those periods. Hall, Edward [d. 1547] (and Richard Grafton, Printer). Reprinted, London, 1809

7 Calendar of State Papers, Domestic, 'James I: Volume 2: June–July, 1603', 17 July: Answers and assertions of Geo. Brooke. Part taken by Lord Grey in the conspiracy.

8 From Sonnet 125.

9 Calendar of State Papers, Domestic: July 10. London.40. J. Chamberlain to Dud. Carleton: He will remain in London till the Coronation. The sickness [plague] increases.

10 See Calendar of State Papers, Domestic, 'James I: Volume 2: June–July, 1603'.

11 Campbell, *Shakespeare's History Plays* and Halliday, *Shakespeare Companion*.

12 See Halliday, *Shakespeare Companion*, p.679 'His [Vergil's] history is particularly valuable for the Yorkist and early Tudor period, and was used by Halle and Holinshed, from whom Shakespeare took most of his material for *Richard III*'.

13 See the Worsley Papers in Lincolnshire Record Office.

14 Ref. 1 Worsley 46.

15 See Preface to Volume of *Winwood's Memorials,* 1725: '... Sir Henry Neville's Negotiations at the French Court in the years 1599 and 1600, together with the Transactions in the Treaty of Bulloign, which immediately succeedded it. I [Edmund Sawyer – editor and compiler] should be ungrateful to my Benefactor, if I did not in this publick manner acknowledge, that for these I am oblig'd to his late worthy great-grandson Grey Neville, Esquire: who, with the greatest freedom and generosity gave me leave to publish them entire from the original MSS. (all wrote by his two Secretaries Mr. Winwood and Mr. Packer;) desiring, that as these two great and worthy statesmen had lived together in the most constant and intimate friendship, their Memoirs and Letters might be jointly delivered to the World.'

16 See letter from Dudley Carleton to Sir Ralph Winwood, *Winwood's Memorials*, vol.3, p.213: London, 28 August 1610 '... I must not forget Mr. Packer, who was fetched by a pursuivant out of the Isle of Wight, where he was making merry with young Worslie, to be imployed in Denmark...'

17 See entry for John Packer, *DNB*.

18 See letter from Lord Pembroke to Oglander, Lord Lieutenant of the Isle of Wight, 11 July 1622, concerning John Packer (IoW Record Office, ref. OG/BB/46).

19 Historical MSS. Collection, 1887, Belvoir Castle, p.136.

20 See Halliday, *Shakespeare Companion*, p.360 '... By a Decree of the Star Chamber of 23 June, 1586, all books had to be licensed for printing by the Archbishop of Canterbury or the Bishop of London'. Plays were later encompassed by the Bishops' authority too, in 1599.

21 Whitgift was the Archbishop of Canterbury at the time of the Essex rebellion, and he had ordered 'offensive publications' to be burned after the performance of *Richard II* (Halliday, *Shakespeare Companion*, p.95).

22 *Iter Boreale* – Richard Eedes' poem about his journey to the north of England, accompanying the new Bishop on his journey to take up his place in Durham.

23 '... many of the writers of Shakespeare's age, English writers at least, wrote spontaneously in a variety of hands: we have come across one case in point ... in the tale of Francis Throckmorton and his conspiratorial papers ...', Bossy, *Giordano Bruno*, p.268.

24 '... I cannot so freely and fiercely express my self by speech unto your lordship as my occasions require, I have had to be content to do yt by writing, humbly praying your favourable interpretation.' *My copy of a letter to a noble lord* from the Neville papers in the Berkshire Record Office, ref. D/EN F6 2/3.

25 The actual letter was pointed out to us by Dr John Rollet. It is in a bound collection in the Cambridge University Library, ref. Dd. 3. 63, on fo. 50 verso. Howard refers to Soughampton's failure to obtain for his 'Dear Damon' (Neville) the office of Secretary of State. The whole business was brought down around Neville's ears partly through the involvement of Henry Howard, a well-known 'dark schemer', with his niece's marriage to the King's then favourite, Robert Carr, Earl of Rochester. This dark affair ended in the murder of Rochester's one-time secretary and (it is rumoured) bedfellow, Sir Thomas Overbury. See Anne Somerset, *Unnatural Murder* (London, 1998). It is important to note that this 'Damon' was also a poet.

26 See Duncan, op. cit.

27 *Winwood's Memorials*, vol.3, p.453.

28 Halliday, *Shakespeare Companion*, p.427.

29 Duncan, op. cit.

Appendix 1 Commendatory verses and the three suns

1 Alison Weir, *Lancaster and York, The Wars of the Roses* (London, 1995), p.261.

2 *An Epitaph on the admirable Dramaticke Poet, W. Shakespeare*, which appeared anonymously in the prefatory matter of the Second Folio of his collected Works (1632).

Appendix 2 Sir Henry Neville and the Essex rebellion

1 Sir Henry Neville's entry, Haslar, *The House of Commons, 1558–1603*.

2 When the King of Spain died, Neville was invited to his funeral. However, he did not want to attend, giving Cecil the explanation that he thought King Phillip II had been too great an enemy to Queen Elizabeth. (One cannot escape the impression, however, that Sir Henry may have been already made enemies of some influential Spaniards and that this was the real reason for his reluctance to go.) However, he finally wrote to Cecil that he did indeed attend, 'but disguised also myself' then 'repented me of my pains, having never seen a poorer thing'. *Winwood's Memorials*, vol.1, p.45.

3 www.philological.bham.ac.uk/camden/1601e.html

4 Letter from Sir Edward Hoby to Robert Cecil, 1595; Halliday, *Shakespeare Companion*. p.294.

5 Francis Meres, *Palladis Tamia*, 1598.

6 The Neville Papers, Berkshire Record Office, ref. D/EN F6 2/3.

7 Lisa Jardine and Alan Stewart, *Hostage to Fortune, the Troubled Life of Francis Bacon* (London, 1998), p.248.

8 Sir Henry Neville's Case, in *Winwood's Memorials*, vol.1, pp.203–5.

9 *Winwood's Memorials*, vol.1, pp.203–5.

10 Ibid., p.291.

11 Ibid., pp.203–5.

12 Ibid., pp.203–5.

13 Montagu House Papers, 1899 edition, vol.1 (HMSO).

14 William Camden, *Annales Rerum Gestarum Angliae et Hiberniae Regnante Elizabetha* (published 1615 and 1625), notes for the year 1601, now made available on the web by the Shakespeare Institute of the University of Birmingham, www.philological.bham.ac.uk (see also chapter 9, note 16).

15 See the family tree chart 'The Killigrew connection', p.xvi, for details.

Appendix 3 Sir Henry Neville's voyage to France, and its double

1 Sir Henry Unton had been the Queen's previous representative in France. He was a friend and neighbour of Neville. Strangely (or perhaps significantly) the famous picture of the marriage celebrations of Sir Henry Unton are often used to illustrate editions of *A Midsummer Night's Dream*. The marriage feast at the end of that play certainly is reminiscent of Unton's, so it is quite possible that it was indeed that wedding which inspired the ending to the play. However, poor Unton's married life was short: he had been taken ill with a serious liver complaint while in France on the Queen's service and had begged to come home. The Queen refused him permission to do so, and the poor man died over there in agony, longing to see his young wife. As Neville was later to find, Unton had found it expensive to live in France, so had had to dip into his own resources. Consequently, Neville had bought some of Unton's neighbouring lands, partly to expand his own but mainly, it seems, to help out his ailing friend. His friend's death, therefore, must have made Neville extremely angry with Queen Elizabeth, even before he went over to France himself. On discovering that he (Neville) was also forbidden by the Queen to return home after the Treaty of Boulogne, he must have been doubly angry, so here no doubt were very immediate causes for him so readily siding with the Earl of Essex in his abortive rebellion.

2 Dover, 27 April 1599, in *Winwood's Memorials*, vol.1, p.26.

3 Ibid.

4 Thomas Edmondes was a friend and protégé of Neville's. The Queen had allowed Neville to take him as his steward in France, which Henry must have appreciated, especially as Edmondes was a frequenter of the Mitre and Mermaid Clubs, and so could converse about plays and players.

5 *Winwood's Memorials*, vol.1, p.55.

6 Ibid., p.50.

7 Ibid., p.45.

8 Ibid., p.17.

9 Ibid., p.26.

10 Ibid., p.49.

11 Ibid., p.45.

12 Ibid., p.271.

Index

For brevity, the following abbreviations are used: FB – Francis Bacon; HN – Henry Neville; WS – William Shakespeare; and HW – Henry Wriothesley, Earl of Southampton.